George B Herbert

The Popular History of the Civil War in America, 1861-1865

George B Herbert

The Popular History of the Civil War in America, 1861-1865

ISBN/EAN: 9783337409470

Printed in Europe, USA, Canada, Australia, Japan

Cover: Foto ©ninafisch / pixelio.de

More available books at **www.hansebooks.com**

THE POPULAR HISTORY

OF THE

CIVIL WAR IN AMERICA

(1861–1865.)

A COMPLETE NARRATIVE OF EVENTS, MILITARY, NAVAL, POLITICAL AND CONGRESSIONAL, THAT OCCURRED DURING THE WAR FOR THE UNION, WITH FULL INFORMATION AS TO THE CAUSES WHICH BROUGHT ON THE REBELLION.

BY CAPT. GEORGE B. HERBERT,

Journalist, of *Philadelphia, Pa.*, and *Author* of " *The Japanese in Philadelphia*," " *Life of Gen. W. S. Hancock*," " *Guiteau, the Assassin*," Etc.

WITH PORTRAITS AND NUMEROUS OTHER ILLUSTRATIONS.

NEW YORK:
F. M. LUPTON, Publisher,
No. 3 PARK PLACE.
1884.

COPYRIGHT, 1884,
BY F. M. LUPTON.

PREFACE.

Nearly twenty years have sped silently away since the closing scenes of the Civil War in America were enacted, and those years, while they have silvered the locks of men who were participants in, or spectators of, the titanic fraternal conflict, have brought to man's estate, or to the very verge of it, almost a nation of young Americans, who were sleeping sweetly in swaddling clothes, while their mothers were waiting, watching and weeping over the news from the various battle-fields. It is to these budding citizens, more especially, that we address and dedicate this volume, in the humble though fervent hope that its pages may give them a fair knowledge and thorough appreciation of the great principles involved in the stupendous and costly National struggle which the cynical cant of the present day too frequently alludes to as "the recent unpleasantness." There have been more ponderous tomes, of inestimable value to the leisurely student, produced by profound scholars and competent critics on this all-absorbing theme; there have been also skeleton "apologies for a History of the Civil War," serving the purpose only of giving the booksellers something to sell. Between these two there is a great gulf. The average reader shrinks from the task of hunting for crisp facts amid the thickets of theory and comment in the more pretentious volumes, and he turns away hungry for information after scanning a mere cartoon of a battle picture. We cannot hope to fill the chasm entirely, but trust that honest effort, supplementing a well-defined purpose, may succeed in throwing a pontoon bridge over it.

It would be well-nigh impossible to present an absolutely accurate and perfectly full report of a war of such magnitude, extending over so wide an area and embracing so long a period, and at the same time to enter fully upon the underlying political details, within the proposed limits of this work; but it is competent, by judicious selection, by condensation where permissible, and by amplification where expedient or necessary, to produce a history at once instructive and interesting. This we have essayed to do. What measure of success we have achieved must be determined by the verdict of our readers, to whom we "submit the case without argument." It may not be a proof of our excess of modesty, but, we desire to add that we do not even throw ourself upon the merciful consideration of the Court. Nor will we appeal to the sympathies or prejudices of the jury, lest, like the immortal twelve wiseacres of Dymnchurch, they should bring in a verdict acquitting the defendant but recommending him to mercy, or, like the modern juries of Pennsylvania (especially those of Bucks County), they should sagely acquit, but put the costs of the trial upon the prisoner. We decline a vindication on any such terms.

In all seriousness, however, we feel that our little volume contains a fair resumé of the causes which led to the war, the salient events of the campaigns, some essential comments and explanations and liberal pictorial embellishment, calculated to make it a covetable possession. So far as it is possible for human nature to be unbiased, or unprejudiced, we have endeavored to maintain the even tenor of our views amid the exciting, and sometimes irritating, narratives of bitter misunderstandings, mutual jealousies and sanguinary conflicts with which the records of American history abound during the period we have been considering. We have endeavored to avoid equally offensive epithets and excessive laudation, but have felt compelled, however, occasionally, to call a spade a spade, in plain, honest American fashion; for this we claim immunity, on the grounds that this is a free country, and that, therefore, we have a right to our own opinions while our readers have the undoubted privilege of dissenting at their own option. All of which, as our late lamented Lincoln would have remarked, reminds us of an anecdote. Singularly enough, it relates to an experience of the martyr in question, and was narrated by him in the following words:

"One day, when I first came here (Springfield, Ill.), I got into a fit of musing in my room, and stood resting my elbows on the bureau. Looking into the glass, it struck me what an awfully ugly man I was. The fact grew on me, and I made up my mind that I must be the ugliest man in the world. It so maddened me that I resolved, should I ever see an uglier, I would shoot him at sight. Not long after this, Andy —— (naming a lawyer present), came to town, and the first time I saw him I said to myself: 'There's the man.' I went home, took down my gun, and prowled around the streets waiting for him. He soon came along. 'Halt, Andy,' said I, pointing my gun at him, 'say your prayers, for I'm going to shoot you.' 'Why, Mr. Lincoln, what's the matter; what have I done?' 'Well, I made an oath that if ever I saw a man uglier than I am I'd shoot him on the spot. You *are* uglier, sure; so make ready to die.' 'Mr. Lincoln, do you really think that I am uglier than you? 'Yes! 'Well, Mr. Lincoln,' replied Andy, deliberately, and looking me squarely in the face, 'if I *am* any uglier, *fire away!*'"

For the application of this we would simply remark, if you find any other history of the Civil War in condensed, compact, handy form, more replete with military, political and social incident—shut us up—we deserve it!

George B. Herbert

PHILADELPHIA, July, 1884.

CONTENTS.

CHAPTER I.

Introductory—Early Indications of Discontent—Gradual Development of Sectional Interests—Causes of the Civil Strife—The State Rights Theory—John C. Calhoun and Nullification—The Tariff and Slavery Questions—Brief Review of Presidential Succession—Election of Abraham Lincoln—Preparing for War, ... 21

CHAPTER II.

Secession Spreading—The Various Ordinances—Treachery in the Cabinet—Anderson and Fort Sumter—His Heroic Action—Confederate Diplomatic Overtures—Cabinet Changes—The Treachery of Twiggs—Close of Buchanan's Administration, ... 32

CHAPTER III.

Biographical Sketch of Abraham Lincoln—His Eventful Journey from His Home to the National Capital—Plots for His Assassination—The Conspirators Foiled—Intrigues at Washington—Precautions Against Revolution—Lincoln's Inauguration—Abstract of his Address, . 51

CHAPTER IV.

Composition of Lincoln's Cabinet—Another Attempt at Southern Diplomacy—The Overtures Rejected—Affairs in Charleston Harbor—The Attack on Fort Sumter—Its Gallant Defense by Anderson—Peril of the Little Garrison—Its Evacuation on April 14th, ... 57

CHAPTER V.

Lincoln's First Call for Troops—The Quotas of the States—Secession Refusals to Respond—The Fatal Riot in Baltimore—First Bloodshed of the War—The Evacuation of Harper's Ferry—Spread of Confederate Sentiment—Lying Rumors of Defections—An Early Specimen of Repudiation Doctrines, ... 67

CHAPTER VI.

Intermediary Events—The Responses of the Loyal States—Unionists Rallying Round the Flag—Men and Money for Government Aid—Excitement in Philadelphia—Meetings Elsewhere—Spread of Southern Secession—Jottings of Events Among the Confederates, . . 77

CHAPTER VII.

Further Outrages at Baltimore—Burning of the Railroad Bridges—Capture of the Gosport Navy Yard—Butler Moves on Baltimore—The City

CONTENTS. XV

PAGE.

Occupied by Federal Troops—The Split in Virginia—Union Sentiment in the Mountain Counties—Organization of West Virginia—The Habeas Corpus Act Disregarded, ... 84

CHAPTER VIII.

The Federal Forces Cross the Potomac—Occupation of Alexandria—Assassination of Colonel Ellsworth—General George B. McClellan—The Battle of Philippi—Butler at Fortress Monroe—The Blunder at Big Bethel—Butler's Report—Confederate Accounts, . . . 100

CHAPTER IX.

Lincoln's Second Call for Troops—The Condition of the Navy—The Special Session of the Thirty-seventh Congress—Abstract of Lincoln's Message—Extracts from Davis' Confederate Message—Proceedings in Congress—Expulsion of Members on Treason Charges—Opposition Tactics of the Minority—The Government Sustained—Vigorous Preparations for War—Adjournment of Congress, ... 114

CHAPTER X.

The Battles of Falling Waters, Rich Mountain and Carrick's Ford—The Skirmish at Screytown—The First Battle of Bull Run—Official Reports—Narrative of an Eye-witness—Terrible Scenes of the Retreat—General McClellan Begins to Organize the Army of the Potomac, . 142

CHAPTER XI.

Movements in Missouri—Governor Jackson's Defiance—McCullough's Texan Rangers—the Battle of Carthage—Engagement at Dug Spring—Battle of Wilson's Creek—Death of Gen. Lyon—Fremont's Operations in St. Louis—Martial Law Proclaimed throughout Missouri, . 156

CHAPTER XII.

General Butler at Fortress Monroe—Relieved by Gen. Wool—The Burning of the Village of Hampton—Magruder Baffled—Butler Assumes the Offensive—Capture of Forts Hatteras and Clark—Capitulation of the Garrisons—Events and Occurrences of a General Character, . 166

CHAPTER XIII.

Movements in Missouri—The Siege of Lexington—Heroism of the Federals—Barbarism of the Confederates—Attack on Sick and Dying in the Hospital—Surrender of Mulligan's Camp—General Ulysses S. Grant at Paducah—His Dash on Belmont—Fremont Superseded—Summary of Subsequent Movements, ... 173

CHAPTER XIV.

Operations in Western Virginia—The Battle of Carnifex Ferry—Death of Colonel Lowe—Floyd's Hasty Flight—Attack on the Summit Post—Repulse of the Confederates—The Kanawha Valley Cleared of Intruders—Movements of McClellan—The Disastrous Battle of Ball's Bluff, ... 180

CHAPTER XV.

Naval Movements—An Incident of To-Day—Fate of the Harriet Lane—Engagements Around Hatteras—The Affair of Santa Rosa Island—Bombardment of Pensacola—The Expedition to Port Royal—Capture of Forts Walker and Beauregard—The Confederates Driven from the South Carolina Coast—Attempted Blockade of Charleston Harbor, . 180

CHAPTER XVI.

The Close of 1861—Permanent Congress of the Confederate States—Cabinet Changes—Specimen of Judah P Benjamin's Consistency—Privateering—The Trent Affair—Capture of Mason and Slidell—Diplomatic Correspondence—The Prisoners Released, ... 194

CHAPTER XVII.

Condition of Affairs in January, 1862—Exertions of the Secessionists in Kentucky—The Forces at Bowling Green—Garfield's Victory at Prestonburg—The Battle of Mill Spring—Death of Zollicoffer—The Burnside and Goldsborough Expeditions—Capture of Roanoke Island—Other North Carolina Victories, ... 200

CHAPTER XVIII.

Important Movements on the Cumberland and Tennessee Rivers—Foote's Flotilla—Capture of Forts Henry and Donelson—Evacuation of Columbus—The "Gibraltar of the West"—General Grant's Brilliant Achievements—Cowardice of Floyd and Pillow—The New Fortifications on the Mississippi—New Madrid and Island Number Ten, . . 207

CHAPTER XIX.

Inaction of the Army of the Potomac—Lincoln's Annoyance—McClellan's Obstinacy—A General Movement Ordered—Advance of McClellan on Yorktown—Siege Operations Begun—The Merrimack, or Virginia, and the Monitor—The Unique Naval Combat in Hampton Roads, . . 216

CHAPTER XX.

The Confederates Abandon New Madrid—Siege and Capture of Island Number Ten—The Wonderful Canal Construction—Grant Moves on Corinth—The Two Days' Battle of Shiloh, or Pittsburgh Landing—The Confederates Finally Driven Back on Corinth—Siege of Corinth—Beauregard's Flight—Occupation of Corinth by the Federals, . . 225

CHAPTER XXI

Stonewall Jackson in the Shenandoah Valley—Operations before Yorktown—Evacuation of Yorktown—Battle of Williamsburg—Flight of the Confederates across the Chickahominy—Surrender of Norfolk—Opening the Navigation of the James River, ... 237

CHAPTER XXII.

Capture of Memphis—Battle of New Berne—Operations along the Carolina Coasts—Capture of Fort Pulaski—Dupont and Sherman in Florida—Butler and Farragut on the Mississippi—Operations against Forts

CONTENTS. xvii

PAGE.

Jackson and St. Philip—Capture of New Orleans—Occupation of the City by General Butler, ... 244

CHAPTER XXIII.

Stonewall Jackson in the Shenandoah Valley—Fight at Winchester—Battle of Cross Keys—McClellan Before Richmond—Retrograde Movement to the James River—The Battle of Glendale—The Fitz John Porter Affair—Battle of Groveton—General Pope Relieved of His Command, ... 253

CHAPTER XXIV

Affairs in Kentucky and Mississippi—Guerrilla Morgan's Raids—The Confederates Capture Lexington and Frankfort—Bragg Retreats into Tennessee—General Buell Relieved—General Rosecrans in Command of the Army of the Cumberland—The Battles at Murfreesboro—Some Very Heavy Fighting, ... 272

CHAPTER XXV.

The Battle of Iuka—Movements Around Corinth—Grant's Communication Severed at Holly Springs—General Sherman at Memphis—The Attack on Vicksburg—Failure of the Movement—Burnside with the Army of the Potomac—Abortive Attack on Fredericksburg—Burnside Relieved of His Command, ... 278

CHAPTER XXVI.

President Lincoln's Emancipation Proclamation—Full Text of the Most Important State Paper in the History of the United States—Effects of Its Promulgation—Condition of the Federal Finances—Further Calls for Troops—Demoralized Condition of Confederate Affairs, . . 284

CHAPTER XXVII.

Running Summary of the Earlier Military Movements in 1863—Siege of Vicksburg—Surrender of Vicksburg by General Pemberton—Guerrilla Morgan's Raids—His Capture, Imprisonment and Escape—The Glorious Federal Achievements at Lookout Mountain and Missionary Ridge, ... 291

CHAPTER XXVIII.

Hooker with the Army of the Potomac—Disastrous Fight at Chancellorsville—Death of "Stonewall" Jackson—Capture of the Heights at Fredericksburg—Lee's Dash Into Pennsylvania and Maryland—Capture of Winchester by the Confederates—Hooker Superseded by General Meade, ... 304

CHAPTER XXIX.

The Confederate Invasion of Pennsylvania and Maryland—Meade's Movements to Check Lee's Advance—Battle of Gettysburg—Defeat of the Confederates—Meade's Leisurely Pursuit—Engagement at Mine Run—Both Armies in Winter Quarters—Close of 1863—Personal Narrative of the Swamp Angel's Construction, . . . 312

CONTENTS.

PAGE.

CHAPTER XXX.

Early Movements in 1864—General Sherman's Expedition from Vicksburg—Capture of Fort Pillow by the Confederates—Brutal Massacre under Orders of General Forrest—The Red River Expedition—Failure of the Movement—Colonel Bailey's Remarkable Engineering on the Red River—General Banks Superseded by General Canby, . . 328

CHAPTER XXXI.

The Rank of Lieutenant-General Revived—General U. S. Grant made General-in-Chief—Retirement of General Halleck—Preparing for a Vigorous Closing Campaign—General Sherman's Movements—The Two Battles Before Atlanta—Sherman's Occupation of Atlanta—Total Destruction of Hood's Army—"Marching Through Georgia," . . 334

CHAPTER XXXII.

Sherman's "March to the Sea"—A Glorious War Record—The Confederates Swept by a Federal Broom—Savannah Captured—Movements in the Carolinas—Capture of Charleston—Surrender of the Confederate General Johnston—Capture of Mobile—Record of the Confederate Privateers—The Beginning of the End, ... 344

CHAPTER XXXIII.

Reorganization of the Army of the Potomac—Battle of the Wilderness—Battle of Spottsylvania Court House—Battle of Cool Arbor—Operations Before Petersburg—Movements in the Valley of the Shenandoah—Battle of Cedar Creek—Sheridan's Famous Ride from Winchester—The Army in Winter Quarters, ... 361

CHAPTER XXXIV.

Events of 1865—The Closing Scenes of the War—Desperate Attempts of the Beleagured Confederates—Evacuation and Burning of Richmond—Occupation of Petersburg—Surrender of Lee to Grant—Dispersion of the Army of Northern Virginia—Closing Battle at Palmetto Ranch, Texas—End of the War, ... 376

CHAPTER XXXV.

Political Matters—Lincoln's Re-election—The Great Conspiracy—Assassination of President Lincoln—Attempt on the Life of Secretary Seward—Flight and Capture of J. Wilkes Booth, the Assassin—Capture, Trial and Execution of the Conspirators—Capture of Jeff Davis—Conclusion, ... 387

Appendix, ... 414

LIST OF ILLUSTRATIONS.

	PAGE.
John Caldwell Calhoun,	24
Stephen A. Douglas,	29
Jefferson Davis,	36
Alexander H. Stephens,	37
Major Robert Anderson,	41
Sand Bag Battery at Fort Moultrie,	45
Scene of the Inauguration,	54
William H. Seward,	57
P. G. T. Beauregard,	59
Fort Sumter after the Bombardment,	65
The Rebel Flag,	67
Destruction of the Bridge over Gunpowder Creek,	84
Union Square, New York, on the 20th of April, 1861,	89
General Benjamin F. Butler,	91
Annapolis Junction in 1861,	92
Federal Hill,	95
Colonel E. E. Ellsworth,	100
Ellsworth Zouaves,	101
General George B. McClellan,	104
Carrick's Ford,	136
Bull's Run Battle Ground,	147
General Franz Sigel,	159
Burning of Hampton,	167
Fort Hatteras,	169
Pontoon Bridge at Paducah,	176
Ulysses S. Grant,	177
General Robert E. Lee,	181
A Hand Litter,	203
Foote's Flotilla,	207
A Mortar Boat,	211
Engagement between the Monitor and Merrimack,	222
Constructing the Canal,	226
Shiloh Meeting House,	229
Burning Horses near Pittsburg Landing,	234
Thomas J. (Stonewall) Jackson,	238
General Nathaniel P. Banks,	239
General Joseph Hooker,	240

LIST OF ILLUSTRATION

	PAGE
General Philip Kearny,	241
General James Longstreet,	242
David G. Farragut,	248
Reconnoitering,	260
General Ambrose E. Burnside,	280
Pickets on Duty,	296
Grant's Headquarters at Chattanooga,	298
General Hugh Judson Kilpatrick,	310
General George G. Meade,	313
General Winfield S. Hancock,	315
General William T. Sherman,	329
Ruins of Charleston,	347
Place of Johnston's Surrender to Sherman,	351
General Philip H. Sheridan,	364

THE POPULAR HISTORY OF THE CIVIL WAR.

CHAPTER I.

INTRODUCTORY—EARLY INDICATIONS OF DISCONTENT—GRADUAL DEVELOPMENT OF SECTIONAL INTERESTS—CAUSES OF THE CIVIL STRIFE—THE STATE RIGHTS THEORY—JOHN C. CALHOUN AND NULLIFICATION—THE TARIFF AND SLAVERY QUESTIONS—BRIEF REVIEW OF PRESIDENTIAL SUCCESSION—ELECTION OF ABRAHAM LINCOLN—PREPARING FOR WAR.

Even the hoarse echoes of the cannon's thunder and the clash of steel have sunk to sleep; the fretful murmurs of semi-satiated passion and prejudice which succeeded the savage frenzy of murderous hate have even been hushed, and the timid tenders of reconciliation have been supplanted by an eager anxiety to proffer and respond warmly to fraternal greetings among the citizens of all sections throughout the now happily re-United States. It is therefore opportune to present a concise, impartial narrative of one of the most important episodes in the history of modern civilization and the development of human liberty. The term episode is not inappropriate in connection with so stupendous an affair as the Civil War in America, since it was, despite its costly magnitude, whether the basis of calculation be that of mere money or those priceless elements, human life and human blood, but one of the incidents of the conflict of opinions which began with the adoption of the Constitution of this Republic.

For the greater part of a century the exigencies of National development were such that the germs of disaffection found no sun of popular feeling to warm them into life and action. They were latent, however, and as surely as the scrub oaks appear when the lofty pines are felled and cleared, so the sturdy sproutings of innate discontent were manifested when social and commercial success had crowned the untiring efforts of a generation of unselfish, patriotic impulses.

But enough of generalization. **The causes of the Civil War**—call it *Rebellion* if you will, deem it *Secession* if you please—had their origin in but one Hydra-headed element, commonly known as State Rights. From the sovereign citizen to the sovereign State, was an easy transition in popular or personal opinion; from property in slaves to property interests in relation to tariff legislation, it was even yet more easy to turn, and therefore, *Nullification*, the earliest exemplar of the latent controversy, is entitled to but subjunctive rank among the cohorts of dissatisfaction. It was, however, the touchstone of the entire matter, and consequently we must begin our history by rapidly recounting the legislation which led up to the bold attempt of John C. Calhoun, of South Carolina, in 1832, to sap the integrity of the Union.

As early as 1812, Calhoun, when taunted by Rear Admiral Stewart with the sham under which the aristocracy of the South, supported absolutely by slave labor, assumed to affiliate with democracy, haughtily retorted. in effect, that such assumption, or pretense, was mere policy designed to aid the South in controlling the Republic; that the compromises of the past would not be repeated, and that any attempt to crush that policy or to abrogate its consequent power of control, would be met by a dissolution of the compact of the States.

Following closely upon the tariff agitation of 1816, a mere preliminary skirmish, came the heated discussions in 1820 on the slavery question, resulting in the Missouri Compromise, by which Missouri was admitted as a slave-holding State in 1821. Subsequent events proved that Calhoun's declaration of hostility towards compromise measures was not a personal feeling merely, nor an unmeaning threat. The issue was merely postponed and the agitation allayed until 1849.

The passage of the tariff act of 1824, which afforded protection to the iron trade of Pennsylvania, the manufacturers of the Eastern States and the Northern and Western wool and hemp interests, revived Southern hostility, and when, in 1828, after a bitter controversy lasting nearly a year, the tariff bill, imposing duties upon an average basis of fifty per cent., was passed, the outspoken indignation of the advocates of the cotton interests was so violent and aggressive that the long-threatened hour of dissolution seemed at hand.

In the fall of 1828, after an exciting Presidential campaign, John Quincy Adams was defeated, and Andrew Jackson, a native of North Carolina, but a resident of Tennessee, was elected, receiving 178 electoral votes against 83 for Adams' re-election. As usual, the mere partisan rancours of a campaign disappeared as easily and as silently as the morning mists. But gathering clouds took their place, the Bank Charter Act and the reopening of the tariff question precipitating another storm. The first annual message of President Jackson opposed the re-chartering of the Bank of the United States, and suggested that the old charter should be allowed to expire by the effluxion of time in 1836. The corporation power was, however, strong enough to set these views aside, and Congress in 1832 passed the bill to re-charter. This was promptly met by a veto, and failing to comand a two-thirds majority, the friends of the bill were compelled to yield.

Meanwhile the agitation on the tariff question had been rapidly spreading, and when, as the result of the session of 1831-32, additional duties were levied upon manufactured goods imported from abroad, the smoldering discontent of the South leaped into flame. It was claimed that again the manufacturing districts were favored at the expense of the agricultural States, and South Carolina, under the lead of John C. Calhoun, with his nullification theory, determined to resist the power of Congress in the premises.

Inflammatory literature was widely disseminated, and other Southern States were invited to join the movement for mutual self-protection. On the 24th of November, 1832, a grand convention was held at Columbia, and the Nullification Ordinance was adopted. This instrument declared that no duties should be paid in South Carolina after a certain date; that no appeal should be permitted to the Supreme Court of the United States in reference to the validity of the ordinance, and that attempts by the United States Government to collect revenue would justify secession and the establishment of an independent government. This ordinance was approved by the Legislature of the State then in session. To emphasize the matter the Legislature ordered the raising, arming and equipping of State forces to resist to the uttermost the exercise of Federal authority.

Mr. Calhoun, then Vice-President of the United States, was named as the head of the proposed State organization, and medals bearing the words, "John C. Calhoun, First President of the Southern Confederacy," were struck off and distributed. In the streets blue cockades, with a center button ornamented with a palmetto, the symbol of the new nation, were freely displayed. Nor did the matter rest here. Colonel Hayne, Senator from South Carolina, boldly advocated, on the floor of the United States Senate, the right of a State, under certain circumstances, to nullify an act of Congress. To his fiery eloquence was opposed the masterly argumentative speech of that master of American oratory, Daniel Webster.

JOHN CALDWELL CALHOUN.

Debate, however, on such a subject, was not President Jackson's mode of meeting and dealing with a crisis. He promptly issued a proclamation, in which he asserted that "to say that any State may at pleasure secede from the Union, is to say that the United States are not a Nation." He declared his intention to collect the revenue under all and any circumstances. This was met by a counter proclamation, in which Governor Hayne, of South Carolina, sustained the Nullification theory, and called for twelve thousand armed volunteers to defend the State against Federal interference. On the 28th of February, 1833, Congress passed the Force bill, which gave jurisdiction to the United

States Courts over cases arising under the revenue laws and materially enlarged the Presidential power in dealing with armed resistance. Thus strengthened, the President dispatched vessels of war to the coast of South Carolina and sent General Winfield Scott to Charleston with troops. Vigorous measures like these, nipped in the bud the immature revolt. The leaders recoiled for the time, the rank and file sullenly subsided, and without bloodshed the point of extreme tension had been reached and passed. Meanwhile Congress considered a bill introduced by the great pacificator, Henry Clay, and in the following spring adopted the measure which, by providing for the gradual reduction of the duties complained of, till at the end of ten years they should reach a basis such as the South had intimated willingness to accept, removed even the shadow of a grievance, on the tariff score, from the restless spirits of South Carolina.

The slavery question, however, was rapidly resuming its position as a burning issue, though the financial panic and the Canadian troubles during the administration of Martin Van Buren (1837-1841), tended to keep it somewhat in the background. The close of this administration by the defeat of Van Buren for re-election, he receiving but sixty electoral votes against two hundred and thirty-four for General Harrison, deprived the Democrats, for the first time in forty years, of the control of the Government.

Inaugurated on the 4th of March, 1841, General Harrison, borne down by the weight of years, died within one month of that date, and on the 6th of April Vice-President John Tyler, of Virginia, took the oath of office as President of the United States.

In the current run of this history, holding its main purpose in view, we have little to consider until in December, 1844, the proposition to admit Texas as a State came before Congress. A clause in the proposed constitution of this State recognized the existence of slavery within its limits. This had been the issue of the Presidential election of that year, and had been the cause of unparalleled excitement. On the 1st of March, 1845, but three days before Tyler's retirement, the annexation bill was adopted, and the prompt assent of the President admitted the "Lone Star State."

The administration of James K. Polk, of Tennessee (1845 to 1849), was chiefly occupied with the Mexican troubles arising out of the Texas boundary question. Towards its close the slavery question again loomed up, David Wilmot, of Pennsylvania, having brought before Congress a bill *to prohibit slavery* in all the territory which might be secured by treaty with Mexico. The defeat of the "Wilmot Proviso," as this measure was termed, led to the formation of a political party, composed of its supporters; and in June, 1848, they nominated ex-President Van Buren, as the Presidential candidate of the "Free Soil Party." Practically this was but the ventilation of an idea, for the campaign turned upon the personal popularity of Generals Cass and Taylor, the latter being elected, by a large majority, with Millard Fillmore, of New York, as Vice-President.

President Taylor's first message paved the way for another struggle. In it he advised the Californians to form a State government in readiness for admission to the Union. In accordance with this a convention at Monterey, in September, 1849, framed a constitution *prohibiting slavery*, and the people adopted it. On the 20th of December, the new Government, with Peter H. Burnet as Governor of the Territory, was organized and a petition was forwarded to Congress asking admission for the State of California.

A bitter controversy was at once initiated and the Missouri experiences were repeated, with this difference, that the North favored and the South opposed the admission. The Southern argument was that with the extension of the Missouri compromise line to the Pacific the right to introduce slavery into California was guaranteed by the general Government, consequently the Constitution of the proposed State should be rejected. The North argued that part of the new State only was affected, that the Missouri Compromise applied only to the Louisiana purchase, and that the people of California had the right to choose their own Constitution. In the bitter debates which followed kindred issues became involved. The South complained that fugitive slaves were aided and encouraged by the North; the Free Soil party demanded the abolition of slavery in the District of Columbia, and Texas added to the imbroglio by claiming New Mexico as part of her territory.

Again the genius of Henry Clay was invoked. Early in 1850 he was appointed chairman of a committee of thirteen to whom all the vexed questions were referred. On the 9th of May he brought forward "The Omnibus Bill" as a compromise. Its provisions were: *First*, the admission of California as a free State; *second*, the formation of new states, not exceeding four in number, out of the territory of Texas, said states to permit or exclude slavery as the people should determine; *third*, the organization of territorial governments for New Mexico and Utah, without conditions on the question of slavery; *fourth*, the establishment of the present boundary between Texas and New Mexico, and the payment to the former of ten million dollars from the public treasury for the surrender of the latter; *fifth*, the enactment of a more vigorous law for the recovery of fugitive slaves; *sixth*, the abolition of the slave trade in the District of Columbia.

During the heated discussion which followed the introduction of the measure, President Taylor died on July 9th, 1850. Mr. Fillmore took the oath of office and appointed Daniel Webster as Secretary of State. The discussion on the Omnibus bill progressed, and on September 18th, 1850, the last clause was adopted. The President immediately approved the measure, and for a time the excitement was again abated. True, it was but a compromise, and did not affect convictions on either side.

Meanwhile, on March 31st, 1850, John C. Calhoun died, and thus the foremost figure in early secession movements passed from the conflict. His influence, however, had left too deep an impression to be easily effaced. Henry Clay followed on the 28th of June, 1852, and Daniel Webster on the 24th of October in the same year. The close of Fillmore's administration introduced a new element, for both the Whig and Democratic platforms affirmed the wisdom of the Compromise Act of 1850; a new party, or rather an extension of the Free Soil organization, denied the wisdom of the Compromise, and declaring that *all* the Territories of the United States ought to be free, put forth their own Presidential candidate. This was John P. Hale, of New Hampshire. The real contest, however, was between General Winfield Scott and Franklin Pierce, of New Hampshire, the latter being elected by a large majority.

The pacification of the Omnibus bill provisions was of very short duration, the anti-slavery party daily growing in determination, if not in actual audacity. In Syracuse, N. Y., a fugitive named Jerry was rescued by force from the Government officers, and the rescue of Anthony Burns was almost effected. In this struggle one man was killed and troops were ordered out to aid in the surrender of the alleged slave. In Ohio, Margaret Garner, another fugitive, killed two of her children to save them from slavery. More legitimate efforts to restrict the operations of the fugitive slave law were made in several States by the enactment of laws to secure at least a jury trial for alleged slaves. Thus steadily and resistlessly the Nemesis of slave-holding brutality was pressing on to the point of actual conflict and its result, the glorious Emancipation Proclamation.

The organization of the vast region west of Minnesota, Iowa and Missouri into Territories was one of the earliest issues of Pierce's Administration. In January, 1854, Senator Stephen A. Douglas, of Illinois, submitted to the United States Senate a proposition to organize the Territories of Kansas and Nebraska. The Kansas-Nebraska bill contained a clause providing that the people of the two Territories, in forming their Constitutions, *should decide for themselves* whether the new States should be free or slave-holding. This was cutting the Gordian knot with a vengeance, for both the new territories lay north of the parallel of thirty-six degrees and thirty minutes, and therefore the proposition absolutely annulled the Missouri Compromise and virtually restored the naked issue of slavery or no slavery. Sectional feeling ran high and debates were bitter, but the bill passed, and in May, 1854, it received the Presidential sanction.

The battlefield was now transferred to Kansas, where a "carpet-bag" element of either faction hastened to control the elections. In November, 1854, a pro-slavery delegate was elected to Congress, and the following year the same party was triumphant in the general Territorial election. The State Legislature met at Lecompton, and framed a Constitution permitting slavery. The Free Soil party denounced the election as illegal, held a convention at Topeka, framed a Constitution excluding slavery, and organized a rival government. From the autumn of 1855 to the summer of 1856, a turbulent civil war raged. This was not quieted until after the appointment, on the 3d of September, of John W. Geary, of Pennsylvania, as Military Governor of Kansas, with authority from the President to restore order and punish lawlessness. This he accomplished locally, but the agitation had spread throughout the Union and the slavery question became the issue of the Presidential election of 1856.

STEPHEN A. DOUGLAS.

Extraordinary combinations and disintegrations of parties marked this campaign. Many Northern Democrats, though opposed to slavery, held that every Territory was entitled to individual choice on the subject, and James Buchanan, of Pennsylvania, with a platform reaffirming the principles of the Kansas-Nebraska bill, became their standard bearer.

The Free Soil party, demanding absolute abolition, nominated John C. Fremont, of California. Another new party, with real purposes which some other historian may be able to comprehend, but which professed to be concerned only with the restriction of foreign influence in the United States, now sprang into being, and called itself, or was christened, the "Native American" or "Know-Nothing" organization. The candidate of this clique was Millard Fillmore. The great majority, however, decided that the vital home question was that of Slavery, and James Buchanan was elected, with John C. Breckinridge, of Kentucky, as Vice-President.

Immediately following the inauguration of President Buchanan, in March, 1857, came the decision of the Supreme Court of the United States in the memorable "Dred Scott" case, which had been pending three years. This deserves more than passing mention.

Dred Scott had been one of the slaves of Dr. Emerson, of Missouri, a United States army surgeon. Emerson moved first to Rock Island, Ill., and then to Fort Snelling, Minn., at which latter place, in 1836, Scott was married to a negro woman whom Emerson had bought. After the birth of two children all the family were taken back to St. Louis and sold. Dred brought suit for his freedom, and after the Circuit and Supreme Courts of Missouri had heard the case, it was, in May, 1854, appealed to the United States Supreme Court. The decision read by Chief-Justice Taney held that "negroes, whether free or slaves, *were not citizens of the United States, and could not become such by any process known to the Constitution*"; that under the laws of the United States "a negro could neither sue nor be sued, and therefore the court had no jurisdiction of Dred Scott's cause"; that "a slave was to be regarded in the light of a personal chattel, and might be removed from place to place by his owner as any other piece of property"; that "the Constitution gave to every slave-holder the right of removing to or through any State or Territory with his slaves and of returning at his will with them to a State where slavery was recognized by law; and that therefore the Missouri Compromise of 1820 and the compromise measures of 1850 were unconstitutional and void."

Six of the associate Justices, Wayne, Nelson, Grier, Daniel, Campbell and Catron concurred, but Judges McLean and Curtis dissented. The President had hoped that this would allay the excitement, but it had a contrary effect. The South affected satisfaction, but the Free Soil party became exasperated, and the passage of Personal Liberty bills resulted in several of the anti-slavery States.

John Brown's raid at Harper's Ferry, Va., October 16th, 1859, was the next excitement for the slave States. The details of the daring attempt, its failure and the trial, condemnation and execution of John Brown and six of his companions are incidents too well and widely known to justify recapitulation here. This affair, and the rapid growth of the Free Soil party in Kansas, while widening the breach between North and South, threw into the nineteenth Presidential election campaign of 1860 the apple of discord destined to precipitate the clash of arms.

With a rapid summary of the features of this campaign we shall close this introductory chapter on the causes which led to the Civil War.

The "People's" party, now called Republican, nominated Abraham Lincoln, of Illinois, with a platform opposing the extension of slavery as the issue of the period. The Democratic Convention met at Charleston in April and split on the slavery question. The Southern delegates withdrew, and, after a meeting in Richmond, organized a separate convention at Baltimore on the 28th of June, and nominated John C. Breckinridge, of Kentucky. The Northern wing remained in session for a time at Charleston, and after some fruitless balloting, also adjourned to Baltimore, where, on June 18th, Stephen A. Douglas was nominated. The American party, now called "Constitutional Unionists," nominated John Bell, of Tennessee. Thus four candidates were in the field.

Abraham Lincoln was elected, having received the electoral votes of all the Northern States, except New Jersey, which were divided between him and two of his opponents. The Southern States mainly supported Breckinridge. Virginia, Kentucky and Tennessee gave their thirty-nine votes to Bell, while Douglas received a scattering vote through nearly all the States.

The South had foreseen the result and energetically provided for it. The words, "ABRAHAM LINCOLN IS ELECTED" became the tocsin of revolt, and the long expected, much dreaded crisis had been reached.

CHAPTER II.

SECESSION SPREADING — THE VARIOUS ORDINANCES — TREACHERY IN THE CABINET—ANDERSON AND FORT SUMTER—HIS HEROIC ACTION—CONFEDERATE DIPLOMATIC OVERTURES—CABINET CHANGES—THE TREACHERY OF TWIGGS—CLOSE OF BUCHANAN'S ADMINISTRATION.

With prompt precision which gave evidence of premeditation, a call was issued in South Carolina, on the day following the general election in November, 1860, for a convention to be held at Columbia, December 17th, to take action in regard to secession. At the appointed time the assemblage was called to order by General D. F. Jamieson, but the men who could calmly contemplate the horrors of civil war trembled at the thought of a pock-marked face, and passed a resolution to adjourn to Charleston in consequence of the prevalence of small-pox in Columbia. After three days' deliberation the following ordinance was passed, shortly after noon, on December 20th, by the unanimous vote of one hundred and sixty-nine members:

"We, the people of the State of South Carolina, in Convention assembled, do declare and ordain, and it is hereby declared and ordained, that the ordinance adopted by us in Convention on the 23d day of May, in the year of our Lord 1788, whereby the Constitution of the United States of America was ratified, and also all Acts and parts of Acts of the General Assembly of this State ratifying the amendments of the said Constitution, are hereby repealed, and that the union now subsisting between South Carolina and other States, under the name of the United States of America, is hereby dissolved."

The fatal plunge had been taken, and on December 24th Governor Pickens issued a proclamation declaring South Carolina "a separate, sovereign, free, and independent State, with the right to levy war, conclude peace, negotiate treaties, leagues or covenants, and do all acts whatever that rightly appertain to a free and independent State."

The dread significance of these measures cannot be overestimated, for the boldness of the declaration and its promptitude proved contagious, and swept away hesitancy or timidity in the other cotton-growing States.

On January 19th, 1861, the Mississippi State Convention, organized the previous day at Jacksonville, with A. J. Barry, of Lowndes, in the chair, passed a secession ordinance, with some slight opposition. The fifteen opposing delegates, however, signed the ordinance next day, making the vote unanimous. South Carolina and Alabama delegations were present and were accorded seats in the Convention.

Florida and Alabama followed, the Convention of the first-named meeting at Tallahassee, and that of the latter at Montgomery, with Wm. M. Brooks in the chair. On the 11th of January both conventions passed secession ordinances, that of Florida by a vote of 62 to 7, and that of Alabama by 61 to 39.

As the Alabama ordinance gives the first indication of Confederacy it may be well to quote it in full:

"*Whereas*, The election of Abraham Lincoln and Hannibal Hamlin to the offices of President and Vice-President of the United States of America, by a sectional party avowedly hostile to the domestic institutions and peace and security of the people of the State of Alabama, following upon the heels of many and dangerous infractions of the Constitution of the United States by many of the States and people of the Northern section, is a political wrong of so insulting and menacing a character as to justify the people of the State of Alabama in the adoption of prompt and decided measures for their future peace and security.

"*Therefore*, Be it declared and ordained by the people of the State of Alabama, in Convention assembled, that the State of Alabama now withdraws from the Union known as the United States of America, and henceforth ceases to be one of the said United States, and is, and of right ought to be, a sovereign independent State.

"Sec. 2. And be it further declared and ordained by the people of the State of Alabama, in Convention assembled, that all power over the territories of said State, and over the people thereof, heretofore delegated to the Government of the United States of America, be, and they are hereby withdrawn from the said Government, and are hereby resumed and vested in the people of the State of Alabama. And as it is the desire and purpose of the people of Alabama to meet the slaveholding States of the South who approve of such a purpose, in order to frame a revisional as a permanent government upon the principles of the Government of the United States, be it also resolved by the people of Alabama, in Convention assembled, that the people of the States of Delaware, Maryland, Virginia, North Carolina, South Carolina, Florida, Georgia, Mississippi, Louisiana, Texas, Arkansas, Tennessee, Kentucky and Missouri be and they are hereby invited to meet the people of the State of Alabama, by their delegates in Convention, on the 4th day of February next, in Montgomery, in the State of Alabama, for the purpose of consultation with each other as to the most effective mode of securing concerted, harmonious action in whatever measures may be deemed most desirable for the common peace and security.

"*And be it further Resolved*, That the President of the Convention be and he is hereby instructed to transmit forthwith a copy of the foregoing preamble, ordinance and resolutions to the Governors of the several States named in said resolutions.

"Done by the people of Alabama, in Convention assembled, at Montgomery, this 11th day of January, 1861."

This extraordinary document is—whether intentionally or accidentally, matters not—a specific admission of the actual purposes and alleged grievances of the South. It will be noticed that "the slaveholding States of the South" are specifically called upon to organize in defense of the peculiar institution.

While this work was being done in Montgomery amid intense excitement, the news had been forwarded to Mobile, where it was received with the wildest demonstrations of enthusiasm, which were intensified by the simultaneous report of the adoption of the Florida ordinance. One hundred and one guns for Alabama and fifteen for Florida were fired, the secession pole was decorated with the Southern flag, and Judge Jones, speaking from the window of the court-room in the Custom-House, announced that the United States Court for the Southern District of Alabama was "adjourned forever." Processions, speeches and busy preparations for illumination occupied the rest of the day. The display at night was simply indescribable within reasonable limits, and thus the long latent theory of a "Southern Confederacy" was forced into practical existence.

There is grim humor in an episode of this period. Governor Pickens, of South Carolina, on January 14th, sent to Washington for a balance of three thousand dollars due him as late minister to Russia. The Department adjusted his accounts by sending him a draft on the Charleston sub-treasury, the money in which had been seized by the State.

Georgia next wheeled into line by passing a secession ordinance on January 19th, by a vote of 208 to 89, and a motion to postpone its operation until March 3d was defeated. Alexander H. Stephens and Herschel V. Johnson were among those voting against passage of the ordinance.

Louisiana followed on January 26th, passing its ordinance by a vote of 113 to 17, a delay motion having been previously voted down. Each member of the Convention was presented with a gold pen with which to sign the ordinance.

Texas came next and on February 1st, at Austin, passed a secession ordinance to be submitted to the people of Texas for their ratification or rejection by the qualified voters on the 23d of February, 1861. If adopted, to take effect and be in force on March 2d, 1861.

The adoption of this ordinance virtually completed the preliminary work of secession, the North Carolina House of Representatives having meanwhile, on February 6th, passed unanimously a declaration that if reconciliation should fail North Carolina would join the other slave States.

Meanwhile several important phases of the controversy had been developed. The Peace Congress, a movement recommended by resolutions of the Legislature of Virginia, met in Washington, February 4th, and organized with ex-President John Tyler, of Virginia, in the chair. Delegates from fourteen free labor and seven slave labor States attended the Conference, being in all 133 Commissioners, representing Maine, New Hampshire, Vermont, Massachusetts, Rhode Island, Connecticut, New York, New Jersey, Pennsylvania, Delaware, Maryland, Virginia, North Carolina, Tennessee, Kentucky, Missouri, Ohio, Indiana, Illinois, Iowa and Kansas. After several days of heated discussion, Mr. Guthrie, as Chairman of the Committee to whom the matter had been referred, reported a plan of adjustment and pacification in seven amendments to the Constitution of the United States.

These several amendments were hotly debated. In effect these propositions provided for the permanent recognition of slavery, with various contingent devices to meet the views of States then existing or to be afterwards admitted.

As these adjustment proposals came to naught it will hardly be necessary to burden our pages with them. It may suffice to state that on the 2d of March, 1861, two days before the adjournment of Congress, the President of the Convention sent a copy of the proposed compromise to Vice-President Breckinridge, who submitted it to the United States Senate. It was referred to a committee of five who reported next day. Mr. Crittenden reported the Convention propositions. Mr. Seward, in behalf of himself and Mr. Trumbull, submitted a substitute providing for a Convention of the States to consider amendments to the Constitution. The Guthrie plan was postponed after a sharp debate, and the Senate concurred in a resolution adopted by the House of Representatives to the effect that "no amendment shall be made to the Constitution which will authorize Congress to interfere within any State with the domestic institutions thereof. All other propositions being also rejected the Peace Congress efforts utterly failed, and the public at large disappointedly found themselves once more face to face with war.

JEFFERSON DAVIS.

Another abortive attempt to effect a separate understanding had also been made by South Carolina. Messrs. R. W. Barnwell, James H. Adams and James L. Orr, styling themselves "Commissioners" from the State of South Carolina, arrived in Washington on the 26th of December, 1860, and prepared to establish themselves as a diplomatic body. On the 28th of December they sent a formal letter to President Buchanan proposing to treat with the Government of the United States for the delivery of the forts, magazines and other public property in South Carolina, and generally to negotiate a treaty between the Commonwealth of South Carolina and the General Government.

They submitted as their basis of recognition the Secession Ordinance. They also referred to the events in Charleston Harbor (hereafter to be related) and requested the withdrawal of all national troops from that point under threats of violence if their demands were not acceded to.

The President courteously but firmly informed them by letter, on December 30th, that he could only meet them as private gentlemen, and could not treat with them as agents of a foreign State. He further called attention to the acts of war committed by South Carolinians in seizing two forts and placing them under the Palmetto flag. He peremptorily refused to withdraw the national troops or personally to enter into negotiations.

On January 1st, 1861, the "Commissioners" wrote a further letter, insolent in tone and matter, declaring that the course of the President had probably rendered civil war inevitable. Simultaneously with the delivery of this letter, the effect of which had doubtless been anticipated, W. H. Trescot, their secretary

ALEXANDER H. STEPHENS.

—a South Carolinian who had been covertly aiding the South while Assistant Secretary of State—started for Charleston. Even the patience of President Buchanan was not proof against the insolence of this second communication, and he returned it with the following indorsement: "This paper, just presented to the President, is of such a character that he declines to receive it." As a matter of course this concluded all pretence of diplomatic intercourse, and the Commissioners, after a ten days' stay in Washington, returned to South Carolina to aid in the Rebellion movements.

On the same day that the Peace Congress met in Washington, quite a different organization was effected in Montgomery, Alabama; in this Convention delegates from the six seceding States commenced the establishment of the Confederate Government. Howell Cobb, of Georgia, was chosen to preside, with Johnson F. Hooper, of Montgomery, as secretary. For several days in secret session the details of the Constitution were discussed, the delegates being far from harmonious in their views, and being more or less actuated by the promptings of personal ambition. On the 8th of February a Provisional Constitution was agreed upon. The next day the members of the Convention took the oath of allegiance to this document, and then proceeded to the election of a President and Vice-President of the Confederacy. Jefferson Davis, of Mississippi, received the six votes of the Convention for President, and Alexander H. Stephens, of Georgia, was similarly elected Vice-President.

The Convention then directed its Chairman to appoint committees on Foreign Relations, Postal Affairs, Finance, Commerce, Military and Naval Affairs, etc. The Finance Committee promptly began to consider a tariff bill and a committee was appointed to draft a constitution for a permanent government. For some days the question of an appropriate flag for the "new nation" was discussed. The first selected had three equal width stripes, one white and two red; a blue union extending the depth of two-thirds of the flag with a circle of six white stars. This was unfurled first on the 4th of March over the State-House at Montgomery. Already, however, grave difficulties were springing up, for South Carolina, though willing to enter a Confederacy, was unwilling to surrender any sovereign rights, especially in regard to the Fort Sumter matter. The inauguration of Davis was the next thing on the programme. He had been at his home in Vicksburg when apprised of his election and he at once started for Montgomery.

On the 18th of February the inaugural ceremonies were conducted in an imposing manner, on a platform in front of the State-House. Davis read his inaugural, recommending the immediate organization of an army and navy, and threw out suggestions of privateering as a means of retaliation on the commerce of an enemy. Howell Cobb, President of the Convention, then administered the oath of office. A full fledged President, he next appointed his Cabinet, selecting for Secretary of State, Robert Toombs; for Secretary of the Treasury, Charles G. Memminger; Secretary of War, Le Roy Pope Walker; Secretary of the Navy, Stephen R. Mallory; and Postmaster-General, John H. Reagan. Subsequently, Judah P. Benjamin was appointed Attorney-General; Wm. M. Browne, Assistant Secretary of State, and Philip Clayton, of Georgia, Assistant Secretary of the Treasury.

The next step after the formal assumption of a national character, was the demanding of recognition by foreign powers, and the following Commissioners were sent to Europe: William L. Yancey, of Alabama, to England; P. A. Rost, of Louisiana, to France; A. Dudley Mann, of Virginia, to Holland and Belgium, and T. Butler King, of Georgia, whose sphere of action was not specially defined.

Vice-President Stephens boldly announced the guiding principle of the Confederacy to be the maintaining of slavery and the continued subjection of the negro to the white race. Although this had long been evident in the course of events, a speech at Savannah, Ga., March 21st, 1861, first placed the matter in an unequivocal light.

Leaving for a time this branch of our subject, we must turn to some of the exciting episodes which marked the closing days of Buchanan's administration. It may be well to note just here the order in which the representatives of the seceding States withdrew from Congress. On January 14th, 1861, Albert G. Brown, Senator from Mississippi, quitted the Capitol, and on the 21st his colleague, Jefferson Davis, after defending his devotion to the doctrine of State Supremacy, also left the Chamber. The representatives of Alabama and Florida left on the same day. On January 28th, Senator Iverson, of Georgia, withdrew after a speech in which he professed faith in the power of "King Cotton" to overthrow northern coercion. Toombs had preceded him and was already engaged in dragooning the Mayor of New York City on the subject of the seizure of arms, on board the steamer Monticello, bound for Savannah, by the

New York police. John Slidell and Judah P. Benjamin of Louisiana quitted the Senate on February 4th, after making characteristic speeches. Miles Taylor, of Louisiana, on quitting the House, made a threatening speech which drew from Representative Spinner, of New York, a vehement protest against treasonable utterances on the floor of Congress. Other representatives quietly drew their pay and retired.

So rapidly and co-incidently was American history being manufactured towards the close of Buchanan's administration, that a running summary of events would prove but an inextricable tangle of exciting incidents. We must, therefore, ask the indulgence of our readers when we drop back, under separate sections, to review momentous phases of the gigantic conspiracy which, like some huge devil-fish, had its tenacious tentacles spread in every direction. We have heretofore briefly adverted to the affairs in Charleston Harbor; we propose now to go into details.

It is necessary here to mention that Buchanan's Secretary of War, John B. Floyd, of Virginia, was perhaps the most treasonably implicated and most dangerous member of the Cabinet. While desiring to avoid stigmatic epithets in general reference to the unhappy struggle in which both North and South were, doubtless from honest convictions, engaged, we cannot close our eyes to the fact that the deliberate betrayal of a sworn National trust is, under any circumstances, treason.

As far back as 1859 Floyd and his confederates were strengthening the resources of the Southern forts in regard to war material and steadily withdrawing Northern or Federal troops. On the 20th of December, 1859, Floyd ordered the transfer of 115,000 muskets and rifles from Springfield and Watertown, Massachusetts, and Watervliet, New York, to the arsenals at Mount Vernon, Alabama; Augusta, Georgia; Fayetteville, North Carolina; Charleston, South Carolina, and Baton Rouge, Louisiana. In addition to this, under a strained construction of the law authorizing the Secretary of War to sell unsuitable military stores, he transferred to private individuals and States a large quantity of altered muskets at a ridiculously low price. In this way over 135,000 small arms were withdrawn from the North and placed in Southern control. Nor was this all; for while Virginia, South Carolina, Georgia, Florida, Alabama, Louisiana, Mississippi and Kansas received at the close of 1860, by the Secretary's orders, their annual quotas of arms for 1861 in advance several of the Northern States had received part only, and some none at all. Even a believer in the theory of a "fortuitous aggregation of atoms" could not accept such a condition of affairs as accidental, but would be forced to recognize conspiracy, and that, too, of a traitorous brand.

We turn now to Charleston Harbor, with its four forts—Moultrie, Sumter, Pinckney and Johnson. Fort Sumter, the largest and strongest, is in the middle of the entrance to Charleston Harbor; Fort Moultrie is on Sullivan's Island, distant four miles from Charleston; Castle Pinckney is near the city, on a strip of marsh, and was never of much importance; Fort Johnson, on James Island, west of Sumter, was of still less consequence. In October, 1860, Floyd, for reasons best known to himself, but open to grave suspicion, removed Colonel Gardner from the command of Fort Moultrie, and sent there Major Robert Anderson, of Kentucky. If there was a special design in this, it was one of the inevitable errors of an over-confident conspiracy, for Major Anderson quickly detected the secession sentiment and penetrated the local designs. He represented the case to the Secretary, and mentioned the weakness of Fort Moultrie in the event of an attack. His fidelity was also a blunder, though an honest one; for, while his appeals for reinforcement were disregarded, he was really informing Adjutant-General Cooper, brother-in-law of Senator Mason, of Virginia, one of the deeply

MAJOR ROBERT ANDERSON.

implicated secessionists, of the weakness of the Federal status at Charleston.

Meanwhile zealous efforts had been made in Congress by Jefferson Davis and others, to stifle official investigation, prevent the strengthening of the defenses at Charleston, and even to procure the removal of troops already there. As time rolled on, Anderson became more convinced of the danger and more urgent in his demands, intimating that he should submit the matter to Lieutenant General Scott. To prevent this he was permitted to send a few men to repair Fort Pinckney, and Floyd further quieted him by summoning Colonel Huger, of Charleston, to Washington, Anderson being directed to confer with Huger on the position of affairs. At an interview with Major Macbeth, Colonel Huger and others, Anderson was bluntly told that after secession the forts would be taken possession of. Still more urgent demands on his part for assistance to enable him to cope with this threat were met by suggestions that it would not do to provoke hostilities, but he was further instructed to defend himself if attacked. Meanwhile the remonstrances of General Scott, and of Secretary of State Cass, had failed to induce President Buchanan to throw off his timid procrastination and reinforce the Southern forts. It is doubtless a fact that other members of the Cabinet, in sympathy, if not in actual league with secession, held him back. As earnest as he was loyal, Major Anderson felt that the period of "waiting for orders" had passed. The repairs of Castle Pinckney and Fort Moultrie were pressed on as fast as his limited resources would permit.

The passage of the South Carolina secession ordinance convinced him that the hour of peril was at hand. An appeal to the government at Washington was entirely unheeded. With military instinct he determined to shift his base to the strongest fort, Sumter, rather than allow himself to be overshadowed by it in a weaker fort. As commander of all the forts he could choose his location. With the utmost caution he first moved the women and children to Fort Johnson, on the 26th of December, sending with them in the vessels ample provisions. The plausible excuse that he had removed them from the scene of a coming conflict satisfied the conspirators in Charleston, who prepared to spring their trap on the little garrison of Fort Moultrie. But they had mistaken their man; as wily as he was loyal, cool and determined, Anderson had ordered that no landing should be made at Fort Johnson, but that a signal of "three guns from Moultrie" should send them on direct to Sumter.

That evening, by moonlight, most of the garrison of Fort Moultrie left for Fort Sumter. The few officers and men remaining gave the concerted signal and then spiked the great guns, destroyed the carriages and cut down the flag-staff. Perfect success crowned this stratagem. The women and children, with their gallant protectors, were safe within the staunch walls of Fort Sumter, provisioned and fairly supplied with ammunition by 8 o'clock P. M.

For skill, daring, chivalry and patriotism, this action of Major Anderson is almost without a parallel in the world's history.

The little party left behind at Fort Moultrie consisted of Surgeon Crawford, Captain Foster, three other South Carolina officers and seven privates.

Immediately after assuming his quarters in the Fort, Major Anderson wrote a brief report to the Adjutant-General, without any comment, except an expression of thankfulness for a safe removal. The foiled and disgusted schemers in Charleston, however, flashed the news to Washington, and the angry Floyd, finding his fiendish plans frustrated, furiously telegraphed as follows: "Intelligence has reached here this morning that you have abandoned Fort Moultrie, spiked the guns, burned the carriages, and gone to Fort Sumter. It is not believed, because there is no order for any such movement. Explain the meaning of this report."

With characteristic coolness Anderson replied: "The telegram is correct. I abandoned Fort Moultrie because I was certain that if attacked my men must have been sacrificed, and the command of the harbor lost. I spiked the guns and destroyed the carriages to keep the guns from being turned against us. If attacked, the garrison would never have surrendered without a fight."

As an indication of the local feeling, we clip the following from newspapers of December 28th. The Charleston *Courier* says: "Major Robert Anderson, U. S. A., *has achieved the unenviable distinction of opening civil war between American citizens by an act of gross breach of faith.*"

Had the writer of this fustian been blessed with a little more piety and patriotism, and a little less treason and tergiversation he would have admitted that "Surely in vain the net is spread in the sight of any bird."

The Charleston *Mercury*, with greater calmness but more guile, remarks: "Major Anderson alleges that the movement was made without orders and upon his own responsibility. He is a gentleman and we will not impugn his word or his motives. But it is due to South Carolina and to good faith that the act of this officer should be repudiated by the government, *and that the troops be moved forthwith from Fort Sumter.*" The italics, in this case, are ours, and comment is needless. On the contrary the Baltimore *American* and the Baltimore *Exchange* admired and warmly commended the movement, as did the Boston *Courier*, while the Boston *Atlas* and *Bee*, going still further, printed in capitals at the end of an editorial the three names "WASHINGTON, GARIBALDI, ANDERSON."

Before quitting Fort Sumter for a glance at the doings in the National Capitol we cannot pass over an impressive scene. Proud of their commander's exploit the brave little garrison desired to salute the rising sun of the 27th, with the fluttering folds of the Stars and Stripes, but Major Anderson refused to allow this till the Chaplain should be present. At noon he arrived; the inmates of the fort were congregated, and as the chaplain offered a fervent prayer, Anderson, kneeling at the foot of the flagstaff, held the halliards. At the conclusion of the prayer he ran up the flag amid the wild enthusiasm of all present. It was a few hours after this that he received and replied to Floyd's telegram.

When on the morning of the 27th of December the people of Charleston became aware of the condition of affairs their rage and disappointment were ungovernable. Governor Pickens at the request of the Secession Convention, at once ordered the military occupation of Castle Pinckney and Forts Moultrie and Johnson. The seizure of the Government arsenal with its arms and ammunition was the first step, in the name of the State. Amid wild excitement six or seven hundred men were armed and equipped from the stores which Floyd had treacherously placed there. In the course of the afternoon the steamers *General Clinch* and *Nina*, under the orders of General R. G. M. Donovant, secession Adjutant General of the State, started for Pinckney and Moultrie. Colonel J. J. Pettigrew captured

SAND-BAG BATTERY AT FORT MOULTRIE.

Castle Pinckney with two hundred men after a sharp resistance by the garrison, though the commandant, Lieutenant R. K. Mead, had escaped to Sumter. The ammunition was gone, the guns were spiked and the carriages ruined, but Pettigrew hastily waved a "Palmetto flag" over the ramparts, amid the shouts of the people along the shore, who wildly cheered the first secession flag over a national fort.

Meanwhile Colonel Wilmot G. De Saussure, with 250 men, proceeded to Fort Moultrie, which was surrendered by the sentinel without opposition. As we have before shown, this fort had been dismantled. The Palmetto was soon floating from this fortification also, and the work of repairing the damage caused by Anderson and his men was immediately commenced. Huge heaps of sand-bags were placed upon the ramparts, and new breast-works, with heavy guns mounted on them, were erected.

About the same time Governor Pickens sent a messenger to Fort Sumter, demanding Major Anderson's immediate evacuation and return to Moultrie, on the allegation that an understanding existed that no re-enforcements were to be sent to any of the forts. Anderson declared that he had no knowledge of any such understanding, and positively refused to heed the demands. Several other messages of like import were treated in a similar manner, and then the indignation of the baffled conspirators in Charleston knew no bounds. On all sides Anderson was denounced as a traitor to the South. But that troubled the brave soldier but little. His most bitter annoyance came from the fact that with the guns of Sumter in position to have dislodged the insurgents from the deserted forts, he did not feel that his powers exceeded the step he had taken in changing his location to a safe vantage ground. Here we must leave him for the present, compelled idly to witness the preparations of the secessionists for the next stirring Fort Sumter episode.

In Washington Secretary Floyd denounced Anderson at a Cabinet meeting and demanded President Buchanan's permission to withdraw the garrison from Charleston harbor. But the mask had been torn off and even Buchanan was mulish and obstinate. The logic of events was too potent for his half-hearted conciliation policy. He refused to listen to Floyd's arguments and a Cabinet disruption followed. Floyd was succeeded on December 31st, 1860, as Secretary of War, by Joseph Holt, of Kentucky, whose first act was to compliment Anderson for his action, which he described as being "in every way admirable, alike for its humanity and patriotism as for its soldiership."

The reorganization of Buchanan's Cabinet was completed early in January, 1861. Attorney-General Black succeeded Cass as Secretary of State; Edwin M. Stanton became Attorney-General; Philip F. Thomas, of Maryland, became Secretary of the Treasury, but soon made way for John A. Dix, of New

York. With cleaner men around him, the President, who had been despondent and inert, became more hopeful and energetic. The merchant steamer *Star of the West* was quietly chartered and provisioned, and on the 5th of January was dispatched from New York. Four officers and 250 artillerists and marines were secretly put on board of the steamer down the bay, under Captain John McGowan, en route for Fort Sumter to re-inforce Anderson. Secretary Thompson, of the Interior Department, however, while writing his resignation, found time to send a dispatch to Judge Longstreet, at Charleston, warning him of the expedition. As a consequence, when the *Star of the West* neared Fort Moultrie, a battery on Morris Island and the guns of the fort opened fire on her. Two tugs also steamed out from Fort Moultrie with an armed schooner to intercept her. Despite the display of an American ensign at the fore in addition to the usual national flag the cannonade was kept up. Finding himself powerless, Captain McGowan reluctantly put about and returned to New York. Though the insurgents, through Cabinet treachery, were aware of the character of the vessel and her mission, Major Anderson was wholly in the dark, and regarded the attack as a wanton outrage upon a merchant vessel and an insult to the flag, which his instructions did not permit him to resent. His guns were in position, shotted and commanding the whole range of the scene of action; his officers and men implored him to let them fire, but he declined the responsibility. His instructions limited him to defense, and the saddened soldier saw the dishonored flag of his nation disappear in the distance.

One other episode remains to be noticed here, before we turn to a rapid review of general affairs during the brief period prior to the inauguration of President Lincoln.

On December 27th, while the occupation of Fort Moultrie was being consummated, Captain N. L. Coste, United States Revenue Service, surrendered the revenue cutter *William Aiken* to the South Carolina authorities. He personally ran up the Palmetto flag, and his crew volunteered to remain with him in the service of the State under the Secession Ordinance. His subordinate officers reported for duty at Washington, and left Captain Coste, of the navy, to share with Captain Dunovant, of the army, the infamy of being the first two commissioned officers of the United States who went into rebel service.

It is but common charity to presume that the magnitude of the crisis through which he was passing had absolutely shattered the nerves of President Buchanan. He dared not grasp the nettle. Thus, when Lieutenant-General Scott suggested the promotion of Lieutenant Anderson for his heroic act, the President evaded the request and referred the matter to his successor in the Presidency.

Meantime, the demand of Governor Pickens for the surrender of Sumter having been sternly refused by Anderson, the Governor sent Isaac W. Hayne as a "Commissioner of South Carolina" to Washington, to treat for the surrender of the fort on a partition basis, in regard to the value of the property, as between the State and the Federal Government. Hayne reached the Capital on January 13th, and three days later Senators Slidell, Fitzpatrick and Mallory submitted the matter to the President. Through Mr. Holt, Secretary of War, he replied, in effect, that he was powerless to consider such a proposition; that he did not deem it needful to reinforce Anderson, but that, should such necessity arise, efforts to aid him would be made. Governor Pickens then instructed Hayne to make a demand for the immediate surrender of Fort Sumter. This was refused in somewhat similar terms, and the onus of a grave responsibility was thrown on South Carolina, should force be attempted.

Co-incidently with this event, the "Commissioner of the sovereign State of Alabama," one Thomas J. Judge, arrived in Washington, and desired to "present his credentials" to the President, being "duly authorized to negotiate with the Government of the United States in reference to the public buildings in Alabama and its position in regard to the debt of the United States." An audience was refused on any diplomatic basis, and Mr. Judge disappeared with Mr. Hayne, disgusted and indignant.

Another base surrender, or betrayal of trust, stains the pages of American history about this period.

General David E. Twiggs, second in rank to Lieutenant-

General Scott, was placed in command of the Department of Texas, early in 1861. It was not long before he began to show signs of disloyalty, even to the extent of warning his subordinates to secure their pay while they could get it. Secretary Holt becoming acquainted with this, issued a general order on January 18th, relieving Twiggs, and turning over the command to Colonel Carlos A. Waite, First Infantry Regiment. The headquarters of Twiggs were at the Alamo, in San Antonio, while Colonel Waite was sixty miles distant, on Verde Creek. Before the orders could reach Waite the treachery of Twiggs was consummated. On the 17th of February, one of two couriers sent out from San Antonio by Assistant Adjutant-General Nicholls delivered the orders to Waite; the other courier had been captured by the conspirators. Twiggs had previously depleted the force under his immediate command, and now he demanded a plausible excuse for surrendering. This was furnished by a dash made on San Antonio on Sunday morning, February 16th, by Ben McCulloch, a Texan ranger, with two hundred mounted men, who seized the arsenal and other buildings. A much larger force then poured into the city, and Twiggs made terms of surrender. By this diabolical act he gave up stores and munitions worth $1,200,000; surrendered all the fortifications and military posts in his command, and all the national forces in Texas, about 2,500 men. He issued a general order to this effect on the 18th instant, and advised his betrayed comrades to make their way to the coast, he having secured permission for them to leave the State with their clothing, arms and subsistence. With the details of the subsequent capture of the Texas forts, we shall have to deal in later pages of this history. When this act of treason became known, the indignation of the Government was intense, and the expulsion of Twiggs was promptly ordered.

The closing days of Buchanan's administration were unmarked by any events of significance. The Confederates were maturing their plans for the coming conflict, and the President, who had degenerated into a despondent old man who had tried to please everybody, and consequently pleased nobody, drifted out of office and into comparative obscurity.

CHAPTER III.

BIOGRAPHICAL SKETCH OF ABRAHAM LINCOLN—HIS EVENTFUL JOURNEY FROM HIS HOME TO THE NATIONAL CAPITAL—PLOTS FOR HIS ASSASSINATION—THE CONSPIRATORS FOILED—INTRIGUES AT WASHINGTON—PRECAUTIONS AGAINST REVOLUTION—LINCOLN'S INAUGURATION—ABSTRACT OF HIS ADDRESS.

It is a relief to turn from records of baseness; from the contemplation of criminal careers and conspiracies, and restfully review, in a brief biographical sketch, the noble character of that sturdy, sterling, rugged representative of nature's nobility, Abraham Lincoln. Upon him fell the brunt of the battle, and we cannot better begin our war history than by rapidly outlining his career. Of Virginia descent, he was born in Larue County, Kentucky, February 12th, 1809. When seven years of age, his struggling, hard-working parents removed to Spencer County, Indiana, and the boy took his share of the toil in the rude cabin amid the partially cleared timber lands. Nine years later the spare, wiry stripling is seen running a ferry, at the mouth of Anderson Creek, across the Ohio, for the modest wage of six dollars per month. The scanty opportunities for education were eagerly seized upon, though it is doubtful whether he had as much as one year's actual schooling. About the time he came to man's estate, his father again shifted his location, settling on the north fork of the Sangamon, ten miles west of Decatur, Illinois. A log cabin, a small clearing and plenty of hard work, would hardly seem to be legitimate preparation for the bar, the Legislature, the White House and the apotheosis of martyrdom; but such were Abraham Lincoln's surroundings and obligations when twenty-one years of age. Flatboating on the Mississippi and clerking in a country store at New Salem, near Springfield, Illinois, were his next experiences. Then, from 1833 to 1836, we find him a merchant, till bankrupted by the dissipation of a worthless partner. The law, always a pet hobby, then claimed its votary, and in 1837, after admission to the bar, he began practice in Springfield. In 1846 his sterling qualities had gained for him such respect that his fellow-citizens sent him to represent them in Congress. We had almost overlooked one other experience, his services as a volunteer during the Black Hawk war. In 1858, during his candidacy for United States Senator from Illinois, the quaint power of his masterly mind was revealed in his oratorical combats with Stephen A. Douglas, who, though a victor by eight votes in the election contest, made for his defeated opponent more political capital than anything else, perhaps, could have done. Elected President of the United States in November, 1860, by a large majority, as the representative of the Republican party, an advanced form of the Free Soil organization, Abraham Lincoln found himself, at the age of fifty-two, the chosen champion of human liberty, the standard-bearer of the Republic of America, the rugged barrier between union and disunion, against which the roaring, seething billows of slavery and secession were to beat fiercely and vainly; save that, in baffled demoniacal malice, the cowardly resort of assassination was invoked, to cause delight among devils and angered anguish amid angels. But Lincoln had not lived in vain, and his death crowned his prestige. However, we are anticipating, and must resume the thread of our narrative.

On February 13th, 1861, the joint convention of the two houses of Congress declared Abraham Lincoln, of Illinois, and Hannibal Hamlin, of Maine, elected President and Vice-President of the United States for the four years from the 4th March next ensuing.

Two days before this, Mr. Lincoln left his home in Springfield, Illinois, accompanied by J. G. Nicolay, his private secretary; Robert T. Lincoln, Major Hunter and Colonel Sumner, United States Army; Colonel E. E. Ellsworth, State Auditor; John K. Dubys, Governor Yates' Aid; Colonel W. H. Lamon, Judge David Davis, Hon. O. H. Browning, E. L. Baker, of the Springfield *Journal*; Robert Irwin, N. B. Budd and George Lotham. It was a notable and representative party. The scene at the depot on his departure was overwhelmingly affecting. The parting words of the President-elect to his assembled fellow-citizens, delivered in tones broken by his emotions, breathed the true spirit of a man equally the servant of his God and of his country. And yet miscreants were already on his track with murder in their hearts, while whispers were heard in various quarters that he would not reach Washington alive. An attempt to throw the train from the track, and the later discovery of an Orsini bomb in the car he was to occupy when leaving Cincinnati, proved that there was more than mere rumor afloat. At many points along the route enthusiastic demonstrations greeted him, but with instinctive caution his utterances, while firm, were guarded. The most that could be made of them was that he would do his duty and defend the Union. In New York the timid demagogue, Mayor Fernando Wood, attempted to counsel the distinguished guest of the city as to his future conduct, but Lincoln looked him through, and discomfited the secession sympathizer by repeating his stereotyped formula. It is difficult to believe that beneath that impassive countenance there were not twitching nerves, and that that bold, brave heart did not at times beat tumultuously, for Lincoln was a keen listener and a close observer; nevertheless he kept cool, and earnestly advised others to do likewise. His reception in the loyal city of Philadelphia, on February 22d, and his participation in the celebration ceremonies of Washington's Birthday, formed the most pleasing episode of his journey. Beyond this point lay his greatest danger, the existence of a plot in Baltimore to precipitate a riot and murder him in the melee having already been ascertained. The shrewd plans of Detective Pinkerton, a Chicago detective, and of Mr. Judd, of the same city, an ardent admirer of Mr. Lincoln, allowed the programme of the journey to be safely carried out. Mrs. Lincoln having joined her husband in Philadelphia, the party proceeded to Harrisburg. There, while the Legislature and citizens were honoring the President-elect, the telegraph wires were cut, to baffle the Baltimore conspirators. A special train, ostensibly to convey a messenger bearing "despatches," rushed through to Washington twelve hours earlier than had been expected, and on the morning of the 23d of February Mr. Lincoln was greeted by Congressman Washburne, of Illinois, who was waiting at the depot in painful suspense. After a brief rest he called on President Buchanan, who joyfully introduced him to the Cabinet, then in session. A great crisis had been met and overcome, and the enthusiasm of loyalty but deepened the contrast with the ill-concealed chagrin of the conspirators. With zealous forethought, General Scott had gathered so strong a force in Washington that any further effort to prevent the coming inauguration would have been worse than futile.

SCENE OF THE INAUGURATION.

It is an open secret, however, that a plan had been formed to seize Washington at this juncture, and inaugurate a revolution. So bold, indeed, were the conspirators, that Senator Wigfall, of Texas, on the 5th of February, had asked in the Senate, and Representative Burnett, of Kentucky, on the 11th, inquired in the House, why troops and munitions had been massed in the National Capital. A resolution was even offered in the House, providing for the removal of the regular troops, but this was laid on the table, and on March 1st President Buchanan simply replied to Congressional inquiry by stating that there were but "six hundred and fifty-three private soldiers in the city, besides the usual number of marines at the navy-yard, intended to act as a *posse comitatus*, in strict subordination to civil authority, should they be needed to preserve peace and order prior to or at the inauguration of the President-elect." Detected and baffled, the iniquitous plot was abandoned.

The inauguration ceremonies were peacefully and impressively conducted. Senator Baker, of Oregon, introduced Mr. Lincoln to the vast throng, and Senator Douglas waited on his late opponent with respectful attention. After reading his memorable inaugural address, Chief Justice Taney administered the oath of office, and President Lincoln went at once to the White House, to begin the most stirring chapter of his life and of the life of this great Republic.

Limited space prevents our incorporating the full text of President Lincoln's inaugural address, but our task would be incomplete did we fail to present its most salient features. After a brief introduction, in which Mr. Lincoln quoted from one of his speeches as follows: "I have no purpose, directly or indirectly, to interfere with the institution of slavery in the States where it exists," he added that those who nominated and elected him did so with a full knowledge of these sentiments. He continued: "And more than this, they placed in the platform for my acceptance, and as a law to themselves and to me, the clear and emphatic resolution which I now read:

"'*Resolved*, That the maintenance inviolate of the rights of the States, and especially the right of each State to order and control its own domestic institutions according to its own judgment exclusively, is essential to that balance of power on which the perfection and endurance of our political fabric depend; and we denounce the lawless invasion by armed force of the soil of any State or Territory, no matter under what pretext, as among the gravest of crimes.'

"I now reiterate these sentiments; and in doing so I only press upon the public attention the most conclusive evidence of which the case is susceptible, that the property, peace and security of no section are to be in anywise endangered by the now incoming Administration."

After elaborating upon this theme, adverting to the troubles which had arisen, the dangerous menaces which had been enunciated and the legitimate methods which existed of meeting and remedying real or alleged grievances, Mr. Lincoln concluded in these words: "I am loath to close. We are not enemies, but friends. We must not be enemies. Though passion may have strained, it must not break our bonds of affection. The mystic cords of memory, stretching from every battle-field and patriot grave to every living heart and hearthstone all over this broad land, will yet swell the chorus of the Union, when again touched, as surely they will be, by the better angels of our nature."

It was a noble appeal, and only hearts, hardened as was that of Pharaoh, could have resisted it. That they did so, however, is all too true. How they did this, and to what dire lengths sectional prejudice and fraternal hate were driven in the ensuing four years, it is our painful task now to trace, step by step, until the saddened citizens of the United States could thankfully, though wearily murmur, "The cruel war is over."

CHAPTER IV.

COMPOSITION OF LINCOLN'S CABINET—ANOTHER ATTEMPT AT SOUTHERN DIPLOMACY—THE OVERTURES REJECTED—AFFAIRS IN CHARLESTON HARBOR—THE ATTACK ON FORT SUMTER—ITS GALLANT DEFENCE BY ANDERSON—PERIL OF THE LITTLE GARRISON—ITS EVACUATION ON APRIL 14TH.

It will be proper to note, just here, who were the men selected by President Lincoln to aid him in the Herculean labors of his administration. His Cabinet was constituted as follows: Secretary of State, Wm. H. Seward, of New York; Secretary of the Treasury, Salmon P. Chase, of Ohio; Secretary of War, Simon Cameron, of Pennsylvania; Secretary of the Navy, Gideon Welles, of Connecticut; Secretary of the Interior, Caleb Smith, of Indiana; Postmaster-General, Montgomery Blair, of Maryland; Attorney-General, Edward Bates, of Missouri. These were loyal and able men, and their first task was to cleanse the Augean official stables of their several departments. These were reeking with corruption and disloyalty.

WILLIAM H. SEWARD.

The first skirmish with secession which the new administration had was a verbal one on the 5th of March. John Forsyth, of Alabama, and Martin J. Crawford, of Georgia, two of the three commissioners appointed by the Confederate Convention at Montgomery, arrived in Washington, and on the 11th attempted to open negotiations. Various communications passed between them and Secretary Seward, but official recognition on a diplomatic basis was denied them, and after a display of arrogant impertinence they quitted the capital on the 11th of April. The details of their fruitless efforts to force in the thin edge of the wedge of recognition are not worth mention. The plan was doubtless to divert attention, as much as possible, from the preparations in the South, especially at Charleston, to which point we must now turn for what is usually accepted as the opening of the war, although the occupation of Moultrie, etc., and the firing on the *Star of the West* might fairly be accorded such notoriety.

On the day of Lincoln's inauguration, Major Anderson's letter of February 28th was received. In it he expressed doubts of the possibility of the needed reinforcements reaching him in time. This matter was the first discussed by the new cabinet. The majority of the members, together with General Scott, favored abandoning the position, but after many discussions extending over several days, the minority, Chase and Blair, particularly the latter, convinced the President that dignity and policy alike demanded that an effort should be made, despite the seeming impractibility of the project. On the 4th of April a written order was given, together with personal instructions, to Gustavus V. Fox (subsequently Assistant Secretary of the Navy) to fit out an expedition for the relief of Sumter. With wonderful tact and promptitude, in the face of official opposition, for General Scott still ridiculed the movement, Mr. Fox had his expedition under way from New York early on the 9th of April. It consisted of the steamer *Baltic*, the U. S. ships *Powhatan*, *Pawnee*, *Pocahontas* and *Harriet Lane*, together with three tugs. Blunders and disasters, however, marred the well-laid plans. The entire details had been secretly arranged, and a consequent confusion of orders enabled Lieutenant Porter to take the *Powhatan*, unknown to Mr. Fox, from the little fleet on its way down New York Bay, in pursuance of instructions to proceed to Pensacola. A storm next drove off the tugs, one going back, another being captured at Wilmington, N. C., and the third being disabled. The expedition arrived too late, and would have been almost useless under any circumstances, as the *Powhatan*, flagship, had carried off the launches designed to land the supplies, etc. With scrupulous honor, in accordance with a previous understanding, the President had notified Governor Pickens of his intention to send supplies to Major Anderson. This courtesy was taken advantage of and the plans of the Confederates were hurried forward.

From the time of the occupation of Castle Pinckney and Fort Moultrie, the greatest activity had been manifested at Charleston. The forts were repaired and partially reconstructed, new batteries had been built, including a formidable floating affair, composed of logs and layers of railway iron. All was in readiness for the capture of Sumter, although it was felt that by this act the Rubicon would be crossed and the momentous issue precipitated. Early in February the women and children had been sent away from the fort, and the little garrison patiently awaited the decree of fate, willing to die but determined to defy dishonor.

P. G. T. BEAUREGARD.

The muster roll numbered only eighty-one persons, including Major Robert Anderson, First Lieutenants Jefferson C. Davis, George W. Snyder, Truman Seymour, Theodore Talbot and Norman J. Hall. Second Lieutenant Richard K. Mead, Assistant Surgeon Samuel W. Crawford, twenty-two non-commissioned officers and fifty-one privates. Opposed to this handful of men the Confederates had grouped a force of 7,000 men under arms, and had 140 pieces of heavy ordnance in position.

The "Charge of the Six Hundred" at Balaklava, brilliant blunder as it was, pales in audacity and heroism when compared with the politic, well-considered, daring defiance of this pigmy garrison to its titanic assailants.

For a brief period the beleagured garrison had but little difficulty in procuring supplies of food, and although it was pretty well understood that all communications with Washington were intercepted and read in Charleston, yet the channel was kept open to a certain extent. At last Anderson was notified by General Beauregard that the Montgomery authorities had ordered the cutting off of all communications between the fort and the main land, and the stoppage of mails and supplies. On the 26th of March, Beauregard had tendered every facility for the evacuation of the fort, on the personal pledge of Anderson that he would leave the defenses in good condition. The offer was peremptorily declined, but meanwhile no instructions were received ; and finally, on the 5th of April, he wrote Adjutant-General Thomas, pleading for orders of some kind as an act of justice, and stating that in a few days, at least, the garrison must starve at its post or abandon the fort.

On the 8th of April the dispatch of President Lincoln to Governor Pickens was received in Charleston, and sent on to Montgomery. In reply, Beauregard was ordered to demand the surrender of Sumter. The critical moment had arrived, and Charleston was aflame with excitement, which was fanned by hot-headed men from other disloyal States anxious to precipitate that state of affairs so admirably described by Talleyrand as that when " All things solid and valuable sink to the bottom and only straws and things valueless float on the surface." Two of these straws were Roger A. Pryor and Edmund Ruffin, of Virginia. The first made an incendiary speech on the evening of the 10th, in which he cursed the Union, urged the excited people to strike a blow at once, and promised the immediate secession of Virginia if it was done. The second of these worthies went beyond mere oratory ; he begged permission to fire the first shot at Fort Sumter, was accorded the coveted boon, and by it covered himself with dishonor only equaled by another shot which he fired on the 17th of June, 1865, at Danville, Va., when, a hoary-headed miscreant of eighty years, ruined by the war he had precipitated, he committed suicide by blowing off the top of his head.

Under the promptings of such men, Charleston became a veritable Pandemonium during the night of the 10th of April and the twenty-four hours following. At 2 P. M. on Thursday, April 11, Beauregard sent a formal demand for the surrender of the fort. Major Anderson promptly replied that he could not, in honor, comply, and added : "I will await the first shot, and if you don't batter us to pieces, we will be starved out in a few days."

At a late hour the same night Beauregard, under orders from Confederate Secretary of War Walker, sent a second communication to Anderson, offering that if he would name a time for the evacuation and consent to suspend hostilities, none should be employed against him. Major Anderson replied that, anxious to avoid bloodshed, he would agree to leave the fort by noon on the 15th, unless he should in the meantime receive supplies or controlling instructions from his government. The night had slipped away, and it was 2 A. M. on the 12th when Anderson gave his written reply, unsealed, by request, to Beauregard's aids, Colonels Chesnut, Chisholm, Pryor and Captain Lee. That the tenor of the reply had been foreseen and preparations made, in accordance with Walker's instructions, to reduce the fort by any means, is proved by the fact that the aids were instructed to require an "unsealed" reply.

These men, in accordance with discretionary powers, read the note, held a hasty consultation within the fort, and by half-past three o'clock had handed to Anderson the following ultimatum: "By authority of Brigadier General Beauregard, commanding the provisional forces of the Confederate States, we have the honor to notify you that he will open the fire of his batteries on Fort Sumter in one hour from this time."

This called for no reply, and the aids at once left the fort. The Stars and Stripes were flung to the breeze of the early dawn; the men were withdrawn from the ramparts and sent to the bomb-proofs in readiness for the attack. It should here be noted that Anderson's messenger to Washington having been trapped on his return journey, the Major was unaware of the relief expedition, while the Confederates not only knew all the details, but were also cognizant of the fact that the *Harriet Lane* and the *Pawnee* were already outside the harbor. In Charleston the bustle and preparation was seen on all sides. Military had been summoned by telegraph, hospital arrangements made, and at midnight the signal of seven guns called the reserves from their quarters. To increase the confusion nature took a hand in the performance, and heaven's artillery crashed and rumbled as a southwest storm came up.

The dreadful suspense of that memorable hour was endured in silence by the patriot band. It passed, and then a signal from a battery near Fort Johnson was followed by a shell from Cummings' Point, which exploded over Sumter.

Ruffin had fired his "first shot at Fort Sumter." Scarcely yet even have its echoes ceased to reverberate.

The first shell was almost immediately followed by a furious cannonade from all the works, new and old, which encircled the fort. For hours the attack was endured without any reply, the storm meanwhile raging with unabated fury.

The garrison in Sumter took their breakfast at the usual hour, 6:30 A. M., and then divided into three reliefs, each to work the guns four hours, the return fire was begun at 7 A. M. on the 12th of April. The lower tier of guns opened on Fort Moultrie, the iron battery on Cummings' point, two batteries on Sullivan's island and the floating battery simultaneously. By this time the pent-up enthusiasm of all had burst the bounds of routine discipline, the two reliefs, officers and men, rushed to the aid of the firing party, and hurled iron defiance at all the leading works of the enemy. It was soon apparent, however, that beyond inflicting slight damage little could be effected towards silencing this formidable attacking force. It was soon found that there was no portion of the fort not exposed to the fire of mortars. The fire of the enemy, which at first had been wild, became more effective as time wore on and began to tell on the walls. Some of the guns were disabled, and soon the barracks were found to be on fire. By active exertion this was subdued, but twice afterwards during that day the terrible experience was repeated. The disadvantages of the garrison were very great; they had no sighting instruments for the guns, nothing with which to weigh powder, and then the cartridges were expended. The men tore up shirts to make cartridge bags. The firing, however, was maintained steadily throughout the day, for although several men had been wounded none were actually disabled. In fact during the whole of the engagement not a man was killed by hostile missiles, on either side. At 6 P. M. the firing from Sumter ceased, but the enemy's batteries were at work all through the night, at twenty-minute intervals. At dawn on the 13th the attack was resumed in earnest, and about an hour later the fort began to reply. At 8 o'clock the officers' quarters were set on fire by a shell, and this compelled a slackening of the firing, as the men were taken away to aid in combatting the flames. The attack became fiercer than ever as the dense volume of smoke arising from the fort gave evidence of the havoc within, and with diabolical malignity red-hot shot were thrown with the utmost rapidity. The spread of the flames soon endangered the magazine and the service powder, some ninety barrels of which had been brought out for use. This was rolled into the sea to prevent explosion. By 12 o'clock the whole roof of the barracks was in flames, and shortly before 1 o'clock the flag staff was shot through and the flag fell in the glowing embers. It was promptly rescued and displayed from the ramparts. Those on shore believed that the flag had been lowered in token of submission, and ex-Senator Wigfall came off in a boat with a white handkerchief as a flag of truce. No heed was taken of this, however, and the volunteer negotiator found himself in imminent peril from the guns of his own party. In frantic terror he asked to be admitted, but was repulsed by the sentinel. Effecting a landing at another point, he finally obtained an interview with Major Anderson, and falsely representing himself as the agent of General Beauregard, began to treat for the surrender. Anderson at length agreed to evacuate the fort at once on the same terms as had been previously proposed, viz., the privilege of saluting and retaining the flag of the fort, removing all company arms and property and all private property, and receiving every facility for reaching any post in the United States that the commander might select. In full faith that Wigfall had power to treat with him, Major Anderson ordered the firing on his side to cease, as it must have done under any circumstances almost immediately, for the extemporized cartridges then in the guns comprised the entire remaining ammunition. A white flag was raised over the fort and Wigfall left. Shortly before two o'clock the official aids of General Beauregard came direct from headquarters to inquire the meaning of the white flag, and then to his infinite disgust Major Anderson found that Wigfall had not seen Beauregard in two days and had no authority whatever. He was furious over the trick played upon him and declared the white flag should come down at once. Yielding to entreaty, however, he consented to let it remain till the officers could personally communicate with their commander. During the rest of the day several attempts were made to modify the terms, but Anderson refused a single point, and at length, about 8 P. M., an official communication from Beauregard arrived at the fort consenting to the terms for which Anderson had contended.

During all this the relief squadron outside had been passive witnesses of the engagement, but the precautions of the enemy were such that no aid could be rendered. The garrison had become aware of their presence and immediately after the agreement had been made with Beauregard a couple of Anderson's staff were sent to the squadron to arrange for the departure of the garrison.

At an early hour on Sunday morning all dispositions had been made within the fort. The messengers of Major Anderson had returned with the Captain of one of the relief squadron, and the steamer *Isabel*, provided by the Charleston military authorities arrived to convey the garrison to the *Baltic*, lying outside the bar. The flag was raised again over the fort and the salute of one hundred guns begun. Before half of this salute had been fired some ammunition exploded, killing private Daniel Hough and wounding several others, including private Edward Gallway, who was mortally injured. This ended the salute, and the Palmetto guard entered the fort to assist in burying Hough. The garrison having evacuated the fort and gone on board the *Isabel*, that vessel remained near the ruined stronghold until tide served on Monday morning, when they were put on board the *Baltic*, from the masthead of which soon fluttered the flag for which they had fought so gallantly against such fearful odds.

In the course of Sunday, Governor Pickens, General Beauregard, and a number of official and private citizens of Charleston, took formal possession of Fort Sumter and soon floated the Palmetto and Confederate flags over it.

FORT SUMTER AFTER THE BOMBARDMENT.

Major Anderson and his associates landed in New York on the 18th, when the "Flag of Fort Sumter" was again displayed from the mast-head of the *Baltic* and saluted by all the forts of that harbor. It is needless to recount the honors which an enthusiastic people showered upon the brave commander and his devoted band; suffice it to say that in addition to the marks of public approval, the President, on May 14th, one month after the evacuation, honored Major Anderson by promoting him to the rank and pay of brigadier general.

We cannot better conclude this chapter of the first actual warfare than by giving Major Anderson's official dispatch to the Secretary of War, which was sent from the *Baltic* when off Sandy Hook. It was in these words:

"Having defended Fort Sumter for thirty-four hours, until the quarters were entirely burned, the main gates destroyed by fire, the gorge wall seriously injured, the magazine surrounded by flames, and its doors closed from the effects of heat, four barrels and four cartridges of powder only being available, and no provisions but pork remaining, I accepted terms of evacuation offered by General Beauregard, being the same offered by him on the 11th inst., prior to the commencement of hostilities, and marched out of the fort Sunday afternoon, the 14th inst., with colors flying and drums beating, bringing away company and private property and saluting my flag with fifty guns."

This brief epitome of a terrible struggle and its results exhibits at once the modesty and the straightforward courage of the noble soldier. Left to his own resources he had defended the honor of the flag till only life remained to defend it longer, yet the dispatch magnifies neither the service nor its fearful peril.

CHAPTER V.

LINCOLN'S FIRST CALL FOR TROOPS—THE QUOTAS OF THE STATES—SECESSION REFUSALS TO RESPOND—THE FATAL RIOT IN BALTIMORE—FIRST BLOODSHED OF THE WAR—THE EVACUATION OF HARPER'S FERRY—SPREAD OF CONFEDERATE SENTIMENT—LYING RUMORS OF DEFECTIONS—AN EARLY SPECIMEN OF REPUDIATION DOCTRINES.

The evacuation of Sumter was an event for which the country was unprepared, although serious trouble in Charleston Harbor had been fully anticipated. The flag of the Union had been insulted; the pride of the nation outraged and the news that the Palmetto flag, an alien symbol, was flying over a Federal fortress filled the cup of humiliation to the brim. Already the "yell of rebeldom" was heard in the exultation of the Southern element, and it was met and answered by the hoarse murmur of indignation throughout the loyal North. The long-threatened sectional issue was an accomplished fact, "and Sumter has fallen" was the tocsin of war which called the merchant from his desk, the clerk from his counter and the farmer from his plough. With that promptitude which was one of his most salient characteristics President Lincoln seized the tide of popular indignation at the flood and issued the following call for troops within three days of the evacuation:

THE REBEL FLAG.

A PROCLAMATION

By the President of the United States.

Whereas, The laws of the United States have been for some time past and are now opposed, and the execution thereof obstructed, in the States of South Carolina, Georgia, Alabama, Florida, Mississippi, Louisiana and Texas, by combinations too powerful to be suppressed by the ordinary course of judicial proceedings, or by the powers vested in the marshals by law; now, therefore, I, ABRAHAM LINCOLN, President of the United States, in virtue of the power in me vested by the Constitution and the laws, have thought fit to call forth the militia of the several States of the Union to the aggregate number of 75,000, in order to suppress said combinations and to cause the laws to be duly executed.

The details for this object will be immediately communicated to the State authorities through the War Department. I appeal to all loyal citizens to favor, facilitate and aid in this effort to maintain the honor, the integrity and the existence of our National Union, and the perpetuity of popular government, and to redress wrongs already long enough endured. I deem it proper to say that the first service assigned to the forces hereby called forth, will probably be to repossess the forts, places and property which have been seized from the Union ; and in every event the utmost care will be observed, consistently with the objects aforesaid, to avoid any devastation, any destruction of, or interference with property, or any disturbance of peaceful citizens of any part of the country ; and I hereby command the persons composing the combinations aforesaid, to disperse and retire peaceably to their respective abodes, within twenty days from this date.

Deeming that the present condition of public affairs presents an extraordinary occasion, I do hereby, in virtue of the power in me vested by the Constitution, convene both Houses of Congress. The Senators and Representatives are, therefore, summoned to assemble at their respective chambers at 12 o'clock, noon, on Thursday, the fourth day of July next, then and there to consider and determine such measures as in their wisdom the public safety and interest may seem to demand.

In witness whereof, I have hereunto set my hand, and caused the Seal of the United States to be affixed

Done at the City of Washington, this fifteenth day of April, in the year of our Lord one thousand eight hundred and sixty-one, and of the Independence of the United States the eighty-fifth.

ABRAHAM LINCOLN.

By the President.
  WILLIAM H. SEWARD, Secretary of State.

The following is the form of the call on the respective State Governors for troops, issued through the War Department :

SIR:—Under the Act of Congress for calling out the militia to execute the laws of the Union, to suppress insurrection, to repel invasion, etc., approved February 28th, 1795, I have the honor to request your Excellency to cause to be immediately detailed from the militia of your State the quota designated in the table below, to serve as infantry or riflemen for a period of three months, unless sooner discharged. Your Excellency will please communicate to me the time at about which your quota will be expected at its rendezvous, as it will be met as soon as practicable by an officer or officers to muster it into service and pay of the United States. At the same time the oath of fidelity to the United States will be administered to every officer and man. The mustering officers will be instructed to receive no man under the rank of commissioned officer who is in years apparently over 45 or under 18, or who is not in physical strength and vigor. The quota for each State is as follows (in regiments): Maine 1, New Hampshire 1, Vermont 1, Massachusetts 2, Rhode Island 1, Connecticut 1, New York 17, New Jersey 4, Pennsylvania 16, Delaware 1, Tennessee 2, Maryland 4, Virginia 3, North Carolina 2, Kentucky 4, Arkansas 1, Missouri 4, Ohio 13, Indiana 6, Illinois 6, Michigan 1, Iowa 1, Minnesota 1, Wisconsin 1.

It is ordered that each regiment shall consist, on an aggregate, of officers and men, of 780. The total thus to be called out is 73,391. The remainder to constitute the 75,000 men under the President's proclamation will be composed of troops in the District of Columbia.

This proclamation and resultant order was followed on the 19th of April by a Presidential proclamation declaring a blockade of the ports of the seceding States in consequence of secession threats to issue "letters of marque" (*i.e.*, pirate licenses).

Simultaneously, General Orders No. 3 of the War Department declared "the Military Department of Washington extended so as to include, in addition to the District of Columbia and Maryland, the States of Delaware and Pennsylvania, to be commanded by Major-General Patterson, Pennsylvania Volunteers."

So thick will be the oncoming cloud of events from this time forward that we must endeavor to forbear from comment and confine ourself to the task of classifying and recording incidents, but we cannot avoid, just here, calling attention to the shrewdness of the President in not only seizing upon the period of fever heat in his demand for troops, but also in appealing to the calmer, though equally powerful, impulses of patriotism by selecting Independence Day for the assembling of Congress. This point has hitherto escaped notice, or at any rate comment, but none can doubt that Lincoln meant to make it.

In the free labor States the call for troops was received with unbounded enthusiasm; the President meant business, and the people were with him. Party lines became confused, even the better elements of the Democracy of the North denouncing rebellion.

In the slave labor States included in the proclamation call the leaven of secession was at once set working. In various tones of insolent defiance the Governors of Kentucky, North Carolina, Virginia, Tennessee, Arkansas and Missouri replied to General

Cameron, refusing to obey the mandate for militia quota. The reply of Governor B. Magoffin, of Kentucky, on the 16th of April, the earliest received, may be taken as the text of the entire set, in spirit, though others, notably those of Governor Letcher, of Virginia, and Governor Ellis, of North Carolina, were more violent in terms.

Governor Magoffin's reply was: "Your dispatch is received. In answer, I say emphatically, Kentucky will furnish no troops for the wicked purpose of subduing her sister Southern States."

That these refusals were based on instructions from the Confederate Congress at Montgomery, Alabama, does not admit of a doubt, many expressions being absolutely identical in sentiment in each case.

The debatable States of Maryland and Delaware, probably on account of nearness to the first brunt of battle in one case and of insignificance in size in the other, were more guarded in language. Governor Hicks, of Maryland, declared that no troops should be sent from the State except to defend the city of Washington. It was a lame dog's limp in the way of refusal or defiance. It was not until the 26th of April that Governor Burton, of Delaware, could settle on his course, or get it settled for him, for there is a suspicious undertone which suggests the latter idea. He informed the Department that he doubted his power constitutionally to comply. At the same time, for the protection of his State and the preservation of the Union, he suggested that he be empowered to organize local volunteer companies, and he issued a proclamation for this purpose.

President Davis had meanwhile, two days after the call for troops, issued a counter proclamation declaring that an intention had been announced to invade the Confederacy, capture its fortresses and subject its free people to the dominion of a foreign power. He invited offers from those desirous of engaging in privateering to apply to him for authority to do so.

This was met by the blockade proclamation. Davis further summoned the Congress of the Confederate States to meet at Montgomery, Alabama, on April 29th. We must here anticipate events, and state that on the 6th of May that body passed an elaborate act recognizing the existence of war between the United States and the Confederacy, providing for letters of marque and authorizing the Confederate President to execute general reprisal against the vessels, goods and effects of the United States, and of the citizens or inhabitants of the States or Territories thereof. In point of fact, upon the "go-as-you-please" theory under which the Confederacy was created, Davis issued privateering permits long before the authority to do so was conferred upon him by his Congress.

In the loyal States, as we shall show in detail later, the greatest activity prevailed in responding to the call for troops. Unfortunately, while the passionate press of the South was breathing defiance, war and bloodshed, that of the North was not one whit behind in its promptings of stern measures of repression, and thus day by day the fearful chasm was widened by those whose solemn, almost sacred, duty it is to conserve commercial interests and heal social and political differences. As a matter of course the fruit of such indiscretion was soon ripe for the picking, and in the city of Baltimore the harvest commenced. Here was shed the first blood of the Civil War.

The concluding paragraph of Governor Hicks' proclamation, dated April 18th, told the people of Maryland that they would shortly have afforded them, in a special election for members of Congress, an opportunity to express their devotion to the Union, *or their desire to see it broken up.* Coincidently Major George W. Brown, of Baltimore, issued a proclamation endorsing the Governor's sentiments, and suggesting that if his counsels should be disregarded "a fearful and fratricidal strife may at once burst forth in our midst."

Within twenty-four hours this sanguinary prediction was verified.

On April 19th, the anniversary of the battle of Lexington, intense excitement prevailed in Baltimore, resulting from incendiary speeches made by Wilson C. N. Carr, William Burns, President of the National Volunteer Association, and others, at a monster secession meeting held the previous night in that city, with T. Purkin Scott presiding.

The Virginia State Convention, held on the 17th of April,

passed the "ordinance to repeal the ratification of the Constitution of the United States of America by the State of Virginia, and to reserve all the rights and powers granted under said authorities." This was to be submitted for ratification on the fourth Thursday in May, and if so ratified to take effect and be an act of the day it was passed by the Convention.

During the afternoon of the 18th the first section of the troops from Pennsylvania, summoned hastily for the defense of the Capital, passed through Baltimore, and though bitterly vituperated had not been physically molested. They reached Washington about seven P. M. and were at once quartered in the Hall of Representatives at the Capitol. It is almost an open secret that they arrived not an hour too soon for the frustration of a plot of gigantic proportions. By this time a delegation from Virginia had reached Baltimore with a demand that neither troops nor munitions of war should pass over the Baltimore & Ohio Railroad. These men, aided by local leaders, fomented the mob spirit which now pervaded the city, and during the night secret meetings were held at which plans for the coming day were matured. At the same time the evacuation and destruction of Harper's Ferry were consummated, and this news still further inflamed the groups which had gathered by early dawn on the 19th. It was known that more troops were en route and a riot was decided on. Shortly after eleven o'clock that morning a train containing portions of the Sixth Massachusetts and the Seventh Pennsylvania arrived at the President street depot from Philadelphia. The Massachusetts Regiment occupied eleven cars, and these were, according to the then existing regulations, drawn through the streets of the city, singly, by horses to the Camden street depot. An ominous-looking mob had assembled, but at first a sullen silence was maintained. Ere the cars had gone a couple of blocks, however, the crowd became so dense that the horses could barely force their way through. Then began a chorus of hoots and yells mingled with threats. The troops remained quiet, and this, instead of appeasing, appeared to anger the rioters. Brickbats and stones were hurled, and it became evident that these missiles were not *accidentally* at hand.

Many of the men were wounded, but the first eight cars reached Camden street depot without serious damage. The ninth car was not so fortunate, for a defective brake caused a halt at Gay street, and the mob, now numbering from 8,000 to 10,000, made a furious onslaught. This car, with some damage, also reached the Camden-street depot. Behind it, however, were two other cars confronted by a barricade hastily constructed of anchors and other materials dragged from the wharf. Finding further transportation impossible, the men were ordered to leave the cars and were formed into close columns under Captain A. S. Follansbee, of Company C, of Lowell. With fixed bayonets they advanced on the double-quick in the direction of the Washington station. The mob closed on them, muskets were snatched away, and amid throwing of missiles, revolver shots, and bullets from the stolen muskets, the patience of the troops at last gave way. Two of their number had been killed and several wounded had been taken within the solid square which was now formed. An order was given to turn and fire singly; there was no platoon firing or the carnage in that dense mass would have been appalling. On Pratt street, near Gay street, one man was crushed by a stone or heavy piece of iron thrown from a window. After a protracted struggle the troops reached the depot, bearing with them their dead, now increased to three, and nine wounded comrades, one of them mortally injured. They were hustled into the train and sent off, but the mob followed for a considerable distance and made frantic efforts to throw the cars from the track. In the streets nine of the Baltimorians had been killed and a great number wounded. The Mayor of Baltimore had headed the column for a short time, but he could not allay the storm he had raised, and finding his person in danger he disappeared.

While this battle was being waged the Pennsylvanian military, wholly unarmed, remained in the freight and passenger cars at the President street station. General Small proposed to retire with them, but before this could be effected a large section of the mob, baffled in attempts to seize arms at the Custom House or at a local armory, rushed upon the defenseless troops with their murderous missiles. Several hand-to-hand fights ensued and many were badly wounded on both sides; but finally, through the efforts of Marshal Kane, the Pensylvanians were placed on board the cars and taken back to Philadelphia.

The mob continued its excesses about the streets of the city, plundering gunsmiths and breathing secession and vengeance.

Mayor Brown and Governor Hicks each sent dispatches to the President, notifying him of the affray and advising him that no more troops could pass through Baltimore without fighting their way.

A meeting of Secessionists was held in Monument Square, at which Mayor Brown, General George H. Stewart and others promised the mob that no troops should pass through the city hereafter and begged them to disperse.

The meeting broke up, but excited gangs prowled around seeking for arms and threatening violence to Union citizens.

We will turn from this scene for the present, and close this chapter with a fragment of concurrent history. We cannot more concisely do this than by quoting Lieutenant Jones' official report:

CARLISLE BARRACKS, Pa., April 20, 1861.
To the Assistant Adjutant-General, Headquarters Army, Washington, D. C.:

SIR: Immediately after finishing my dispatch of the night of the 18th inst., I received positive and reliable information that 2,500 or 3,000 State troops would reach Harper's Ferry in two hours from Winchester, and that the troops from Halltown, increased to 300, were advancing, and even at that time—a few minutes after 10 o'clock—were within 20 minutes' march of the Ferry. Under these circumstances, I decided that the time had arrived to carry out my determination, as expressed in the said dispatch above referred to, and accordingly gave the order to apply the torch. In three minutes, or less, both of the arsenal buildings, containing 15,000 stand of arms, together with the carpenter's shop, which was at the upper end of a long and connected series of workshops of the armory proper, were in a complete blaze. There is every reason for believing the destruction was complete. After firing the buildings, I withdrew my command, marching all night, and arrived here at 2½ P. M. yesterday, where I shall await orders. Four men were missing on leaving the armory and two deserted during the night.

I am, sir, very respectfully, your obedient servant,
R. JONES, First Lieutenant R. M. Rifles,
Commanding Dept. Rect.

As in Anderson's case at Sumter, so in this, the Government

appreciated the ready tact and sterling pluck which contrasted so nobly with opposing treachery. Lieutenant Jones was promoted on the 22d of April to be Assistant Quartermaster General, with the rank of Captain.

Almost simultaneously with the attack on Harper's Ferry, another Virginia raid was made on the Gosport Navy Yard, opposite Norfolk, on the Elizabeth River, the particulars of which we shall note in a subsequent chapter. On all sides the Confederates were active, and giving evidence of long-contemplated, well-laid plans for the seizure of the National capital. To increase the general consternation, lying rumors of important defections were set afloat, the most serious being a positive announcement made at Montgomery, on April 22d, that General Scott had resigned his position in the army and tendered his sword to his native State—Virginia. This canard was emphasized by the firing of one hundred guns at Mobile "in honor of Scott's resignation."

This was promptly met by a speech delivered in Ohio by Senator Douglas, who, alluding to the rumor, stated that he had seen and conversed with the chairman of the committee appointed by the Virginia Convention to tender the command of the forces of that State to General Scott. The General, after patiently listening to the infamous proposal, replied: "I have served my country under the flag of the Union for more than fifty years, and as long as God permits me to live I will defend that flag with my sword—even if my own native State assails it." About the same time General Scott, on April 21st, telegraphed to Senator Crittenden, of Kentucky: "I HAVE NOT CHANGED: HAVE NO THOUGHT OF CHANGING: ALWAYS A UNION MAN."

Though promptly contradicted, the poison of these artful rumors vitiated public confidence, even brothers looked askance at each other, and every face was eagerly scanned to try and penetrate a probable mask. The "times that tried men's souls" in the days of Washington were hours of comfort compared with those which ushered in the four years' fratricidal strife.

It may be pertinent here to note a sample of correspondence which fell into the hands of a New York journalist at this period, as giving an indication of the spirit animating all. It was a letter from a merchant in a Tennessee town, dated April 20, 1861, and ran thus:

"GENTLEMEN: Our note to you for $187.12, due to-day, has not been paid. We deeply regret the necessity that impels us to say, *that during the existence of this war* we are determined to pay no notes due our Northern friends."

Whatever else these worthies had omitted to learn, or had wilfully forgotten, it is quite plain that the example of the Israelites, at the period of the Exodus, had been remembered and was being carefully imitated. They were determined to "spoil the Egyptians" so far as they had any power to do so.

CHAPTER VI.

INTERMEDIARY EVENTS — THE RESPONSES OF THE LOYAL STATES — UNIONISTS RALLYING ROUND THE FLAG — MEN AND MONEY FOR GOVERNMENT AID — EXCITEMENT IN PHILADELPHIA — MEETINGS ELSEWHERE — SPREAD OF SOUTHERN SECESSION — JOTTINGS OF EVENTS AMONG THE CONFEDERATES.

To keep pace, as nearly as may be, with the rapidly rushing current of exciting events, we must turn aside from the struggle in Maryland and Virginia for a kaleidoscopic chapter of incidents in various localities, disconnected in themselves, yet all having a bearing more or less direct on the war now actually begun.

Throughout the North in the early days of April the responses to the President's call for troops were ample and enthusiastic, banks, corporations and wealthy citizens were liberal in their tenders of the sinews of war, and impressive Union meetings passed resolutions in which all partisan feeling was thrown to the winds and undying fidelity to the President and the Constitution was pledged in the most unequivocal terms. In Philadelphia the publication of some alleged newspapers, termed respectively *The Palmetto Flag* and *The Southern Monitor*, brought out an excited crowd and for a time rioting was feared. The office of the first named paper, at Fourth and Chestnut streets, was surrounded, and it would probably have been gutted but for the merely money-making character of the proprietor being evidenced in his display of the American flag, and his throwing into the street, along with the objectionable periodical, copies of the *Stars and Stripes*, another of his productions. The crowd laughed — and that always ends the malice of a mob. A good laugh is certainly a great institution. The *Southern Monitor* man had admonished himself, and probably taken shelter under the actual "Palmetto;" at any rate the angry loyalists did not find him, and their expenditure on the stout hemp with which they were amply provided was so much money wasted. As the paper had been suspended and the editor could not be, the only other possible alternative was adopted, and that was to prevent the continued hanging of the sign-boards he had left behind him. These were smashed, and then the crowd hurried to the residence of General Patterson, at Thirteenth and Locust streets. Evil tongues had slandered the brave, bluff, rugged son of Tyrone, and had dared to impute secession sentiments to the gallant Irishman. The terrified imprudence of a domestic who slammed the door in the faces of the excited throng well-nigh brought about the sacking of the mansion. The Mexican hero, however, appeared at a window, bearing the colors of his regiment, and a few of his sturdy sentences converted groans and yells into cheers. General Cadwallader, another Mexican veteran, was next visited. A stanch Union speech and the display of the National flag satisfied the crowd here. Meantime Mayor Henry had hoisted the stars and stripes and quieted the people by a ringing speech, in which, after the emphatic declaration, "By the grace of Almighty God treason shall never rear its head nor have a foothold in Philadelphia," he counselled all good citizens to prove their loyalty by going quietly to their homes and leaving the constituted authorities to do, as they certainly would, their sworn duty of preserving the peace and preventing every act which could be construed into treason to their country. While the mob spirit was quelled, however, an undercurrent of indignation still ran swiftly, and so-called Vigilance Committees warned prominent Southerners, including Robert Tyler, that their suspected Secession proclivities might endanger their safety. On the 19th of April the City Councils of Philadelphia appropriated $1,000,000 to equip volunteers and support their families during their absence. The atmosphere of the City of Brotherly Love was decidedly unhealthy for the cultivation of the Palmetto species of vegetation.

A few days before this a war bill, with an appropriation of $3,000,000, had been passed by the New York Legislature, and signed by the Governor. The authorities of Boston appropriated $100,000, and those of Lowell, Massachusetts, $8,000 for enlistment and support purposes. Norwich,

Connecticut, gave $14,000 for the same objects. Fall River, Massachusetts, not only voted $10,000 for immediate use, but an enthusiastic meeting urged the payment of $20 per month to each volunteer in addition to Government pay. In New Jersey, Governor Olden's message to the Legislature recommended a loan of $2,000,000 for war purposes, a State tax of $100,000 per annum, the thorough arming of the State, and the raising of four regiments additional to those called for. Among private offers was that of Colonel Samuel Colt, of Hartford, Connecticut, who, on the 25th of April, offered the executive of that State his services in organizing a regiment of ten companies equipped with his revolving breech rifles, with saber bayonets, at a personal cost of over $50,000. To sum up, we will mention that the contributions of the citizens of the North during the three weeks preceding May 7th, 1861, amounted to $23,277,000. Pennsylvania led the column with a free gift of $3,500,000. New York and Ohio gave $3,000,000 each; Connecticut and Illinois, $2,000,000 each; Maine, $1,300,000; Vermont and New Jersey, $1,000,000 (the Legislature of the latter State modified the Governor's suggestions); Wisconsin and Rhode Island, $500,000 each; Iowa, $100,000. The contributions of the principal cities were: New York, $2,173,000; Philadelphia, $330,000; Boston, 186,000; Brooklyn, $75,000; Buffalo, $110,000; Cincinnati, $280,000; Detroit, $50,000; Hartford, $64,000.

Enough has been shown to demonstrate that the loyalty of the North was substantial, and, with the record of a few significant episodes, we will leave this part of our subject and glance at matters within the Confederate lines.

On the 17th of April the bark *Manhattan* arrived at Boston from Savannah floating a Secession flag. A crowd promptly collected at the wharf and compelled Captain Davis to replace the obnoxious emblem by the Stars and Stripes. No further violence was offered.

On the 19th of April a meeting of merchants of New York City was held at the Chamber of Commerce of that city, with Mr. Peletiah Perit presiding. Patriotic speeches were made by the Chairman, George Opdyke, James Gallatin, Royal Phelps,

S. B. Chittenden, Prosper M. Wetmore, George W. Blunt, John E. King, William E. Dodge, John A. Stevens, R. H. McCurdy and others. Resolutions upholding the Federal Government and urging a strict blockade of all ports in the Secession States were unanimously adopted. An announcement that several regiments needed assistance to enable them to leave was responded to by donations, within ten minutes, of over $21,000. A committee of influential capitalists was also appointed to use their exertions towards the immediate taking of the $9,000,000 remaining of the Government loan. From a window in Trinity Church steeple, 240 feet above Broadway, an American flag forty feet long by twenty feet wide was flung out upon a huge flagstaff. Another was displayed over the portico of St. Paul's Church. The chimes of Trinity meantime played "Yankee Doodle," the "Red, White and Blue," and concluded with "All's Well." Despite a factious minority, it was evident that the great heart of a great metropolitan city beat strongly in response to the most patriotic impulses. One single thought stirred the masses, and that was, "*the Union must be preserved.*"

We will now turn our attention to the Confederacy, and by a running summary of movements and events in the Secession section, come up abreast with the Baltimore riot.

While the loyalty of the North was being so amply demonstrated, the troops in Texas, trapped by the treachery of Twiggs, were suffering sad humiliation and privation. Isolated and deserted, the officers at various points made gallant efforts to hold their positions, but overwhelming force compelled the evacuation of the several posts. Then another trouble arose. The Confederates had treated with a traitor, and at once absolved themselves from any inconvenient pledges they had made to him. He could not compel them to keep faith, and their theory was, "Might Overcomes Right." The Nemesis of this detestable doctrine they had to face later in the war.

The promised facilities for the transportation of the evacuating troops were withheld, and while the disheartened little bands were toilsomely wending their way seaward, Major Earle Van Dorn, a Mississippian who had deserted the Union flag and accepted a Colonel's commission from Davis, attempted to seduce the stragglers from their allegiance to the Union. Failing in this, the Confederates resolved to employ harsher means. On the 17th of April the *Star of the West* was captured off Indianola, with all her stores, some 900 barrels of provisions, by volunteers from Galveston. This vessel, under convoy of the *Mohawk*, had been sent to bring away troops under Major Sibley. A few days later Major Sibley, after waiting vainly for the expected succor, had embarked his seven companies of national troops on a couple of schooners and attempted to pass down Matagorda Bay, but he was met by four heavily-armed steamers with a large force of men under Van Dorn, and compelled to surrender off Saluria. Besides prisoners, the Confederates thus captured the camp equipage and some 300 rifles. Colonel Waite, with his staff and other officers, were insultingly made prisoners at San Antonio about the same time, and then Colonel Reese, with the remainder of the national troops, was outnumbered and compelled to surrender to Van Dorn, at a point near San Lucas Springs, in middle Texas. All these officers were paroled; the men, after a short period of irritating captivity, were released on their oaths not to again bear arms against the Confederacy. Thus Texas, by Twiggs' treachery, was torn from the control of the Federal Government. Continuing the work of spoliation and outrage in other quarters, Sherrard Clemens, late member of Congress for Richmond, Virginia, was imprisoned there for Union sentiments; the Custom House and Post-Office of the city were seized, as were also the New York packet steamer *Jamestown* and a packet schooner from Maine.

At Liberty, Missouri, the United States Arsenal, with its 1,300 small arms, 12 cannon and quantities of ammunition, was seized and a garrison of 100 Missourians placed to guard it.

At Charlotte, North Carolina, the United States Branch Mint was seized and occupied by Colonel Bryce and a military force, under orders of Governor Ellis.

At Lynchburg, Virginia, Andrew Johnson, United States Senator from Tennessee, was mobbed, and an effort made to capture him, the mob asserting that he had promised the required quota of men from Tennessee. Shortly after this General

Harney, on his way from Wheeling, Virginia, to report at Washington, was taken from the train at Harper's Ferry by a body of State troops, and held prisoner by the Virginia authorities. About this time a strong Union sentiment began development in Western Virginia, and a meeting held at Clarksburg, Harrison County, denounced the course of Governor Letcher, and appointed delegates to confer at Wheeling, on May 13th, with delegates from Eastern Virginia. An important accession to the Confederate ranks must be recorded just here. On the 20th of April, Colonel Robert Edmund Lee, of Virginia, sent to General Scott, from his home on Arlington Heights, his letter of resignation from the Union army. Two days later he attended the Virginia Convention, and accepted the position of General-in-Chief of that State, the Secession Ordinance having been passed on the 17th. That this was part of a matured scheme, is shown by the fact that Alexander H. Stephens, Vice-President of the Confederacy, was present to welcome him. Thus as the Alpha, and subsequently as the Omega, of rebellion, the name of General Robert E. Lee passes into the history of the war.

The surrender of the United States Arsenal at Fayetteville, North Carolina; the capture of Fort Smith, Arkansas, by the State troops, together with property valued at $300,000; the seizure of the steamship *Cahawba*, at New Orleans, by Captain Shivers of the Cadds Rifles, and of the steamships *Texas, Tennessee* and *G. W. Hewes* at the same port, later, by order of Governor Moore, were events which followed in rapid sequence, and kept up the excitement of the period.

By this time the rebel army stationed at Richmond numbered three thousand and seventy-two men, of whom about six hundred were South Carolina troops, under command of Brigadier General M. L. Bonham.

With a quotation from the Southern press we can conclude this chapter of jottings.

The Charleston *Mercury*, of April 22d, concluded an article headed "PRESIDENT LINCOLN A USURPER," with these words: "He will deplore the 'higher law' depravity which has governed his counsels. Seeking the sword, in spite of all moral or constitutional restraints and obligations, *he may perish by the sword*. He sleeps already with soldiers at his gate, and the grand reception-room of the White House is converted into quarters for troops from Kansas—border ruffians of Abolitiondom."

Such an article speaks volumes, and, as we shall have occasion to show in the narrative of a personal reminiscence, in its proper place later on, indicates that assassination had even now entered into the speculations, at least, of the Secessionists.

CHAPTER VII.

FURTHER OUTRAGES AT BALTIMORE—BURNING THE RAILROAD BRIDGES—CAPTURE OF THE GOSPORT NAVY YARD—BUTLER MOVES ON BALTIMORE—THE CITY OCCUPIED BY FEDERAL TROOPS—THE SPLIT IN VIRGINIA — UNION SENTIMENT IN THE MOUNTAIN COUNTIES—ORGANIZATION OF WEST VIRGINIA—THE HABEAS CORPUS ACT DISREGARDED.

On the night of the 19th of April, 1861, while the excitement in Baltimore was still seething, Bradley Johnson, of Frederick County, telegraphed Marshal Kane, offering armed aid to resist the passage of troops through the city. This offer fitted in

DESTRUCTION OF THE BRIDGE OVER GUNPOWDER CREEK.

nicely and was promptly accepted by wire. In the course of the next day Johnson, with a body of men hastily armed and ready for any deed of violence, reported to Kane and assumed quarters opposite the marshal's office. Meantime Kane and ex-Governor Lowe had broken in on the slumbers of Mayor Brown and Governor Hicks, and wrung from them quasi authority to destroy railroad communication between Philadelphia and Baltimore. It was convenient afterwards to repudiate that authority, but Kane was too wary a man to have acted without colorable permission, at least, from the Governor, for the work of destruction contemplated was beyond the city limits. It was not difficult to get the secession sympathies of Mayor Brown enlisted in this work, and shortly after midnight Canton bridge, three miles beyond the city on the Philadelphia, Wilmington and Baltimore Railroad was destroyed. An approaching train was fired upon and the engineer compelled to back his train, conveying the marauders to the bridges over the Gunpowder and Bush Creek arms of Chesapeake Bay. To these the torch was applied, and while they were burning, two wooden bridges on the Northern Central, fifteen miles north of the city, on the road to Cockeysville, were also destroyed. All the telegraph wires out of Baltimore, except the one connecting the Maryland rioters with the Confederates at Richmond, via Harper's Ferry, were cut.

While this was going on, the Committee sent from Baltimore were in conference with the President in Washington, urging that the passage of troops through Baltimore should be prohibited. The evasive answer of the President that a route around Baltimore should be adopted, did not meet the views of those whose real object was to cripple the Capital. They declared that the soil of Maryland should not be invaded, and extensive preparations were made to meet any emergency. In the small hours of Sunday morning, April 21st, the President, anxious to avoid a conflict, telegraphed for Hicks and Brown. The latter only was able to respond. Taking with him Messrs. S. T. Wallis, Brune and Dobbin, Mayor Brown presented himself at the White House by 10 A. M. During the conference which ensued, General Scott proposed that troops should reach Annapolis by water, and march thence to Washington. But this involved passing through Maryland, and again the Mayor insisted upon the sacredness of the soil being preserved. The conference was futile, and the Baltimoreans withdrew. They quickly returned, however, having learned before reaching the cars that a body of troops had arrived at Cockeysville, en route for Baltimore. The result of a further conference was that General Scott, at the pacific and earnest request of the President, sent orders for the return of the troops to Harrisburg. Encouraged by this, a further demand was made on the 22d for a comprehensive order forbidding future passage of troops through any portion of Maryland, and the withdrawal of those already at Annapolis. Nor was this all; the daring conspirators ventured to suggest that Lord Lyons, the British Minister, be requested to mediate between Maryland and the Federal Government and arrange the terms of a truce. In this the old-time anxiety to obtain even the shadow of belligerent rights was so palpable as to be absolutely insolent.

Secretary Seward now took a hand in the matter, and scathingly rebuked Governor Hicks for the impertinent indecency of his proposition. He pointed out that, beyond the insolence of assumed sovereignty, the suggestion of the employment of a foreign power to regulate domestic differences was too humiliating to be for a moment entertained. Another alleged attempt at diplomacy was made, and this time on an assumed basis of religious sentiment. Rev. Dr. Fuller, of the Baptist Church, Baltimore, with delegations from several of the Young Men's Christian Associations of the city, waited on the President and made lamb-like bleatings for peace and the avoidance of bloodshed, which they assured him could be secured by his recognition of the independence of the Southern States and their accomplished autonomy. Grimly amused by this wolf-in-sheep's-clothing style of argument, Mr. Lincoln politely but sternly reminded them that the safety of the Capital, and his own life, were endangered by the South Carolinians now pouring through Virginia. In his quaint, determined manner, he added, "I must have troops; they can neither crawl under Maryland nor fly over it, they must come across it." To such an ultimatum there could be no reply but that of armed resistance, and the doves of peace returned to consort with the wolves of rapine and organize sanguinary defiance. Diplomatically, Baltimore was not heard from again.

We have already noticed the Harper's Ferry affair, and must now record an incident of even more importance—the occupation of the navy yard at Gosport, on the Elizabeth River, opposite Norfolk, Virginia. The seizure of this was planned at the same time as that of Harper's Ferry, and on the 16th of April a couple of vessels were sunk in the channel of the river, blocking the passage of the ships at the navy yard. At this point were the following vessels, afloat or on the stocks, and in varying conditions as to service: The three-decker *Pennsylvania*, 120 guns; *Columbus*, 80 guns; *Delaware*, 84; and *New York*, 84—these latter were ships of the line—*United States*, *Columbia* and *Raritan*, frigates of 50 guns each; *Plymouth* and *Germantown*, sloops of 22 guns each; the brig *Dolphin*, 4 guns, and the steam frigate *Merrimack*. The navy yard itself, of immense area and fitted with all the most approved appliances, contained also some 2,000 heavy cannon, including 300 new Dahlgren guns. In all, the Government property at this point was worth at least ten millions of dollars. The designs of the Confederates were at least suspected, at Washington, and as early as the 10th of April orders had been given to rush in work and quietly prepare for defense. Commodore McCauley, however, made haste so slowly that Engineer-in-Chief B. F. Isherwood was sent to press the work forward. His efforts were quietly frustrated by McCauley, and even when, by personal supervision, Isherwood had got the *Merrimack* ready for sea by the 17th, delay was interposed and the fires were not lighted until the next day. Even then, despite the warnings and remonstrances of Isherwood, who was cognizant of obstructions planned by the Confederates at Sewell's Point and Craney Island, the Commodore kept back his orders and finally extinguished the fires. He claims to have been misled by his subordinates, chief among whom was Lieutenant M. F. Maury, a Virginian, but only the wildest stretch of charity could excuse such culpable folly, if not criminal indiscretion. On the 18th, these subordinate officers having accomplished their designated task of treachery, sent in their resignations, and the same evening General Taliaferro, in command of the forces in southwestern Virginia, took up quarters in Norfolk. The deserters joined him, and the next day the workmen in the yard were absent from roll-call. On the 20th, Taliaferro had mustered, for the attack on the yard, the military companies of Norfolk and Portsmouth, six hundred men from Petersburg, and the Richmond Grays, with fourteen heavy rifled cannon and ample ammunition. McCauley, finding resistance would be useless, sent a message to Taliaferro, promising that the vessels should not be moved, and that no shot should be fired, except for self-defense. His next work, either from excess of caution or from some other motive, was to order the scuttling of all the ships. This was done, except in the case of the *Cumberland*, which was saved by the opportune arrival of Captain Paulding, with orders to relieve McCauley, repel force at all hazards, and defend the public property. The time for efficient action, however, had passed, and Paulding proceeded to complete the work of absolute destruction by burning the sinking ships, to reduce the advantage which the enemy might obtain by getting possession of them. He further ordered the demolition of the cannon, and made arrangements for an extensive conflagration. At 2 A. M. on the 21st, having got his men, troops, marines and a few loyal workmen on board the *Cumberland* and the *Pawnee*, he gave a rocket signal from the deck of the *Pawnee*, when Commander Rogers and Captain Wright fired the trains of powder leading in all directions. The resultant blaze was appalling, and the roaring of the flames spread terror for miles around. It was a sacrifice to Moloch on the most gigantic scale. Towed by the *Yankee*, under Captain Germain, the *Cumberland* and *Pawnee* went down the river, but the two brave officers in charge of the torch, Rogers and Wright, were unfortunately left behind, and were subsequently made prisoners by the Confederates.

Breaking through the obstructions at Sewell's Point, the *Cumberland*, *Pawnee* and *Yankee* made their way to Hampton Roads.

Despite the elaborate plans for the destruction of the yard, they failed to achieve their full purpose, and the Confederates obtained possession of the principal works, officers' quarters and the dry dock. The partially disabled ordnance was speedily repaired, with the aid of the appliances at hand, and from this point heavy guns were sent to many Southern fortifications. Of the vessels, some were totally and others partially burned. The *Columbus*, *Delaware* and *Plymouth* were merely scuttled and sunk, the latter being afterwards raised and repaired. The

Merrimack, burned to her copper line and sunk, but, being reconstructed, became at a later period famous in history for the memorable conflict with the *Monitor.* Old Fort Norfolk, with an enormous store of powder, shells, etc., was next seized, and then the hulk of the old *United States* was sunk in the channel a mile below the fort. Heavy batteries on Craney Island and Sewell's Point completed the defenses, and troops from Georgia

UNION SQUARE, NEW YORK, ON THE 20TH OF APRIL, 1861.

and lower Virginia were rapidly rushed in to garrison this important capture.

Meanwhile the insurgent troops were being massed at other points, and by the 20th of May some eight thousand men, comprising South Carolinians, Alabamians, Virginians and Kentuckians, had been posted at Harper's Ferry, on Maryland Heights, and in fortifications on both sides of the Shenandoah and Potomac rivers.

But the North was not idle. On the 20th of April, while stirring events were happening elsewhere, and the safety of the Capital itself was imperiled, a monster meeting in Union Square, New York, had resulted in the formation of the Union Defense Committee, an organization of responsible citizens of all political shades. Major-General Wool, commander of the Eastern Department, after a conference with Governor Morgan at Albany, proceeded to New York. Here he held a conference with the Defense Committee and Governor Morgan on the 23d, and perfected arrangements for the relief of Washington, and also for the protection of the Government property at St. Louis, believed to be threatened by the Missouri Secessionists. Colonel Ellsworth's Zouaves, recruited mainly from the New York firemen, were sent on to Washington, and their arrival in all probability prevented a national disaster. All this was necessarily done on personal responsibility, and in excess of any existing authority—facts which led to a slight misunderstanding with the War Department; but as this was afterwards rectified, we need not go into details. It will suffice to say that the aid thus rendered by General Wool, with the co-operation of Commodores Breeze and Stringham and the titanic labors of the Union Defense Committee, was of incalculable value towards the ultimate preservation of the Union.

We turn now to equally energetic movements in other directions. The Seventh New York Regiment, which had started on the 19th of April, was joined by the Eighth Massachusetts and a company from Springfield, and, with General B. F. Butler, had arrived in Philadelphia. The news of the Baltimore riot had just been received, and Butler, whose instructions had been to march through that city, found a lion in his path. A hurried consultation with General Patterson and Commodore Dupont, of the Philadelphia Navy Yard, resulted in a plan to take the troops by water from Perryville, at the mouth of the Susquehanna, to Annapolis, and thence to Washington across Maryland. General Patterson, as commander of the "Department of Washington," ordered Butler to seize Annapolis and Annapolis Junction and maintain a military highway to the Capital. At a council of war in the Girard House that evening, Colonel

Lefferts, of the Seventh New York, demurred to the plan of Butler, and the latter made arrangements for pushing on with his Massachusetts troops. At 11 A. M. on the 20th, Butler and his troops had reached the Susquehanna, where rumor had located a hostile force. The men were ordered from the cars in readiness for battle, but there was no enemy in sight. The Philadelphia, Wilmington and Baltimore huge ferryboat *Maryland*, however, was in waiting at Perryville, and by midnight the troops were off Annapolis. Here a surprise awaited them.

GEN. BENJAMIN F. BUTLER.

The Secessionists were in possession of the town and the Naval Academy, waiting reinforcements from Baltimore to seize the old frigate *Constitution*, then used as a school ship. The arrival of Butler put an end to this little plot, and with the aid of the *Maryland*, after opening communication with Captain Blake, Superintendent of the Academy, the *Constitution* was towed from the wharf to a point out beyond the bar. In doing this the *Maryland* grounded, and the troops, who had all along suspected the captain, at once made him prisoner. Meanwhile Butler had gone ashore and held a conference with the Mayor of Annapolis and Governor Hicks. The latter protested against the landing of Northern troops, and the former assured him that the hungry troops could not purchase food there. Butler swept aside both these cobwebs in his characteristic way. He told the Governor he had no "Northern troops," but a part of the militia of the United States obeying the call of the President. He reminded the Mayor that hungry soldiers were seldom particular about paying for necessary rations, and then, in general terms, announced his intention to land, under any and all circumstances, and push on to the Capital. The discomfited State and city authorities could only shrug their shoulders and protest. The *Maryland*, however, was still aground, but at dawn on the 22d the *Boston* hove in sight. On board was Colonel Lefferts, with the Seventh New York Regiment, he having become convinced that a passage through Baltimore was impracticable. After vain efforts on the part of the *Boston* to float the *Maryland*, the Seventh New York were landed, and then the *Boston* took off the Massachusetts men from the stranded steamer The

ANNAPOLIS JUNCTION IN 1861.

buildings of the Academy were converted into quarters and the two well-nigh famished bodies of men divided the rations with which the Seventh were provided.

Meanwhile the Secessionists had torn up the rails and scattered them and dismantled the locomotives. The troops were now stranded ashore. This check was of short duration, for luckily the Massachusetts troops were composed mainly of artisans, one of whom, Charles Homans, of the Beverly Light Guard, had been employed in the machine shops in which one of the dismantled engines had been built. He promptly announced his ability to reconstruct it. Butler detailed him for the work, and as there were others nearly as well skilled around, the locomotive was rapidly got into working order.

The hidden rails were ferreted out and replaced. On the evening of the 23d Butler took possession of the Annapolis and Elk Ridge Railroad. A protest from Governor Hicks, drew, as usual, a sneering response from the General, and the troops commenced their forward movement. Bridges were repaired and the tracks relaid as the little army moved steadily, but cautiously, onward throughout the day and night of the 24th. A sharp watch was kept for Southern skirmishers, but these wisely refrained from useless interference. Up to this time Colonel Lefferts with the Seventh New York had co-operated, but on the morning of the 25th, on reaching Annapolis Junction, the New Yorkers pressed on for Washington, leaving Butler and his men to hold the position and keep open the line of communication. General Scott then procured the creation of the " Department of Annapolis," and placed Butler in absolute command of a district extending to Bladensburg, and stretching twenty miles on either side of the railroad. This was precisely what he wanted, and having obtained the dictum from headquarters that his power was absolute, except where his views controverted specific orders or military law, he prepared to carry out his own plans for the humbling of Baltimore and avenging the murder of the men of the Sixth Massachusetts. He knew of the plans of his Commander-in-Chief, but they were of too slow a character to suit Butler's dash and energy. By the end of April the National Capital was well guarded, and although Baltimore in the hands of the Secessionists was constantly adding to its threatening force, Butler had, under various pretexts, obtained permission to concentrate troops and locate them at discretion, until he had ten thousand men at Annapolis, and had stationed a force at the Relay House, on the Baltimore and Ohio Railroad, ostensibly to cut rebel communication with Harper's Ferry. In reality this was part of his plan for a descent on Baltimore, which he found to be within his Military Department.

The Maryland Legislature, which had been called to meet at Annapolis on the 27th, found it convenient to select Frederick as the place of meeting instead. There was not room enough at Annapolis for Butler and secession legislation, at one and the same time, the more especially as Butler had promised steel bracelets to those who talked treason, in or out of legislative session. Instead of pressing a secession ordinance the disunionists fell back on strategy, assumed a virtue if they had it not, talked buncombe about the danger of revolution, and then appointed a State Board of Safety, the members of which, while intrusted with almost absolute power over the resources of the commonwealth, were not required to swear allegiance to the United States. General Butler keenly noted all this, and prepared for his grand *coup*. He knew there was a strong Union under-current in Maryland, and he relied on its development when he afforded the opportunity. On the 4th of May his preparations were complete. Under his orders the Eighth New York, Sixth Massachusetts, and Cook's Battery of Boston Light Artillery, left Washington by train early on the morning of the 5th of May, and, reaching the Relay House, nine miles from Baltimore, after a two hours' ride, seized that point, and then rapidly occupied positions commanding the viaduct over the Patapsco Valley, which was the junction point of the Baltimore and Ohio and the roads to Baltimore and Harper's Ferry. During the following week Butler remained at the Relay House, quietly perfecting his scheme, and taking the utmost care that General Scott should not issue orders which would impede him. In fact, the headquarters orders were drawn up by Colonel Schuyler Hamilton, of the staff of the General-in-Chief, a man who, probably, more than suspected Butler's designs, and cordially approved of his dash and enterprise. These orders gave Butler permission, in general terms, to arrest Secessionists, instructed him to prevent accessions to the rebel force at Harper's Ferry, to seek for concealed ammunition, alleged to be stored in Baltimore for insurgent purposes, and thus in all but specific terms instructed him to use force in the very direction he had planned to exercise it.

These schemes were materially aided by the movements of General Patterson, who sent the First Pennsylvania Volunteer Artillery and Sherman's Battery, under Colonel Francis E. Patterson, his son, to force their way, if necessary, through Baltimore. On the 9th of May, this force of nine hundred and thirty men, with a portion of the Third Infantry, regulars, landed at Locust Point, near Fort McHenry, from the steamers *Fanny Cadwallader* and *Maryland*, the debarkation being effected under cover of the guns of a gunboat and those of the *Harriet Lane*. The presence of Butler's troops at the Relay House, the shifting tide of public opinion, and other prudential views, prevented opposition, though the Mayor, Marshal Kane, and the Police Commissioners were on hand. Kane even had the impertinence to tender assistance to Major Sherman, but on making himself known received such a repulse that he desired

FEDERAL HILL.

no employment in the military aid department just then. The passage of these troops through Baltimore, amid every demonstration of welcome from the loyal element, diverted attention at the Capital from Butler and his plans. Meantime Ross Winans, of Baltimore, had manufactured a steam gun, supposed to be something remarkable, for city defense, and had sold it to the Baltimore authorities. This man Butler was determined to capture, if possible, as an example. On the 13th of May some fifty men were sent on to Frederick by train to arrest Winans, behind them was a train containing Butler and a force of one thousand men, with two field pieces. The train headed for Harper's Ferry, but subsequently backed till the Camden street depot, Baltimore, was reached. A thunder-storm was in progress, and thus the arrival escaped general notice, though a spy had warned the Mayor of some such movement. The force, however, had disappeared in the darkness, and their whereabouts could not be ascertained until at daylight they were discovered encamped on Federal Hill and in command of the city. Butler promptly issued a proclamation announcing his occupation of the city, and determination to cause the laws to be enforced and respected. He forbade the display of secession flags, and alluding to the force he had with him, mentioned it merely as a guard, though he announced his ability to concentrate thousands of troops if necessary. Ross Winans having been captured and confined in Fort McHenry, General Butler was about to try him before a military tribunal, when one of those almost fatal blunders, for which this period was remarkable, was perpetrated by General Scott. He recalled General Butler, or rather, prevailed upon the President to do so, under the impression that so absolute an exercise of discretionary powers was a dangerous precedent. It may be permissible to doubt whether the forestalling of the General-in-Chief's more leisurely campaign did not lend a coloring of personal pique to an act which in all human probability prevented the strangling of the Rebellion in the cradle of its infancy.

The humiliation of Butler's recall was tempered by his being commissioned Major-General of Volunteers and placed in command of a military district, including Eastern Virginia and the Carolinas, with headquarters at Fortress Monroe.

The troops, however, were withdrawn from Baltimore, and the district assigned to General Cadwallader, of Philadelphia.

Coincident with these events the Legislature of Maryland had adjourned, and Governor Hicks, on the 14th of May, issued a proclamation, in response to the President's call for troops, dated April 15th. In this the Governor called upon loyal citizens to volunteer to the extent of four regiments to serve for three months within the limits of Maryland, or for the defense of the Capital of the United States, but not beyond those limits, and to be, under such conditions, subject to the orders of the Commander-in-Chief of the United States.

This last straw broke the back of the conspirators; the Union sentiment, which had only been kept down by the threats of a disloyal clique aided by alien agitators, reasserted itself, and Maryland once more stood up boldly and proudly under the flag of the Union. At the same time, to put a finishing touch upon the work of regeneration, Major Morris, commanding Fort McHenry, refused to obey a writ of habeas corpus issued by Judge Giles, of Baltimore, for the release of one of the Maryland State Militia then confined in Fort McHenry. The Major in a lengthy letter recapitulated the disturbances and treasonable acts of the past few weeks, and asserted that the exigencies of the case set all questions of precedent aside. On the 27th of May General Cadwallader refused to obey a similar writ issued by Judge Taney, in the case of John Merryman, a Baltimore secessionist, also confined in Fort McHenry. Judge Taney issued an order of attachment for General Cadwallader, and the Marshal made return that he had been denied admission to Fort McHenry. Judge Taney in an elaborate statement denied the power of the President to suspend the privilege of the writ of habeas corpus, or to authorize any military officer to do so. In the face of an overpowering force, however, he would not call out a posse comitatus to enforce the decrees of the Court, and he therefore relieved the Marshal of further liability under the order. Judge Taney further stated that he should prepare an opinion, and call on the President to do his constitutional duty in maintaining the supremacy of the civil over the military authority.

The condition of affairs at this time was not favorable for legal hair-splitting, and as a result the Chief-Executive had, in the coming eventful days, to frequently exceed constitutional authority and rely upon Congressional action to sustain him thereafter.

We have, perhaps, been prolix in handling some of these details, but have deemed the investigation of the mainsprings and minor movements of the great controversy of equal importance at this stage, as affording the key to many matters which will arise in the course of this history when the smoke of battle comes upon us. Already the bayonets are being fixed for the first actual clash of arms, and therefore with a brief résumé of the events leading to the split in the State of Virginia we shall close this chapter.

As before noted, the secession sentiment was almost powerless in Northwestern Virginia, and it was still further subdued by meetings held at various points prior to May 23d, the time at which a vote of the State was to be taken on the Secession ordinance. On the other hand, Senator James M. Mason, of Winchester, had written an open letter in which he declared that those who opposed the ordinance must prepare to leave the State.

At the Wheeling Convention, which met on the 13th of May, the long-cherished project of a division of the State was the main topic of discussion. There was no bond of sympathy between the counties of the mountain region and the slave-labor section to the eastward. The result of the deliberations was that resolutions denouncing secession were adopted, with a call for a Provisional Convention to meet at the same place on June 11th, should the ordinance obtain a majority vote of the State at large. As was expected, Eastern Virginia, under the control of the Confederate leaders at Montgomery, swamped the vote of the free-labor section.

The Provisional Convention met at Wheeling, June 11th, with Arthur J. Boreman, of Wood County, as permanent president. On the 13th, an ordinance vacating all offices of the State held by officers hostile to the Federal Government was reported, and on the 17th the Convention, by the unanimous vote of the fifty-six members, declared for independence of Governor Letcher, who had, the resolution alleged, abdicated his authority and protection, and assumed an attitude of hostility. On the 20th, the separation of Western from Eastern Virginia was agreed to by a unanimous vote, and on the same day a Provisional Government was organized, with Francis H. Pierpont, of Marion County, as Governor; Daniel Polsley, of Mason County, Lieutenant-Governor, and an Executive Council of five members. The work of organization was pushed forward, and a Legislature elected which met at Wheeling July 1st, and chose as Senators to the United States Senate, John S. Carlile and Waitman G. Willie. On the 20th of August the convention re-assembled and passed an ordinance for the formation of a new State. This was ratified by the people in October, and thus were set in train the proceedings which resulted in the admission, on the 3d of June, 1863, of the State of West Virginia, to the muster roll of the Union.

CHAPTER VIII.

THE FEDERAL FORCES CROSS THE POTOMAC—OCCUPATION OF ALEXANDRIA—ASSASSINATION OF COLONEL ELLSWORTH—GENERAL GEORGE B. M'CLELLAN—THE BATTLE OF PHILIPPI—BUTLER AT FORTRESS MONROE—THE BLUNDER AT BIG BETHEL—BUTLER'S REPORT—CONFEDERATE ACCOUNTS.

While measures were being energetically prosecuted for the defense of Washington the Confederates were far from idle in pushing forward their plan for its capture, and secured a commanding position at Manassas Junction, on the Orange and Alexandria Railroad, some thirty miles from the capital. They then began works on Arlington Heights and had pushed their picket line to the Virginia shore of the Potomac, and covering that end of the Long Bridge, which connects with Washington City. It was evident that the time for action had arrived, and on the 23d of May an order was given for a general movement into Virginia. General Butler, with twelve thousand men, already held Fortress Monroe, at the mouth of the James River, and had made a successful reconnoissance of Hampton with Colonel Phelps' Vermont regiment, defeating the plans of the rebels for the destruction of the bridge connecting the Fortress with the village across the bay. Just prior to this two Confederate companies who had the temerity to enter Clarksburg, Harrison County, had been compelled to surrender to Captains

COL. E. E. ELLSWORTH.

A. C. Moore and J. C. Vance, who had promptly mustered a couple of Union companies to attend to the unwelcome visitors.

At 1:20 A. M. on the 24th of May one of the most important of the early Federal movements was begun. At that hour the New York Seventh Regiment left their camp at Washington, each man having sixty rounds of ball cartridge. These reached Virginia soil by 4 A. M., and camped near the Alexandria end of the bridge. Meanwhile other large bodies of troops were in motion; in fact, almost simultaneously, by way of the Long Bridge and the Aqueduct Bridge at Georgetown, and by water on a couple of vessels, a combined force numbering about thirteen thousand men were poured into the rebellious State. This force was made up of the New York Seventh, Sixty-ninth and Twenty-eighth regiments; two companies each of the New York Second, Fifth, Twelfth, Twenty-fifth; three companies of the New York Seventy-first and the New York Fire Zouaves; the Fifth Massachusetts; Rhode Island First, with the Rhode Island batteries; the New Jersey Second, Third and Fourth; the Michigan Third; three companies of an Ohio regiment, some United States cavalry, and a large contingent of District of Columbia troops. The Loudon and Hampshire Railroad was first seized, and then the New York Sixty-ninth took a position on the Orange and Manassas Gap railroad, running out of Alexandria. By this last movement the fugitives from that city, some seven hundred in all, including three hundred men, were captured and held as hostages. Shortly before 5 A. M. the commander of the United States steamship *Pawnee*, lying off Alexandria, sent a

ELLSWORTH ZOUAVES.

flag of truce, giving the rebels one hour to quit the town. The steamers *Baltimore* and *Mount Vernon* made fast to the wharf and landed the New York Fire Zouaves. The rebel sentinels fired on the landing party and retreated. The Zouaves at once proceeded to destroy the railroad track to Richmond, and meanwhile Colonel Ellsworth, with his aid, Lieutenant Winser, and a file of men, started for the telegraph office to cut the wires. On their way they noticed a large secession flag on the Marshall House—this had been observed in Washington for several days. Colonel Ellsworth halted his men and entered the house. A man came rushing down stairs, and in reply to the Colonel's inquiry, "Who put up that flag," replied: "I don't know; I am only a boarder." He was allowed to pass, but he subsequently proved to be J. W. Jackson, the proprietor. Colonel Ellsworth, Lieutenant Winser, Chaplain House and four privates made their way to the roof and cut down the flag. Coming down the stairs, Colonel Ellsworth was rolling up the flag, when Jackson rushed out from some hiding-place and leveled a double-barreled gun at Private Brownell, who was leading the party. Brownell attempted to strike the weapon up with his musket, but Jackson pulled both triggers and the contents of the two barrels were lodged in the body of the Colonel, entering between the third and fifth ribs. Ellsworth fell dead and Brownell at once discharged his musket at Jackson, who fell dead with a ball through his brain. The enraged soldier, to make sure of the fellow, ran a bayonet through his body. The guard at the door, becoming alarmed at the firing and protracted absence of the party, disobeyed orders and entered the house. They brought the body of their dead Colonel out on a litter of muskets and carried it to the steamer for conveyance to Washington. The rage of the Zouaves was such that they threatened to burn the town, and it was found necessary to put them on board a steamer anchored in the river to prevent their avenging their colonel's murder.

Meanwhile the First Michigan had entered Alexandria by the road from the Long Bridge and captured the railroad depot, together with one hundred rebel cavalry, with horses and equipments. Various other points, including Arlington Heights, were taken possession of by other detachments, and thus all the positions commanding the capital were in the hands of the Federal troops. The completion of earthworks and batteries was pushed forward, and in a few days an almost impregnable barrier was placed between Washington and Manassas Junction, the grand Confederate rendezvous.

On the 27th of May, General McDowell, U. S. A., was placed in command of all the national forces in Virginia.

Many minor movements were carried on about this period, including the passage of the Potomac flotilla to Washington, and its severe encounters with rebel batteries on the banks, one engagement off Acquia Creek lasting over five hours. There was also a sharp reconnoissance at Fairfax Court House, carried out by Lieutenant Charles H. Tompkins, of the Second United States Cavalry.

It was clear that war was now the deliberate choice, if not the stern necessity, on either side, and the Southern press was not slow to begin the work of fomenting the troubles. The Richmond *Enquirer*, of May 25, in a violent article starting out with the words, "The Rubicon has been passed," went on to denounce the occupation of Alexandria as a flagrant outrage on Virginia soil, and added: "Virginians, arise in your strength and welcome the invader with 'bloody hands to hospitable graves.' The sacred soil of Virginia, in which repose the ashes of so many of the illustrious patriots who gave independence to their country, has been desecrated by the hostile tread of an armed enemy, who proclaims his malignant hatred of Virginia because she will not bow her proud neck to the humiliating yoke of Yankee rule. Meet the invader at the threshold. Welcome him with bayonet and bullet. Swear eternal hatred of a treacherous foe, whose only hope of safety is in your defeat and subjection." The Richmond *Examiner* called the murderous act of Jackson a "trait of true heroism," and with willful falsehood represented him as "standing alone against thousands" when he shot that "chief of all scoundrels, called Colonel Ellsworth." Such pleasant terms as "jail-birds," "execrable cut-throats," and "Federal hirelings" were thrown in at random till the editorial columns of the Richmond papers resembled no other species of journalism than that which might emanate from a lunatic asylum.

On the 14th of May a conspicuous figure was added to the commanders of the Union forces. General George B. McClellan, a Philadelphian and a West Point graduate, was commissioned Major-General of Volunteers, and assigned to the command of the Department of Ohio, comprising that State, Western Virginia, Indiana and Illinois. He promptly issued addresses complimenting the loyal citizens of Western Virginia and at the same time warning his troops against excesses. His first movements in Virginia were directed against Harper's Ferry, but first it was necessary to dispose of Colonel Porterfield, who, with a force of Confederates, was stationed at Grafton under orders from General Lee to muster volunteers at that point.

GEN. GEO. B. M'CLELLAN.

Colonel B. F. Kelley, of the First Virginia, a regiment organized at Camp Carlile, in Ohio, crossed to Wheeling and moved on Porterfield, who retreated to Philippi, a little town on a branch of the Monongahela, about twenty miles from Grafton. The Ohio and Indiana troops were also pushing in the same direction. On the 2d of June General Morris and Colonel Kelley held a conference at Grafton, where a plan for the capture of Porterfield and his troops at Philippi was decided on. This provided for the simultaneous movement of two columns, one under Colonel E. Dumont, and the other under Colonel Kelley, by different routes, with Philippi as the objective point. Colonel Kelley's division, consisting of the First Virginia, a portion of the Ohio Sixteenth, and the Indiana Ninth, commanded respectively by Colonels Irwin and Milroy, moved east by railroad toThornton, and thence marched twenty-two miles to Philippi. Dumont's column consisted of eight companies of the Seventh Indiana Volunteers, which moved westward on the Northwestern Virginia Railroad to Webster, and at this point he was reinforced by four companies of Ohio Volunteers under Colonel Steedman, with artillery under the immediate command of Lieutenant-Colonel Sturgis and four companies Sixth Indiana Volunteers under Colonel Crittenden. Colonel F. W. Lander, of McClellan's staff, was also with Dumont's column and led the advance from Webster. A terrible march of twelve miles, in a furious storm, on a dark night, brought this column at 5 A. M. on the 23d of June near the bridge leading into Philippi. The enemy were now in sight, and Dumont's men made a rush for the bridge over the Valley River, a narrow, double-passage structure about four hundred feet in length. One of the passages was found to be barricaded, but through the other dashed the Seventh Indiana, followed in rapid succession by the detachment of the Fourteenth Ohio, commanded by Colonel Steedman, and close on their heels followed Colonel Crittenden with the Sixth Indiana. The enemy, however, were in full flight, and Dumont's column pursued them with a running fire for several miles. A number of wagons with munitions of war, clothing, baggage and provisions were captured, being left behind in the precipitate flight, the horses having been cut loose and mounted by some of the fugitives. At this juncture Colonel Kelley's division appeared on the heights to the left, and giving a friendly cheer made a rapid descent on the retreating enemy. The pursuit was kept up toward Beverly, a point some thirty miles distant, for which Porterfield's disorganized men were heading. In a running engagement, during which many of the rebels were killed and wounded, Colonel Kelley received a severe pistol-shot wound in the breast and for a time he was believed to be mortally wounded. The shot was fired by Assistant-Quartermaster Simms, of the Confederate forces, after the actual engagement had ceased. Simms was captured, and with difficulty saved from immediate mutilation by the exasperated Virginians of Kelley's command. Among the prisoners taken was Colonel W. J. Willey, upon whose person were found papers of importance, besides his commission in the Confederate army, from Adjutant-General Garnett. Dumont proposed to hold Philippi and push on to Beverly, but the difficulty of moving among the mountains with inefficient transportation trains compelled a return to Grafton, which for some time thereafter became the headquarters in Western Virginia. The secession flag at Philippi was captured by Captain Ferry of the Seventh Indiana, and the colors presented by the ladies of Aurora to that regiment were the Stars and Stripes that first floated over the captured town. Among the papers found upon Colonel Willey was a letter from Colonel Porterfield, in which, under instructions from Governor Letcher, he was ordered to destroy the bridges on the Baltimore and Ohio Railroad as far west as possible. Other papers seriously compromised Major A. Loring, and he was promptly arrested by United States officers at Wheeling. Governor Letcher's instructions also included the seizure of arms sent to Wheeling by Secretary Cameron.

On the 6th of June Governor Pickens, of South Carolina, issued a characteristic proclamation, in which he said: "I have understood that many good people have been remitting funds to creditors in Northern States. In the existing relations of the country such conduct is in conflict with public law, and all citizens are hereby warned against the consequences." Side by side with the howls of execration on the part of the Southern press, because of the invasion of the sacred soil of Virginia, such a document stands out as a piece of unequaled effrontery.

Next in order comes the disastrous affair of Big Bethel, on the 10th of June, but some preliminary movements must be mentioned. General Butler, who had taken command at Fortress Monroe on the 22d of May, at once began to lay plans for the capture of Richmond, Va., which the Confederates had selected as their seat of government. After a reconnoissance of Hampton by Colonel Phelps the Fortress Monroe end of

Hampton Bridge was covered by a two-gun redoubt, and Camp Hamilton was formed and occupied by the Second New York and a Vermont regiment. A few days later Camp Butler was formed at Newport News by Colonel Phelps and Lieutenant John S. Greble. A strong position, however, was held by the Confederates at Pig Point, and the *Harriet Lane*, United States steamer, was sent to test its metal. After a short engagement the *Harriet Lane* withdrew, having been unable to shell the battery and having sustained some damage, five of her crew being wounded.

While Greble was fortifying Newport News, Colonel Duryee, with a Zouave regiment, the Fifth New York Volunteers, had arrived and been placed in command of Camp Hamilton.

Meanwhile General J. B. Magruder, who had been a Lieutenant Colonel of Artillery in the United States Army and loud in his professions of loyalty up to the moment when he deserted and joined the Confederate army, had taken up a position at Yorktown, and had also established posts at Little Bethel, a small church eight miles from Newport News, and another at Big Bethel, a larger church near the north branch of Back River. From these points foraging parties were sent out to annoy the picket guards at Hampton and Newport News, capture slaves of Union men, and even carry off citizens whom they forced to work in the intrenchments of Williamsburg and Yorktown. Butler became convinced that Magruder's plan was to seize Newport News and Hampton, and thus hem him in at Fortress Monroe. A prompt aggressive policy was decided on. The plan was to advance on the two Bethels, in two converging columns. The details were carefully mapped out, and but for gross blundering negligence that which proved a galling defeat would have been a decisive victory. General Butler's design can best be shown by his official report to Lieutenant-General Scott dated June 10th, 1861. After describing the annoyances already referred to he says:

"I ordered General Peirce, who is in command of Camp Hamilton, at Hampton, to send Duryee's regiment of Zouaves to be ferried over Hampton Creek at one o'clock this morning, and to march by the road up to Newmarket Bridge, then crossing the bridge, to go by a by-road and thus put the regiment in the rear of the enemy, and between Big Bethel and Little Bethel, in part for the purpose of cutting him off, and then to make an attack upon Little Bethel. I directed General Peirce to support him from Hampton with Colonel Townsend's regiment, with two mounted howitzers, and to march about an hour later. At the same time I directed Colonel Phelps, commanding at Newport News, to send out a battalion composed of such companies of the regiment under his command as he thought best, under command of Lieutenant-Colonel Washburn, in time to make a demonstration upon Little Bethel in front, and to have him supported by Colonel Bendix's regiment, with two field pieces. Bendix's and Townsend's should effect a junction at a fork of the road leading from Hampton to Newport News, something like a mile and a half from Little Bethel. I directed the march to be so timed that the attack should be made just at daybreak, and that after the attack was made upon Little Bethel, Duryee's regiment and a regiment from Newport News should follow immediately upon the heels of the fugitives, if they were enabled to cut them off, and attack the battery on the road to Big Bethel while covered by the fugitives; or, if it was thought expedient by General Peirce, failing to surprise the camp at Little Bethel, they should attempt to take the work near Big Bethel. To prevent the possibility of mistake in the darkness, I directed that no attack should be made until the watchword should be shouted by the attacking regiment, and, in case that by any mistake in the march the regiments that were to make the junction should unexpectedly meet and be unknown to each other, also directed that the members of Colonel Townsend's regiment should be known, if in daylight, by something white worn on the arm. The troops were accordingly put in action as ordered, and the march was so timed that Colonel Duryee had got in the position noted upon a sketch herewith inclosed, and Lieutenant-Colonel Washburn, in command of the regiment from Newport News, had also got into position indicated, and Colonel Bendix's regiment had been posted and ordered to hold the fork of the road, with two pieces of artillery, and Colonel Townsend's regiment had reached a point just behind, and were about to form a junction as the day dawned. Up to this point the plan had been vigorously, accurately, and successfully carried out; but here, by some strange fatality, and as yet unexplained blunder, without any word of notice, while Colonel Townsend was in column en route, and when the head of the column was within one hundred yards, Colonel Bendix's regiment opened fire with both artillery and musketry upon Colonel Townsend's column, which, in the hurry and confusion, was irregularly returned by some of Colonel Townsend's men, who feared they had fallen into an ambuscade. Colonel Townsend's column immediately retreated to the eminence near by, and were not pursued by Colonel Bendix's men. By this almost criminal blunder two men of Colonel Townsend's regiment were killed and eight more or less wounded. Hearing this cannonading and firing in his rear, and Lieutenant-Colonel Washburn, not knowing but that his communication might be cut off, immediately reversed his march, as did Colonel Duryee, and marched back to form a junction with his reserves. General Peirce, who was with Colonel Townsend's regiment, fearing that the enemy had got notice of our approach, and had posted himself in force on the line of march, not getting any communication from Colonel Duryee, sent back to me for reinforcements, and I immediately ordered Colonel Allen's regiment to be put in motion, and they reached Hampton about seven o'clock. In the meantime, the true state of facts having been ascertained by General Peirce, the regiments effected a junction and resumed the line of march. At the moment of the firing of Colonel Bendix, Colonel Duryee had surprised a part of an outlying guard of the enemy, consisting of thirty persons, who have been brought to me. Of course, by this firing, all hope of a surprise above the camp at Little Bethel was lost, and, upon marching upon it, it was found to have been vacated, and the cavalry had pressed on towards Big Bethel. Colonel Duryee, however, destroyed the camp at Little Bethel and advanced. General Peirce then, with the advice of his colonels, thought best to attempt to carry the works of the enemy at Big Bethel, and made dispositions to that effect. The attack commenced about half-past nine o'clock. At about ten o'clock General Peirce sent a note to me saying there was a sharp engagement with the enemy, and that he thought he should be able to maintain his position until reinforcements could come up. Acting upon this information, Colonel Carr's regiment, which had been ordered in the morning to proceed as far as Newmarket Bridge, was allowed to go forward. I received this information about twelve o'clock. I immediately made disposition from Newport News to have Colonel Phelps form the four regiments there, and forward aid if necessary. As soon as this order could be sent forward I repaired to Hampton for the purpose of having proper ambulances and wagons for the sick and wounded, intending to go forward and join the command. While the wagons were going forward a messenger came announcing that the engagement had terminated, and that the troops were returning in good order to camp. I remained upon the ground at Hampton, personally seeing the wounded put in boats and towed round to the hospital, and ordering forward Lieutenant Morris with two boat howitzers to cover the rear of the returning column in case it should be attacked. Having been informed that the ammunition of the artillery had been expended, and seeing the head of the column approach Hampton in good order, I waited for General Peirce to come up. I am informed by him that the dead and wounded had all been brought off, and that the return had been made in good order, and without haste. I learned from him that the men behaved with great steadiness, with the exception of some few instances, and that the attack was made with propriety, vigor and courage; but that the enemy were found to be supported by a battery, variously estimated at from fifteen to twenty pieces, some of which were rifled cannon, which were very well served and protected from being readily turned by a creek in front.

"Our loss is very considerable, amounting perhaps to forty or fifty, a quarter part of which you will see was from the unfortunate mistake—to call it by no worse name—of Colonel Bendix. I will, as soon as official returns can be got, give a fuller detail of the affair, and will only add now that we have to regret especially the death of Lieutenant Greble, of the Second Artillery, who went out with Colonel Washburn from Newport News, and who very efficiently and gallantly fought his piece until he was struck by a cannon shot. I think, in the unfortunate combination of circumstances, and the result which we experienced, we have gained more than we have lost. Our troops have learned to have confidence in themselves under fire, and the enemy have shown that they will not meet us in the open field, and our officers have learned wherein their organization and drill are inefficient."

We have given this remarkable report at full length for several reasons. First, because it is due to General Butler to show his military talent in planning a movement, and next to give a first general outline of an engagement which has been considerably tangled by various narrators. It is also interesting as showing that then, as now, General Butler was the champion formulator of "views" adapted to the exigencies of any subject or the condition of it.

The full official returns give the Union losses in this disastrous affair, the first actual reverse of the Federal troops, at sixteen killed, thirty-four wounded and five missing. The Confederate loss, according to the correspondent of the Richmond *Dispatch*, was one killed and three wounded. They claimed to have taken six prisoners.

Before closing we will cull one or two episodes from other sources believed to be authentic. It is but simple justice to Colonel Bendix to show how the terrible blunder came about. Acting Assistant Quartermaster Captain Peter Haggerty, of General Butler's staff at Fortress Monroe, was the officer who had been instructed to give the watchword, and the order for wearing the white badges; he forgot both in the excitement of ordering the advance from Newport News. The Confederates, whose dress was similar to that of Townsend's men, wore white bands on their hats and of this Bendix was aware. In the gray dawn the white badges ordered by General Butler, of which Bendix knew nothing, at once confounded them with Magruder's troops, and the blunder was deepened by the fact that Peirce and Townsend, with their respective staffs, mounted, in advance of the column, were mistaken for cavalry, of which service none had been ordered on the expedition, while Magruder was known to have a good force of this class with him at Big Bethel.

Besides the gallant Greble, the Union forces suffered a severe loss in the death of Major Theodore Winthrop, one of General Butler's aids. He was leading a company of the New York Seventh and attempted to take the redoubt on the left. He mounted one of the logs and, waving his sword, shouted, "Come on, boys: one charge, and the day is ours." A North Carolina drummer boy borrowed a gun, leaped on the battery and shot him deliberately in the breast. He fell nearer to the enemy's works than any other man went during the fight. On the 17th of June Lieutenant George H. Butler was sent with an escort to Big Bethel to recover the body of Major Winthrop. At Little Bethel a picket took their message to Magruder, who sent Captain Kilsen, of Louisiana, to receive them. Two hours later Magruder himself came with Colonel De Rusey, brother of the Chief of the Engineers at Fortress Monroe; Colonel Hill, of North Carolina, and other late officers of the United States Army. Magruder received the party handsomely and presently his men, three hundred in number, appeared with the wagon bearing the remains, over which they fired a volley. Magruder spoke in the highest terms of Major Winthrop's bravery and offered an escort to Hampton, but this was declined. On the other hand, none of Butler's men were allowed to go near the batteries. At the time Winthrop fell he was wearing the sword of Colonel Wardrop, of the Third Massachusetts, and this was sent to North Carolina as a trophy.

Under reserve, but by way of giving the reverse of the medal, we quote from the correspondent of the Richmond *Dispatch*, who participated in the Big Bethel battle, under date of June 11th, from Yorktown. After describing the earlier movements, he says:

"The men did not seem able to stand fire at all. About one o'clock the guns were silenced, and a few moments after their infantry retreated precipitately down the road to Hampton. Our cavalry, numbering three companies, went in pursuit and harassed them down to the edge of Hampton. As they retreated many of the wounded fell along the road and died, and the whole road to Hampton was strewn with haversacks, overcoats, canteens and muskets which the men had thrown off in their retreat. After the battle I visited the position they held. The houses by which they had been hid had been burned by our troops. Around the yard were the dead bodies of the men who had been killed by our cannon, mangled in the most frightful manner by the shells. The uniforms on the bodies were very different, and many of them are like those of the Virginia soldiery. A little further on we came to the point to which they had carried some of the wounded who had since died. The gay-looking uniforms of the New York Zouaves contrasted greatly with the pallid, fixed faces of their dead owners. Going to the swamp through which they attempted to pass to assault our lines another bloody scene was presented. Bodies dotted the black morass from one end to the other. I saw one boyish, delicate-looking fellow lying in the mud, with a bullet-hole through his breast. His hand was pressed on the wound from which his life-blood had poured, and the other was clenched in the grass that grew near him. Lying on the ground was a Testament which had fallen from his pocket, daubed with blood. On opening the cover I found the printed inscription: "Present. d to the Defenders of their Country by the New York Bible Society." A United States flag was also stamped on the title page. Among the haversacks picked up along the route were many letters from the Northern States, asking if they liked the Southern farms, and if the Southern barbarians had been whipped out yet. The force the enemy brought against us was 4,000, according to the statement of the six prisoners we took. Ours was 1,100. Their loss in killed and wounded must be nearly 200; our loss is one killed and three wounded. * * * As there was force enough at Old Point to send up to Bethel and surround us, we took up the line of march and came up to Yorktown, where we now are."

Allowing for exaggeration and bias, this memorandum from across the lines is interesting as showing how differently the same thing may look when seen through another pair of spectacles.

Just here, and before we turn from the field of battle to the forum, we should mention that it was during the preliminary movements, when Phelps made his reconnoissance of Hampton, that some of Colonel Mallory's negroes escaped and sought protection in the Union lines from the Confederate scouts who had been capturing their fellow slaves and forcing them to work in the intrenchments. What to do with these fugitives was a problem till Butler solved it by one of his "views": "These men are contraband of war: set them at work." Thus while the poor fellows were freed from Confederate labor they still found the curse of the Ishmaelite was upon them. The term "contraband," however, passed into war vernacular and had much to do with hastening forward that bold stroke of the pen which, while it emancipated the "contraband," dealt a deadly blow at the power of the South by stripping it of its living chattels.

Here we must turn from scenes of bloodshed to note the proceedings of the special session of Congress summoned for July 4th.

CHAPTER IX.

LINCOLN'S SECOND CALL FOR TROOPS—THE CONDITION OF THE NAVY—THE SPECIAL SESSION OF THE THIRTY-SEVENTH CONGRESS—ABSTRACT OF LINCOLN'S MESSAGE—EXTRACTS FROM DAVIS' CONFEDERATE MESSAGE—PROCEEDINGS IN CONGRESS—EXPULSION OF MEMBERS ON TREASON CHARGES—OPPOSITION TACTICS OF THE MINORITY—THE GOVERNMENT SUSTAINED—VIGOROUS PREPARATIONS FOR WAR—ADJOURNMENT OF CONGRESS.

On the 3d of May, 1861, President Lincoln issued another proclamation embodying a further call for troops, and also for men for the naval service. This second call was for forty-two thousand and thirty-four volunteers, to serve for a period of three years, unless sooner discharged, to be mustered into service as infantry and cavalry. He also directed the regular Army of the United States to be increased by the addition of eight regiments of infantry, one regiment of cavalry and one regiment of artillery, making altogether a maximum aggregate increase of twenty-two thousand seven hundred and fourteen officers and enlisted men. He further directed the enlistment, for not less than one nor more than three years, of eighteen thousand seamen, in addition to the present force, for the naval service of the United States.

It will be pertinent here to glance at the condition of the Navy, a branch of the public service heretofore but incidentally mentioned. The treachery which had permeated the Buchanan Cabinet, took especial care to weaken this important department in various ways, either by gross neglect in the ship-yards or by the dispatch of serviceable ships to foreign stations. At the incoming of the Lincoln administration there were but forty-two vessels in commission out of the ninety of all classes which were supposed to constitute the United States Navy. Upon utterly absurd pretexts the bulk of those in commission had been stationed in remote foreign waters, the *Brooklyn*, of twenty-five guns, and the storeship *Relief*, of two guns, being all that the Government could command for immediate use when the Secession movement was initiated. Of these, the *Relief* was under orders with stores for the coast of Africa, and the *Brooklyn*, from her great draught, was useless for the waters of Charleston Harbor, the first objective point of the Confederate movement. The cunning of the conspirators and the imbecility of Buchanan are painted in vivid colors by this brief résumé. Two thousand, four hundred and fifteen guns was the standard armament of the United States, but eight hundred and seventy-four guns were out of service, because twenty-eight dismantled hulks were rotting in port, and in such condition generally that months of vigorous work would be needed to put them afloat. Sailor life being in accord with the easy-going Southern propensities, the Navy, such as it was, had drawn its officers largely from the now seceding States, and the defections were large and rapid. It was a pitiful spectacle upon which Gideon Welles gazed, and of which he had to report to his disgusted Chief, when he assumed the Secretaryship of the Navy under Lincoln. There was no weeping over spilt milk, however, and by the time Congress met in extraordinary session, July 4th, 1861, there were two squadrons, the Atlantic, under Flag Officer Silas H. Stringham, and the Gulf Squadron, under Flag Officer William Mervine, comprising in all forty-three armed vessels engaged in blockade duty and coast defense, with a force of thirty-three hundred men and two hundred and ninety-six guns. Even more promptly, perhaps, than in the Army requisitions, that is relatively, recruits flocked to the standard of the Navy, and though nearly three hundred officers had resigned, or been dismissed, a very satisfactory make-shift service had been organized. The removal of the Naval School from Annapolis to Newport, Rhode Island, had insured the safety of public property and the regular continuance of marine training. Much of this had been done outside of strict constitutional authority, as indeed many other things were of necessity done in this exceptional period, but the rebel element had been largely eliminated from Congress by its own action, and the little leaven left was insufficient to create any serious difficulty. That greater liberties were not taken with the alleged prerogatives of the people may be fairly credited to the scrupulous fidelity of the patriotic President, whose calm, cool judgment tempered the indignant zeal of his Cabinet.

The Congress which met in extraordinary session on Thursday, July 4th, was the Thirty-seventh in point of nomenclature, and its assembling marked the eighty-fourth anniversary of the Declaration of Independence. Upon this momentous gathering were fixed the eyes not alone of the entire people of this country, but of the whole civilized world.

Twenty-three States were represented in the Senate by forty Senators, and twenty-two States and one Territory by one hundred and fifty-four Representatives in the lower house, on the first day of the session. The Union sentiment prevailed by a large majority. The States of North and South Carolina, Georgia, Alabama, Florida, Louisiana, Arkansas, Texas, Mississippi and Virginia were conspicuously absent from choice, and Tennessee was also unrepresented in the House in consequence of its Congressional elections not having been held. In this State, although a secession ordinance had been passed, the sentiment in favor of disunion was not universal, and consequently when in August the elections were held three of the eastern districts chose representatives to Congress. One of these was captured by the Confederates while on his way to the Capitol, and carried to Richmond. There he professed allegiance to the Southern Confederacy. This was Thomas A. R. Nelson. In the Senate Andrew Johnson appeared as the Senator from Tennessee. We may take occasion, presently, to quote from his powerful speech in defense of the Union, delivered in the Senate on the 27th of July.

The organization of the two houses at the opening of this the Thirty-seventh Congress was as follows: Hannibal Hamlin, Vice-President of the United States, President of the Senate by virtue of his office, and Galusha A. Grow, of Pennsylvania, Speaker of the House of Representatives, by election of that body. On the second day of the session President Lincoln sent in his message. From this important document it would seem expedient to quote.

After logically, clearly, and historically narrating the events of the few previous months, events which we have endeavored to place before our readers, and, therefore, need not recapitulate here, the President said :

"It is believed that nothing has been done beyond the Constitutional competency of Congress. Soon after the first call for militia, it was considered a duty to authorize the commanding general, in proper cases, according to his discretion, to suspend the privilege of the Writ of Habeas Corpus; or, in other words, to arrest and detain, without resort to the ordinary processes and forms of law, such individuals as he might deem dangerous to the public safety. The authority has been exercised but very sparingly. Nevertheless, the legality and propriety of what has been done under it are questioned, and the attention of the country has been called to the proposition that one who is sworn to take care that the laws be faithfully executed, should not himself violate them. Of course some consideration was given to the questions of power and propriety before this matter was acted upon. The whole laws which were required to be executed were being resisted, and failing of execution in nearly one-third of the States, must they be allowed to finally fail of execution, even had it been perfectly clear that by use of the means necessary to their execution, some single law, made in such extreme tenderness of the citizen's liberty, that practically it relieves more of the guilty than the innocent, should to a very great extent be violated ? To state the question more directly, are all the laws but one to go unexecuted, and the Government itself go to pieces lest that one be violated ? Even in such a case would not the official oath be broken if the Government should be overthrown when it was believed that disregarding the single law would tend to preserve it ?

But it was not believed that this question was presented. It was not believed that any law was violated. The provision of the Constitution, that the privilege of the writ of habeas corpus shall not be suspended unless when, in cases of rebellion or invasion, the public safety may require it, is equivalent to a provision that such privilege may be suspended when, in cases of rebellion or invasion, the public safety does require it. It was decided that we have a case of rebellion, and that the public safety does require the qualified suspension of the privilege of the writ, which was authorized to be made. Now, it is insisted that Congress, and not the Executive, is vested with this power. But the Constitution is silent as to which or who is to exercise the power ; and as the provision was plainly made for a dangerous emergency, it cannot be believed that the framers of the instrument intended that in every case the danger should run its course until Congress could be called together, the very assembling of which might be prevented, as was intended in this case by the rebellion. No more extended argument is now offered, as an opinion at some length will probably be presented by the Attorney-General. Whether there shall be any legislation on the subject, and, if so, what, is submitted entirely to the better judgment of Congress. The forbearance of this Government had been so extraordinary, and so long continued, as to lead some foreign nations to shape their action as if they supposed the early destruction of our National Union was probable. While this, on discovery, gave the Executive some concern, he is now happy to say that the sovereignty and rights of the United States are now everywhere practically respected by foreign powers, and a general sympathy with the country is manifested throughout the world."

After alluding to the accompanying reports of the Secretaries of the Treasury, War and Navy, and promising any further information needed, the Message proceeds:

"It is now recommended that you give the legal means for making this contest a short and decisive one ; that you place at the control of the Government for the work at least 400,000 men and $400,000,000 ; that number of men is about one-tenth of those of proper ages within the regions where apparently all are willing to engage, and the sum is less than a twenty-third part of the money value owned by the men who seem ready to devote the whole. A debt of $600,000,000 now is a less sum per head than was the debt of our Revolution when we came out of that struggle, and the money value in the country bears even a greater proportion to what it was then than does the population. Surely each man has as strong a motive now to preserve our liberties as each had then to establish them.

"A right result at this time will be worth more to the world than ten times the men and ten times the money. The evidence reaching us from the country leaves no doubt that the material for this work is abundant, and that it needs only the hand of legislation to give it legal sanction, and the hand of the Executive to give it practical shape and efficiency. One of the greatest perplexities of the Government is to avoid receiving troops faster than it can provide for them; in a word, the people will save their Government if the Government will only do its part indifferently well. It might seem at first thought to be of little difference whether the present movement in the South be called Secession or Rebellion. The movers, however, well understand the difference. At the beginning they knew they could never raise their treason to any respectable magnitude by any name which implies violation of law ; they knew their people possessed as much of moral sense, as much of devotion to law and order, and as much pride in its reverence for the history and government of their common country, as any other civilized and patriotic people. They knew they could make no advancement directly in the teeth of these strong and noble sentiments. Accordingly they commenced by an insidious debauching of the public mind ; they invented an ingenious sophism, which, if conceded, was followed by perfectly logical steps through all the incidents of the complete destruction of the Union. The sophism itself is that any State of the Union may, and therefore lawfully and peacefully, withdraw from the Union without the consent of the Union or of any other State.

"The little disguise that the supposed right is to be exercised only for just cause, themselves to be the sole judges of its justice, is too thin to merit any notice with rebellion. Thus sugar-coated they have been dragging the public mind of these sections for more than thirty years, and until at length they have brought many good men to a willingness to take up arms against the Government the day after some assemblage of men have enacted the farcical pretense of taking their State out of the Union, who could have been brought to no such thing the day before. This sophism derives much, perhaps the whole of its currency, from the assumption that there is some omnipotent and sacred supremacy pertaining to a State, to each State of our Federal Union. Our States have neither more nor less power than that reserved to them in the Union by the Constitution, no one of them ever having been a State out of the Union. The original ones passed into the Union before they cast off their British Colonial dependence, and the new ones came into the Union directly from a condition of dependence, excepting Texas, and even Texas in its temporary independence, was never designated as a State. The new ones only took the designation of States on coming into the Union, while that name was first adopted for the old ones in and by the Declaration of Independence. Therein the United Colonies were declared to be *free* and *independent* States. But even then the object was not to declare their independence of one another—of the Union, but, directly the contrary, as their mutual pledge and their mutual action, before, at the time, and afterward, abundantly show. The express plight of faith by each and all of the original thirteen States in the Articles of Confederation two years later, that the Union shall be perpetual, is most conclusive. Having never been States, either in substance or in name, outside of the Union, whence this magical omnipotence of State rights, asserting a claim of power to lawfully destroy the Union itself? Much is said about the sovereignty of the States, but the word is not in the National Constitution, nor, as is believed, in any of the State constitutions. What is sovereignty in the political sense of the word? Would it be far wrong to define it as a political community without a political superior? Tested by this, no one of our States, except Texas, was a sovereignty; and even Texas gave up the character on coming into the Union, by which act she acknowledged the Constitution of the United States; and the laws and treaties of the United States, made in pursuance of States, have their status in the Union, made in pursuance of the Constitution, to be for her the supreme law. The States have their status in the Union, and they have no other legal status. If they break from this they can only do so against law and by revolution. The Union, and not themselves separately, procured their independence and their liberty by conquest or purchase. The Union gave each of them whatever of independence and liberty it has. The Union is older than any of the States, and, in fact, it created them, as States. Originally, some dependent Colonies made the Union, and in turn the Union threw off their old dependence for them and made them States, such as they are. Not one of them ever had a State Constitution independent of the Union. Of course it is not forgotten that all the new States formed their constitutions before they entered the Union, nevertheless, dependent upon and preparatory to coming into the Union. Unquestionably the States have the powers and rights reserved to them in and by the National Constitution.

"But among these surely are not included all conceivable powers, however mischievous or destructive, but at most only such as were known in the world at the time as governmental powers, and certainly a power to destroy the Government itself had never been known as a governmental, as a merely administrative power. This relative matter of national power and State rights as a principle is no other than the principle of generality and locality. Whatever concerns the whole should be conferred to the whole General Government, while whatever concerns only the State should be left exclusively to the State. This is all there is of original principle about it. Whether the National Constitution, in defining boundaries between the two, has applied the principle with exact accuracy is not to be questioned. We are all bound by that defining without question. What is now combated is the position that secession is consistent with the Constitution, is lawful and peaceful. It is not contended that there is any express law for it, and nothing should ever be implied as law which leads to unjust or absurd consequences. The nation purchased with money the countries out of which several of these States were formed. Is it just that they shall go off without leave and without refunding? The nation paid very large sums, in the aggregate I believe nearly a hundred millions, to relieve Florida of the aboriginal tribes. Is it just that she shall now be off without consent or without any return? The nation is now in debt for money applied to the benefit of those so-called seceding States, in common with the rest. Is it just either that creditors shall go unpaid or the remaining States pay the whole? A part of the present national debt was contracted to pay the old debt of Texas. Is it just that she shall leave and pay no part of this herself? Again, if one State may secede, so may another, and when all shall have seceded, none is left to pay the debts. Is this quite just to creditors? Did we notify them of this sage view of ours when we borrowed their money? If we now recognize this doctrine by allowing the seceders to go in peace it is difficult to see what we can do if others choose to go, or to extort terms upon which they choose to remain. The seceders insist that our Constitution admits of secession. They have assumed to make a National Constitution of their own, in which, of necessity, they have either discarded or retained the right of secession, as they insist exists in ours. If they have discarded it they thereby admit that on principle it ought not to exist in ours; if they have retained it by their own construction of ours that shows that to be consistent, they must secede from one another whenever they shall find it the easiest way of settling their debts, or effecting any other selfish or august object. The principle itself is one of disintegration, and upon which no government can possibly endure. If all the States, save one, should assert the power to drive that one out of the Union, it is presumed the whole class of seceder politicians would at once deny the power, and denounce the act as the greatest outrage upon State rights. But suppose that precisely the same act, instead of being called driving the one out, should be called the seceding of the others from that one, it would be exactly what the seceders claim to do, unless, indeed, they made the point that the one, because it is a minority, may rightfully do what the others, because they are a majority, may not rightfully do.

These politicians are subtle and profound in the rights of minorities. They are not partial to that power which made the Constitution and speaks from the preamble, calling itself 'We, the people.' It may well be questioned whether there is to-day a majority of the legally qualified voters of any State, except, perhaps, South Carolina, in favor of disunion. There is much reason to believe that the Union men are the majority in many, if not in every one of the so-called seceded States. The contrary has not been demonstrated in any one of them. It is ventured to assert this, even of Virginia and Tennessee, for the result of an election held in military camps where bayonets are all on one side of the question voted upon, can scarcely be considered as demonstrating popular sentiment. At such an election all that large class who are at once for the Union and against coercion would be coerced to vote against the Union. It may be affirmed, without extravagance, that the free institutions we enjoy have developed the powers and improved the condition of our whole people beyond any example in the world. Of this we now have a striking and impressive illustration. So large an army as the Government has now on foot was never before known, without a soldier in it but who has taken his place there of his own free choice. But, more than this, there are many single regiments whose members, one and another, possess full practical knowledge of all the arts, sciences, professions, and whatever else, whether useful or elegant, is known in the whole world, and there is scarcely one from which there could not be selected a President, a Cabinet, a Congress, and perhaps a Court, abundantly competent to administer this Government itself. Nor do I say this is not true also in the army of our late friends, now adversaries, in this contest. But it is so much better the reason why the Government, which has conferred such benefits on both them and us, should not be broken up. Whoever in any section proposes such a government would do well to consider in deference to what principle it is that he does it. What better is he likely to get in its stead, whether the substitute will give, or be intended to give, so much of good to the people. There are some foreshadowings on this subject. Our adversaries have adopted some declarations of independence in which, unlike the good old one penned by Jefferson, they omit the words 'All men are created equal.' Why? They have adopted a temporary National Constitution, in the preamble of which, unlike the good old one signed by Washington, they omit 'We, the people' and substitute 'We, the deputies of the sovereign and independent States.' Why? Why this deliberate pressing out of view the rights of men and the authority of the people? This is essentially a people's contest on the side of the Union, it is a struggle for maintaining in the world that form and substance of government whose leading object is to elevate the condition of men, to lift artificial weights from all shoulders, to clear the paths of laudable pursuits for all, to afford all an unfettered start and a fair chance in the race of life, yielding to partial and temporary departures from necessity. This is the leading object of the government for whose existence we contend.

"I am most happy to believe that the plain people understand and appreciate this. It is worthy of note that while in this, the Government's hour of trial, large numbers of those in the army and navy who have been favored with the offices, have resigned and proved false to the hand which pampered them, not one common soldier or sailor is known to have deserted his flag. Great honor is due to those officers who remained true despite the example of their treacherous associates, but the greatest honor and the most important fact of all, is the unanimous firmness of the common soldiers and common sailors. To the last man, so far as known, they have successfully resisted the traitorous efforts of those whose commands but an hour before they obeyed as absolute law. This is the patriotic instinct of plain people. They understand without an argument that the destroying the Government which was made by Washington means no good to them. Our popular government has often been called an experiment. Two points of it our people have settled, the successful establishing, and the successful administering of it. One still remains. Its successful maintenance against a formidable internal attempt to overthrow it. It is for them to demonstrate to the world that those who can fairly carry on elections can also suppress a rebellion; that ballots are the peaceful successors of bullets, and that when ballots have fairly and constitutionally decided, there can be no successful appeal back to bullets; that there can be no successful appeal except to ballots themselves at succeeding elections. Such will be a great lesson of peace, teaching men that what they cannot take by an election neither can they take by a war, teaching all the folly of being the beginners of a war.

"Lest there be some uneasiness in the minds of candid men as to what is to be the course of the Government toward the Southern States after the rebellion shall have been suppressed, the Executive deems it proper to say it will be his purpose then, as ever, to be guided by the Constitution and the laws, and that he probably will have no different understanding of the powers and duties of the Federal Government relatively to the rights of the States and the people under the Constitution than that expressed in the inaugural address. He desires to preserve the Government that it may be administered for all, as it was administered by the men who made it. Loyal citizens everywhere have the right to claim this of their Government, and the Government has no right to withhold or neglect it. It is not perceived that in giving it there is any coercion, any conquest, or any subjugation, in any sense of these terms.

"The Constitution provided, and all the States have accepted the provision, 'that the United States shall guarantee to every State in the Union a republican form of government,' but if a State may lawfully go out of the Union, having done so it may also discard the republican form of government. So that to prevent its going out is an indispensable means to the end of maintaining the guarantee mentioned; and when an end is lawful and obligatory the indispensable means to it are also lawful and obligatory. It was with the deepest regret that the Executive found the duty of employing the war power in defense of the Government forced upon him; he could but perform this duty or surrender the existence of the Government. No compromise by public servants could in this case be a cure; not that compromises are not often proper, but that no popular Government can long survive a marked precedent that those who carry an election can only save the Government from immediate destruction by giving up the main point upon which the people gave the election. The people themselves, and not their servants, can safely reverse their own deliberate decisions.

"As a private citizen the Executive could not have consented that these institutions shall perish, much less could he in betrayal of so vast and so sacred a trust as these free people had confided to him. He felt that he had no moral right to shrink, nor even count the chances of his own life in what might follow.

" In full view of his great responsibility he has so far done what he has deemed his duty. You will now, according to your own judgment, perform yours. He sincerely hopes that your views and your actions may so accord with his as to assure all faithful citizens who have been disturbed in their rights, of a certain and speedy restoration to them under the Constitution and laws, and having thus chosen our cause without guile, and with pure purpose, let us renew our trust in God, and go forward without fear and with manly hearts."

We do not deem an apology necessary for having taken up so much of our space in quoting thus fully from this remarkable and valuable document; since the scope of our plan in this volume is not confined to a mere routine record of battles and hostile movements during the Civil War, but is purposed to convey a definite idea of the motives and impulses of the great contention, as specifically set forth by the chief actors in it.

The logical, cogent arguments of President Lincoln ; the unerring accuracy with which every weak joint in the armor of his adversaries is assailed; the noble, patriotic resolves which are announced and the lucid exposition of the true condition of affairs in general, render this message an epitome of this phase of American history, which can be read with profit over again even by those to whom its language is as a twice-told tale ; while to the rising generation, already disposed to class the events of this period among legendary lore, it will prove invaluable as a guide to their duty in shaping those destinies of this great Republic which must, in the course of nature, fall upon their shoulders. We would simply, just here, call attention to the guarded, but emphatic, implication of the monarchical tendencies of the Southern movement which the President conveyed in the sentences which show the subordination of " we, the people, " to "the sovereign States," and in the theorem that, " if a State may lawfully go out of the Union it may also discard the republican form of government." It was doubtless the perception of this subtle contingency that secured for Secession that keen sympathy which the Tory party in England, monarchical and aristocratic, if not actually despotic in its tradition, so freely afforded.

Before resuming the thread of Congressional proceedings it may be well, as a fitting pendant to the foregoing message, to quote from the message delivered to the Congress of the Confederate States, at Richmond, on July 20th.

Addressing the body as " Gentlemen of the Congress of the Confederate States of America," Jefferson Davis said :

"I have again to congratulate you on the accession of new members to our Confederation of free and equally sovereign States. Our loved and honored brethren of North Carolina and Tennessee have consummated the action foreseen and provided for at your last session, and I have had the gratification of announcing, by proclamation, in conformity with law, that these States were admitted into the Confederacy. The people of Virginia, also, by a majority previously unknown in our history, have ratified the action of her convention, uniting her fortunes with ours. The States of Arkansas, North Carolina and Virginia have likewise adopted the permanent Constitution of the Confederate States, and no doubt is entertained of its adoption by Tennessee, at the election to be held early in next month.

"I deemed it advisable to direct the removal of the several executive departments, with their archives, to this city, to which you have removed the seat of Government. Immediately after your adjournment the aggressive movements of the enemy required prompt, energetic action. The accumulation of his forces on the Potomac sufficiently demonstrated that his efforts were to be directed against Virginia, and from no point could necessary measures for her defense and protection be so effectually decided as from her own capital. The rapid progress of events, for the last few weeks, has fully sufficed to lift the veil, behind which the true policy and purposes of the Government of the United States had been previously concealed. Their odious features now stand fully revealed. The message of their President and the action of their Congress during the present month confess their intention of the subjugation of these States by a war, by which it is impossible to attain the proposed result, while its dire calamities not to be avoided by us will fall with double severity on themselves.

"Commencing in March last with the affectation of ignoring the secession of seven States, which first organized this Government ; persevering in April in the idle and absurd assumption of the existence of a riot, which was to be dispersed by a *posse comitatus*, continuing in successive months the false representation that these States intended an offensive war, in spite of conclusive evidence to the contrary, furnished as well by official action as by the very basis on which this Government is constructed, the President of the United States and his advisers succeeded in deceiving the people of these States into the belief that the purpose of this Government was not peace at home, but conquest abroad; not defense of its own liberties, but subversion of those of the people of the United States. The series of manœuvres by which this impression was created, the art with which they were devised, and the perfidy with which they were executed were already known to you, but you could scarcely have supposed that they would be openly avowed and their success made the subject of boast and self-laudation in an executive message."

The message then quotes from that of President Lincoln as to the details of the Charleston Harbor affairs, and the provisions of Congress for increasing the United States forces to half a million of men. It then proceeds as follows:

"These enormous preparations in men and money for the conduct of a war, on a scale more grand than any which the New World ever witnessed, is a distinct avowal, in the eyes of civilized man, that the United States are engaged in a conflict with a great and powerful nation. They are at last compelled to abandon the pretense of being engaged in dispersing rioters and suppressing insurrections, and are driven to the acknowledgment that the ancient Union has been dissolved They recognize the separate existence of these Confederate States, by an interdictive embargo and blockade of all commerce between them and the United States, not only by sea, but by land; not only in ships, but in cars; not only with those who bear arms, but with the entire population of the Confederate States; for they are waging an indiscriminate war upon them all, with savage ferocity, unknown in modern civilization.

"In this war rapine is the rule; private houses in beautiful rural retreats are bombarded and burnt; grain crops in the field are consumed by the torch; and when the torch is not convenient, careful labor is bestowed to render complete the destruction of every article of use or ornament remaining in private dwellings after the inhabitants have fled from the outrages of brutal soldiery, * * * But who shall depict the horror they entertain for the cool and deliberate malignity which, under pretext of suppressing insurrection (said by themselves to be upheld by a minority only of our people), makes special war on the sick, including women and children, by carefully-devised measures to prevent them from obtaining the medicines necessary for their cure. The sacred claims of humanity, respected even during the fury of actual battle, by careful diversion of attack from hospitals containing wounded enemies, are outraged in cold blood by a Government and people that pretend to desire a continuance of fraternal connections. All these outrages must remain unavenged, save by the universal reprehension of mankind. In all cases where the actual perpetrators of the wrongs escape capture they admit of no retaliation. The humanity of our people would shrink instinctively from the bare idea of waging a like war upon the sick, the women and the children of our enemy. But there are other savage practices which have been resorted to by the Government of the United States, which do admit of repression by retaliation, and I have been driven to the necessity of enforcing the repression. The prisoners of war taken by the enemy on board the small schooner Savannah, sailing under our commission, were, as I am credibly advised, treated like common felons, put in irons, confined in a jail usually appropriated to criminals of the worst dye, and threatened with punishment as such." The message then details alleged applications for the exchange of prisoners to which no reply had been received, and continues: "As measures of precaution, however, and until this reply is received I still retain custody of some officers captured from the enemy, whom it had been my pleasure previously to set at large on parole, and whose fate must necessarily depend on that of prisoners held by the enemy."

The message then complains of the suspension of habeas corpus, and says: "We may well rejoice that we have for ever severed our connection with a government that thus trampled on all principles of constitutional liberty, and with a people in whose presence such avowals could be hazarded." After alluding to the necessity for raising additional forces and funds, the message compliments the seceded citizens on "their attitude of calm and sublime devotion to their country, the cool and confident courage with which they are already preparing to meet the invasion in whatever proportions it may assume." The message closes in the following words:

"To speak of subjugating such a people, so united and determined, is to speak in a language incomprehensible to them; to resist attack on their rights or their liberties is with them an instinct. Whether this war shall last one, or three, or five years is a problem they leave to be solved by the enemy alone. It will last till the enemy shall have withdrawn from their borders; till their political rights, their altars and their homes are freed from invasion. Then, and then only, will they rest from this struggle, to enjoy, in peace, the blessings which, with the favor of Providence, they have secured by the aid of their own strong hearts and sturdy arms."

It will be noted that this document, while purporting to comment on President Lincoln's message, does not attempt to answer it on the grave charges advanced. The sneer, the whimper and the mutter of discontent and defiance are frequent, but the argument, the logic and even the plea of justification are conspicuously absent. Federal harshness is condemned as inhuman, but is coupled with a threat of at least equal inhumanity. How this threat was carried out the horrors of the Andersonville shambles subsequently demonstrated. No shadow of Right is advanced, save that which depends on Might, and yet the same course of action is imputed to the United States as a crime. It is almost amusing also to find a complaint of the interdiction of commerce emanating from the same sources that had but recently denounced the payment of northern commercial debts as a crime against the community.

However, we must leave the two documents to stand on their respective merits and return to the proceedings in Congress.

Accompanying the President's message were the Departmental Reports, which we will briefly summarize.

Secretary of the Treasury Chase asked for $240,000,000 for war purposes and $80,000,000 for general purposes for the current fiscal year ending June 30, 1862. These amounts he proposed to raise as follows: for general purposes, by increased duties according to a stated schedule, and further by direct taxation of real and personal property or by certain internal revenue levies. For the war credit he proposed a national loan of $100,000,000 in Treasury notes bearing interest at the rate of $7\frac{3}{10}$ per cent. per annum, and further the issuance of bonds to the same amount, redeemable at Government pleasure after thirty years at 7 per cent. interest. Also Treasury notes, not exceeding $50,000,000, at $3\frac{65}{100}$ per cent. interest, exchangeable for those of the first issue at will of the holder.

Secretary Welles, of the Navy, asked Congressional sanction for acts in excess of authority compelled by the Rebellion exigencies; an increase of staff and the appointment of commissioners to investigate the subject of iron-clads and floating batteries.

Secretary Cameron, of the War Department, recommended an increase of clerical force; a bounty of one hundred dollars for three-year enlistments in the regular Army; for a liberal supply of improved arms and appropriations for telegraph and railroad purposes for Government use.

Congress got rapidly to work and promptly prohibited parliamentary filibustering by a House resolution declaring only measures of military, naval and financial character pertinent to the current session. All other business was referred to committees for action at the next regular session. This resolution cleared the decks for action. In the Senate Mr. Wilson, Chairman of the Committee on Military Affairs of that body, gave notice of the immediate introduction of the following six measures: To ratify and confirm certain acts of the President for the suppression of insurrection and rebellion; to authorize the employment of volunteers to aid in enforcing the laws and protecting public property; to increase the present military establishment of the United States; providing for the better organization of the military establishment; to promote the efficiency of the army; and, lastly, for the organization of a volunteer militia force, to be called the National Guard of the United States.

When these measures came up for consideration, the Secession element yet remaining in Congress offered its opposition to the strengthening of the hands of the Executive, under the leadership of Clement L. Vallandigham, of Ohio, in the House, and John C. Breckinridge, of Kentucky, in the Senate. Despite Vallandigham's impassioned oratory and unscrupulous condemnation of the Presidential policy and conduct, a loan bill authorizing the Secretary of the Treasury to borrow $250,000,000 for the support of the Government and the prosecution of the war was passed, under the previous question. The following day an army appropriation bill for $161,000,000 was passed by 150 yeas to 5 nays, the latter being Benjamin Wood, of New York; Norton and Reid, of Missouri; Burnett, of Kentucky; and Vallandigham, of Ohio. The latter had vainly attempted to add a proviso prohibiting the use of the money for operations against the Seceded States, or for interfering with African slavery. On the 13th the measure authorizing the contingent of 500,000 men was passed, as was also a bill introduced by Mr. Hickman, of Pennsylvania, defining and punishing conspiracies against the United States. On the 15th a resolution was adopted, by which the House agreed to sanction unlimited appropriation of money, and unlimited employment of men, in such numbers as might become necessary for the suppression of rebellion. Wood and Vallandigham in every instance offered factious opposition, and endeavored to incorporate provisos looking to an armistice; to diplomatic relations with Jefferson Davis and to a general convention at

Louisville for peace purposes. As a matter of course all these efforts, mustering at the most but seven supporters, were summarily disposed of by being tabled. On the 19th John Jay Crittenden, of Kentucky, offered the following joint resolution to the effect that:

"The present deplorable civil war has been forced upon the country by the communists of the Southern States now in revolt against the Constitutional Government, and in arms around the Capitol, and that, in this National emergency, Congress, banishing all feeling of mere passion or resentment, will recollect only its duty to its country; that this war is not waged, on our part, in any spirit of oppression, nor for any purpose of conquest or subjugation, nor purpose of overthrowing or interfering with the rights or established institutions of those States; but to defend and maintain the supremacy of the Constitution, and to preserve the Union, with all the dignity, equality and rights of the several States unimpaired; and as soon as these objects are accomplished the war ought to cease."

This was laid over till Monday, the 22d. (Meanwhile the disastrous first Battle at Bull's Run was fought, but of this we shall treat in a separate chapter.) On coming up for action Mr. Crittenden's resolution was passed by a vote of 117 to 2. The House also passed a resolution on the same day declaring unswerving determination to support the Constitution and execute its laws, and pledging to the country the employment of every resource, national and individual, for the suppression, overthrow and punishment of rebels in arms. On the 5d of August a Senate bill providing for the confiscation of property used for insurrectionary purposes, to which Mr. Trumbull had added an amendment providing that the master of any slave who should employ him for insurrectionary purposes should forfeit all right to his service or labor thereafter, came up in the House for consideration. Bitter opposition to the Trumbull amendment specially was manifested, and then the Committee on the Judiciary, to whom the bill had been recommitted, modified the amendment so as to apply it only to slaves whose labor for insurrectionary purposes was employed in any military or naval service against the Government and authority of the United States. It was a distinction, certainly, and it made just difference enough to secure the passage of the bill by 60 to 48. It is not quite easy to understand the animus of so large a minority vote, but men, even in those days of peril, appeared to pet their hobbies almost as much as in times of ease and prosperity. The attempts of the Secession faction to introduce compromise measures were unceasing until swept aside by the accepted sentiment of a proposed resolution by Mr. Diven, of New York, that such suggestions were either cowardly or treasonable. With the authorization of the proposed loan of $250,000,000, and the passage of an act imposing additional duties on imports of foreign articles of luxury and necessity, with a further proviso for a direct tax of $20.000,000 on real estate, as per schedule, in each State not in rebellion, the work of the House of Representatives for the special session was accomplished. It should be noted that on the 13th of July John B Clark, of Missouri, was expelled the House as a traitor.

Turning to the work of the Senate we note that within six days of the opening of the session James Chesnut, Jr., of South Carolina; Thomas L. Clingman and Thomas Bragg, of North Carolina; John Hemphill and Louis T. Wigfall, of Texas; James M. Mason and Robert T. M. Hunter, of Virginia; A. O. P. Nicholson, of Tennessee; William K. Sebastian and Charles B. Mitchell, of Arkansas, were all expelled by virtue of a resolution which declared them to be engaged in a conspiracy for the destruction of the Union and the Government. On the 18th the bill providing for the reorganization of the army passed the Senate, after a Secession restriction process by Powell, of Kentucky, had been defeated, and a substitute by Sherman, of Ohio, had been adopted, declaring the purposes of the act to be the preservation of the Union, the defense of the property and the maintenance of the authority of the Government. On the 24th of July a resolution, identical with Mr. Crittenden's in the House, was adopted, and on the 6th of August the amendments of the House to the bill confiscating insurrectionary property being concurred in by a vote of 24 to 11, the bill received the President's sanction and became law.

All other business arising in the House having been, with slight changes, concurred in by the Senate, an adjournment of the special session was agreed to on the 6th of August, after the passage of a joint resolution requesting the President to appoint a day of public fasting, humiliation and prayer for the safety and welfare of the Union and the speedy restoration of peace. To this request the President responded by a proclamation on the 12th of August, appointing the last Thursday in September as such day of national religious observance.

Thus ended one of the most important sessions of the Congress of the United States, after thirty-three days of unremitting labor, performed with dignity, calmness and decorum, despite the fact that a serious reverse to the Union arms had been sustained meanwhile, and that outside those legislative halls excitement was at fever heat; that the streets of Washington were thronged with men, ragged and wounded in the rout of battle, and that the safety of the Capital itself was believed to be seriously imperilled. They had nobly done their duty and had conferred upon the Executive and his Cabinet almost limitless powers in furtherance of that deathless sentiment, "THE UNION MUST AND SHALL BE PRESERVED."

CHAPTER X.

THE BATTLES OF FALLING WATERS, RICH MOUNTAIN AND CARRICK'S FORD—THE SKIRMISH AT SCREYTOWN—THE FIRST BATTLE OF BULL RUN—OFFICIAL REPORTS—NARRATIVE OF AN EYE-WITNESS—TERRIBLE SCENES OF THE RETREAT—GENERAL M'CLELLAN BEGINS TO ORGANIZE THE ARMY OF THE POTOMAC.

The results of the battle at Big Bethel on June 10th, while disheartening to the people at large and creating much chagrin among the authorities at Washington, merely served to inflame the enthusiasm and valor of the troops elsewhere who were clamoring to be led against the enemy. Butler remained for the present inactive at Fortress Monroe, but Major-General Patterson was moving upon Harper's Ferry, which General Joseph E. Johnston held with a considerable force. On the 6th of June the Eleventh Indiana Regiment, under Colonel Wallace, had been ordered from Evansville, Ohio, to report to Patterson, and the order was executed with a promptness which evidenced the anxiety of officers and men for action. Hurrying on to Grafton and thence to Cumberland, which was reached on the night of the 9th, Colonel Wallace rested his men and then resolved to make a dash at the Confederate force stationed at Romney. Disguising his plans, under pretense of seeking a camping ground, Wallace, with about eight hundred men, pushed on to New Creek by rail. A perilous and fatiguing night's march brought the troops, on the morning of the 11th, to the bridge crossing the south branch of the Potomac. In spite of opposition, this was crossed on the run and the bewildered insurgents, wholly uninformed as to the strength of their assailants, fled in all directions. Wallace, having but a small force and no cavalry, contented himself with this scare and got back to Cumberland in good condition. He had, however, effected far more than he anticipated or hoped for.

General Johnston, apprised of this movement, and wholly unable to account for it, feared a surprise, and at once resolved to evacuate Harper's Ferry. His troops left in two columns, one going toward Winchester, with intent to join the force at Manassas Junction; the other retreating through Loudon County toward Leesburg. Before quiting, however, all public property in the vicinity was destroyed. The bridge, including the Winchester span, one thousand feet in length, was burned, and an attempt made to blow up the piers. The railroad bridge at Martinsburg, and the turnpike bridge over the Potomac at Shepherdstown, were also destroyed. The armory buildings were burned, the machinery having been removed to Richmond. Not content with the destruction of the bridges General Johnston blocked the railway and canal by blasting huge rocks overhanging near the Ferry. Among the other obstructions an immense boulder, weighing about one hundred tons, known as Bolman's Rock, was overturned and hurled from Point of Rocks on to the Baltimore and Ohio Railroad. This was removed by blasting on June 14th, and the road reopened to Harper's Ferry. Meantime Johnston had pitched his camp at Charlestown, on the road to Winchester. General Patterson was then at Hagerstown, Md., and at once pushed forward with some nine thousand troops, and on the 16th and 17th of June forded the river at Williamsport, twenty-six miles above where Johnston had been encamped. Patterson's force at this time consisted of the Pennsylvania First, Second, Third, Seventh, Eleventh, Thirteenth and Twenty-fourth regiments together with the First Rhode Island Regiment, two regiments of United States regulars and seven hundred United States cavalry. Included in this force were Captain Doubleday's corps and McMullen's company of Philadelphia Rovers. The fording of the river was accomplished under the superintendence of General Thomas. The men dashed into the stream in high glee, singing "Dixie" and other popular airs with unusual vim; they were generally above their hips in water, and sometimes it reached their arm-pits. General Patterson intended to make Harper's Ferry his base, to open communication along the Baltimore and Ohio, maintain a strong force at Martinsburg and Charlestown, and then by a steady advance toward Winchester and Woodstock, break the insurgent line of communication with Northwest Virginia. These plans, however, were upset by orders from headquarters, and, in spite of urgent remonstrances, he was compelled to obey General Scott's imperative orders and send to Washington all the regulars, horse and foot, in his command, together with Burnside's Rhode Island regiment. Left without artillery, only one cavalry regiment, barely drilled, and a total force not exceeding ten thousand men, General Patterson was obliged to recall his men from the Virginia side. At this time General Cadwallader had marched to Falling Waters, on the way to Harper's Ferry. The Confederates, some fifteen thousand strong, well drilled, with about twenty field pieces and a large body of cavalry, were encamped under General Joe Johnston only a few miles off. It was a perilous position, yet Patterson was obliged to remain inactive until the beginning of July. The impatience and peremptory orders of General Scott, which thus thwarted a bold scheme and brought much undeserved censure upon Patterson, can only be ascribed to the panic which prevailed at the Capital about the time of the assembling of Congress. It was pretty generally believed that General Beauregard, who was in command at Manassas Junction, had been ordered to attack Washington and prevent the assembling of Congress. It was also rumored that a plot to blow up the Capitol while Congress was in session had been devised, and that it had been submitted to Davis and his Attorney-General, Judah P. Benjamin. In the light of later revelations there is not much doubt but both these projects were really entertained. In his eagerness to prevent so dire a catastrophe General Scott appears to have lost sight of every other consideration, and thus lost the chance to prevent the junction of Beauregard's and Johnston's forces.

On the 1st of July General Patterson made a reconnoissance and on the following day crossed the Potomac at the Williamsport Ford and took up the line of march for Martinsburg. Colonel John J. Abercrombie led the advance, and at Falling Waters, five miles from the ford, came in contact with a force under General Thomas Jonathan Jackson (afterward known as "Stonewall" Jackson). This was Johnston's advance and consisted of Stuart's cavalry, between three and four thousand infantry and Pendleton's field battery, Abercrombie at once gave battle. Lieutenant Hudson, with a section of Perkins' battery, took the roadway, supported by the Philadelphia City First Troop of cavalry, and advance, in the face of a brisk fire. The First Wisconsin, the Eleventh Pennsylvania and McMullen's Philadelphia Rovers (or Rangers) also participated. After half an hour's sharp cannonading the guns of the rebels were silenced and the approach of Colonel George H. Thomas' brigade convinced even Jackson that discretion was the better part of valor. He made a rapid retreat to Hainesville, the pursuit being maintained for about five miles. Jackson then pushed on to Bunker's Hill, where Johnston sent reinforcements, and as the Confederate troops had previous to this largely outnumbered the Federal force Abercrombie did not deem it wise to force the fighting any further. In this memorable little battle of Falling Waters the Confederate loss was about eighty killed and wounded and the Union forces had three killed and ten wounded.

On the 3d of July General Patterson entered Martinsburg and a few days later was reinforced by Colonel Stone with the Ninteenth and Twenty-eighth New York and General Sanford with the Fifth and Twelfth New York regiments. The troops, however, needed rest, and supplies of every kind were running low, therefore it was decided to wait at this point for a couple of weeks.

The other engagement about this time, preceding the important fight at Bull Run, was the battle of Rich Mountain, Virginia, on July 11th, between a detachment of Union troops under General Rosecrans and about one thousand Confederates under Colonel Pegram. There had been a skirmish on the previous day on the Staunton road. The battle of the 11th was short and sharp, the Confederates losing some 150 killed and wounded, including several officers. General McClellan, who had been encamped at Roaring Run, at once prepared to attack Pegram's camp. This movement, however, was detected and Pegram, under cover of darkness, broke camp and made for Laurel Hill, where General Robert S. Garnett, who had succeeded Colonel Porterfield in the command of Northwestern

Virginia, was encamped. But Garnett had also taken the alarm and was making for Staunton, by way of Beverly. This avenue of escape, however, was blocked by McClellan's rapid advance, and Garnett, passing through Leedsville gap, made for the Cheat Range of mountains and thence to Carrick's Ford on the Cheat River. Meantime Rosecrans had taken possession of Pegram's camp, and on the 14th of July Pegram, with some 800

CARRICK'S FORD.

of his disorganized and half-starved, troops, surrendered to McClellan at Beverly.

General Garnett had encamped after crossing Carrick's Ford, but General Morris, with his four thousand men and a detachment of McClellan's column under Captain H. W. Benham, pressed him closely, and on the 13th a decisive engagement was fought at Carrick's Ford in which Garnett was killed and some thirty of his men shared the same fate. A large number were wounded and the rest were dispersed in great disorder. During the three days' fighting the Union forces lost but thirteen killed and had about forty wounded. About seven cannon, a large quantity of provisions and several wagons were captured by the Unionists.

In another direction ex-Governor Henry A. Wise, now holding a Confederate brigadier's commission, was engaged terrorizing the loyal citizens in the Great Kanawha Valley and proposed to effect a junction with Garnett, crossing over by the headwaters of the Gauley River. To check this McClellan sent General J. D. Cox with a detachment. Cox crossed at the mouth of the Guyandotte River and captured Barboursville. Colonel Lowe had meanwhile attacked Wise at Screytown, Va., one of his outposts, but had been repulsed with a loss of nine killed and forty wounded and missing. The arrival of General Cox, however, so alarmed Wise that he hastily retreated to Lewisburg, destroying Gauley Bridge, near the mouth of Gauley River, on his retreat. This ended the career of General Wise: his men, disgusted with his want of skill and tact, deserted in large numbers, and he was replaced by Brigadier-General John B. Floyd, who had been Confederate Secretary of War.

We must now turn back to note the formation of the army which was soon to take the field under Brigadier-General Irwin McDowell, who had previously been placed in command of the Department of Virginia. McDowell, a native of Ohio, graduated from West Point in 1838 and remained there for some years as instructor of infantry tactics; he afterward served with considerable credit in the Mexican War, and his talent for organization had commended him specially to the notice of General Scott, whose health was such that active service in the field was impossible. McDowell had been, throughout the month of June, actively engaged in preparing for field operations, and though men were coming forward freely, there was much trouble in effecting the details of the equipments necessary for the extensive operations contemplated. Then, again, many of the three-months men were nearing the end of their term. The public meanwhile, under the incitement of the press of the country, were clamoring for some decisive action and the cry of "On to Richmond" was heard on every side. The troops also were eager for the fray, and thus it was that a large force was put in motion early in July, not nearly so well prepared for work as its commander desired.

McDowell's force amounted to about forty-five thousand men. This force rested on the Potomac from Alexandria, nine miles below Washington, to a point about five miles above that city. General Patterson, stationed at Martinsburg, had about eighteen thousand men. His force also had the Potomac behind it. The Confederate forces in the Shenandoah Valley and at Manassas Junction, according to the most reliable estimates, numbered about ninety thousand men, pretty equally divided between the commands of Generals Beauregard and Joe E. Johnston. The latter had his headquarters at Winchester, where he was heavily intrenched. His scheme of operations from this base was to prevent a junction of the columns of McClellan and Patterson. Beauregard's position at Manassas Junction was considered almost impregnable, the natural defenses of wooded hills surrounding the plateau in which the main army was encamped having been strengthened by engineering works of great military value. The naval battery, armed with Dahlgren guns, part of the spoils of the Norfolk Navy Yard, was a formidable work, well-manned and commanded by naval officers who had been thoroughly trained in the United States service. Thus it will be seen that on the eve of actual hostilities in the field the Confederate army was fully as well equipped and as efficient as that of the United States.

Up to this time the main anxiety had been for the defense of the Capital, and as a consequence the guarding of the Long Bridge, the Aqueduct, and the Chain Bridge were deemed of the first importance. Block-houses and batteries on Arlington and Georgetown Heights and Fort Corcoran covered the Aqueduct Bridge, while Forts Jackson, Runyon and Albany protected the Long Bridge connecting with Washington City at Maryland avenue and Fourteenth street. The Chain Bridge was well covered on the Maryland side by a couple of batteries commanding its whole length, and a substantial barrier, pierced for musketry, had been erected about midway, for the Virginia end was beyond the Union lines and therefore open to rebel approach. This was the condition of affairs at the beginning of July, when public opinion, inspired by the press of the country, compelled aggressive action on the part of the Government.

On the 15th of July all preparations for breaking camp were completed, and shortly after two o'clock the next afternoon the advance was begun. General Mansfield, with about fifteen thousand men, was left to guard the Capital, while McDowell's five divisions under Brigadier-Generals Daniel Tyler and Theodore Runyon and Colonels S. P. Heintzelman, David Hunter, and Dixon S. Miles made the forward movement. Tyler, with the right wing, moved on to Vienna and there encamped that night, pushing on the next morning along the Georgetown road, the objective point by the entire advance being Fairfax Court House. On the 17th, at daybreak, the other columns advanced in the following order : Miles along the Braddock road ; Hunter along the Leesburg and Centreville road ; Heintzelman by the Little River turnpike. The temporary obstructions thrown up by the Confederates were speedily removed, and before midday Centreville, which had been abandoned by the rebels, was occupied by the Federal forces. Germantown Village, two miles beyond, was next occupied by McDowell's and Tyler's divisions. Failing to meet with serious opposition the troops, partly demoralized by the fact that the three months' service had nearly expired with many of them, indulged in excesses which the Commanding General found it necessary to sharply rebuke and punish.

While this advance was being made, General Patterson, at Martinsburg, was expected to prevent the junction of Johnston's force with that of Beauregard's at Bull Run. This duty, however, he was unable to perform, and for this failure he was subjected to sharp criticism. It is but a matter of justice to record that fuller information proved the fallacy of the hasty public judgment of a man whose military ability, indomitable pluck and dogged Irish obstinacy can never be honestly assailed. He was hampered by orders not to fight unless success was certain ; was being hourly weakened by the departure of men whose three months' time was up, and, in addition to all this, he was without direct communication with the main army for several days preceding the disaster at Bull Run. Whether blame attaches for his having allowed Johnston to elude him, or whether the grounds of humanity and expediency are sufficient to justify him for not risking an isolated engagement with a superior force, are matters which more able military critics may discuss among themselves. As we shall have to notice presently, however, Johnston, with six thousand infantry, did reinforce Beauregard on the 20th, and thus render possible the defeat of the next day.

To return to the main advance which we left at Centreville and Germantown. McDowell, on the 18th, made a reconnoissance in connection with his intended movement to turn the Confederate right flank at Manassas. Tyler at the same time pushed on to the vicinity of Bull's Run, where the rebels had thrown up earthworks. Pushing still further Tyler made a reconnoissance to Blackburn's Ford. Every Union movement, however, was communicated to Beauregard, and as a consequence Tyler found himself in an ambuscade. The Second Michigan encountered the first brush with the concealed foe. The Third Michigan, the Twelfth New York, and the First Massachusetts were sent to their assistance, and at once received a severe musketry fire from the woods, supplemented by the fire of a masked battery near the Ford. Tyler's movement having been foreseen, Longstreet had massed his own and some of Early's men to meet it, and the Federal forces in some confusion, for a time, fell back behind Ayres' battery. On the arrival of Colonel W. T. Sherman with his brigade, Corcoran's New York Sixty-ninth leading, the attack was resumed and kept up till 4 o'clock P. M. At this hour the rebel batteries were still active, and McDowell, finding the Manassas position could not be turned, resolved to fall back to Centreville. In this engagement, which the Federals called the Battle of Blackburn's Ford, and which the Confederates claimed as a victory and termed the Battle of Bull's Run, the loss on the Union side was 19 killed and 64 wounded and missing. General Beauregard's official report of Confederate losses quotes 13 killed, 2 missing and 53 wounded, many of whom afterward died. He also claims to have found and buried 64 corpses, to have taken 20 prisoners and 175 stand of arms, besides a quantity of accoutrements and blankets, and one hundred and fifty hats. It must be conceded that it was a slight reverse to the Federal arms, but the usual exaggerations of the rebels magnified the affair to an extent wholly disproportionate to the real facts. Still the effects were depressing to the Union army, and tended toward a shrinkage of force which a victory might have prevented.

McDowell, however, knew that a decisive blow must at least be attempted at once, ere the expiry of the three months' term deprived him of a large proportion of his force. He planned an attack on the 20th, having made a careful reconnoissance on the previous day. His force at this time massed around Centreville was about thirty thousand, and Runyon, with another five thousand, was near at hand. Delays in the transmission of supplies from the Capital postponed his advance and meanwhile some ten thousand men claimed their discharge. Plenty of hard work and but little glory seemed to be the prospect, and rose-colored promises from headquarters as well as from the commander in the field failed to propitiate them. Among those who thus quit the service at a critical moment were Varian's battery of the New York Eighth Regiment and the Fourth Pennsylvania. War was a new trade, with more kicks than pennies in it, and there is every excuse to be made for the men. These defections left McDowell with but 28,000 men and 49 guns at the close of the 20th of July. His own desire was to push forward that night and attempt to turn the Confederate left by occupation of the Stone Bridge and the Warrenton turnpike, and then seizing the Manassas Gap Railroad place himself between Johnston and Beauregard. In deference to the views of his officers the advance was postponed until Sunday morning. In the meantime Beauregard's strength, which on the 19th had been inferior to McDowell's, had been, as we have previously shown, augmented by Johnston's strategic detour around Patterson with six thousand men through Ashby's Gap to Piedmont and thence by rail to Manassas. Thus, while McDowell was losing strength and was ignorant of Johnston's movements, Beauregard was not only being largely reinforced, but was also cognizant, through treachery, of all the details of his adversary's condition.

McDowell's plans were laid for an advance at 2 A. M. on Sunday, July 21st. A still, clear night with the bright light of a full moon wrestling with expiring camp fires around Centreville gave a weird aspect to the scene of great bustle in the Federal lines. Precisely at the appointed hour the advance was begun in three divisions; after crossing Cub Run, Tyler's division with Ayres' and Carlisle's batteries and Schenck's and Sherman's brigades wound along the Warrenton turnpike to accomplish their mission, a feigned attack on the Stone Bridge at daybreak to cover the real attack of Hunter and Heintzelman on the rear and flank of the enemy's left wing. The want of promptness on the part of undisciplined troops, however, delayed this operation until past six o'clock, more than two hours later than should have found Tyler in position and threatening his objective point.

Nor was this the only misadventure which foreshadowed the disasters of the day, for Hunter and Heintzelman, misled as to distance and compelled to traverse a difficult route, were fully four hours behind their appointment. In addition to all this the Confederates, so far from being taken by surprise, had been planning an attack on the Federal position at Centreville. The official dispatches of General Beauregard show that this scheme was reluctantly abandoned on account of the condition of the roads and that the main details of McDowell's intended movement having been betrayed to the Confederate Commander, he formed his plans to receive the Federal attack at Bull Run, and then to throw forward a sufficient force by converging roads to attack the Federal reserve at Centreville so soon as the main attacking force was inextricably engaged on the left. This duty was assigned to General Ewell, but it would seem that the orders did not reach him, for late in the day, finding that Ewell, posted on the extreme right of the line, had not advanced according to programme, Beauregard sent a courier to ask the reason, and then for the first time learned that the previous order had miscarried. It was too late then, as it would take three hours for Ewell to reach Centreville, and consequently the plan was abandoned and General Johnston was directed to change front on the left, bring up Ewell's reserves and thus meet the attack which had become strong. The failure of this order to reach Ewell thus prevented a still more disastrous blow to the Union arms.

The accounts of the battle of Bull Run present so many discrepancies that we can best give our idea of it by quoting first from General McDowell's official report, and supplementing that by the statements of eye-witnesses and extracts from Confederate official reports.

General McDowell, after detailing the advance from camp, substantially as we have given it, says :

"General Tyler commenced with his artillery at half-past six A. M., but the enemy did not reply, and after some time it became a question whether he was in any force on our front, and if he did not intend himself to make an attack and make it by Blackburn's Ford. After firing several times and obtaining no response I held one of Heintzelman's brigades in reserve, in case we should have to send any troops back to reinforce Miles' division. The other brigades moved forward as directed in general orders. On reaching the ford at Sudley's Spring, I found part of the leading brigade of Hunter's division (Burnside's) had crossed, but the men were slow in getting over, stopping to drink. As at this time the clouds of dust from the direction of Manassas indicated the immediate approach of a large force, and fearing it might come down on the head of the column before the division could all get over and sustain it, orders were sent back to the heads of regiments to break from the column and come forward, separating as fast as possible. Orders were sent to the reserve brigade of Heintzelman's division to come by a nearer road across the fields, and Brigadier Tyler was directed to press forward his attack. The ground between the stream and the road leading from Sudley's Spring south and over which Burnside's brigade marched, was for about a mile from the ford thickly wooded, whilst on the right of the road for about the same distance the country was divided between fields and woods. About a mile from the road the country on both sides of the road is open, and for nearly a mile further large rolling fields extend down to Warrenton turnpike, which crosses what became the field of battle through the valley of a small watercourse, a tributary of Bull Run.

"Shortly after the leading regiment of the First Brigade reached the open space, and whilst others and the Second Brigade were crossing to the front and right, the enemy opened his fire, beginning it with artillery and following it up with infantry. The leading brigade (Burnside's) had to sustain this shock for a short time without support, and did it well. The battalion of regular infantry was sent to sustain it, and shortly afterward the other corps of Porter's Brigade, and a regiment detached from Heintzelman's Division to the left, forced the enemy back far enough to allow Sherman's and Keyes' Brigades of Tyler's Division to cross from their position on the Warrenton road. These drove the right of the enemy from the front of the field and out of the detached woods, down to the road, and across it up the slopes on the other side. While this was going on. Heintzelman's Division was moving down the field to the stream, and up the road beyond. Beyond the Warrenton road, and to the left of the road down which our troops had marched from Sudley's Spring, is a hill with a farm-house on it. Behind this hill the enemy had, early in the day, some of his most annoying batteries planted. Across the road from this hill was an elevated ridge or table of land. The hottest part of the contest was for the possession of the hill with the house upon it. The force engaged here was Heintzelman's division. Wilcox's and Howard's brigades on the right, supported by part of Porter's brigade and the cavalry under Palmer, and Franklin's brigade of Heintzelman's division, Sherman's brigade of Tyler's division in the centre and up the road, while Keyes' brigade of Tyler's division was on the left attacking the batteries near the Stone Bridge. The Rhode Island battery of Burnside's brigade also participated in this attack by its fire from the north of the turnpike. Ricketts' battery, together with Griffin's battery, was on the side of the hill, and became the object of the special attention of the enemy, who succeeded—our officers mistaking one of his regiments for one of our own, and allowing it to approach without firing upon it—in disabling the battery, and then attempted to take it. Three times was he repulsed by different corps in succession and driven back and the guns taken by hand (the horses being killed) and pulled away. The third time it was supposed by us all that the repulse was final, for he was driven entirely from the hill, and so far beyond it as not to be in sight, and all were certain the day was ours. He had before this been driven nearly a mile and a half, and was beyond the Warrenton road, which was entirely in our possession from the Stone Bridge westward, and our engineers were just completing the removal of the abatis across the road to allow our regiments (Schenck's brigade and Ayres' battery) to join us.

"The enemy was evidently disheartened and broken. But we had been fighting since half-past ten o'clock in the morning, and it was now after three in the afternoon. The men had been up since two in the morning, and had made what seemed to those unused to such things a long march before coming into action, though the longest distance gone over was not more than nine and a half miles; and though they had three days' provisions served out to them the day before, many no doubt either did not eat them or threw them away on the march or during the battle, and were therefore without food. They had done much severe fighting. Some of the regiments which had been driven from the hill in the first two attempts of the enemy to keep possession of it, had become shaken, were unsteady, and had many men out of the ranks.

"It was at this time that the enemy's reinforcements came to his aid from the railroad train, understood to have just arrived from the Valley with the residue of Johnston's army. They threw themselves in the works on our right and towards the rear of our right, and opened a fire of musketry on our men, which caused them to break and retire down the hill-side. This soon degenerated into disorder for which there was no remedy. Every effort was made to rally them, even beyond the reach of the enemy's fire, but in vain. The battalion of regular infantry alone moved up the hill opposite the one with a house on it, and there maintained itself until our men could get down to and across the Warrenton turnpike, on the way back to the position we occupied in the morning. The plain was covered with the retreating troops, and they seemed to infect those with whom they came in contact. The retreat soon became a rout, and this degenerated still further into a panic.

"Finding the state of affairs was beyond the efforts of all those who had assisted so faithfully during the long and hard day's work in gaining almost the object of our wishes, and that nothing remained on the field but to recognize what we could no longer prevent, I gave the necessary orders to protect their withdrawal, begging the men to form in line, and offer the appearance, at least, of organization. They returned by the fords to the Warrenton road, protected by Colonel Porter's force of regulars. Once on the road and the different corps coming together in small parties, many without officers, they became intermingled and all organization was lost.

"According to general orders, while the operations were going on in front an attack was to be made at Blackburn's Ford, by Richardson's brigade. This was well carried out, and succeeded for a considerable time in deceiving the enemy and keeping in check part of his force.

"At the time of our retreat, seeing great activity in this direction, much firing and columns of dust, I became anxious for this place, fearing if it were turned or forced the whole stream of our retreating mass would be captured or destroyed. After providing for the protection of the retreat by Porter's and Blenker's brigades, I repaired to Richardson's and found the whole force ordered to be stationed for the holding of the road from Manassas by Blackburn's Ford to Centreville on the march, under the orders of the division commander, for Centreville. I immediately halted it and ordered it to take up the best line of defense across the ridge that their position admitted of, and subsequently taking command in person of this part of the army, I caused such disposition of the forces, which had been added to by the First and Second New Jersey and the De Kalb regiments, ordered up from Runyon's reserve before going forward, as would best serve to check the enemy. The ridge being held in this way, the retreating current passed slowly through Centreville to the rear. The enemy followed us from the ford as far as Cub Run, and, owing to the road becoming blocked up at the crossing, caused us much damage there, for the artillery could not pass, and several pieces and caissons had to be abandoned. In the panic the horses hauling the caissons and ammunition were cut from their places by persons to escape with, and in this way much confusion was caused, the panic aggravated and the road encumbered. Not only were pieces of artillery lost, but also many of the ambulances carrying the wounded.

"By sundown most of our men had gotten beyond Centreville bridge, and it became a question whether we should or not endeavor to make a stand there. The condition of our artillery and its ammunition, and the want of food for the men, and the utter disorganization and consequent demoralization of the mass of the army, seemed to all who were near enough to be consulted—division and brigade commanders and staffs—to admit of no alternative but to fall back: the more so as the position at Blackburn's Ford was then in possession of the enemy and he was already turning our left. On sending the officers of the staff to the different camps they found that our decision had been anticipated by the troops, most of those who had come from the front being already on the road to the rear, the panic with which they came in still continuing and hurrying them along.

"Shortly afterward the rear guard (Blenker's brigade) moved, covering the retreat, which was effected during the night and next morning. The troops at Fairfax station, leaving by the cars, took with them the bulk of the supplies which had been sent there."

This report quotes the number of killed at nineteen officers and four hundred and sixty-two non-commissioned officers and privates, and the wounded at sixty-four officers and nine hundred and forty-seven non-commissioned officers and privates.

Subsequent official reports give the following figures: Union loss, 481 killed, 1,011 wounded and 1,460 missing. There were also lost 4,000 muskets and 4,500 sets of accoutrements, 20 cannon and a large quantity of ammunition. The Confederate loss is stated at 378 killed, 1,489 wounded and 30 missing.

The officers commanding divisions and brigades during this engagement were as follows: Brigadier General Daniel Tyler, Connecticut Volunteers; Colonel David Hunter, Third Cavalry, severely wounded at the head of his division; Colonel S. P. Heintzelman, Seventeenth Infantry, wounded in the arm while leading his division into action on the hill; Brigadier General Robert Schenck, Ohio Volunteers, commanding Second Brigade, First Division; Colonel E. D. Keyes, Eleventh Infantry, commanding First Brigade, First Division; Colonel W. P. Franklin, Twelfth Infantry, First Brigade, Third Division; Colonel W. T. Sherman, Thirteenth Infantry, commanding Third Brigade, First Division; Colonel Andrew Porter, Sixteenth Infantry, commanding First Brigade, Second Division; Colonel A. E. Burnside, Rhode Island Volunteers, commanding Second Brigade, Second Division; Colonel O. B. Wilcox, Michigan Volunteers, commanding Second Brigade, Third Division, who was wounded and taken prisoner while on the hill in the hottest of the fight; Colonel O. O. Howard, Maine Volunteers, commanding Third Brigade, Third Division; Colonel J. B. Richardson, Michigan Volunteers, commanding Fourth Brigade, First Division; Colonel Louis Blenker, New York Volunteers, commanding First Brigade, Fifth Division; Colonel Thomas A. Davies, New York Volunteers, commanding Second Brigade, Fifth Division.

Of General McDowell's staff, his official report gives the following list: First Lieutenant H. W. Kingsbury, Fifth Artillery,

BULL'S RUN BATTLE GROUND.

aide-de-camp; Major Clarence S. Brown, New York Militia Volunteers, aide-de-camp; Major James S. Wadsworth, New York Militia Volunteers, aide-de-camp. He had a horse shot under him in the hottest of the fight. Captain James B. Fry, Assistant Adjutant-General; Captain O. H. Tillinghast, Assistant Quartermaster, who was mortally wounded while acting with the artillery; Captain H. F. Clark, Chief of Subsistence Department; Major Meyer, Signal Officer, and Major Malcolm McDonnell, acting as aides; Surgeon W. S. King and Assistant

Surgeon Magruder, Medical Department ; Major J. G. Barnard, Engineer ; First Lieutenant Fred. S. Prima, Engineers ; Captain A. W. Whipple, First Lieutenant H. L. Abbott and Second Lieutenant H. S. Putnam, Topographical Engineers ; Major W. F. Barry, Fifth Artillery, Chief of Artillery ; Lieutenant George C. Strong, Ordnance Officer ; Major W. H. Wood, First Infantry, Acting Inspector-General. Second Lieutenant George Henry also joined McDowell in the field and acted as aide-de-camp.

It is doubtful whether any chosen detail of the day's fighting would give a clearer conception of the humiliating disaster to the Federal arms, and as General McDowell, irritated by the slowness of the advances of Hunter and Heintzelman had actually passed them on the road with his staff and was consequently an attentive spectator as well as an actor in the events of the battle, the clear-cut narrative of his report may be accepted in its entirety. The language, though guarded, amply indicates that the troops left the field a routed rabble.

In a further section of his report McDowell states that he crossed Bull Run with 18,000 men of all arms, and he justly claims that the force attacked, when reinforced by those whom Patterson had failed to intercept, was largely in excess of the attacking army. He also states that among the missing were many surgeons who, remaining in attendance on the wounded, were, against the rules of modern warfare, made prisoners.

Turning from the dry routine recital of this reverse, it will be interesting to quote from the vivacious correspondent of the New York *World*, whose letter, dated July 22, bristles with the excitement of the scenes he had just passed through. Skipping his narrative of the details of the projected advance, which have already been covered in these columns, we will start with him on the "Midnight march." He says :

"There was moonlight, and no moonlight scene ever offered more varying themes to the genius of a great artist. Through the hazy valleys and on hill slopes, miles apart, were burning the fires at which forty regiments had prepared their midnight meal. In the vistas opening along a dozen lines of view, thousands of men were moving among the fitful beacons ; horses were harnessing to artillery, white army wagons were in motion with the ambulances—whose black covering, when one thought about it, seemed as appropriate as that of the coffin which accompanies a condemned man to the death before him. All was silent confusion and intermingling of moving horses and men. But forty thousand soldiers stir as quickly as a dozen, and in fifteen minutes from the commencement of the bustle every regiment had taken its place, ready to fall into the division to which it was assigned. General McDowell and staff went in the centre of Tyler's, the central column. At 2.30 A.M. the last soldier had left the extended encampments, except those remaining behind on guard. * * * * * * * The spirit of the soldiery was magnificent. They were all smarting under the reproach of Thursday and longing for the opportunity to wipe it out. There was growing rivalry among the men of different States. 'Old Massachusetts will not be ashamed of us to-night.' 'Wait till the Ohio boys get at them.' 'We'll fight for New York to-day.' and a hundred similar utterances were shouted from the different ranks. The officers were as glad of the task assigned them as the men. I rode a few moments with Lieut.-Col. Haggerty, of the Sixty-ninth. He mentioned the newspaper statement that he was killed at the former battle, and laughingly said he felt very warlike for a dead man, and good for at least one battle more. This brave officer was almost the first victim of the day. The cheery voice of Meagher, late the Irish, now the American patriot, rang out more heartily than ever. Then there were Corcoran, and Burnside, and Keyes, and Speidel, and many another skilled and gallant officer, all pushing forward to the first fruition of the three months' patient preparation. * * * General McDowell's carriage halted at the junction of two roads, a place most favorable for the quick reception of despatches from all portions of the field. The column assigned to Colonel Hunter here divided from the main body and went on its unknown, perilous journey around the enemy's flank."

After describing the opening of the battle he says :

"Meantime Richardson, on the extreme left, could not content himself with 'maintaining his position,' for we heard occasional discharges from two of his guns. From the hill behind we could see long columns advancing, and at first thought they were Richardson's men moving on Bull Run ; but soon discovered their true character. Indeed, from every southward point the enemy's reinforcements began to pour in by thousands. A person who ascended a lofty tree could see the continual arrival of cars at the nearest point on the Manassas railroad with hosts of soldiers, who formed in solid squares and moved swiftly forward to join in the contest. It was hard for our noble fellows to withstand these incessant reinforcements, but some of our regiments whipped several corps opposed to them in quick succession, *and whenever our forces, fresh or tired, met the enemy in open field, they made short work of his opposition.*

"At 10:30 A. M. Hunter was heard from on the exreme right. He had previously sent a courier to General McDowell, reporting that he had safely crossed the Run. The General was lying on the ground, having been ill during the night, but at once mounted his horse and rode on to join the column on which so much depended. From the neighborhood of Sudley

Church he saw the enemy's left in battle array, and at once advanced upon them with the Fourteenth New York and a battalion of regular infantry—Colonel Hunter ordering up the stalwart Rhode Island regiments, the Second New Hampshire and the New York Seventy-first. Governor Sprague himself directed the movements of the Rhode Island brigade, and was conspicuous throughout the day for gallantry. * * * * As soon as Hunter was thus discovered to be making his way on the flank, General Tyler sent forward the right wing of his column to co-operate, and a grand force was thus brought to bear on the enemy's left and centre. The famous Irish regiment, 1,600 strong, claimed the honor of a share in the hard fighting and led the van of Tyler's attack, followed by the Seventy-ninth (Highlanders), the Thirteenth New York and Second Wisconsin.

"It was a brave sight—that rush of the Sixty-ninth into the death struggle! With such cheers as those which won the battles in the Peninsula, with quick step at first and then a double quick, and at last a run, they dashed forward and along the edge of the extended forest. Coats and knapsacks were thrown to either side, that nothing might impede their work, but we knew that no guns would slip from the hands of those determined fellows, even if dying agonies were needed to close them with a firmer grasp. As the line swept along Meagher galloped toward the head, crying : ' Come on, boys ! You've got your chance at last !' Tyler's forces then moved forward for half a mile, describing quite one-fourth of a circle on the right, until they met a division of the enemy, and, of course, a battery of the enemy's most approved pattern. It was noon, and now the battle commenced in the fierceness of the most extended fury. * * * For some time the fight raged at a distance from the non-combatants, but the battle on the hilltop could be seen. * * * Then the battle began to work down the hill, the returning half of the circle which the enemy, driven before the desperate charges of our troops, described during the day, until the very point where Tyler's advance commenced the action. Down the hill and into the valley thickets on the left, the Zouaves, the Connecticut, New York and Rhode Island regiments drove the continually enlarging, but always vanquished, columns of the enemy. It was only to meet more batteries, earthwork succeeding earthwork, ambuscade after ambuscade. Our fellows were hot and weary, most had drunk no water during hours of dust and smoke and insufferable heat. No one knows what choking the battle atmosphere produces in a few moments until he has personally experienced it. And so the conflict lulled for a little while. It was the middle of a blazing afternoon. Our regiments held the positions they had won, but the enemy kept receiving additions and continued a flank movement toward our left—a dangerous movement for us, a movement which those in the rear perceived and vainly endeavored to induce some general officer to guard against. *Here was the grand blunder, or, misfortune of the battle.* A misfortune that we had no troops in reserve after the Ohio regiments were again sent forward, this time to assist in building a bridge across the run on the Warrenton road by the side of the Stone Bridge known to be ruined. A blunder in that the last reserve was sent forward at all. It should have been retained to guard the rear of the left, and every other regiment on the field should have been promptly recalled over the route by which it had advanced and ordered only to maintain such positions as rested on a supported, continuous line. But McDowell tried to vanquish the South in a single struggle, and the sad result is before us.

"As it was, Captain Alexander, with his sappers and miners, was ordered to cut through the abatis by the side of the ruined bridge and lay pontoons across the stream. Carlisle's artillery was detailed to protect the work and the Ohio and Wisconsin reserve to support the artillery. Meanwhile in the lull I have mentioned the thousand heroic details of Federal valor and the shamelessness of rebel treachery began to reach our ears. We learned of the loss of the brave Cameron (brother of the Secretary of War), the wounding of Heintzelman and Hunter, the fall of Haggerty and Slocum and Wilcox. We heard of the dash of the Irishmen and their decimation, and of the havoc made and sustained by the Rhode Islanders, the Highlanders, the Zouaves and the Connecticut Third—then of the intrepidity of Burnside and Sprague—how the devoted and daring young Governor led the regiments he had so munificently equipped again and again to victorious charges, and at last spiked, with his own hands, the guns he could not carry away.

"At this time, near four o'clock, I rode forward through the open plain to the creek, where the abatis was being assailed by our engineers. The Ohio, Connecticut and Minnesota regiments were variously posted thereabouts; others were in distant portions of the field; all were completely exhausted and partly dissevered; no general of division, except Tyler, could be found. Where were our officers? Where was the foe? Who knew whether we had won or lost? The question was quickly decided for us. A sudden swoop, and a body of cavalry rushed down upon our columns near the bridge. They came from the woods on the left, and infantry poured out behind them. Tyler and his staff, with the reserve, were apparently cut off by the quick manœuvre. I succeeded in gaining the position I had just left, there witnessed the capture of Carlisle's battery in the plain, and saw another force of cavalry and infantry pouring into the road at the very spot where the battle commenced, and near which the South Carolinians, who had manned the battery silenced in the morning, had doubtless all day been lying concealed. The ambulances and wagons had gradually advanced to this spot, and of course instantaneous confusion and dismay resulted. Our own infantry broke ranks in the field, plunged into the woods to avoid the road, got up the road as best they could, without leaders, every man serving himself in his own way. * * * In his account of the panic-stricken flight he says: 'I saw officers with leaves and eagles on their shoulder-straps, majors and colonels who had deserted their commands, pass me galloping as if for dear life. No enemy pursued just then, but I suppose all were afraid that his guns would be trained down the long, narrow avenue, and mow the retreating thousands, and batter to pieces army wagons and everything else which crowded it. Only one field officer, so far as my observation extended, seemed to have remembered his duty. Lieut.-Col. Speidel, a foreigner attached to a Connecticut regiment, strove against the current for a league. I positively declare that all other efforts made to check the panic before Centreville was reached were confined to *civilians*. I saw a man in citizen's dress, who had thrown off his coat, seized a musket and was trying to rally the soldiers who came by at the point of the bayonet. In reply to a request for his name, he said it was Washburne, and I learned he was the member by that name from Illinois. The Hon. Mr. Kellogg made a similar effort. Both these Congressmen bravely stood their ground till the last moment, and were serviceable at Centreville in assisting the halt there ultimately made.' * * * * *

"The right of Miles' reserve, drawn up on the hills at Centreville, supporting a full battery of field pieces, and the efforts of the few officers still faithful to their trust, encouraged many of the fugitive infantry to seek their old camps and go no further. But the majority pushed on to a point near the late site of Germantown, where Lieutenant Brisbane had formed a line of Hunt's artillerists across the road and repulsed all who attempted to break through. While he was thus engaged, a courier arrived with the news that Colonel Montgomery was advancing with a New Jersey Brigade from Falls Church, and that the retreat must be stopped, only wagons being allowed to pass through. Some thousands of the soldiery had already got far on their road to Washington. Poor fellows! who could blame them? Their own colonels had deserted them, only leaving orders for them to reach Arlington Heights as soon as they could. A few miles further I met Montgomery swiftly pressing to the rescue, and I reported the success of Lieutenant Brisbane's efforts. And so I rode along as well as my weary horse would carry me, past groups of straggling fugitives, to Fairfax, where Colonel Woodbury was expecting, and guarding against, a flank movement of the enemy, and on again to Long Bridge and the Potomac. But the van of the runaway soldiers had made such time that I found a host of them at the Jersey intrenchments begging the sentinels to allow them to cross the bridge. To-day we learn of the safe retreat of the main body of the army; that they were feebly followed by the rebels as far as Fairfax, but are now within the Arlington lines, and that McDowell, a stunned and vanquished general, is overlooking the wreck of his columns from his old quarters at the Custis Mansion."

We must turn from this sad spectacle to note the results at the Capital, the streets of which were swarming with the tattered, footsore and disheartened men who had so recently started thence flushed with hope and wild with the excitement of anticipated victory and glory.

The stunning blow fell on the Administration like a thunderbolt from a clear sky, and in an instant, the entire nation awoke from its dream of a three-months' campaign, to a realization of the fact that a bloody war was to be fought, rather than that a paltry insurrection was to be put down. The dejection, however, was brief, and the exultant shouts of the Confederates aroused a fierce determination to accept the issue and abide all consequences. That marvelous elasticity which is so peculiarly a characteristic of the American people, and which exhibits itself, in peaceful times, by the prompt good nature which follows the most heated political contest when the verdict of the ballot boxes has been registered, at once came to the rescue of the nation. The three-months' men, some seventy-five thousand in number, took their discharges, it is true, upon the principle that "a singed cat dreads the fire," but their places were eagerly filled by others. Many went coolly from a sense of duty, but very many more felt that to stay at home was to earn an ineffaceable stigma. Public opinion no longer clamored for "On to Richmond," but it sternly pressed forward its best bone and sinew to the field, anywhere, everywhere, so that the insult to the Union might be wiped out. It was with very different feelings, however, that the new recruits entered upon their self-imposed task; there were no more sneers at the Confederate cause, but "for three years or for the war," was the ready response of those who, appreciating that the Southerners were no insignificant foemen, were resolved that, cost what it might, the great peril of free institutions, popular sovereignty and human rights must be averted.

In Washington the first feeling was of dread lest the enemy should push on and capture the Capital, but when, after a brief pause, it was found that the Confederates proposed to content themselves with shouting, the Administration, keenly alive to the disgrace of its own misjudgment, retreated from its position of arrogant egotism and gladly welcomed the offers of troops which the loyal States had eagerly, though vainly, proffered before. On the 23d of July, the day after the disastrous defeat, General George B. McClellan was summoned to Washington from the scene of his dashing movements in West Virginia and placed in full command of the Army, on the retirement of McDowell, who, though certainly blameless, felt that the loss of his prestige would impair his value even with new troops. The Departments of Washington and of Northeastern Virginia were created, and McClellan, with headquarters in Washington City, at once commenced the task of building up that phenomenal organization thereafter to be known as the "Army of the Potomac." It was a "labor of Hercules," but the gallant young Philadelphian, then in the thirty-fifth year of his age only, was equal to the task, spurred on, as he was, by his own fearless ambition and the plaudits of the public. The new "Departments" were announced on the 25th of July, and on the 27th McClellan, having turned over his previous command to Brigadier-General Rosecrans, assumed full charge. A rapid review of the nucleus of the shattered Army disclosed not more than 50,000 infantry, no cavalry, barely seven hundred artillerymen and about thirty guns. Looking closer into matters, he found the men ready enough, but wholly incompetent and demoralized by laxity of previous discipline. This he at once began to remedy; it was henceforth to be soldiering, and the officers whose only ambition was to wear shoulder-straps, were sent back to their desks and workshops. A speech made by McClellan when passing through Philadelphia, on July 25, may be taken as the text of his operations. In response to the calls of an enthusiastic crowd assembled at the depot, he said: "My friends and old townsmen, I thank you for your reception, and might reply if this were not a time for action and not for speech. Your applause, as I take it, is intended for my brave soldiers in Western Virginia. I am going to fulfill new duties, and I trust that your kindness will give me courage and strength. Good by."

Calling to his aid Major J. G. Barnard and Major W. F. Barry, he gave the latter charge of the artillery details and the former he assigned to the duty of protecting the City of Washington by elaborate works on either side of the Potomac.

His own work, after weeding out the incompetents, was to establish a thorough code of discipline and perfect the army details. Four regiments were constituted a brigade and three brigades a division, with four batteries, one served by regulars and three by volunteers, the captain of the regulars in chief command of all the artillery. Within fifty days he had mustered 100,000 men, most of whom were fit for immediate service. His recommendations to the President for the constituent elements of the main army were 250 regiments of infantry, 28 regiments of cavalry, 5 regiments of engineers, 100 field batteries, comprising 600 guns, to be served by 15,000 men, a total of 273,000 men. (This standard was nearly reached in March following.)

While McClellan was thus arranging for men, Secretary Cameron was looking around for arms. The loss of the Gosport Navy Yard and the destruction at Harper's Ferry had somewhat crippled the productive resources of the Government. Supplies, however, were speedily obtained abroad, the appropriations of Congress being immediately available, and at a cost of $2,044,931 Colonel George L. Schuyler purchased in Europe 116,000 rifles, 10,000 cavalry carbines, 10,000 revolvers and 21,000 sabres.

Alarm for the safety of the Capital speedily abated as McClellan's vigorous measures were noted and appreciated, and throughout the country, while the tension was still severe, the people breathed more easily; but they had settled down to the conviction that there were many vicissitudes in store before peace could be even hoped for.

In another chapter we will glance at concurrent events in other disturbed districts and peep within the Confederate lines.

CHAPTER XI.

MOVEMENTS IN MISSOURI—GOVERNOR JACKSON'S DEFIANCE—M'CULLOUGH'S TEXAN RANGERS—THE BATTLE OF CARTHAGE—ENGAGEMENT AT DUG SPRING—BATTLE OF WILSON'S CREEK—DEATH OF GEN. LYON—FREMONT'S OPERATIONS IN ST. LOUIS—MARTIAL LAW PROCLAIMED THROUGHOUT MISSOURI.

We must now trace up the movements in the Mississippi Valley. As far back as April 18, Governor Claiborne F. Jackson, of Missouri, had replied to Secretary Cameron's requisition for troops under President Lincoln's first call that "the requisition is illegal, unconstitutional, revolutionary, inhuman, diabolical, and cannot be complied with." As if the Governor's reply was not sufficiently explicit, the Charleston *Mercury*, of April 19th, in quoting the refusal, adds—"Missouri won't furnish a single man for such an unholy crusade." Although Missouri was not admitted to the Confederacy till August 19th, the secession sympathies and the deep laid schemes of Governor Jackson had been matters of notoriety very early in Lincoln's administration, and it was suspected that one of the earliest movements would be an attack on the United States arsenal at St. Louis. This was the contingency against which General Wool had endeavored to provide by instructing Governor Yates, of Illinois, to send a force to guard it. It was, however, deemed better to remove a large portion of the arms secretly rather than precipitate matters by openly strengthening the local military. Captain Nathaniel Lyon and Colonel Frank P. Blair, the former in command of the post, and the latter busily engaged in organizing a regiment of loyal Missourians, were keenly watching the Secession meetings; and, finally, on April 30th, obtained an order from the President empowering Captain Lyon to enroll ten thousand loyal citizens of St. Louis in the service of the United States. But Governor Jackson, at the instigation of Brigadier-General Daniel M. Frost, of the militia, had called the State troops into camp by the 3d of May. The camp was termed "Camp Jackson," and two of its principal avenues were named "Beauregard" and "Davis." Some two weeks later, Captain Lyon learned that cannon and mortars, with appropriate ammunition, had been secretly landed from a steamer and taken to Camp Jackson. In female disguise he examined the preparations at the camp, and feeling sure that an attack on the arsenal was imminent, he determined by initiating hostilities to put an end to the scheme. Accordingly on the 11th he surrounded the camp with six thousand men, and placed heavy guns in position to command the entire grove. Frost was fairly trapped, and finding resistance unavailing, despite the frenzy of a mob which had rushed out from the city to join in the expected mêlée, he surrendered, on demand, with his 1,200 men, each armed with a new rifle, twenty cannon, and a quantity of ammunition which had been taken from the Baton Rouge arsenal. The prisoners declining release on parole, were marched to the arsenal. Riotous demonstrations *en route* were followed up during the night by a collision between the troops and the Secessionists, in which several persons were killed. About this time General Wm. S. Harney assumed the command of the Department of the West, and finding that the Missouri Legislature had passed a military bill authorizing the Governor to contract a State loan for war purposes and to call all able-bodied men out for the defense of the State, promptly issued a proclamation denying its validity and terming it a Secession ordinance. He, however, entered into negotiations with General Sterling Price, chairman of the late convention, looking to a compromise by which neutrality was pledged. It was well known by the loyalists that no pledges would bind Jackson and his Secession advisers, and the Administration being warned of this, recalled Harney and placed Lyon, with the rank of Brigadier General, in command of the "Department of Missouri." Governor Jackson still held on his course, declaring that the people of his State should not be subjugated, and finally, after a meeting between the Governor, with his Secretary, T. L. Smead, and General Price and the Federal Commander Lyon, accompanied by Colonel Blair, an open rupture was initiated. Jackson demanded that Federal troops should quit the State, and this being peremptorily refused, the Governor retired to Jefferson City, called out 50,000 State troops, and in his proclamation defied the Washington authorities. He appointed General Sterling Price Military Commander of the State forces, and prepared, as he said, to resist invasion, but really to raise the standard of revolt.

In General Lyon, however, he met his match. Having first fortified Bird's Point opposite Cairo, he next sent Colonel Franz Sigel to protect the Pacific Railroad from St. Louis to the Gasconade River and to prepare for checking the advance of Ben McCullough, the Texan ranger, who had crossed the Arkansas border with eight hundred men and was pushing for Springfield. On the 13th of June, Lyon with about two thousand men; Missouri Volunteers, under Colonels Blair and Boernstein; regulars under Captain Latrop, and artillery under Captain James Totten, started in two steamers from St. Louis for Jefferson City. Ere their arrival on the 15th, Price and Jackson had evacuated the city and after destroying the bridges along the railroad had made a stand near Booneville, some forty miles from Jefferson City. Lyon, however, pushed after them on three steamers, so that the bridge burning was mere reckless destruction. On the 17th Lyon found the enemy under command of Colonel Marmaduke a few miles below Booneville. A brisk attack and a vigorous cannonade from Totten's artillery supplemented by an unexpected fire from the river, where the transports were engaged in silencing a small shore battery, completely demoralized the rebels, who fled in all directions, leaving the camp and its stores in the hands of the Federals. Governor Jackson who had watched the fight, retreated hastily to Warsaw on the Osage River. Totten pursued for some distance, but Jackson with about five hundred men kept on a headlong flight to Montevallo, in Vernon County, where General Price joined him on July 3d, he having been at Lexington under pretense of illness when the camp was taken. General G. J. Rains was also pressing on to the same point. Jackson's next efforts were directed toward a junction with McCullough's rangers with a view to making the southwestern section of the State his base of operations, for he had by this

THE BATTLE OF CARTHAGE.

time discovered that the "Palmetto" principles would not thrive among the loyalists of northern Missouri.

Meantime Sigel had pushed on to Springfield, whither he was advised that McCullough was heading. Finding, on arrival at this point, that Governor Jackson and General Price were moving in a southwesterly direction, Sigel pushed on to Sarcoxie, reaching there late on the 28th. Here he learned that General Price with nine hundred men had encamped at Pool's Prairie, and that Jackson and Rains were moving to join him. Hastily forming a plan to cut up Price before he could be reinforced, Sigel started at once, but soon heard that Price had fled to Elk Mills, thirty miles south of Neosho, the capital of Newton County. Pushing on to this point, he found the insurgents had been pillaging there and had gone on. Leaving a small force at Neosho, and keeping open a communication with Sarcoxie, Sigel, reinforced by Colonel Salomon and his Missouri battalion, advanced to Carthage, the capital of Jasper County, and encamped on the south fork of the Spring River late on the 4th of July. But while Sigel was looking for Price, that worthy, with Rains, Clark, Parsons and Stack, and a force of some six thousand men, under the immediate command of Governor Jackson, was on the still hunt for Sigel. The troops with the latter numbered in all about 1,500 men, with eight field pieces. On the morning of the 5th of July, Sigel, having learned that this force was about ten miles off, determined to attack it, though he knew the disproportion of the two commands. Some nine miles north of Carthage, after passing Dry Fork Creek, Sigel came upon his foe drawn up to receive him on a small eleva-

GEN. FRANZ SIGEL.

tion. That he was vastly outnumbered was evident to Sigel, but he quickly noted that the enemy were badly off for artillery, and he at once began battle with his field pieces. The Confederates, however, had plenty of cavalry, and these, under Rains, attempted a flanking movement right and left. Good artillery service kept them at a distance, but a retreat was imperative, and this was effected in an orderly manner under cover of the field pieces. Near Dry Fork Creek the rebel cavalry passed round to the front of the retreating Federals, but a vigorous canonading and a brisk infantry charge cleared the road. After a running fight Sigel attempted to halt at Carthage, but was so closely pressed by the cavalry that he was compelled to push on to Sarcoxie. The little party of ninety men under Captain Conrad left to guard Neosho, had meanwhile been surprised and taken prisoners. In this engagement, known as the Battle of Carthage, the Federal loss was 14 killed and 31 wounded; they also lost four field pieces, nine horses and one baggage wagon. The Confederate loss in killed and wounded was not far short of 600; they also lost 80 horses, a lot of shot-guns and had 45 men taken prisoners. Fearing to be pressed still harder with his small force, Sigel pushed on through Mount Vernon to Springfield. Here he halted to await General Lyon, feeling sure that a junction of the Confederate commands could not be prevented. Meanwhile, Lyon, who left Booneville on July 3d, had been joined by Major Sturgis with three thousand men, and the united force pushed on to the ferry on the Grand River, and thence reached the Osage River late in the night at a point some eight miles from Springfield. Here they heard of Sigel's battle at Carthage, and his retreat. This somewhat changed Lyon's plans, and, hurrying to Sigel's relief, the troops made a forced march of fifty miles in twenty-four hours in the direction of Springfield. On the 13th Lyon came up with Sigel, and, encamping, took the chief command. Offensive operations were almost impossible, since the men's enlistment terms were expiring, and all appeals for reinforcements were unanswered.

The Confederate forces, however, were being regularly consolidated, and by the 29th Price, McCullough, Pearce and

McBride had effected a junction at Cassville, and with 20,000 men of all arms prepared to overwhelm Lyon, Sigel and Sturgis, who could only muster some fifty-five hundred infantry, four hundred cavalry and eighteen guns. The Confederates' plan was to invest Springfield by converging columns, one advancing from Sarcoxie and the other from Cassville. Becoming aware of this, Lyon resolved to abandon his defensive position and risk open battle. Accordingly, on the 1st of August, he moved south with his entire force to look for the enemy at Cassville. Early on the morning of the 2d of August, at Dug Springs, nineteen miles southwest from Springfield, they encountered a large force under General Rains, and a sharp engagement ensued. The heroism of Captain Stanley's Fourth Cavalry (regulars) routed the Confederate infantry, but their flight was covered by a large body of cavalry which suddenly emerged from the woods. Being well shelled, however, by Captain Totten from a neighboring hill, these were in turn thrown into confusion, and Lyon's forces were left in possession of the valley. The Confederates lost about eighty killed and wounded, and the Federals eight killed and thirty wounded. After feeling vainly for the enemy for a couple of days, Lyon moved back on Springfield and occupied his old camp again on the 6th. The battle of Dug Springs, while it had encouraged the Federal troops, had taught McCullough a lesson, and he favored a retrograde movement. Price, however, dissented, and while the two leaders were at odds on the question, Major-General Leonidas Polk, commanding the Confederate Department, ordered McCullough to advance on Lyon. This brought matters to an issue, and resulted in McCullough taking the chief command. At midnight on the 7th, the entire force of 20,000 men in three columns, under McCullough, Pearce and Price, broke camp and began an advance on Springfield. They had miscalculated Lyon's movements, and therefore when on the 9th they reached Wilson's Creek, some nine miles south of Springfield, they had seen nothing of the Federal troops.

General Lyon, apprised of the advance and conscious of the weakness of his position at Springfield, had to choose between the alternatives of a hasty retreat, or a bold advance to meet the foe and give him battle. Lyon determined on the latter course, and on the night of the 9th he resolved to surprise the Confederate camp at two points simultaneously.

McCullough, on his part had resolved on a somewhat similar plan, with four columns, but postponed the attack on account of a storm, and having drawn in his pickets ready for an advance next morning, had actually played into Lyon's hands in a most unexpected manner.

The two Federal columns under Lyon and Sigel left Springfield during the afternoon and evening of the 9th, and in the small hours of the next morning each was in the positions selected; Lyon within sight of the camp-fires on the Confederate front, and Sigel in the rear by way of their right.

At 5 o'clock on the morning of the 10th, Lyon, with Major Sturgis as his second in command, dashed on Rains' camp on the extreme north, and was within musket shot before the approach had been observed. Thoroughly alarmed, Rains called on Price for aid. Meantime Lyon was pressing on supported by Totten's battery, while Dubois' battery was attending to a concealed Confederate battery across the ridge. While the battle was at its hottest on the right, a body of Confederates carrying a Union flag got close to Totten's battery, and but for detection would certainly have captured it. The trick being discovered, however, the rebels were made to pay dearly for their audacity. In the meantime General Sigel with his little force of 1,200 men and six guns, opened fire on the rear of the Confederate camp almost simultaneously with Lyon's attack in front. After vigorously shelling the camp, which was the first notice of his approach, Sigel's men dashed over the creek and into the camp from which the Texas rangers and mounted Missourians had hastily escaped. After reforming his men, Sigel moved along the Fayetteville road, and seeing a large body of men advancing toward him under a Union flag, naturally supposed them to be a portion of Lyon's force. He gave orders to cease firing in that direction, and suddenly a Confederate banner was raised—the treacherous foe were in his midst, hacking down his men and artillery horses. It was an instant rout. The regimental flag and five of his guns had been captured and three-fourths of his men killed or dispersed. Unaware of Sigel's mischance, Lyon was sturdily battling against enormous odds on the extreme right, and was frequently wounded. Totten's battery had hurled back several Confederate charges, and the conflict had raged over four hours, when Colonel Mitchell, of the Second Kansas, was wounded and disabled. General Lyon, bleeding from wounds on the leg and head, dashed to the front to lead on the Kansas troops, when a rifle ball pierced his heart. The death of General Lyon and the absence of General Sigel threw the immediate command upon Major Sturgis. This was at about 9 A. M., and the fierce fighting had ceased for a time. While Sturgis was holding a hasty council with his brother officers, while the question of immediate retreat was under discussion, a body of men, supposed to be Sigel's, came from the direction where Sigel's battery was understood to be, and the waving of a Union flag again covered a Confederate advance. At the same time Sigel's captured guns again opened fire on the Federal forces. Another hand-to-hand struggle ensued, and Sturgis' line was well nigh broken, when Captain Granger, supported by Dubois' battery, came hurrying forward and instantly turned the tide of battle. The Confederate right wavered, then fell back, and the confusion spread along the whole line, which hastily sought refuge in the woods.

The battle of Wilson's Creek was over, but the Confederates remained masters of the field, the shattered remnant of the Federal forces being unable to dislodge the enemy, and having no alternative but to fall back to Springfield. On the retreat Sigel, with his three hundred men, joined Sturgis. Reaching their old camp in the early evening the troops were rested till 3 A. M. on the 11th, when the line of march was taken up for Rolla, 125 miles distant. Here, on the 19th, they arrived without molestation, and established "Camp Good Hope," having direct railway communication with St. Louis. The Federal loss in killed, wounded and missing was placed at 1,256 men, while the Confederates lost nearly eighteen hundred men.

The Confederates were boastful of their great victory, but as they made no attempt to follow up the retreating force, with its valuable Government train, estimated at a million and a half of dollars, it is clear that they were only entitled to score a drawn game. The boastful attitude of McCullough provoked Price, and a wrangle ensued, in consequence of which the Texas guerrilla left the State in search of some more congenial field of action.

Meanwhile the political affairs of the State were in almost inextricable confusion. The Loyal Convention had deposed Governor Jackson and substituted Hamilton R. Gamble as Provisional Governor, and this official issued a temperate proclamation assuring the citizens that slaveholding interests should be protected. This was promptly met by a counter proclamation on the part of the deposed Lieutenant-Governor, who announced the severance of Missouri from the Union and the appointment of General Pillow, of Tennessee, assisted by M. Jeff Thompson and Brigadier W. J. Hardee as the military rulers of the State.

At this time John C. Fremont, Major General of Volunteers, had been appointed by the Federal Government to the command of the Western Department, with headquarters at St. Louis, He had a difficult task before him, but with characteristic energy set about frustrating the plans of Pillow, and on the 30th of July started an expedition to strengthen Bird's Point and Cairo. This accomplished, he returned to St. Louis, appointing General McKinstry Provost Marshal. This quelled the incipient revolt in that city. On the 31st of August General Fremont issued another proclamation extending the operation of martial law throughout Missouri, and threatening the confiscation of the property of all rebels for public use, and the emancipation of all slaves held by them; it also made the destruction of bridges, railways and telegraphs capital offenses, punishable by death. This intimation of reprisals by slave emancipation was deemed premature, and awoke a storm of indignation, under pressure of which the President requested Fremont to modify his proclamation. As he declined to do so, President Lincoln himself issued an order providing that only slaves compelled to act in the military service of the Confederacy were declared free. The mistake in this matter, if mistake there was, certainly did not rest on Fremont's shoulders, since the principle involved was one which, sixteen months later, was adopted by the Administration as one of the most powerful engines for the suppression of the Rebellion.

Such was the condition of affairs in Missouri at the end of August.

In the meantime, however, on the 16th of August, President Lincoln had issued a proclamation, in accordance with the act of Congress approved July 13th, 1861, declaring the inhabitants of Georgia, South Carolina, Tennessee, Alabama, Louisiana, Texas, Arkansas, Mississippi, Florida and Virginia (except that part of the latter State lying west of the Alleghany Mountains) in a state of insurrection against the United States, declaring all commercial intercourse with such States unlawful until such insurrection shall have ceased or been suppressed, and declaring further that all goods and chattels, wares and merchandise coming from any of the said States into other parts of the United States without the special license and permission of the President, or proceeding to any of the said States by land or water, together with the vessel or vehicle conveying the same or conveying passengers to or from the said States, will be forfeited to the United States; and that from and after fifteen days from the issuing of this proclamation all ships and vessels belonging in whole or in part to any citizen or inhabitant of any of the said States found at sea or in any port of the United States will be forfeited to the United States.

Taking all in all, August was a busy month, and at its close the nation had settled down to the conviction that a stubborn war was to be waged.

CHAPTER XII.

GEN. BUTLER AT FORTRESS MONROE—RELIEVED BY GEN. WOOL—THE BURNING OF THE VILLAGE OF HAMPTON—MAGRUDER BAFFLED—BUTLER ASSUMES THE OFFENSIVE—CAPTURE OF FORTS HATTERAS AND CLARK—CAPITULATION OF THE GARRISONS—EVENTS AND OCCURRENCES OF A GENERAL CHARACTER.

We left General Butler in command of Fortress Monroe, with Camp Hamilton, on the outskirts of Hampton, covering his position. The camp had been assigned to Colonel Max Weber. The disastrous battle of Bull Run had compelled Butler to close in his lines and abandon Hampton on the other side of the creek. The old Confederate plan of an attack upon Fortress Monroe was again conceived by General Magruder, in command at Yorktown. On Monday, August 5, he left Yorktown with two Tennessee, one Georgia and one Alabama regiment, some other infantry, and a small force of cavalry: about 6,000 men in all, with eight guns, one rifled. Encamping at Great Bethel on Tuesday, Magruder pushed on next day to Newmarket Bridge, about two and one-half miles from Hampton, reaching there about 11 A. M. The intent was to attack Newport News and Fortress Monroe simultaneously, but Magruder supposed that Butler would come out to attack him and consequently formed his men in line of battle at Newmarket Bridge. Mr. Mahew, formerly of Bath, Maine, who had removed to Georgia and had there been pressed into the rebel service, was one of the Georgia regiment. A thorough loyalist, Mr. Mahew saw his opportunity to render the Federals a service, and escaping to the woods, he swam the creek and gave himself up to the pickets with a request to be taken at once to General Butler. The information he gave as to Magruder's plans was at once telegraphed to Colonel Phelps at Newport News and preparations were made to meet the combined attack. It is possible that Mahew's desertion and its motives were at once apprehended, for an advance into Hampton was made by the Rebels, their advance guards entering the village about 4 P. M. Late in the evening,

THE BURNING OF HAMPTON.

General Butler having visited Camp Hamilton, ordered the force holding Hampton Bridge to resist any attempt to pass or destroy it. About 25 feet of the planks on the Hampton village end were torn up and a barricade erected which was held by a detachment of Colonel Weber's riflemen. These preparations were but just completed when the rebels attacked the bridge, but being picked off by the marksmen, retired after a sharp interchange of shots. Returning to the village, orders were given by Magruder to apply the torch and

BURNING OF HAMPTON.

totally destroy the place. There were rebel sympathizers in Hampton, and these, though property-owners themselves, lent their aid in the fiendish work. So quickly were the flames kindled that the terrified inhabitants had no opportunity to save their furniture, getting off at best with a few portable valuables. At the house of Mr. Joseph Segar, a faithful old negro undertook to get out some special treasures, when the rebel incendiary assigned to the destruction of this particular property warned him to desist or he would be shot. The imperturbable negro coolly replied: "Can't help dat; massa's things must be got out." The resultant shot missed the faithful old fellow, who then fled, considering he had gone as far in the line of duty as could reasonably be expected. The houses near the bridge were first set fire to, and then the rebels returned to the attack on the bridge, their own fiendish work, however, behind them, casting a lurid glare which rendered them admirable targets for Colonel Weber's German marksmen. The barricade was fairly riddled with rebel bullets, but no Federal casualties resulted. Repulsed at this point, the rebels drew off and set to work in earnest to destroy the remainder of the village. In a short time an immense mass of flame lit up the heavens so that it was light enough to read a newspaper as far off as Newport News. Every house was gutted save about five at the north and south ends of the town, and these only escaped in consequence of a southwest wind driving the flames from them, and the continued peppering of Weber's men kept the rebels from approaching them again. This work of destruction accomplished, Magruder retired to Big Bethel and Yorktown, finding that all his other schemes had been detected and thwarted.

On the 19th of August General Butler was relieved of his command by Major-General John E. Wool, who gave General Butler command of the volunteer forces outside the fortress.

In the meantime, Commodore Stringham, whose fleet was in Hampton Roads, learned by means of an escaped Union prisoner that English blockade-runners were landing supplies of every kind through Hatteras Inlet, which was covered by the rebel Forts Hatteras and Clark, on the western end of Hatteras Island. This information was sent on to Butler, and by him communicated to Washington, together with a plan for the reduction of the forts in question by the aid of the Hampton Roads fleet. The project was approved, and General Butler was ordered to take the forts and destroy them, preparatory to closing the inlet. On the 26th of August, with nine hundred men, General Butler put his expedition in motion. Under command of Commodore Stringham the little squadron, consisting of the flag-ship *Minnesota*, the frigate *Cumberland*, the transports *George Peabody* and *Adelaide*, made Pamlico Sound by the afternoon of the 27th. The *Susquehanna*, *Pawnee*, *Wabash*, *Monticello* and *Harriet Lane* also participated in the movement.

FORTS HATTERAS AND CLARK CAPTURED.

While the frigates opened fire on the forts, the troops landed two miles above on the morning of the 28th at daybreak. After four hours' fighting Fort Clark was captured and held by some of Colonel Weber's men. As Fort Hatteras was silent, the attacking party ceased firing also. The *Monticello* and the *Harriet Lane* proceeded up the inlet, when suddenly the fort batteries were brought to bear on them. The squadron at once reopened on the fort, and another engagement began. This lasted till evening, when the squadron drew off without

FORT HATTERAS.

much damage, though the safety of the *Monticello* was at one time a matter of grave concern.

During the night Commodore Samuel Barron, in command of the Confederate squadron in Pamlico Sound, and Major W. S. G. Andrews, arrived at Fort Hatteras, and the command was turned over to Barron. Supposing that Butler's troops were holding Fort Clark, the guns were trained on this, but it was only waste of powder, for Weber had withdrawn from so perilous a position.

Next morning at an early hour the contest was renewed and maintained until nearly noon, the Federal Squadron and a land battery handled by Lieutenant Johnson, of the Coast Guard, shelling the fort so severely that Barron, after a futile attempt to entrap the attacking force, exhibited a white flag. At the same time his vessels on the sound made off out of reach of the Federal squadron. Terms of capitulation were signed on board the *Minnesota*, by which the forts and the entire garrisons, with all munitions, etc., were surrendered. Commodore Barron attempted to capitulate with leave to retire, but Butler was firm and the entire Confederate force surrendered as "prisoners of war." Only a few of the Federals were wounded and none killed, while the Confederate loss was 49 killed and 51 wounded. The prisoners numbered 691 officers and men, and the capture included 29 cannon, 1,000 stand of arms, 6 regimental colors and a large amount of military stores. The principal officers taken prisoners were Major W. S. G. Andrews, Colonel W. F. Martin and Commodore Samuel Barron.

The chagrin of the Confederates over this serious blow was deepened by the fact that General Butler, instead of destroying the forts according to orders, reported his victory personally at Washington, and succeeded in obtaining orders to garrison the captured works. Supplies were promptly sent forward to Colonel Hawkins, who, with part of the Ninth New York, had been left in charge, and thus Hatteras Island and Inlet were stopped from further use by the blockade-runners. One back alley-way had been closed, and the position proved the key to future operations of a more important character, to which we shall refer later on,

Turning aside, restfully, for a brief space from the din of battles, we may note a few straws indicative of the state of public feeling about this time. On the 20th August, Ambrose L. Kimball, editor of the Essex County *Democrat*, at Haverhill, Mass., who had been publishing Secession articles, was taken from his home, tarred and feathered, and ridden on a rail through the town, until he consented to apologize on his knees and promise not to repeat the offense. In West Chester, Pa., about the same time, the office of the *Jeffersonian* was visited by a mob who cleaned out the establishment as a kind of gentle remonstrance against the principles of the newspaper. No tar: no feathers. At Danville, Ky., on the same day, 240 loyal fugitives from East Tennessee, men of all ages, were fed in the Seminary yard. The barefooted, weary victims enlisted in the United States service at Camp Dick Robinson, Kentucky. At Philadelphia, Pa., Pierce Butler, whose letters giving information to the rebels had been intercepted, was arrested by the United States Marshal and taken to New York. At Alexandria, Va., Miss Windle, an accomplished authoress, formerly of Delaware, but afterwards of Philadelphia, was arrested when about to start for Washington. She had been in correspondence with the rebel leaders and boldly avowed her Secession sympathies. At Newport, Rhode Island, United States Marshal Albert Sanford captured Louis de Bebian, claiming to be a French citizen, but a resident of Wilmington, N. C. He took passage from Wilmington on the British vessel *Adelso*, bound for Halifax, N. S., to meet a Cunard steamer, but the vessel put into Newport in distress. He complained of his arrest, stating he was on his way to Europe to see his family, but among his effects were letters of credit amounting to $40,000, with which he was to purchase clothing, arms and iron for shipment to Wilmington, N. C., and other Southern points. On the 16th of August, the Grand Jury of the Circuit Court for the Southern District of New York, sitting in New York city, made presentment against the New York daily and weekly *Journal of Commerce*, the daily and weekly *News*, the daily and weekly *Day Book* and the *Freeman's Journal*, of New York city, and the daily and weekly *Eagle*, of Brooklyn, charging these periodicals with affording encouragement to the rebels, the first-named paper having also published a list of newspapers in the Free States opposed to what it termed "the present unholy war." The Court said he would turn the presentment over to Judge Wilson at the October term. In sharp contrast to this, on the 21st of August, the Executive Committee of the New York Union Defense Committee reported that up to that date it had spent in the equipment of various regiments $581,689; for arms and ammunition, $26,589, and for relief to soldiers' families, $230,000. In Philadelphia, August Douglas, a Baltimore merchant, was arrested on a charge of attempting to induce Lieutenant Hain to join the rebels, under promise of higher rank and pay.

While treason was thus at work in every direction, it is not to be wondered at that the Department of State gave notice that "no person will be allowed to go abroad from a port of the United States without a passport either from this Department or countersigned by the Secretary of State; nor will any person be allowed to land in the United States without a passport from a Minister or Consul of the United States, or, if a foreigner, from his own Government, countersigned by such Minister or Consul."

These few extracts from the newspapers of the period tell their own story, and give a faithful reflex of the condition of society at that period.

CHAPTER XIII.

MOVEMENTS IN MISSOURI—THE SIEGE OF LEXINGTON—HEROISM OF THE FEDERALS—BARBARISM OF THE CONFEDERATES—ATTACK ON SICK AND DYING IN THE HOSPITAL.—SURRENDER OF MULLIGAN'S CAMP—GENERAL ULYSSES S. GRANT AT PADUCAH—HIS DASH ON BELMONT—FREMONT SUPERSEDED—SUMMARY OF SUBSEQUENT MOVEMENTS.

Early in September, after the Texan ranger McCullough had left Missouri, General Price, pluming himself on what he was pleased to call the "great victory on Wilson's Creek," which, however, he had not dared to follow up, began an advance on Lexington, the capital of Lafayette County, on the southern bank of the Missouri River. After a skirmish at Drywood Creek with a small Union force under General James H. Lane, whom he forced to retire, Price moved on to Warrensburg, which he reached on the 11th of September. But Fremont had early intimation of this advance, and divined its purpose. He consequently sent Colonel James A. Mulligan, of the Chicago "Irish Brigade," or Twenty-third Illinois, with the Thirteenth Missouri and the First Illinois Cavalry, to hold Lexington. On the 9th of September, two days before Price left Warrensburg, Mulligan reached Lexington, and at once began throwing up works on an elevation to the northeast of the city. The intrenchments were rapidly being pushed forward when Price, on the morning of the 12th, drove in the extreme picket line and opened fire on the camp. Little was done, and Price drew off before dark. The entire force with Colonel Mulligan did not number over 2,800 men, and it was clear that the enemy with a much larger force would resort to a siege. To meet this contingency energetic preparations were made, and urgent appeals for reinforcements were sent to Jefferson City. None came, but the little band resolved to hold the position at all hazards. On the 17th, Price, who now mustered 25,000 men, began closing in on the camp. The messengers sent by Mulligan had been captured on the river forty miles below, and Price felt himself master of the situation. Entering the town and cutting off all communication. Price disposed his forces for a regular siege. On the southwest General Parsons with Captain Guibor's battery poured a continuous fire into the works, while picked marksmen made targets of individuals incessantly. On the northeast General Rains, with a heavy force, and Clark's and Bledsoe's batteries were equally active. During the hottest of the fight Brigadier-General Harris, one of Governor Jackson's special associates, performed the characteristic feat of assaulting and capturing the hospital, killing and wounding the attendants, the sick and wounded in their cots, and generally exhibiting the ferocity of the Blackfeet Indians. This revolting scene stirred the Hibernian blood of the Montgomery Guards, and Captain Gleason with eighty men dashed on the fiends, regardless of a fierce fusilade, and drove them like sheep down the bluff. Gleason lost thirty men and received two bullet wounds, but covered himself with glory and the cowardly rebels with shame and disgrace. In the camp, the heroic little band fought like devils; parched with thirst, their water supply being cut off by the investing force, but from 9 A. M. on the 18th till 2 P. M. on the 20th they worked and fought, by day and by night, in an oven-like atmosphere at night and under a fierce sun by day. The sublime heroism of the gallant band under the inspiration of their dauntless officers is worthy of deathless record. When at the hour last named the beleaguered garrison were confronted by one of those devices which the erratic genius of this country could alone achieve, to wit, a movable line of well-wetted hemp bale breastworks, advanced to within almost pistol shot of their lines, a longer resistance would have converted heroism into suicidal folly. Reinforcements could not reach them and the enemy were in overwhelming force. On his own responsibility Major Becker, of the Eighth Missouri Regiment, raised a flag of truce, and though reprimanded by Colonel Mulligan for so doing, his act was shortly after accepted as the only alternative. The garrison surrendered, and Colonels Mulligan, Marshall, White, Peabody and Grover, with Major Van Horn and 118 non-commissioned officers, became prisoners of war. About forty men had been killed and three times that number wounded. The losses of the enemy were probably about the same. The Union loss in material was very heavy, some 3,000 muskets and rifles, 5 cannons, 750 horses, a large number of wagons, vast quantities of munitions and accoutrements falling into the hands of the Confederates. They also captured $900,000 in money from the banks, the protection of which had been Fremont's main object in sending Mulligan forward. While Colonel Mulligan was awarded the thanks of Congress, and promotion for his gallantry, the alleged negligence of Fremont was censured bitterly, but unjustly, for he had in his entire department only 56,000 men, and these were scattered at remote points, harassed by roving bands of Confederates. Upon this small force even, continual demands were being made by General Robert Anderson, who wanted aid to protect Louisville, Kentucky; by General Ulysses S. Grant, who was in command of the district around Cairo, and located at Paducah, at the mouth of the Missouri River, and was threatened by Confederates on his flank from Columbus; and by the repeated demands of General Scott for immediate dispatch of troops to aid in guarding the Capital. These facts, however, were not appreciated, even at military headquarters; and Fremont, piqued by the treatment he was receiving, organized a force of 20,000 men under Generals Hunter, Pope, Sigel, McKinstry and Ashboth, and on the 27th of September began an advance with this army and some eighty-six guns. Pushing on to Jefferson City, he forced Price back and Lexington was abandoned on the 30th, the Union prisoners there being left under guard. On the 16th of October Major Frank J. White put the guard to flight by a bold surprise, released the prisoners and captured some seventy Confederates. He then pushed on to join Fremont, who was now at Warsaw preparing to cross the Osage River, which Sigel had already passed. Heavy rains had meantime swollen the stream, and a log bridge was hastily improvised, over which some five days later Fremont's force, now increased to 30,000 men, safely crossed. His plan in brief was to scatter Price's force, capture Little Rock, Arkansas, cut off Polk, Pillow, Thompson and Hardee, and with the aid of a flotilla from St. Louis push straight on for New Orleans for a decisive battle. But Secretary Cameron and Adjutant-General Thomas, who had chosen to disapprove his plans, were hastening after him, to see for themselves how matters stood. Aware of this, Fremont hurried on, but Cameron and Thomas came up with him at Tipton on the 13th of October. They came, saw and went away without disclosing their intent, but on their return published an unfavorable report and on the 2d of November sent an order directing Fremont to turn over his command to General David Hunter.

Just before this was received Fremont had sent orders to General Grant at Paducah to co-operate in the movements projected.

PONTOON BRIDGE AT PADUCAH.

In accordance with these orders an immense pontoon bridge was constructed across the Ohio, half a mile below Paducah. Smithfield, near the mouth of the Cumberland River, was also occupied, and the Confederate base of supplies from Kentucky and Tennessee was thus cut off. Fremont had made his dispositions to attack Price then marching on Springfield, with his vanguard, at Wilson's Creek and McCullough's supporting force at Dug Springs. At about midnight on the 3d of November, however, General Hunter arrived and disapproved the plans. In fact, there was to be no chance for Fremont to reap laurels. The next official stab was a coldly polite refusal by General McClellan to allow him to retain his Cavalry Corps Body-guard and the subsequent mustering of them out of service on the 28th of November.

Fremont took leave of the army on the 4th of November, and on the 8th was received in St. Louis by a public demonstration which went far to atone for the willful or ignorant discourtesy of his official superiors.

In pursuance of Fremont's orders, General Grant had sent Colonel Oglesby to intercept Jeff. Thompson, and had detailed General Charles F. Smith to make a demonstration in the direction of Columbus and keep Polk from interfering with the pursuit of Thompson. At the same time Grant, with three thousand men, dropped down the Mississippi in four steam transports and, at dawn on the 7th of November, landed at Hunter's Point on the Missouri, and leaving a battalion to guard the transports, pushed on to the village of Belmont, opposite Columbus.

ULYSSES S. GRANT.

The gunboats *Tyler* and *Lexington*, which had acted as convoy, opened fire on the Confederate batteries a short distance above Columbus, and at the same time Grant, throwing his men forward in skirmishing line, drove in the Confederates, and charging over the abatis captured the intrenched camp of Belmont. Polk, who had only been looking for Smith's attack from Mayfield in the rear, was taken completely by surprise.

It was not possible to hold Belmont, as it was covered by the batteries on the Columbus bluffs, consequently, after destroying everything in the camp, Grant fell back with his prisoners, captured horses and artillery to the landing place. Polk, however, sent General Cheatham to intercept him, and crossed himself to join Pillow in the attack, while the Columbus batteries kept up a heavy fire. The gunboats did efficient service, and by dint of hard fighting Grant reached his flotilla and returned to Cairo. His loss had been heavy, amounting to about 580, but the Confederate losses were still greater. Two of Beltzhoover's heavy guns were carried away by Grant's troops.

We left General Hunter in command of the army from which Fremont had been relieved, but his tenure was short, for on the 9th of November General Henry Wager Halleck was appointed to the command of the Department of Missouri, and Hunter was assigned to the Department of Kansas.

General Hunter had meantime led his troops back from Springfield to St. Louis, and General Price cautiously followed the retreating Federals, and soon all southwestern Missouri was in Confederate grasp.

Several other fields of operation demand our attention. Therefore, with a hasty summary of other fighting and of administrative measures we must with this chapter close the record of events in Missouri for the year 1861.

On December 17th and 18th, two brigades of General Pope's command, under Colonels Steele and Jeff. C. Davis, surprised rebel camps at Osceola and Milford, securing 360 Confederate prisoners at Osceola and 1,300 Confederates, with 1,000 stand of arms, 400 wagons, and a large amount of camp equipage and stores, at Milford. The Union loss was two killed and seventeen wounded.

At Mount Zion, in Boone County, on December 28th, a sharp engagement occurred between a detachment from the command of General Prentiss, consisting of five companies of cavalry under Colonel Glover, and five companies of sharpshooters under Colonel Birge. The enemy were strongly posted in some woods near Mount Zion Church. A battle at close quarters for over two hours was ended by a bold movement on the part of Colonel Glover, who turned the position and sent the rebels flying in total disorder. The Union loss was but two killed and eleven wounded, while the Confederates lost in killed and wounded about 200 men. The Federal forces took thirty prisoners and the entire camp equipage and stores. There were several intervening minor skirmishes, but their details are not of interest.

On assuming command in Missouri General Halleck determined not only to improve the morals of his army but also to teach the wavering citizens that allegiance to the Union was their most economic policy. Finding himself hampered with fugitives from all sections of the State, he instructed Brigadier-General Curtis, Provost-Marshal of St. Louis, to levy on disloyal citizens for the support of such fugitives, and to inflict penal damages on such as resisted the levy. He then cleared his camp of the spies who, in the guise of fugitives, were daily penetrating the lines. He applied military law to such cases without respect to age or sex. While his harshness in this respect has been the subject of much hostile comment, it would be but fair to apply the test of "Put yourself in his place," when at a distance and in cold blood the actions of a much-harassed military man are under discussion.

He also dispatched General John Pope on a kind of roving commission to break up Confederate camps, giving him general command of all the National troops between the Missouri and Osage Rivers. Pope did his work well, and effectually blocked the operations of Price, by depriving him of communication with recruiting points and forcing him to seek safety on the Arkansas border. We have noted the results of his movements in the two preceding engagements.

We have noted other military changes of command west of the Alleghanies, and it remains only to mention that General Don Carlos Buell had superseded General Sherman in command of the Department of the Ohio, embracing that State and the portion of Kentucky lying east of the Cumberland River, and that Colonel E. R. S. Canby had been appointed to the command of the Department which included the Territory of New Mexico only.

CHAPTER XIV.

OPERATIONS IN WESTERN VIRGINIA—THE BATTLE OF CARNIFEX FERRY—DEATH OF COLONEL LOWE—FLOYD'S HASTY FLIGHT—ATTACK ON THE SUMMIT POST—REPULSE OF THE CONFEDERATES—THE KANAWHA VALLEY CLEARED OF INTRUDERS—MOVEMENTS OF M'CLELLAN—THE DISASTROUS BATTLE OF BALL'S BLUFF.

We must now fall back, chronologically, to note events in Virginia, Kentucky and Tennessee.

We have already noted the military changes in July, by which the retirement of General McDowell placed General McClellan in chief command, and we left the vigorous young commander busily perfecting the organization of the Army of the Potomac. Among the changes at this time were those included in General Order No. 46, by which Major-General Robert Patterson and Brevet Major-General Cadwallader, of the Pennsylvania Volunteers, were honorably discharged, and Major-General N. P. Banks was ordered to assume command, in the Valley of Virginia, of the army from which Patterson was relieved, the Department of the Shenandoah being created, with headquarters in the field. Major-General John A. Dix relieving Banks at Baltimore, and assuming command of the Department of Maryland. McClellan's command, as we have seen, was turned over to Brigadier-General Rosecrans, and we

GEN. ROBERT E. LEE.

will for a brief space note his operations in Western Virginia, where General Robert E. Lee was making vigorous efforts to obtain a footing in conjunction with Brigadier-General John B. Floyd, late Confederate Secretary of War, who had succeeded that vainglorious military bubble, General Wise, after the battle of Carrick's Ford.

Early in August, Lee, with 1,600 men, was at Huntersville, in Pocahontas County, and his plan was to sweep down on Wheeling and threaten Western Pennsylvania. Floyd had taken command at Lewisburg, the capital of Greenbrier County, and intended to push through the Kanawha Valley and dislodge General Cox, who had crossed the Ohio River, and, after capturing Barboursville, had pushed on to the Kanawha River.

Leaving a force at Pickett's Mills to prevent Cox turning his flank from Hawksnest, Floyd moved to Carnifex Ferry, on the Gauley River, but in making his dispositions there, came to grief by the upsetting of a ferry-boat, and thus had his artillery and most of his cavalry on one side the river, while his infantry and the remaining cavalry were on the other side. Colonel Tyler hearing of this mischance, started from Summersville, hoping to surprise Floyd and take him at a disadvantage, but Floyd, who was wily, if nothing else, turned the tables on him and dispersed his force, with the loss of fifty men, on the morning of August 26. General Cox had meantime moved along the Kanawha Valley and scattered the Confederates at all points, until by the end of July he had entered the abandoned Confederate intrenchments at Charleston, near the New and Gauley rivers. The Elk River Suspension Bridge had been destroyed by Wise previously, and Cox accordingly fortified his position and awaited developments.

General Rosecrans determined to drive Floyd from Carnifex Ferry, and leaving General Reynolds at Cheat Mountain with orders to check Lee's advance, he pushed forward by a difficult route across the Gauley Mountain range to Summersville. By noon on the 9th of September he had reached the summit of the range, and soon encountered the outlying pickets. After a short skirmish these were driven in. The next morning, General Benham's brigade leading the advance, the Federals passed through Summersville and pressed on to the works which Floyd had thrown up on a hill commanding the approach to the Ferry. The Confederates opened a heavy fire on Colonel Lytle's skirmishers, and for a time threw the line into confusion. The batteries of Schneider and McMullen, however, went to their support and the men quickly rallied. General Benham then sent the Twelfth and Thirteenth Ohio regiments to attack Floyd's right wing, and Colonel Lytle, with the Tenth Ohio, made a dash on the centre. In this, however, he was severely wounded and his horse was killed. Colonel Smith, with the Thirteenth, and Colonel Lowe, with the Twelfth, under the direction of Adjutant-General Hartsuff, made a desperate attack on the right flank of the Confederates, in which Lowe fell with a bullet through his brain. Meanwhile Rosecrans had organized a column, composed of the Third, Ninth and Twenty-eighth Ohio regiments, with Scammon's brigade in reserve. Colonel Robert L. McCook, with his regiment of Germans, the Ninth Ohio, was assigned the post of honor. With a wild cheer, in response to his cry of "Forward, my bully Dutch!" the men plunged down upon the enemies' intrenchments. But Rosecrans had conceived the idea that the plans of Hartsuff involved too much peril, and checked the advance at the moment when to all appearances the works would have been successfully stormed. Thus, after about four hours' fighting and with a loss of fifteen killed and seventy wounded, the Federals did not seem to have accomplished much. They had, however, done more than they hoped for, Floyd having been wounded and so terribly scared that before daybreak he fled across the Gauley in confusion, leaving all his camp stores, ammunition and equipage behind. He destroyed the bridge of logs and the ferry-boat, and did not rest till he had put thirty miles between his men and the Federal forces. His first halt was on Big Bethel Mountain, near New River, from whence he pushed on to Meadow Bluff. General Wise, who had refused to aid Floyd at Carnifex Ferry, held the position on Big Bethel Mountain and established "Camp Defiance."

General Reynolds, who had been left at Cheat Mountain Pass,

had disposed his forces to guard the pass and check General Lee, whose main object was to secure this line of communication with the Shenandoah Valley. On the 11th of September Lee left Huntersville and prepared for a simultaneous attack on the pass, the outpost at Elk Water, held by Colonel Kimball with the Fourteenth Indiana, and the Summit post, Kimball's headquarters. On the morning of the 12th, Colonel Kimball found that Captain Coons was invested on a ridge near the pass by a large body of Confederates. Hurrying up with the Fourteenth Indiana and a handful of dragoons, Kimball routed these and released Coons. At the same time another body of Confederate troops on the front and flank of Kimball's position, near the Cheat River, were utterly routed, and fled in disorder. About 5,000 Confederates under General Anderson, of Tennessee, were thus foiled in their attempt on the Summit post by something like six hundred Federals. General Lee, on the failure of this scheme, withdrew from Cheat Mountain, and reached Meadow Bluff on the 20th of September to join Floyd. General H. R. Jackson had been left to watch Reynolds, with a few thousand men, on the Greenbriar River. Lee then concentrated the forces of Floyd and Wise with his own, and assuming chief command, strengthened the works on Big Bethel Mountain.

On October 3d, Reynolds made an attack on Jackson's intrenched camp on the Stanton pike, and a sharp engagement, lasting seven hours, inflicted severe loss on the Confederates, about two hundred of them being killed in the trenches. The Federals, however, were repulsed with the loss of ten killed and thirty-two wounded.

The troubles in the Confederate camp between Wise and Floyd led to the recall of the former, and Lee was soon afterwards sent to take charge of the South Carolina and Georgia coasts, his failure to strike Rosecrans having bitterly disappointed the Confederate authorities. Floyd was thus left in sole command, and during October he erected batteries on the left bank of the New River, near its junction with the Gauley, thus commanding the road to Rosecrans' camp. On the 12th of November a vigorous and successful attack was made for the purpose of dislodging him. General Schenck and Major Leeper were to have struck Floyd's front and rear at the same time, but a flood cut off Schenck, and Leeper with the First Kentucky achieved the victory by a bold dash on the front near the mouth of the Gauley. Floyd fled with such precipitation that he eluded General Benham, who had crossed below the mouth of New River to intercept him. With headlong haste he pushed on through Fayetteville and Raleigh till he reached Peterston, some fifty miles south of his abandoned position. In his flight Floyd threw away ammunition, camp equipage and tents. General Benham closely pressed him as far as Raleigh, some thirty miles down the valley. This decisive stroke left Rosecrans in clear possession of the Kanawha Valley, and broke the Confederate grasp, for the time at least, in Western Virginia. The finishing blow was given by Brigadier-General Robert H. Milroy, who first attacked Colonel Edward Johnston, of Georgia, who had been left by Jackson to hold the Alleghany Summit. This engagement on the 12th of December was a stubborn affair, the fortunes of the day wavering in the balance for some hours. The attempt to capture the battery commanding the Staunton pike failed, however, and the Federals retired in good order. The loss in killed and wounded amounted to about two hundred on each side. Toward the end of December Milroy sent an expedition under Major Webster, of the Twenty-fifth Ohio Regiment, to break up a Confederate post at Huntersville, about fifty miles distant. This was accomplished after a heavy march through deep snow, the Confederates were scattered, the military stores destroyed and the jail wrecked. This ended military operations in this section for that year.

We must now turn to the movements of General McClellan, whom we left organizing the Army of the Potomac, and which by the middle of October consisted of some 75,000 men, in splendid condition, ready for the field. Every department had been thoroughly organized and the defense of Washington City had been elaborately completed, extensive earthworks and a number of strong forts having been constructed. The main body of the army was close to the city, with outposts as far down the Potomac as Liverpool Point and away up the river to Williamsport, above Harper's Ferry.

The Confederates meanwhile had not been idle. General Johnston was within six miles of Washington City, at Munson's Hill, having advanced from Centreville and Fairfax Court House. Batteries had been planted on Matthias' Point and others were erected below Occoquan Creek, cutting off communication by water with the Capital. This blockade was very irritating and divers plans were formulated for breaking it up, but divided counsels upset every project, and before the month of October the Potomac was closed as an avenue of approach to Washington.

During the month of August there were several skirmishes between the outposts of the two armies, and on the 12th of September a sharp engagement was had between a Federal reconnoitering party and some Virginia cavalry under Colonel J. E. B. Stuart. The Federals, however, came out of this with but little loss. On the 15th of September Colonel John W. Geary's pickets, at Darnestown, Maryland, were attacked by Virginia troops who had crossed the Potomac. Soon afterward Lewinsville, Vienna and Fairfax Court House were occupied by the Federals. The Confederates had evacuated Munson's Hill some three weeks before, and its formidable-looking batteries of "Quaker guns," *i. e.*, painted logs and stove-pipes, became as much objects of amusement as they had been for nearly two months previously objects of dread by the troops facing them.

A sharp encounter between the troops under Colonel Geary and a large body of Confederates occurred on the 5th of October for the possession of Bolivar Heights, but the enemy were thoroughly routed and driven up the valley some six miles to Charlestown.

The most important, and at the same time disastrous affair occurred on the 21st of October, being the battle of Ball's Bluff. An unconfirmed report of the evacuation of Leesburg by the Confederates induced McClellan to order a reconnoissance in force and he sent General McCall to occupy Dranesville, a point midway between Leesburg and the Chain Bridge. General Banks having repeated the rumor on the strength of a dispatch from Sugar Loaf signal station, McClellan instructed Brigadier General Charles P. Stone, commanding an army of observation between Conrad's and Edwards' Ferries, to feel for the Confederate left under General N. G. Evans, advising him also of McCall's movements. Stone made a feint at each of the two ferries, General Gorman operating at Edwards' Ferry and Colonels Lee and Cogswell attending to the movement at Conrad's Ferry. Colonel Devens went in flat boats with his command to Harrison's Island. A reserve force of about 3,000, including the First California, commanded by Colonel E. D. Baker, Senator from Oregon, was held in readiness should the enemy force fighting. McCall's movements had been closely watched by the Confederates and they sent out a scouting party which General Gorman managed to disperse. Devens sent out a scouting party under Captain Philbrick towards Leesburg, by way of Ball's Bluff, and he reported a small camp in sight. Stone then ordered Devens to cross from Harrison's Island at dawn on the 21st and take the alleged camp, Colonel Lee meantime occupying the island. When the advance was made the camp could not be found and Devens halted within a mile of Leesburg. Colonel Baker with the reserve was ordered to move on Conrad's Ferry, from which point another feint was to be made to ward off attention to the movement of Devens. McClellan had not intended anything beyond a demonstration, and supposing this to be understood by General Stone, had ordered McCall to fall back from Dranesville, but of this Stone was ignorant. The Confederates had not been deceived by these feints but had kept a close watch upon Devens, and about noon on the 21st Colonels Jenifer and Hunton, with infantry and cavalry fell on his front and left in an open field. Colonel Baker, finding that Devens was attacked by a superior force, hurried to his aid. Devens had fallen back on Colonel Lee and was stubbornly facing his foe. Transportation was difficult, and Baker, finding the battle waxing hot, crossed the river in a skiff, left his artillery to come on and pushed forward to join Devens. Colonel Cogswell's Tammany Regiment and a couple of howitzers under Lieutenant French had already come up when Baker reached the field and assumed command. Expecting the aid of McCall, a line of battle was formed in the open field. Evans quickly accepted the challenge and attacked the front and left flank with great fury. Then it was found that the woods which surrounded the field on three sides were absolutely alive with men. The battle began soon after three o'clock in the afternoon, and by five o'clock Colonel Baker fell riddled with bullets. Colonel Cogswell took command and ordered a movement to the left, in order to cut through the enemy to Edwards' Ferry. At this moment a Confederate officer rode to the head of the Tammany Regiment and gave the order to "Charge," the trick succeeded, the men dashed forward with the Fifteenth Massachusetts only to find themselves exposed to a galling fire along the whole line. The day was lost and Cogswell ordered an immediate retreat to Harrison's Island. The scene which follows beggars description—the Confederates pressed in upon the disorganized mass and at the point of the bayonet forced them down the bluff to the banks of the turbulent river. The only boat there was speedily sunk and swimming the river was the only means of escape. Colonels Cogswell and Lee were taken prisoners, together with between four and five hundred of their men. Colonel Devens swam the river on horseback. The men who essayed to cross were either picked off by the Confederates or swept away by the current. The loss in killed was 223 and 266 were wounded. The Confederate loss was about 350 killed and wounded. The entire Federal force did not exceed 1,900 while that of the Confederates was fully 4,000.

All this time General Stone had been within easy reach with 7,000 men, but had relied on the co-operation of McCall, who, as we have seen, was nowhere near.

The news of the disaster came on him like a thunder clap and he hastily made arrangements to cover the retreat of Gorman's Brigade, whom he had sent to Edwards' Ferry. In the course of the night General Banks relieved him of his command and orders came from McClellan to hold the island and the Virginia shore till reinforcements could arrive.

This disaster roused public indignation and the blame was liberally showered upon all those in command. The House of Representatives, representing popular feeling demanded an investigation, but McClellan opposed this as likely to affect the service injuriously. He maintained that Stone was free from blame and this threw the weight of public indignation on the General-in-Chief.

The sequel of the matter was the arrest of General Stone on February 8th, 1862, and his incarceration for six months in Fort Lafayette without a trial. His release, as unceremonious as his arre t, may be taken to indicate that he suffered unjustly.

McClellan's first orders for holding the Virginia shore proved that even then he had not been fully informed of the condition of affairs, and when on the 23d of October he arrived at Poolesville he countermanded all orders for an advance and withdrew the entire force to the Maryland side of the river.

Their success at Ball's Bluff and the falling back of McCall vastly encouraged the Confederates. They again occupied Dranesville and, pushing their pickets forward to the verge of the Federal lines, ravaged the surrounding country.

McCall getting tired of this, obtained McClellan's permission to attack Dranesville, where the Confederate reserve was quartered. Accordingly Brigadier General E. O. C. Ord with about 4,000 men was intrusted with the expedition to Dranesville on the 20th of December, and was supported by Brigadier General Reynolds. About two miles out of Dranesville General J. E. B. Stuart with some 2,500 men came up from Centreville and a hot engagement followed. The Confederates, flushed by recent successes, were over-confident and had this time undertaken too big a contract. They were utterly routed with the loss of 43 killed and 143 wounded. The Federal loss was 7 killed and 61 wounded. McCall did not attempt to hold the position but fell back to his encampment, taking with him twenty-two wagon loads of corn and sixteen of hay. Although this spirited affair somewhat moderated the public annoyance over recent events, yet there was much murmuring at the general inaction of so large a body of troops, now amounting to some 200,000 men, while the Confederate force surrounding the capital was understood to be not much more than one fourth of that number.

We must again shift the scenes and turn our attention to naval operations on the coast of North Carolina and on the Gulf of Mexico.

CHAPTER XV.

NAVAL MOVEMENTS—AN INCIDENT OF TO-DAY—FATE OF THE HARRIET LANE—ENGAGEMENTS AROUND HATTERAS—THE AFFAIR OF SANTA ROSA ISLAND—BOMBARDMENT OF PENSACOLA—THE EXPEDITION TO PORT ROYAL—CAPTURE OF FORTS WALKER AND BEAUREGARD—THE CONFEDERATES DRIVEN FROM THE SOUTH CAROLINA COAST—ATTEMPTED BLOCKADE OF CHARLESTON HARBOR.

We have noted the capture of Forts Hatteras and Clark, at Hatteras Inlet, on the 29th of August, and their subsequent occupation, under the advice of General B. F. Butler, by Colonel Hawkins, of the Ninth New York Zouaves, and will now trace the operations along the coast which grew out of this capture.

Just here we must interpolate an incident which at this writing (June, 1884) is reported by cable from London in the following words: "Bark *Elliot Ritchie*, Captain Perkins, from Brunswick, March 22, for Buenos Ayres, has been abandoned at sea, water-logged, and crew landed at Pernambuco." The reader will naturally ask, "What has that to do with the Civil War?" In reply we shall connect this cablegram directly with the events under notice. The vessel in question was once the smart revenue cutter *Harriet Lane*, converted into a cruiser at the beginning of the war, and was one of the craft most prominent in the engagement off the Hatteras forts. Originally named after Miss Harriet Lane, a niece of President Buchanan, this cruiser was captured off Galveston by General John B. Magruder about the last of December, 1862, having been run into by the Confederate steamer *Bayou City*, after a sharp engagement. Captain Semmes, of the *Alabama*, afterward took the *Harriet Lane* to Havana, where she was turned into a sailing vessel and re-christened the *Elliot Ritchie*. Thus we justify the introduction of this despatch, and link the events of the war with the commercial records of to-day.

Colonel Hawkins having been reinforced by the Twentieth Indiana Regiment, under Colonel Brown, planned the closing up of Pamlico and Albemarle Sounds, and thus gaining the command of the North Carolina coast. The *Susquehanna* and the tug *Fanny*, with a portion of the Naval Brigade under Lieutenant J. T. Maxwell, disabled the deserted Forts Ocracoke and Morgan, on Beacon Island, and then Colonel Brown, with the Twentieth Indiana, started for Chicomico-comico to check the Confederate operations on Roanoke Island. This expedition, however, was a sad failure, for on the 1st of October the *Fanny*, with stores, intrenching tools and equipage, was captured, and three days later six Confederate steamers landed two thousand troops above and below Brown's position. In the enforced retreat to Hatteras about fifty of the Indianians were taken prisoners. The Confederates, however, did not attempt to push their advantage, but retired to Roanoke Island.

Although the Navy Yard at Pensacola, Fla., had been surrendered to the State authorities in January, Fort Pickens, on Santa Rosa Island, had remained in Federal possession, and had been garrisoned in April by Colonel Harvey Brown, after Lieutenant Slemmer had been relieved. Later in the Summer, the New York Sixth, Wilson's Zouaves, established a camp on the island close to the fort. No serious engagements had occurred, although sharp skirmishes had happened, until early in September, when a couple of night expeditions inflicted considerable damage on the Confederates in the Navy Yard. This provoked reprisals, and on the ninth of October some fourteen hundred men, under Generals Ruggles and Anderson, landed on Santa Rosa Island, on which Fort Pickens stands, and in three columns marched upon the Zouaves' camp. Colonel William Wilson being an object of intense hatred to the Floridians, the intent was not only to break up his camp, but, if possible, to capture him. The expedition was well planned and the surprise was complete. The pickets were driven in and the Zouaves forced from their camp, which was fired by the insurgents. Wilson's men, infuriate at the insults which the invaders heaped upon their Colonel, fought every inch of the retreat until they were reinforced by four companies from the fort under Majors Arnold and Vogdes. This turned the tide of battle, the Confederates were soon in full retreat to their launches, but in such confusion that many of them fell beneath the bullets of their comrades. Their total loss was about 150. In the confusion of the retreat Major Vogdes was made prisoner and carried off by the retreating Confederates. The total Federal loss was about sixty-four.

Following this, in November, Colonel Brown, assisted by the blockading squadron, *Niagara*, *Richmond* and *Montgomery*, bombarded the Confederate works and silenced Forts McRee and Barrancas, the two principal forts which defended the Navy Yard, and which, together with a number of smaller batteries, were held by General Braxton Bragg with some seven thousand men. Besides silencing the forts the heavy, continuous fire of the squadron and Fort Pickens laid the greater part of the Navy Yard and adjacent villages in ashes.

Towards the end of October more important operations were in progress on the South Carolina coast. A fleet of fifty war vessels and transports under Captain S. F. Dupont had been collected in Hampton Roads, and a land force of 15,000 men under Brigadier-General W. T. Sherman had been assembled at Annapolis, Maryland. At dawn, on the 29th of October, this formidable armament put to sea, but its destination was as impenetrable a mystery to the loyalists of the North as it was to the alarmed Confederates. Not only had the secret been well kept, but all the contingencies of such an expedition had been provided for by the astute Secretary of the Navy. Each vessel carried sealed orders, only to be opened at a certain point, or under peculiar and adverse circumstances. The wisdom of this precaution became evident when, after passing in safety the turbulent Cape Hatteras, a fearful storm scattered the fleet during the night of November 1st.

At dawn next morning the *Wabash*, which had led the expedition, was alone in the angry waters. An inspection of the sealed orders disclosed the plan of the expedition, a rendezvous off Port Royal; thither the *Wabash* steered her course, and on the 4th came to anchor. Many of the other vessels now came up, only four transports having been actually lost. In passing Charleston Harbor, Dupont had called off the *Susquehanna*, engaged in blockade duty. Along that ugly coast, however, the Confederates had destroyed all buoys, beacons and other aids to navigation, but fortunately there were those on board the fleet who were efficient pilots, and the channel entrance was soon located. There were other obstacles to be encountered in the shape of formidable works thrown up by the Confederates. On the south side of the entrance, near Hilton Head, was Fort Walker, and opposite, at Bay Point, was Fort Beauregard. There was also a small flotilla of eight armed steamers under Commodore Josiah Tatnall, but a few shots sent this incompetent individual in search of personal safety.

On the 5th Dupont made a reconnoisance, and early on the 7th the Federal fleet got under way. Shortly after 9 o'clock the engagement commenced, the two forts being attacked simultaneously, the *Wabash* and the *Susquehanna* being not more than from six to eight hundred yards from the works. At first the fire was briskly returned and the vessels suffered considerable damage, the *Wabash* in particular being badly cut up. The battle plan had been admirably arranged, the ships, one after the other, getting the range of the forts and shelling them for about twenty minutes at each turn. After four hours of this severe cannonading Fort Walker was silenced, and shortly afterward the firing from Fort Beauregard closed also. Both had been hastily abandoned and were strewn with dead and dying. The flagstaff of Fort Walker had been shot away early in the action, but from that of Fort Beauregard still floated the Confederate flag. To the halliards of this was attached an infernal machine, but it fortunately failed to carry out its devilish purpose.

The land force under Sherman had remained on the transports during the operations of the fleet. They were now landed, but the enemy had cleared out. From Fort Walker General T. F. Drayton had taken his men, on the run, across Hilton Head Island to Seabrook, whence they took passage for Savannah. From Fort Beauregard Captain Stephen Elliott got across to Port Royal Island and thence reached the Charleston and Savannah Railroad on the mainland. The Federal loss was eight killed and twenty-three wounded and that of the Confederates about fifty killed and wounded.

Fort Walker was occupied on the evening of the 7th and the

Stars and Stripes once more floated over South Carolina soil. General Horatio G. Wright, with his brigade, established headquarters here, and the following morning General Isaac I. Stevens, with the Seventy-ninth New York and the Eighth Michigan Regiments, occupied Fort Beauregard.

The blow to the Confederate cause was so disheartening that General Ripley, commanding the seacoast district, fell back to the mainland and advised the abandonment of the entire section.

General Sherman at once began to fortify Hilton Head, and took possession of the city of Beaufort, all the white inhabitants having fled. A large quantity of arms and ammunition also fell into the Federal hands. Meanwhile, Dupont sent exploring parties along the coast and took possession of the islands. He then occupied Big Tybee Island at the mouth of the Savannah River, effectually precluding blockade-running. On the last day of the year a land force, under Brigadier-General Stevens, and a naval force, under Commander Rogers, dislodged Generals Gregg and Pope with a Confederate force of some 8,000 men from Port Royal Ferry, after a sharp encounter, and thus the whole of this region was again brought under Federal control.

Meantime, an attempt was made to close up Charleston Harbor by sinking several old vessels laden with stone on the bar, but the operation was a failure, though the attempt was made a pretext for an appeal by the Confederates to the sympathies of Europe.

CHAPTER XVI.

THE CLOSE OF 1861—PERMANENT CONGRESS OF THE CONFEDERATE STATES—CABINET CHANGES—SPECIMEN OF JUDAH P. BENJAMIN'S CONSISTENCY—PRIVATEERING—THE TRENT AFFAIR—CAPTURE OF MASON AND SLIDELL—DIPLOMATIC CORRESPONDENCE—THE PRISONERS RELEASED.

Having thus noted, in as full detail as our space will permit, the principal warlike movements, military and naval, of the year 1861, we will hastily glance at other current events so as to close the record of the first year of the war.

We have incidentally mentioned the meeting of the Provisional Congress of the Confederate States at Montgomery in May, and the removal of the seat of government subsequently to Richmond, Va., where, on July 20th, the Third session was begun. We have also noted the message by which Jefferson Davis sought to reply to that of President Lincoln. In the course of this session an act was passed for the banishment from the limits of the Confederate States of every masculine citizen of the United States, except citizens of Delaware, Maryland, Kentucky, Missouri, the Territories of New Mexico, Arizona, the District of Columbia, and of Indian Territory south of Kansas. The act provided for the arrest as "alien enemies" of all such as remained over forty days after its passage, and also for the confiscation of all property belonging to such "alien enemies." The Confederate President was by other enactments authorized to call for four hundred thousand volunteers, in addition to the existing force, to serve for not less than twelve months nor more than three years; also to send additional commissioners to Europe, and he was further invested with discretionary powers to inflict retaliation upon prisoners of war. By a reorganization of the Cabinet, R. M. T. Hunter, of Virginia, was made Secretary of State; Judah P. Benjamin was transferred from the position of Attorney-General to that of Secretary of War, and ex-Governor Thomas Bragg assumed the portfolio relinquished by Benjamin.

[As we write we are reminded of the death of Judah P. Benjamin, in France, two weeks since, and it is a somewhat significant circumstance that prior to his death he had destroyed all his private papers. Had they been preserved, it is just possible that they would have cast a lurid light on some other personal records.]

As a rebellion War Secretary Benjamin was probably a success, for a time. At any rate, he saliently illustrated the inconsistencies of the Secession theories. We have noted how, immediately after the Baltimore riots, an era of bridge-burning and general devastation was inaugurated by the Secessionists, yet, when in November, 1861, some loyalist Tennessee citizens were arrested and charged with being accessories to certain military operations in which bridges were burned to cut off communication with Virginia, Benjamin wrote to Colonel Wood, at Knoxville, in regard to the prisoners, as follows : "All such as can be identified in having been engaged in bridge-burning, are to be tried summarily by drum-head court martial, and, if found guilty, executed on the spot by hanging. It would be well to leave their bodies hanging in the vicinity of the burned bridges." Such ferocity is hardly in keeping with the protests sent to European Courts against the "barbarous warfare" which sought to destroy Charleston Harbor by sinking the Stone fleet on the bar. However, the Confederate consistency was never strikingly developed.

The "Provisional" Congress reassembled at Richmond on the 18th of November, and when its time ran out on the 18th of February, 1862, it was immediately succeeded by a Congress under the Permanent Constitution of the Confederate States, in which Alabama, Arkansas, Florida, Georgia, Louisiana, Mississippi, North Carolina, South Carolina, Tennessee, Texas and Virginia were represented. Thomas S. Bocock, of Virginia, was elected Speaker of the House of Representatives. Jefferson Davis was then unanimously elected President for six years (without even the saving clause, "or so long as the Confederacy shall last"). Other Cabinet changes were made, Judah P. Benjamin, of Louisiana, becoming Secretary of State ; George W. Randolph, of Virginia, Secretary of War; S. R.

Mallory, of Florida, Secretary of the Navy : C. G. Memminger, of South Carolina, Secretary of the Treasury ; and Thomas H. Watts, of Alabama, Attorney-General. The proceedings of this Congress we may take occasion to make note of later on.

The authority which had been given Davis to issue letters-of-marque had been anticipated by him long before the forms of the alleged government had legalized it, and one of the first vessels which commenced privateering was the *Sumter*, commanded by Captain Raphael Semmes. She was a packet steamer, but heavily armed and carrying a crew of sixty-five seamen and twenty-five marines. Running the blockade of the Mississippi River, on the 30th of June, 1861, she began her operations on the American mercantile marine among the West India Islands and on the Spanish main, and it was while searching for her that Captain Charles Wilkes, of the United States steam sloop *San Jacinto*, performed the act which, while it obtained for him the enthusiastic admiration of the loyalists, very nearly precipitated a war between the United States and Great Britain. This was the capture of Commissioners Mason and Slidell, on board the British mail steamer *Trent*.

The circumstances of this affair deserve more than mere mention. We have noted that immediately after the Secession ordinance of Alabama and the resultant assembling of the Conference at Montgomery, certain commissioners were sent abroad to the various governments of Europe. These men, hastily selected, were unequal to the work cut out for them, and consequently, under the provisions of the Third session of the Provisional Congress, other and shrewder men were appointed with ambassadorial powers. Two of these were, first, James Murray Mason, formerly a Virginia Senator, and the man who in April had declared that all Virginians who refused to vote for Secession should be compelled to leave the State if they would save their lives, and second, John Slidell, who, when withdrawing from the National Senate with Judah P. Benjamin, as Senators from Louisiana, made an insolent speech, in which he threatened the United States with war, and declared that its mercantile marine would be compelled either to sail under foreign flags or to rot at the wharves. Mason was accredited to Great Britain and Slidell to France. But getting into such offices and getting out of America were affairs of very different calibre. The Southern ports were closely blockaded, and outside of the Confederate lines on land neither of these men dared venture. At length, during the wet, dark night of October 12th, they slipped out of Charleston Harbor on the steamer *Theodore* and successfully ran the blockade. It was not a dignified proceeding on the part of high diplomatic functionaries, but expediency may be charitably pleaded for them. Slidell had with him his wife and four children, besides his secretary, Eustis; Mason had his secretary, McFarland, only. Reaching Havana, they embarked on the 7th of November for St. Thomas by the British mail steamer *Trent*. From St. Thomas they proposed to take the packet line to Southampton. Captain Wilkes, as we have remarked, was on a still hunt for the *Sumter*, and putting in at Havana became cognizant of the departure and plans of the Confederate Commissioners. He decided to intercept the *Trent* and arrest them and their secretaries. About midday on the 8th of November he sighted the *Trent* in the Bahama Channel and signaled her to heave to. Mail steamers do not, however, stop to pick up transient guests, and consequently the *Trent* steamed ahead. As a gentle hint, Wilkes sent a shell across her path and Captain Moir concluded he might as well be interviewed by the Yankee. A couple of boats, with a force of marines, under Lieutenant D. M. Fairfax, were soon alongside. The errand being explained, Captain Moir declined to afford any information as to his passengers. Fairfax called on his marines, under Lieutenant Greer, and the matter began to assume a serious aspect. To end the controversy, Mason and Slidell came forward, but protested against arrest. This was, of course, unavailing, and Fairfax used technical force, by putting his hand on the shoulder of Mason, who then went quickly to the boat. Slidell was more obstinate, but a file of marines put an end to his resistance. The two secretaries philosophically followed the fortunes of their superiors, though one of them, Eustis, had to leave his wife in the company of Slidell's family. Captain

Wilkes took his prisoners to New York, whence they were sent to Fort Warren, on George's Island, Boston Harbor.

While Wilkes was receiving public ovations, and the thanks not only of the Secretary of the Navy, but also of Congress, the press and the public of Great Britain were furious in their denunciations of the alleged outrage.

The British Government, under the spur of popular indignation, made a great show of warlike preparations, and the sensational section of the press flamed with appeals to the latent prejudices of the people. On the other hand, Abraham Lincoln, never cooler than when in the midst of the excitement of others, kept a level head and controlled his Cabinet.

Meanwhile a distorted version of the affair had been communicated to the British Government, and Lord John Russell, Foreign Secretary, instructed the British Ambassador at Washington, Lord Lyons, to demand the restoration of the prisoners to the protection of the British flag, and a suitable apology for the aggressions which had been committed.

When this demand was communicated to the Government at Washington, the masterly policy of Lincoln dictated that while the prisoners should be given up, yet Great Britain should be placed in an equivocal position by demonstrating that the "right of search" which that government had so autocratically insisted on was an indecent, infamous and preposterous claim. We need not follow out the diplomatic wrangle which ensued, but terminate this narrative by stating that after Secretary Seward, in an able and exhaustive resumé of the subject, had shown all these bearings, he concluded by saying: "If I decide this case in favor of my own Government, I must disallow its most cherished principles, and reverse and forever abandon its essential policy. The country cannot afford the sacrifice. If I maintain these principles and adhere to that policy, I must surrender the case itself. It will be seen, therefore, that this Government could not deny the justice of the claims presented to us in this respect upon its merits. We are asked to do to the British nation just what we have always insisted all nations ought to do unto us." He further intimated that the individuals were of little or no consequence anyhow, and with covert sarcasm reminded the British Minister of some little affairs in the past which were about as palatable as Dead Sea apples, just at that time. He then announced that the prisoners would be cheerfully liberated and placed at the disposal of Lord Lyons.

In accordance with this, the British gun boat *Rinaldo* was ordered to Provincetown, Massachusetts, and Mason, Slidell, Eustis and McFarland were escorted on board on the 1st of January, 1862.

The result of this matter, while proving that it does " make a great difference whose ox is gored," really satisfied nobody but the President and Cabinet of the United States. They had vindicated a great principle in a diginfied way. The hot heads among the Northerners fumed over what they considered truckling to British arrogance; the scheming Southerners saw their hopes of a war, which must have inured to their advantage, blown to the winds, and the high and mighty Ambassadors themselves found they were, personally, very much like "a chip in porridge," of no account anyhow.

We can here close our record of the troublous, eventful year 1861.

CHAPTER XVII.

CONDITION OF AFFAIRS IN JANUARY, 1862—EXERTIONS OF THE SECESSIONISTS IN KENTUCKY—THE FORCES AT BOWLING GREEN—GARFIELD'S VICTORY AT PRESTONBURG—THE BATTLE OF MILL SPRING—DEATH OF ZOLLICOFFER—THE BURNSIDE AND GOLDSBOROUGH EXPEDITIONS—CAPTURE OF ROANOKE ISLAND—OTHER NORTH CAROLINA VICTORIES.

At the opening of the New Year, 1862, Congress, which met December 2d, 1861, was engaged in the consideration of questions relating to Slavery, the stormy debates incident to the "*Trent* affair" having subsided. The thin end of the wedge, which, when subsequently driven home by the Emancipation Proclamation, lifted forever a great stigma from this nation, had been introduced in the shape of bills, which subsequently became enactments, one providing for the confiscation of rebel property and for giving freedom to those held in slavery by such persons, and another which made it a penal offense for any one in the naval or military service of the United States to capture and return fugitive slaves. As, however, these were merely preliminary measures, we will not do more than mention them here.

We will turn to affairs in Kentucky, where a section of the people, on November 20th, 1861, had assumed to represent the entire State, and after adopting a Secession ordinance and the usual buncombe Declaration of Independence, organized a Provisional Government, with George W. Johnson, of Scott County, as Governor, and Bowling Green as the seat of government. On December 16th the formalities preceding admission to the Confederate Congress were completed, and representatives of the "Legislative Council of Ten" were sworn in. Prior to this a vigorous effort had been made by the National Government to encourage the latent loyalty of the mass of Kentucky citizens, ex-Governor Morehead, accused of treason, had been arrested in Louisville and confined in Fort Lafayette, New York. His chief offense, and a grave one, had been the aiding of Captain Simon B. Buckner, of the National service, in recruiting from the State guard for the Confederate service, though he failed in a scheme to secure an appropriation of $3,000,000 from the State Legislature for the purpose of sending these recruits armed and equipped to Jefferson Davis. This arrest scared the Secession clique in Kentucky, and they scattered for safety. Ex-Vice-President John C. Breckinridge, ex-Congressman Humphrey Marshall, became Brigadier-Generals in the Confederate army, and Captain John Morgan became the guerrilla commander, whose daring dashes and hairbreadth escapes will be the theme for stories of adventure for generations. Captain Buckner, compelled to throw off the mask, had also become a Confederate general, and was for a time with General Johnston at Bowling Green, until superseded by General Hardee.

The Federal forces under General Buell had been well organized at Louisville, and in the latter part of December General Alexander D. McCook, with some 40,000 men, had pushed toward Bowling Green, and after a skirmish driven Terry's Texas Rangers back on that position.

Early in January, General Humphrey Marshall, with 25,000 men, had encamped near the Big Sandy River, near Paintsville, on the Kentucky and Virginia boundaries. To dislodge him the Fourteenth Kentucky and the Forty-second Ohio infantry, with a few hundred Virginia cavalry, were sent under command of James A. Garfield—then only a Colonel, but subsequently a Brigadier-General, and still later our second Presidential martyr.

It was bitter weather thus early in January, but Garfield pushed on, and Marshall, who knew the resistless, quiet energy of the young Ohioan, moved hastily up the river. Garfield sent his Virginia cavalry in hot haste after him, and on the 7th of January they struck him heavily at Jennis' Creek. On the 10th, Colonel Garfield came upon Marshall's forces, some 2,500 strong, with three cannon, a few miles above Prestonburg. Marshall's position was well chosen on a small eminence, but Garfield, with only some 1,100 men, attacked him with such impetuosity that before the afternoon closed a fight of about three hours had driven him from his position. Reinforcements about 700 strong coming up, Garfield was enabled to make the battle of Prestonburg a thorough rout, capturing several prisoners, some stores and horses. The Federal loss was but two killed and a few wounded, while Marshall lost sixty killed besides those wounded and taken prisoners. The gallantry of this affair earned for Garfield a commission as Brigadier-General.

During the same month a sharp engagement took place at Mill Spring, Pulaski County, on the Cumberland River. Near here, at Beech Grove, ex-Congressman General Felix K. Zollicoffer, of Tennessee, had late in 1861 formed an intrenched camp and had considerably extended his works. On the 6th of January Major-General George B. Crittenden assumed command and began to make himself conspicuous, as usual. In the force under General Buell was his brother, Brigadier-General Thomas L. Crittenden. Buell's force at that time numbered about 114,000 men, with seventeen batteries of artillery. The division commanders were Brigadier Generals George H. Thomas, Ormsby M. Mitchell, Thomas L. Crittenden and Alexander McDowell McCook. The bluster of the Confederate Crittenden speedily drew attention to him, and General Thomas' division was instructed to operate against his works. Assigning a portion of his command to General Schoepf, Thomas moved forward and on the 17th was at Logan's Cross Roads, ten miles from Beech Creek. In the meantime Crittenden had ordered Zollicoffer forward to prevent, if possible, the junction of Thomas and Schoepf, feeling satisfied that his defensive works were unable to resist a combined attack. On the evening of the 18th Zollicoffer's advance came upon the cavalry pickets of Thomas' column, and as arranged these retired, the Confederates following them up. On Sunday morning, the 19th of January, General Thomas, after a hasty reconnoisance, ordered the advance of the Tennessee brigade and made other dispositions for immediate battle. The firing opened about daybreak and for some hours the fortunes of the day were about evenly balanced, but in the contest for an important strategic position Zollicoffer was killed at the head of his column. This began to turn the tide, for Crittenden, who assumed Zollicoffer's position, was more capable of issuing buncombe proclamations than he was of giving battle orders. After another two hours of sharp fighting the bayonets of the Ninth Ohio turned the Confederate flank, and Crittenden made a hasty retreat toward Beech Grove. By nightfall the Federals were in possession of Moulden's Hill, which commanded the Confederate camp. During the night General Schoepf and other reinforcements came up. Before daybreak, however, the entire Confederate force had evacuated their intrenchments and crossing the river had scattered in all directions, leaving everything behind them as booty for the victorious Federals. Besides Zollicoffer, General Peyton was killed in this engagement. The total Confederate loss was 192 killed, 62 wounded and 89 taken prisoners. The Union loss was 39 killed and 203 wounded. The captures in the works included 8 cannon, 1,000 stand of arms, 1,700 horses and mules, a drove of cattle, 100 wagons, quartermasters' stores, camp equipage, intrenching tools.

A HAND-LITTER.

Crittenden made his way to Gainesborough in direct communication with Nashville, but the Confederate line in Kentucky was hopelessly broken and the rebuff was keenly felt. In the North the victory was justly appreciated, and a general order, by command of the President, complimented the troops on their brilliant achievement.

Perceiving the exigency of the situation General Beauregard was hastily ordered up from Manassas, for the Confederates evidently hoped, by keeping up vigorous action in this section, to prevent the tide of war rolling southward.

While these operations were in progress another expedition had been organized at Annapolis and Hampton Roads, the land forces at the former place being under command of General Ambrose Everett Burnside, and the naval armament at the latter point, consisting of thirty-one gunboats and a number of tugs, transports, etc., being under the orders of Flag Officer Louis M. Goldsborough, of the North Atlantic Naval Station. On the 11th of January the combined expedition put to sea, its destination being Pamlico Sound, though this was only known to those in command. On the night of the 12th, before Hatteras Inlet was reached, a severe storm was encountered, and Cape Hatteras scored another of its dreary records. Fortunately no lives were lost, but several of the transports, etc., with a large quantity of supplies, went down beneath the gale. The delay thus created enabled the Confederates to advance preparation of their defenses on Roanoake Island and on Roanoake and Croatan Sounds. These consisted of heavy batteries on Roanoke Island commanding the Sound, and similar works on the mainland commanding Croatan Sound. There was also an intrenched camp and a redoubt near the middle of the island. Obstructions had also been placed in the channels, and a flotilla of eight small gunboats, under Lieutenant W. F. Lynch. Colonel H. M. Shaw, in the absence of Brigadier-General Wise, commanded the Confederate land forces.

The Federal military force numbered about 11,500 men and was fully equiped with a heavy battery adapted for land and naval service. These were divided into three brigades. The effects of the storm prevented the concentration of the fleet until the beginning of February, but on the 5th Goldsborough felt justified in commencing operations. The fleet had been divided into two sections under Commanders Stephen C. Rowan and S. F. Hazard. On the 6th the leading division under Rowan was in Croatan Sound six miles below Roanoke. On the 7th at about 10 A. M. the advance commenced, and an hour later the bombardment of Fort Barton was begun. an attempt by Lynch's flotilla to participate was speedily checked and Fort Barton was soon after reduced to a heap of burning ruins. While this engagement between the fleet and the shore batteries was in progress, the transports came up with the land force. Attempts to prevent the landing at Ashby's Harbor were made by the Confederates but by midnight Generals John G. Foster, John G. Park and Jesse L. Reno had landed their respective brigades, amounting to about 11,000 men. It was a difficult task, as the shelving shore compelled the men to wade from the boats and the swampy marshes presented no cover. The men were, however, in splendid spirits, and in the early morning light Foster, closely followed by Reno and Park, with a howitzer battery of six guns, pushed on and drove in the enemy's pickets. A stubborn fight was made, but the constant coming up of reinforcements told heavily on the Confederates, who bravely held their ground until Major E. A. Kimball, of Hawkins' Zouaves, sought and obtained permission to charge on the works. The word had hardly been given when the whole battalion dashed forward with exultant shouts, their gleaming bayonets striking terror into the Confederate troops. Colonel Hawkins joined in the exciting dash, and the Zouaves swept all before them just as the Fifty-first New York and the Twenty-first Massachusetts stormed the Confederates out of their position on the right. The success was complete; the uninjured battery was left with only the dead and dying within the works. Foster and Reno, reforming their brigades, pressed after the fugitives. The former captured about 2,000 men of Colonel Shaw's command, and the latter about 800 of Colonel Jordan's men. No terms of capitulation would be listened to, and the bitter dose of unconditional surrender was the medicine of the flushed and exultant victors. General Foster then sent a force to occupy the ruins of Fort Barton, and before sunset the Stars and Stripes floating over the fort proclaimed the completeness of the victory. Colonel Hawkins had meantime intercepted some Confederate fugitives, about 200 in number, headed by Captain O. J. Wise, son of the Brigadier-General. In all the Confederate prisoners were between two and three thousand. **Despite** the sharp fighting the actual casualties had been small on the Confederate side, their loss being 5 killed and 18 wounded. The Union loss was 212 wounded and 50 killed, among the latter being Lieutenant-Colonel Monteuil, shot through the head during the gallant charge of Hawkins' Zouaves, and Colonel Charles S. Russell. By the victory 40 guns, 3,000 small arms, a quantity of ammunition and other stores fell into Federal hands, there having been no time to spike guns or destroy property when the Zouave bayonets came bristling over the works.

Captain Rowan overtook Lynch's flotilla on the Pasquotank River, where Lynch had taken refuge beneath the guns of a shore battery below Elizabeth River. Rowan made a simultaneous attack on flotilla and battery; the former was speedily silenced, and the vessels were run aground and burned.

Rowan first took possession of Edenton, near the western end of Albemarle Sound, then sunk obstructions in the Chesapeake and Albemarle Canal, and finally destroyed Plymouth on the Roanoke, and partly demolished Winton on the Chowan River. The approach of the Federal troops was everywhere the signal for precipitate retreat on the part of the armed Confederates, while the less partisan citizens were anxious to do all in their power to terminate hostilities.

A conciliatory proclamation issued by the Federal commanders was met by an inflammatory appeal by Governor Clark, but the moral and material effect of the recent victories had greater weight than all the incendiary literature that the desperate Confederate leaders could circulate.

CHAPTER XVIII.

IMPORTANT MOVEMENTS ON THE CUMBERLAND AND TENNESSEE RIVERS—FOOTE'S FLOTILLA—CAPTURE OF FORTS HENRY AND DONELSON—EVACUATION OF COLUMBUS—THE "GIBRALTAR OF THE WEST"—GENERAL GRANT'S BRILLIANT ACHIEVEMENTS—COWARDICE OF FLOYD AND PILLOW—THE NEW FORTIFICATIONS ON THE MISSISSIPPI—NEW MADRID AND ISLAND NUMBER TEN.

The next important movements of combined military and naval forces were those of General U. S. Grant and Commodore Andrew H. Foote, against Fort Henry on the Tennessee River, and Fort Donelson on the Cumberland River. General Halleck,

FOOTE'S FLOTILLA.

commanding the Department of the Missouri, found it expedient to subdivide the enormous range of territory included in it, and toward the close of 1861 had extended the division assigned to General Grant until it covered all Southern Illinois, Kentucky west of the Cumberland River, and that portion of Eastern Missouri south of Cape Girardeau. For several months there had been in preparation at St. Louis and Cairo some novel armored craft, composed of adapted river steamers and newly built vessels designed for river service, with the special views of attack on shore batteries and resistance of shot and shell from the forts attacked. By the beginning of February, Commodore Foote, United States Navy, had at his disposal twelve of these formidable vessels, of such light draft, despite their heavy armor, that they were capable of being operated in the comparatively shallow waters of the Tennessee and Cumberland rivers. "Foote's Flotilla," as it came to be called, was a decided novelty in marine construction. Of great breadth of beam, to insure steadiness when cannonading, seven of these floating batteries had iron plates sloping upward and downward at angles of forty-five degrees, and they were of triple strength at the bows. The design was to prevent any direct impact of shot or shell, by causing projectiles to glance either upward or into the water. The intent was, further, to keep them "stem on" when attacking, so as to offer the least possible target for an enemy. These twelve vessels carried 126 guns in all, of calibres ranging from 32-pounders to rifled 84-pounders. A thirteen-inch calibre mortar was also a part of the armament of each.

After reconnoisances to feel the strength of the enemy on the Tennessee and Cumberland rivers, General Grant obtained permission from Halleck to carry out the expeditions planned by him in conjunction with Foote. On the 2d of February, Foote, with four armored and three other vessels of his flotilla, moved from Cairo to the Tennessee River, and at daybreak on the 3d was a short distance below Fort Henry. The land forces, in transports, under convoy of the gunboats, consisting of McClernand's and Smith's divisions, debarked a few miles below the fort, and while some of the flotilla were seeking for torpedo obstructions, others were shelling the woods to ascertain the enemy's outlying defenses.

About noon on the 6th the gunboats opened on Fort Henry, the intervening days having been occupied in disposing the land forces so as to sever communication between Forts Henry and Donelson. The fort vigorously returned the fire at the beginning of the assault, but the attack was so determined and the fire so well directed that in about an hour General Tilghman ran up a white flag and surrendered. It would have been useless to offer further resistance, for, although the land forces of the Federals had not arrived, the Confederates outside the fort had beat a hasty retreat towards Fort Donelson, most of the gunners in the fort were wounded and nearly all the guns dismounted. General Tilghman and forty of his men were taken prisoners, but the others managed to elude the land troops and escape the observation of the gunboats as they fled along the upper road. In the mean time Smith's division had taken, without resistance, Fort Hieman, an unfinished work upon the hill overlooking Fort Henry.

The loss of this important position was a great blow to the Confederates, and led to much wrangling among the leaders. In the North the victory which restored the flag of the Union to a distinguished position on the soil of Tennessee was hailed as a prestige of future success.

General Grant now determined to attack Fort Donelson and dispatched Lieutenant-Commander Phelps on a reconnoisance with a part of the flotilla up the Tennessee River, while Foote returned to Cairo to prepare mortar boats for the new expedition. Phelps made a successful run as far as Florence, Alabama, seizing and destroying Confederate property along the route. On his return his report made it clear that not only could the capture of the fort be accomplished, but that there was a widespread Union sentiment among the non-combatant citizens.

Fort Donelson was built on a high river bank, about a mile below Dover, in Stewart County, Tennessee. Two powerful shore batteries at the foot of the hill were so arranged that their guns commanded the turn of the river just below. Fieldworks, intrenchments and rifle pits guarded the rear of the fort, and a small creek lent additional protection. Some twenty thousand men had been massed here by orders of General Johnston, who knew its importance with reference to the safety of Nashville and Bowling Green. General Gideon J. Pillow had been placed in command of Fort Donelson, but was superseded a few days later by General John B. Floyd, and and General Simon B. Buckner had also been sent from Bowling Green with some sixteen thousand men of Johnston's division as reinforcements, till, as we have stated, the combined

Confederate force at this point was about twenty thousand men.

Meanwhile General Grant had completed his plans and sent forward Generals McClernand and Smith, with fifteen thousand men and an advance cavalry force. While these divisions were marching across the country to the rear of the fort, the flotilla under Foote was coming along the Cumberland River, together with the transports bearing the troops to form the third division. On the morning of February 13th the First Division, under Colonels Oglesby and Wallace, drove in the Confederate pickets and assumed the positions assigned them, viz.: McClernand's division on the right and Smith's division on the left. The Confederate land batteries were speedily at work, and during the early part of the day a desultory engagement was kept up, but no general attack was made, as Grant, who had taken up his headquarters near the head of Hickman's Creek, determined to await the arrival of the gunboats and Wallace's Third Division. Towards mid-day McClernand ordered a dash on the middle redoubt, separating the Confederate right wing from the centre. The Seventeenth, Forty-eighth and Forty-ninth Illinois went at the works with vigor, but, failing to envelop them, the Forty-fifth Illinois went to their support on the right. The attack, however, failed, and the Federals fell back with considerable loss. The night which followed was a bitter trial, for the temperature fell to within ten degrees of zero and a severe sleet and snow storm prevailed. By noon on the 14th the garrison from Fort Henry, which had been sent for by Grant, arrived and the gunboats and transports also came up. General Wallace was placed in command of the Third Division, which had debarked three miles below the fort, and then General Grant completed his investment of the entire works from the land side. A few hours later the flotilla under Foote began the attack, but the heavy shore batteries played sad havoc with it. After enduring the iron hail for over an hour Foote was obliged to retire, with the loss of fifty-four killed and wounded and several of the vessels seriously damaged. Foote at once returned to Cairo to repair damages and superintend the completion of the mortar

SORTIE OF THE GARRISON.

boats* which he had previously put under way. During his absence General Grant made arrangements to shut off all communication, and thus starve out the Confederates. This was quickly appreciated by the besieged, and a grand sortie was decided on as the only hope of deliverance, before the gunboats should return to the attack. This scheme was put in operation at 5 o'clock on the morning of the 15th, some ten thousand men under Generals Pillow and Bushrod R. Johnston making an impetuous attack on the right (McClernand's Division). So sudden and furious was the attack that Oglesby's Brigade on the extreme right at length gave way, except the Thirty-first Illinois, under Colonel John A. Logan. This, forming the extreme left of the First Division, maintained its position, but the constant pouring forward of fresh Confederate troops soon placed the whole of the line in peril. McClernand called on General Wallace, of the Third Division, for assistance, but the absence of General Grant caused delay. A more imperative demand from McClernand induced Wallace to assume the responsibility

A MORTAR BOAT.

---

* These mortar boats were a special outgrowth of the inventive spirit of the period. On a broad, flat, barge-like float sloping walls of heavy timber, forming a six-sided inclosure, were built. These were iron-plated. The slope was inward, at an angle of about 45 degrees, thus preventing direct impact of the enemy's shot. One heavy mortar, a magazine below water-line and shelter tents comprised the entire equipment of these peculiar but effective naval nondescripts.. The annexed engraving gives a clear idea of their construction.

of ordering the brigade of Colonel Cruft to support the right, and this changed the programme on this wing. At this time, in accordance with the Confederate scheme, General Buckner fell heavily on the left centre, and for a few moments it seemed as if absolute confusion must result. General Wallace saw the peril of the position, and he threw his brigade between the retiring Federals and the advancing foe; rapidly formed a new line of battle with the Chicago Artillery in the centre, supported by the First Nebraska, Fifty-eighth and Thirty-second Illinois and Fifty-eighth Ohio. He also ordered up ammunition, McClernand's troops having exhausted theirs. A reserve force of the Forty-sixth and Fifty-seventh Illinois was held in readiness. This disposition had hardly been completed when the Confederates under Buckner and Pillow dashed furiously upon the centre. The charge was nobly met and the Confederates, after a brief struggle, fell back in considerable confusion to their trenches about noon. Later in the afternoon, while Grant was hesitating about following up this success, a chance remark in reference to the possibility of a Confederate escape to Clarksville, over the ground which McClernand had yielded, suggested a further plan of action. This was to retake McClernand's old position and at the same time attack the Confederate right. Both these operations were successfully carried out, and by nightfall the Confederates had been driven from their intrenchments, over which the Stars and Stripes were speedily floating.

The Confederate commanders, finding that all hope, even of escape, was gone, held a hasty council and decided to capitulate. Floyd and Pillow, terror stricken, resigned their commands to Buckner, who placed himself in communication with Grant. In the meantime, during the night Floyd and Pillow ignominiously escaped, leaving the troops to their fate. On Sunday morning, February 16, a white flag floated over the fort, and Grant, finding that Wallace had full possession of Dover, refused to make any terms with Buckner, but demanded "unconditional and immediate surrender." There was no help for it, and Buckner, deserted by his cowardly companions in arms, was compelled to yield. About fourteen thousand prisoners, a large number of cannon, muskets, horses and military stores were thus surrendered to the victorious Federals. The loss of the Union troops was 321 killed, 1,046 wounded and 150 missing. The Confederate loss in killed and wounded was about the same.

The moral and material effect of this crushing defeat was terrible on the Confederate troops, and the indignation of the leaders at Richmond was unbounded. Davis ordered that Floyd and Pillow should be relieved of their commands at once, pending investigation, and all the efforts of Johnston to obtain a mitigation of this censure were unavailing.

In the North, the victory at Fort Donelson was rapturously received, and in army circles, its full importance being thoroughly appreciated, plans were at once laid for pressing on to reap its fruits.

General Mitchell, of Buell's command, moved upon Bowling Green, from his camp at Bacon's Creek, near Mumfordsville, but although he made a forced march of 32 hours, it was not quick enough to come up with Johnston, who had precipitately fled southward, with some seven thousand of his men, after destroying all that he could in Bowling Green. As a consequence, when Mitchell took possession of the position there was but a small amount of commissary stores and one gun left as spoils. The importance of this occupation, however, was enhanced by the panic at Nashville. Governor Harris and his Legislature fled from that city to Memphis, after gathering up all the state papers they could find, and a general exodus of the disloyal citizens was inaugurated.

On Sunday evening, February 23, Colonel Kenner, of the Fourth Ohio Cavalry, Mitchell's Division, entered Nashville and calmed the apprehensions of the citizens. On the 25th, General Buell reached the camp at Edgefield, opposite Nashville, where his advance had pitched tents, and there, on the following morning, Mayor R. B. Cheatham, and a delegation of Nashville citizens, formally tendered the submission of the city. Meantime, Commodore Foote had sent the *St. Louis* up the Cumberland River, and destroyed the Bessemer Iron Works, which had been actively employed in the Confederate service.

On the 19th, Foote, with the gunboats *Cairo* and *Conestoga*, went up the river to Clarkesville to attack a partly-completed fort at the mouth of the Red River. Here, again, all was panic. The garrison fled, burning the railway bridge behind them. The fort was taken possession of by Colonel Webster, Grant's Chief of Staff, and Foote went on to the city. Finding none but loyal and terrified citizens there, he issued a pacific proclamation, but warned the citizens against any display of Secession symbols. General Smith, with the advance of Grant's army, then came up and took command, while Foote returned to Cairo. Tennessee being now relieved from the incubus of the rebel Governor Harris, it was decided to appoint a military governor and put the State under martial law. In pursuance of this purpose, Andrew Johnson, then a loyal United States Senator from that State, was so appointed, with the rank of Brigadier-General, on March 4.

In the meantime General Polk had been preparing for the evacuation of Columbus, known as the "Gibraltar of the West," it being evident that the position was no longer tenable. Accordingly, under instructions from Beauregard, the sick and wounded were removed from the city toward the close of February, and on the 2d of March, after firing the military buildings, from which the stores had been removed to Jackson, Tennessee, Polk and his staff quitted the post. The troops had been previously sent off, some by steamer to New Madrid and others by land to Union City, Tennessee. Unaware of this evacuation, Foote, with a flotilla of six gunboats, four mortar-boats and three transports, the latter conveying about 2,000 troops under Brigadier-General W. T. Sherman, moved from Cairo early on the morning on the 4th of March. On reaching Columbus the Union flag was seen floating over the Confederate works. Deeming this to be a trick, preparations were made for immediate attack. A loyalist on shore declared that the troops had fled, but still caution was necessary, for the "Union flag trick" had been too frequently played by the wily Confederates. Colonel Buford and some of the Twenty-seventh Illinois were landed, and then it was found that a scouting party of the Second Illinois Cavalry, sent out the previous night from Sherman's command at Paducah, had found the works evacuated and had hoisted the Stars and Stripes. Thus, on the evening of the 4th of March, General Halleck was enabled to telegraph to General McClellan that Columbus had been occupied and Kentucky was free. The evacuation had been hasty and a large quantity of stores had been left behind, but a train had been laid for the explosion of the magazine. This was fortunately discovered and the disaster prevented.

By Beauregard's orders Polk had selected a defensive position below Columbus, and had thrown up works on the mainland in Madrid Bend and New Madrid, and had strongly fortified "Island Number Ten," 40 miles below Columbus in the Mississippi. New Madrid, 10 miles below this, had strong military works, including Fort Thompson. There was also a flotilla of six gunboats, and as the position was at a sharp bend of the river, it was considered the key of the lower Mississippi. Leaving Polk at this point we will turn to events in other directions.

CHAPTER XIX.

INACTION OF THE ARMY OF THE POTOMAC—LINCOLN'S ANNOYANCE—M'CLELLAN'S OBSTINACY—A GENERAL MOVEMENT ORDERED—ADVANCE OF M'CLELLAN ON YORKTOWN—SIEGE OPERATIONS BEGUN—THE MERRIMACK, OR VIRGINIA, AND THE MONITOR—THE UNIQUE NAVAL COMBAT IN HAMPTON ROADS.

While these vigorous movements were in progress in Tennessee and Kentucky, the Army of the Potomac, though recruited up to a high standard, had remained inactive. Edwin M. Stanton had succeeded Simon Cameron as Secretary of War on January 13th, but still the mysterious McClellan neither moved nor gave his reasons. In vain the President urged some action, not alone from his own convictions of the necessity for it, but partly in deference to the mutterings of the people. The General-in-Chief was neither to be coaxed nor bullied; he very plainly intimated that the less civilians had to do with the military dispositions the better. In fact, the conduct of McClellan about this time appeared to indicate that he considered civility and civilians alike repugnant to army discipline. President Lincoln, however, was determined that something must be done, and he called Generals McDowell and Franklin to his aid, intimating that if McClellan would not use the army, somebody else should borrow and employ it. After several conferences during which an immediate advance upon Manassas was recommended, a meeting was arranged between the President, the Cabinet, the General-in-Chief, Generals McDowell and Franklin, with the intention of reaching some decision. Instead of sharing in the discussion, McClellan sulked, and still refused to give direct answers to the various questions put to him. This meeting was on the 13th of January. At length McClellan reluctantly blurted out that movements in Kentucky must precede any others. While this appeared unsatisfactory then, the events of the next few months, as we have shown in the preceding chapter, fully justified McClellan's anticipations in that quarter. The President, however, insisted on some disclosure of the plans for the employment of the Army of the Potomac. As a matter of course this demand had to be met, and McClellan shortly afterward submitted a plan for moving upon Richmond by way of the lower Chesapeake. This involved greater delay than accorded with the President's views, and with his customary decision, when the breaking point of his patience had been reached, he took the bull by the horns as Commander-in-Chief of the Army and Navy of the United States, and issued "General War Order No. 1," on the 27th of January, in which he ordered a general movement of the land and naval forces of the United States against the insurgents, to begin on February 22d. In order that there might be no mistake about the position he had taken up, he intimated that the Secretaries of War and the Navy, the General-in-Chief and all subordinates would be held to a strict accountability for prompt obedience. On the 31st of January the President issued a special order to McClellan, instructing him to form the Army of the Potomac, after providing for the defense of Washington, into an expedition to seize and occupy a point on the railroad southwest of Manassas Junction. McClellan remonstrated, and finally President Lincoln, though very unwilling to yield a point, consented to refer his own and General McClellan's plans to a council of twelve officers. This council, composed of Generals Fitz John Porter, Franklin, W. F. Smith, McCall, Blenker, Andrew Porter, Naglee, Keyes, McDowell, Sumner, Heintzelman and Barnard, met at headquarters on the 27th of February, and after careful consideration, the eight first-named Generals approved McClellan's plan, the minority of four holding to the President's views. As usual the President yielded to the question of ballots, even where bullets were concerned, for he was ever as consistent as he was stubborn. The War Department at once issued orders for transports, and on the 8th of March the President, in General Order No. 2, directed the division of the Army of the Potomac into four corps, under Generals Keyes, Sumner, Heintzelman and McDowell respectively. It is not a little significant that these were the four generals who voted against McClellan's plans and in favor of Lincoln's, but, of course, the President *may* have been swayed by other and quite different considerations. That he still doubted the wisdom of McClellan's views was shown by another order, in which it was provided that not more than 50,000 troops should be moved on the proposed expedition until the Potomac should be cleared of obstructions, and further that a competent force should be left to guard Washington. He also directed, peremptorily, that the new movement on Chesapeake Bay should begin not later than March 18th.

While these arrangements were being made by the Federal forces, the Confederates had not been idle. Johnston had for weeks been secretly removing his stores and munitions from Manassas and Centreville, and on the 9th of March his troops suddenly abandoned both of those positions and fell back slowly on Richmond. They did not quit the immediate locality for some days, but lingered around Warrenton Junction.

As soon as this retrograde movement came to the knowledge of McClellan, he ordered an advance of the entire army on the abandoned posts. The advance crossed the Potomac and occupied Centreville on the 10th, and General Stoneman, with a cavalry force, was sent to harry the retreat. The movement, however, was not followed up, and after a reconnoissance in force toward the Rappahannock, McClellan ordered the main body of the army back to Alexandria. Stoneman's cavalry also retired, and the Confederates, after a halt at the Rappahannock, encamped beyond the Rapidan.

The futility of this movement convinced the President that McClellan had quite as much as he could manage in directing the field movements. He therefore issued an order on the 11th of March, relieving McClellan of all the military departments except the Department of the Potomac. Halleck was assigned to the command in the Valley of the Mississippi, and Fremont was given command of the "Mountain Department" (a new creation), comprising the region between the Mississippi and the Potomac; the order further directed all reports to be made directly to Secretary of War Stanton.

General McClellan now decided that his plans must be modified, and called a council of war at Fairfax Court House. Here it was decided to go down the Chesapeake, debark at Fortress

Monroe, and from thence press on to Richmond. The President approved this, on condition that Washington was properly protected and Manassas Junction held by a competent force.

Preparations for the new movement were pushed on, and troops were rapidly forwarded to Fortress Monroe. McClellan left Washington on April 1st, and on reaching the Fortress found 58,000 men and 100 cannon already there.

In the meantime, General J. B. Magruder had been busy also; he had about 11,000 Confederate troops on the Virginia peninsula between the James and York rivers, and had strongly fortified his headquarters at Yorktown. The concentration at Fortress Monroe of McClellan's troops compelled Magruder to change his tactics somewhat. He placed garrisons at Yorktown, at Gloucester Point and on Mulberry Island, on the James River, and distributed his remaining force, about five thousand men, along a line of thirteen miles of earthworks.

McClellan, estimating the opposing force at far greater numbers, moved forward very cautiously, but he was impressed with the necessity for an attack on Magruder before Johnston could reinforce him. He divided his command into two columns; one led by General Heintzelman, on the right, moved along the old Yorktown road; this comprised the divisions of Generals Fitz John Porter and Hamilton, of the Third Corps, and Sedgwick's divison of the Second Corps. The other column, led by General Keyes, consisted of the divisions of Generals Couch and W. F. Smith, of the Fourth Corps. The advance was begun on April 3d, and on the following day the right column was at Big Bethel, McClellan being with this column. At the same time the left column reached Warwick Court House. On the afternoon of April 5th each column had reached Magruder's fortified lines, the right being near Yorktown, on the York River, and the left being at Winn's Mill, on the Warwick River. Further advance being checked, McClellan began a regular siege, the intrenching works being placed in charge of General Fitz John Porter. This work engaged the army, which was constantly being augmented, for one entire month. Here we will leave them for the present, and note the movements of the other divisions of the Army of the Potomac and the memorable engagement between the *Mer-*

rimack and the *Monitor*, which was one of the events which led to McClellan's change of plans.

In describing the destruction of the vessels in the Gosport Navy Yard in April, 1861, by Captain Paulding, we mentioned that the *Merrimack* had been burned to her copper line and sunk, and that she had been subsequently raised when the rebels got possession of the place. In the early part of 1862 Captain Marston, commanding the United States squadron in Hampton Roads, became acquainted with the fact that this vessel had been reconstructed into some kind of a marine monster, and that the Confederates were chuckling over a projected expedition against Newport News, in which this novel craft was to play a prominent part. About the beginning of March it was learned that preparations were complete, and on the 8th of March the *Virginia*, as the Confederates called her, hove in sight of the squadron from the Elizabeth River. The destructive genius of John M. Brooke, ex-lieutenant United States Navy, had utilized old iron rails and heavy oak timbers. These formed a sort of conical roof, rising almost directly from the water line, and presenting the appearance of a submarine house. The timbers were twenty-eight inches thick, and outside this came six inches of iron rails, bars and plates. A ram of oak and iron, thirty-three feet long, projected from a heavy false bow. Her armament consisted of stem and stern guns capable of throwing one-hundred-pound solid shot, and four rifled cannon, eighty-pounders, projected from each side, half-way up the sloping roof. Below water line were two powerful engines, and the furnaces were also arranged for the production of red-hot shot; another apparatus was designed for the discharge of huge streams of boiling water. A more utterly demoniac, uncouth, ruthless floating battery had never been created. The Federal vessels nearest the approaching monster were the sloop *Cumberland* and the frigate *Congress*. These were lying off Newport News, at the mouth of the James River. With grim determination the *Virginia* went straight at the *Cumberland*, taking no more heed of the iron hail which Lieutenant George M. Morris poured upon his assailant than if it had been ocean spray. One blow of that formidable ram opened a gap in the side of the *Cumberland* and let in an avalanche of water; simultaneously her heavy guns poured in their fire at close quarters. Lieutenant Morris fought his ship with desperate pluck, but she was filling fast, and was evidently about to sink. Morris told his men to leap overboard, and, with a parting shot, took to the billows. The *Cumberland* went down in fifty-four feet of water, with the dead and wounded and several of the crew who were entangled in the wreck. Of 376 men on board, 140 were missing. A couple of gunboats which accompanied the *Virginia* had in the meantime attacked the *Congress*. Lieutenant Joseph B. Smith handled his assailants vigorously until the fate of the *Cumberland* warned him to seek shelter, and he ran his ship aground under the guns of Newport News. The *Virginia* now began to pay attention to the *Congress*, and soon set her on fire, and Lieutenant Pendergast, who had taken command after Smith was wounded, hoisted a white flag and surrendered. In the meantime the steam frigate *Minnesota* had come up, the *Roanoke* (flagship) being at Fortress Monroe with disabled machinery. The *Minnesota* ran aground, and while in this condition Captain Van Brunt gallantly met the attack of the *Virginia* and the two gunboats, damaging the latter so seriously that they hauled off for Norfolk. During the night the *Virginia* returned, and with red-hot shot set fire to the stranded *Congress*. The work of destruction was completed when her magazine exploded. Over two hundred of her crew were killed or missing.

But inventive genius had been at work for the Federals also, for about the time the *Merrimack* had been converted into the *Virginia*, Captain John Ericsson had produced the *Monitor* at Greenpoint, Long Island. This remarkable production consisted of a flat-bottom float, 124 feet long and 34 feet wide on the water surface, with a superstructure projecting about three and a half feet at the sides and twenty feet at each end beyond the actual hull; this upper shell was five feet high, while the depth in the water of the floating portion was six and a half feet. In the centre was a round, revolving turret twenty feet in diameter and ten feet high. The hull was pointed at each end, and the projecting upper works not only covered the propelling and steering gear, but rendered perforation below the water line almost impossible. Built of three-inch iron, it floated like a cork. The upper portion was constructed of oak, thirty inches thick, covered by six-inch iron armor. The turret, made of eight thicknesses of one-inch iron plate, was connected, for revolving purposes, with the propelling engine. It contained two heavy guns moving on slides, so as to run out to the port holes. The upper deck was bombproof, as was also the turret roof, through which was the only entrance, by a sliding hatch. The smokestack, by a telescope arrangement, could be lowered out of

ENGAGEMENT BETWEEN THE MONITOR AND MERRIMACK.

harm's way when necessary. Vague reports of the strange craft had been circulated, and its coming was eagerly looked for in Hampton Roads, where the *Virginia* had spread terror on every side. About midnight on Saturday it came in sight, towed by the *Seth Low*. By two o'clock on Sunday morning its commander, Lieutenant John L. Worden, United States Navy, was in conference with Captain Van Brunt, of the *Minnesota*, now helplessly aground. As had been expected, it was hardly daylight when the formidable *Virginia* and her satellite gunboats returned to the attack on the *Minnesota*; but circumstances alter cases very frequently, and in this case the potent giant of the previous day found a pigmy monster prepared to change the record. The *Monitor* ran alongside the *Virginia*, and from her revolving tower poured a stream of heavy shot, which was answered by the terrible broadsides of the Confederate craft. Almost muzzle to muzzle the heavy guns were worked without any apparent effect. Then, like gladiators taking breath, the monsters separated, while, to continue the simile, each was looking for an advantage in the next grip. It mattered not in what position the *Monitor* was, her two guns were steadily pointing at and pounding the *Virginia*, which of course, on the other hand, was frequently unable to deliver a broadside. At length Captain Buchanan became convinced that he was losing time and wasting ammunition on the tormenting puzzle, so he again returned to the attack on the *Minnesota*. The broadsides of Van Brunt fell harmless, but the *Virginia's* terrible shells went entirely through the *Minnesota* and set her on fire. This unequal contest did not last long, for the vigorous little *Monitor* slid in between the *Virginia* and *Minnesota*, and in turning to escape this attack the *Virginia* grounded. Before she could get off again the *Minnesota* had poured in a heavy broadside, probably with some effect, for the *Virginia*, getting afloat, made off for Norfolk, with the *Monitor* in hot pursuit. This continued attention irritated Buchanan, and turning about, he dashed at the *Monitor* with his powerful ram. He had met more than his match, however, for his prow slid over the *Monitor's* roof, and while in that position the turret guns sent a shot through the *Virginia's* armor. A savage broadside answered this, and then another brief but violent combat ensued. The *Virginia* by this time had got enough for this round; her ram was twisted, several of her steam and smoke pipes were shot through, her commander was severely, if not mortally wounded, and six of her crew had been killed. She made off for Norfolk with her attendant gunboats, in one of which six men had been killed. The *Monitor* did not follow her, but went on to Fortress Monroe, Lieutenant Worden having been injured by some splinters which for a time blinded him. This was the only injury of any account sustained on board the *Monitor*. Although the Federal loss during the two days was heavy—some four hundred men being killed, drowned or severely wounded—the frigates *Congress* and *Cumberland* and the tug *Dragon* sunk or destroyed, and the *Minnesota* badly damaged, yet it was felt that further peril at this point was averted. The *Minnesota* was floated early on Monday morning, and the dreaded *Virginia* (or *Merrimack*, as the Federals continued to call her) had been taught a lesson which was likely to inspire caution in the future. There was now hope, at least, that the James River might be freed from Confederate control, and in official circles this was felt to be all important. It was this conviction that brought about the change in McClellan's plans, which we have already noted.

In official circles and among the general public, the gallantry of Worden and the genius of Ericsson were the themes of the hour this side the Atlantic, while all Europe was wondering what manner of men were these who could, on either side of the great controversy, rise to the needs of the hour with heroic sublimity and boundless fertility of expedient.

Even to-day the words "*Monitor* and *Merrimack*" awake lurid memories all over the civilized world.

CHAPTER XX.

THE CONFEDERATES ABANDON NEW MADRID—SIEGE AND CAPTURE OF ISLAND NUMBER TEN—THE WONDERFUL CANAL CONSTRUCTION—GRANT MOVES ON CORINTH—THE TWO DAYS' BATTLE OF SHILOH, OR PITTSBURG LANDING—THE CONFEDERATES FINALLY DRIVEN BACK ON CORINTH—SIEGE OF CORINTH—BEAUREGARD'S FLIGHT—OCCUPATION OF CORINTH BY THE FEDERALS.

We have shown that when Columbus was abandoned by the Confederates, a position had been chosen at Madrid Bend, below, and strongly fortified. General Halleck had long been meditating a blow at New Madrid, and when that position and Island Number Ten were made rallying points, his attention was concentrated on the work of dislodging the enemy from both of these important posts. General Pope was charged with this work about the end of February, and he pushed on from St. Louis, encountering M. Jeff. Thompson, whom he put to flight. Pressing onward over a heavy route, his main column reached the outskirts of New Madrid on the 8th of March, but the post had been so materially strengthened that additional siege guns were necessary. While awaiting the arrival of these from Cairo, he sent Colonel J. B. Plummer to plant a battery at Point Pleasant, ten miles below, so as to check the throwing in of supplies to Island Number Ten. Then on the 13th, having received his siege train, he opened fire on Fort Thompson and on Hollins' flotilla. The enemy replied with considerable spirit, but the Federal batteries were steadily pushed forward throughout the day, and at the same time General Paine was vigorously attacking the Confederate right. During the night Generals McCown, Stuart and Gantt, the Confederate commanders in New Madrid, concluded that the position was no longer tenable, and they fled to Island Number Ten. The next morning the place was found to be abandoned, and Major-General Schuyler Hamilton sent Captain Mower to take possession. On the 15th, Commodore Foote with a powerful flotilla arrived, and after reconnoitering Island Number Ten, decided to begin the attack next morning. At daybreak the cannonade began, and a battery which had been landed on the Missouri shore also did good work in attacking Hollins' flotilla. The works, however, had been well planned, and were heavily equipped, and they withstood the siege for the best part of a month. In the meantime **Pope** was at New Madrid, unable to do more than command the river. He desired to attack

CONSTRUCTING THE CANAL.

the island in the rear, but was unable to cross the river in the face of the heavy batteries, and Foote could not be induced to run the gauntlet for the purpose of affording his troops transportation. At this juncture General Hamilton submitted a plan for the construction of a canal, from a bend of the Mississippi near Island Number Eight, through the swamp and lake, across the peninsula, so as to afford a passageway for gunboats, transports, etc., thus to flank Island Number Ten. It should be noted that the islands on the Mississippi, from the mouth of the Ohio River downward, are numbered in rotation. Hamilton's plan involved a stupendous undertaking, the intended channel being twelve miles in length through swamps, dense vegetation, tree stumps, some of these being six feet in girth, and masses of driftwood and fallen timber. Pope eagerly embraced the proposal, but after some conference it was arranged to modify the plans so as to provide for the passage of transports and barges only. The work was intrusted to Colonel Bissell, and in nineteen days this herculean engineering feat was accomplished. The giant stumps were sawed off four feet below the surface, while men on rafts and flats pushed aside the driftwood and fallen timber. Some light draft steamers and barges hauled out the débris. This work completed, some floating batteries, barges and four steamers were brought through the canal on the 5th of April, and concealed in a bayou near New Madrid. The Confederates had been apprised of this work, but doubted the truth of the report. Foote, meantime, had not been idle, for on the night of April 1, five boats with picked crews from his flotilla, and forty men under Colonel Roberts of the Forty-second Illinois, had stormed Rucker's battery, one of the seven on the Kentucky shore, and spiked all the guns. Two nights afterward the *Carondelet* ran by the Confederate forts and reached New Madrid, the expedition having been planned by Captain Walke, who wrung a reluctant consent from Foote to go in response to Pope's repeated request. The next day Foote made such a vigorous attack on a huge floating battery that the Confederates were obliged to abandon it, and it floated down stream. It was now time for a decided blow, and on the morning of the 6th the *Carondelet* reconnoitered and found batteries on the Kentucky and Tennessee shores for about fifteen miles. After destroying one of these near Point Pleasant, the *Carondelet* returned. At night another of Foote's boats, the *Pittsburg*, ran past the Confederate works, and next morning Captain Walke silenced the batteries at Watson's Landing, below Tiptonville. The coast was now clear for the use of the transports, etc., brought through the improvised canal, and at noon the troops began to cross the river. The Confederates on Island Number Ten, convinced, when too late, of the success of the flanking movement, at once abandoned all hope of holding their position. Quitting the island in hot haste, they sunk their transports and other vessels in the stream to impede navigation, and started for Union City. Beauregard had left the island on the 4th with a large body of troops, turning over the command of the position to Generals McCall and McCown. While Foote was receiving the surrender of the island, General Pope had sent on troops to intercept the fugitives. This movement was also successful, and, driven into the swamps, the entire body of fugitives unconditionally surrendered. There was but a small force on the island, for McCall had followed Beauregard's example, and made his way to the Tennessee shore. The entire number of prisoners, however, was 7,273, including three generals and 273 officers. About seven thousand small arms, 123 cannon, a large quantity of ammunition, wagons, stores, etc., and four steamers, were also captured. This crushing defeat was keenly felt by the Confederates everywhere, while the glorious Federal victory not only spread joy throughout the North, but had a marked effect on the value of Government securities.

We must now turn to events of equal importance in other directions occurring about the same time, and then, after describing the battle of Shiloh, or Pittsburg Landing, as it is sometimes called, considerations of space will compel us to present in a condensed form, save in a few of the more important engagements, a running summary of the military movements up to the close of 1862.

We have seen that General Grant, after the fall of Fort Donelson, had been placed in command of the new District of West Tennessee, embracing the territory from Cairo, between the Mississippi and Cumberland rivers, to the northern borders of the State of Mississippi. General Grant had made his headquarters temporarily at Fort Henry, while preparing for the seizure of Corinth, Mississippi, at the intersection of the Charleston and Memphis and Mobile and Ohio railroads, when he was surprised by an order from General Halleck to turn over his command to General C. F. Smith. The real cause of this strange order was never made quite clear, but it is surmised to have been caused by a distorted report of the conference between Grant and Buell at Nashville in the latter part of February. Grant's indignant demand to be entirely relieved from duty, and the murmurs of the public, who had thus early begun to recognize Grant's splendid talents, brought about a reversal of the order, and after ten days' suspension General Grant was restored to chief command.

In the meantime General Smith, with about 30,000 troops, moved up the Tennessee on transports and landed at Savannah, the capital of Hardin County, Tennessee, on the 10th of March. General Lewis Wallace was sent on to Purdy, between Humboldt and Corinth, to destroy the bridges, it being known that Beauregard was endeavoring to concentrate at Corinth. Wallace accomplished his work and then remained at Crump's Landing to cover the river communications between Pittsburg Landing and Savannah. General Sherman started for Tyler's Landing, further up the river, but being hindered by floods, returned and took position near Shiloh Meeting-House, about two miles from the Tennessee River. This was a primitive log structure, belonging to Methodists, and giving its name to the country around. General Stephen A. Hurlbut took possession of Pittsburg Landing. Reserves were left at Nashville under command of General James S. Negley. On the 17th of March General Grant arrived at Savannah and made his headquarters a few miles below Pittsburg Landing. Before he arrived General Smith had posted the army with Snake Creek on its right and Lick Creek on its left. Thus matters remained until Sunday morning, April 6, at which time Sherman's division was behind Shiloh Meeting-House, Prentiss' division across the road to Corinth and McClernand's behind his right. Hurlbut's and Smith's divisions were in the rear near Pittsburg, and **Stuart's** brigade was on the Harrisburg road near Lick Creek,

SHILOH MEETING-HOUSE.

Behind the army was the Tennessee River, but no preparation had been made to guard against an attack in front.

The Confederates meanwhile had massed a force of some forty-five thousand men under Johnston and Beauregard, who had effected a junction on the 1st of April, and their line lay from Corinth south to Bethel and east to Iuka, on the two lines of railroad.

General Buell was advancing toward Savannah, and he had sent General Ormsby M. Mitchell toward Huntsville, Alabama. His successes in this direction we shall note later on.

The Confederate forces under Johnston and Beauregard were daily receiving reinforcements all this time, and were waiting the arrival of Van Dorn and Price from Arkansas, when they learned of Buell's approach. A hasty council was held on the night of April 5, and it was resolved to make an attack next morning. Accordingly, before dawn the Confederates moved forward in three divisions, commanded respectively by Generals Hardee, Bragg and Polk, with Breckinridge bringing up the rear with the reserves. So secretly had this movement been arranged that the Union forces had not the slightest premonition of danger, when Hardee's division fell on Sherman's left and then struck Prentiss' division, dashing into the camp on the heels of a murderous hail of shells and bullets. Wholly unprepared, the Union troops were but partly dressed and many were cooking breakfast. The confusion was fearful. Hildebrand's Brigade, of Sherman's Division, was driven from its camp, and only the heroic exertions of General Sherman prevented those of Buckland and McDowell from the same instantaneous rout. McClernand came to the support of Sherman's division, and for a time stemmed the tide of battle; but this did not last long, and Sherman was compelled to fall back under the pressure of Bragg's advance. Meanwhile, Polk's division was pushing for Sherman's rear, to cut off his communications. This was prevented, and then the whole Confederate force fell upon Prentiss' division. A gallant struggle was made, but, overpowered by numbers, the line was broken up, and later in the day Prentiss and about two thousand of his troops were taken prisoners and sent to Corinth. McClernand had brought up his whole division and stubbornly contested his position till Sherman's retrograde movement exposed his right flank, which the Confederates at once assailed with terrible fury. McClernand was forced back to a line with Hurlbut. The Confederate reserves—infantry and cavalry—meantime had fallen on Stuart's brigade on the extreme left, and after severe fighting forced that back also. By noon the Confederates held the camps of Sherman, McClernand, Prentiss and Stuart, and occupied the whole line from which the Federal forces had been driven.

General Grant reached the field about eight o'clock in the morning, having been at his headquarters, eight miles away, when the conflict began. He joined Sherman in reforming the shattered brigades. Generals Hurlbut and W. H. L. Wallace bore the brunt of the battle after the other divisions had fallen back, and prevented the rush of the Confederates through the centre. About four o'clock, however, General Wallace fell, mortally wounded, and was borne from the field on a hand litter. The combined Confederate force now pressed on Hurlbut and he was forced further back toward the river. All this time General Lewis Wallace had been anxiously looked for, but a blundering messenger sent by General Grant had led Wallace into error and he had been marching and countermarching over a route of about sixteen miles, so that it was not until after nightfall that he came up.

Under the direction of Colonel Webster, Grant's chief of staff, earthworks were thrown up during a lull in the battle about sunset, and preparations were made to hold the Confederates in check till Buell could come up. It was known that his advance was at Savannah. Hardly had the twenty-two heavy guns been placed in position when the Confederates made another attack, expecting to drive the Union army into the river. This attack, however, was repulsed, and soon afterward the gunboats *Tyler* and *Lexington* came up and began shelling the Confederates. Before midnight the fighting ceased, the Confederates feeling confident that they could finish their work at daybreak, while Grant felt equally sure that great as had been the peril and the loss, the worst was over. During the day the Confederate General Gladden had been killed, and

General A. S. Johnston, Commander-in-Chief, had been mortally wounded.

Throughout the night Buell's troops were arriving by land and water from Savannah, and the gunboats kept up such a constant fire upon the Confederate position that they were compelled to fall back, and thus they lost nearly all the advantage of position that they had acquired throughout the heavy day's fighting. During the night, General Lewis Wallace had disposed his division on the extreme right; the centre and left wing was composed of Buell's forces, consisting of three divisions under Generals William Nelson, Thomas T. Crittenden and Alexander McDowell McCook. This line was about one mile in length, stretching from the Hamburg road across the Corinth road. It should be mentioned here that the road from Pittsburg Landing to Corinth, twenty miles distant, divides about two miles from the river, one fork running to Lower Corinth. The Hamburg road runs from Hamburg Landing, some miles up the river. Before dawn Wallace began to shell the enemy, and thus opened the battle of April 7. As soon as his guns were heard Nelson and Crittenden moved their divisions forward. General Grant then ordered Wallace to attack the Confederate left. Wallace made short work of Ruggles' division of Bragg's command, and occupied the hill from which this force was driven. In attempting to follow up his advantage, Wallace broke his intended connection with Sherman's advance. The Confederates promptly attempted to profit by this and turn his right, but the effective work of Thompson's and Thurber's batteries kept them in check.

Sherman meantime had been moving to retake his camp of the previous day. After fighting hard for an hour and a half, expecting Sherman, Wallace advanced on the enemy, who were posted near Shiloh Meeting-House on a wooded ridge. A tremendous fire drove Sherman back, and Wallace halted. Bartlett's Ohio Battery, and Mendenhall's Battery, of the regular service, had meantime been having an artillery duel in front of Nelson's and Crittenden's divisions, and then Terrell's Battery came into play on Nelson's left. Batteries were taken and lost as the line swayed to and fro, but at length all three of the Confederate batteries were silenced by the concentrated fire of Mendenhall and Terrell.

The Confederate centre, commanded by Beauregard, Bragg, Polk and Breckinridge had been meanwhile fiercely attacked by McCook's Division, and had been steadily forced back. Foiled at this point, the Confederates made a desperate attack on Wallace and Sherman, driving the latter back and placing Wallace in imminent peril. The coming up of the Seventy-eighth Ohio, reserves, under Colonel Woods, prevented disaster, and then a gallant bayonet dash of the Thirty-second Indiana, under Colonel August Willich, completed the confusion of the Confederates and allowed Sherman to reform his line. Wallace then pressed on, and the rebel lines, stubbornly resisting, were forced back along their whole length. At length, driven through the Federal camps they had captured on the 6th, the Confederates gave up all pretense of making a stand. The Federal reserve cavalry was now thrown at them, hoping to turn the defeat into a rout, but Breckinridge, under Beauregard's orders, interposed, and a sharp artillery fire warned Buell that the cost of pursuit would be too heavy. He called a halt, and the Confederates, still protected by Breckinridge's rear guard, made their way to the heights of Monterey, on the road to Corinth. The Federal disaster of the 6th had thus been nobly redeemed on the 7th, but the carnage and losses generally had been frightful. Beauregard acknowledged a loss of 1,728 killed, 8,012 wounded and 959 missing, but the probabilities are that the total loss was not far short of fifteen thousand. The Union loss was 1,700 killed, 7,495 wounded and 3,022 taken prisoners. George W. Johnston, Provisional Governor of Kentucky, was among the Confederate killed during the second day's fighting.

On the 8th of April, Beauregard sent a flag of truce to General Grant, asking permission to send a force to the late battle fields and bury his dead. Grant informed him that this duty had already been performed, and declined to allow his men to approach. In fact, not only had the dead of both armies been buried, from motives of humanity, but the carcasses of the horses had been burned, to prevent danger to the health of the troops, who might have to remain on the spot for some time. It was well that this was done, for when General Halleck arrived at Pittsburg Landing and took command, on the 12th of April, he opposed an immediate advance, though Grant had prepared the way by sending Sherman along the Corinth road to drive in Breckinridge's rear guard, and afterward had dispatched him up the Tennessee with the gunboats to cut off Corinth from Tuscumbia by destroying the Memphis and Charleston Railroad bridge over Big Bear Creek.

BURNING HORSES NEAR PITTSBURG LANDING.

We have mentioned General Mitchell's successful movements upon Huntsville, from which point he had sent Colonel Sill to the eastward, and Colonel Turchin to the westward, the latter capturing the towns of Stevenson, Decatur and Tuscumbia. It was to protect Turchin's stores at this point that Grant sent Sherman to cut off the communication with the rebel forces at Corinth. On the 24th of April, however, a Confederate force drove Turchin from this point, but he carried off his stores, crossed the Tennessee at Decatur, and burned the bridge. Turchin joined Sill, and some sharp fighting was had between

Stevenson and Bridgeport, but Mitchell hurried to their support, and having driven the Confederates beyond the river, was in full possession of Huntsville, Bridgeport, and all Alabama north of the Tennessee, by the 1st of May. On this day also the Confederates had been driven from Monterey, but nothing else had been done by Halleck's troops, though General Pope, with 25,000, forming the Army of Missouri, had joined Halleck on April 22. Between the restless dash of Grant, with his unscrupulous disregard of the value of human life in military operations, and the methodical caution of Halleck, there was room for a middle course, but Halleck was chief in command, and, consequently, though he had now about one hundred and eight thousand troops at his disposal, it was the 3d of May before he began to feel his way from Monterey toward Corinth.

The delay had been of great advantage to the Confederates, for Beauregard had been reinforced by Generals Price, Van Dorn and Mansfield Lovell, the latter bringing the New Orleans troops. In addition, several bodies of militia from other States had been sent forward, so that within the intrenchments at Corinth there were now about 65,000 men. With Beauregard were, in addition to those generals just mentioned, Generals Polk, Hardee, Breckinridge and Bragg, the latter being next in rank to Beauregard and in command of the Army of the Mississippi. The bluster of Beauregard had done much to restore the shattered nerves of the Confederate soldiers, but they were yet to learn the difference between words and deeds.

General Halleck, on his part, had reorganized his forces and consolidated the various divisions into the Grand Army of the Tennessee, with General Grant as second in command. The forward movement began by a skirmish at Farmington, from which part of Pope's Division drove General Marmaduke. This post, however, was retaken on the 9th by a large force under Van Dorn, who in turn, about a week later, was driven out by the advance of Pope's entire division. Shortly after this regular siege operations were begun and pushed forward day by day, the intrenching works being covered by skirmishing parties. On the 28th the army was within thirteen hundred yards of the enemy's lines, and on the 29th Pope drove the

Confederates from their advance batteries, while Sherman got his heavy guns in position within a thousand yards of Beauregard's left.

During the night Beauregard, despite all his boasting, had evacuated Corinth, leaving his pickets wholly unaware of the movement. The Federal sentinels had reported strange rumbling noises during the night, and at dawn, when Sherman began to move, explosion after explosion was heard, and soon dense masses of smoke hung over Corinth. It was soon ascertained that the position was wholly abandoned, that the stores, ordnance, etc., had been sent off several hours before in the direction of Mobile, and that after applying the torch to the magazines and principal buildings, the rear guards and Beauregard had fled in the same direction. Pursuit was made for some forty miles, but the fugitives had a good start and only a few stragglers were captured.

Beauregard, after collecting his troops at Tupelo, turned over the command to General Bragg and went to Alabama for rest, a proceeding which so incensed Jeff. Davis that he vowed never to reinstate him.

Although the siege and capture of Corinth, bloodless as it was, passed for a victory in the eyes of the public, and the possession of the post was of considerable consequence from a military point of view, yet the escape of the Confederate army with its guns and stores was an event which caused deep chagrin among army men. There is probably little doubt that Grant, unhampered by Halleck's colder blood, would have captured or killed nearly the whole of the force thus hemmed in and driven to bay. As it was, Halleck proceeded to strengthen the works, restore railroad communications, and for a time fighting was over in this immediate locality.

CHAPTER XXI.

STONEWALL JACKSON IN THE SHENANDOAH VALLEY—OPERATIONS BEFORE YORKTOWN—EVACUATION OF YORKTOWN—BATTLE OF WILLIAMSBURG—FLIGHT OF THE CONFEDERATES ACROSS THE CHICKAHOMINY—SURRENDER OF NORFOLK—OPENING THE NAVIGATION OF THE JAMES RIVER.

We left McClellan intrenching before Yorktown, and must now return to the operations in this locality. Before doing so, however, we will pick up a few threads of our narrative. In the early part January the Confederate General Thomas Jonathan Jackson, better known by the soubriquet of "Stonewall" Jackson, had been active in endeavors to retrieve the blundering of Floyd and Wise in the Shenandoah Valley. To thwart his operations, General Fred. W. Lander was assigned to the task of protecting the Baltimore and Ohio Railroad. With a sort of independent command, this brave and spirited officer kept his troops moving, and on February 14 he fell on Jackson at Blooming Gap, driving him out with the loss of seventeen officers and sixty privates. General Lander, however, died on March 2, from the effects of a wound received at Edwards' Ferry about the time of the Ball's Bluff battle. General James Shields succeeded him, and took up the work of watching the wily "Stonewall." When Johnston evacuated Manassas, "Stonewall" Jackson fell back to Winchester from the positions he had held in front of Major-General Nathaniel P. Banks, who at that time occupied the heights near Harper's Ferry, together with Charlestown, Leesburg and other points on the Blue Ridge. A further advance of Union troops sent "Stonewall" forty miles further back, to Mount Jackson, from whence he had direct communication with Luray and other posts near Thompson's Gap on the eastern side. On the 19th of March General Shields feigned an attack on this point, and then fell back to Winchester. In the meantime the movement of McClellan had been inaugurated, and, according to the plan of operations agreed upon at Fairfax Court House, General Banks withdrew most of his troops for operations around Manassas. Turner Ashby's cavalry, of "Stonewall" Jackson's division, immediately began to harass Shields and his little force at Winchester and drive in his pickets. This movement was not deemed of importance, but, to check it, a brigade under Colonel Kimball was pushed forward to Kernstown. Neither Banks nor Shields suspected that near this point the daring "Stonewall" had massed about six thousand men, in addition to the dashing cavalry of Ashby. The Federals had barely taken up position when Jackson's artillery opened on them. A sharp engagement followed, but the Confederates failed to turn Kimball's left. Jackson then threw his forces on the right wing, but Colonel E. B. Tyler's brigade came to the rescue. The Federals now in turn made the attack, and after a desperate struggle at a stone fence, Jackson's brigade fell back. Federal reinforcements were rapidly sent up, and the Confederates retreated up the valley in good order, leaving the Union forces in possession of the ground on which the battle of Kernstown had been fought. General Banks became satisfied that Jackson was too powerful a foe to be left unwatched, and therefore he recalled his first division, under General Williams, which had been sent on to Centreville. General James Wadsworth was made Military Governor of the District of Columbia, with command of the troops left by Banks for the protection of Washington City. At the same time Blenker's division was withdrawn from McClellan's command and assigned to the support of Fremont's Mountain Department. General McDowell's corps was also retained for the additional protection of the Capital and to aid in checking the irrepressible Jackson.

THOMAS J. ("STONEWALL") JACKSON.

We have thus covered the ground up to the time of McClellan's advance, and will now join him in the trenches which Fitz John Porter had been working at for several weeks. On April 16 a reconnoissance in force was attempted before Yorktown, at Dam No. 1, on the Warwick River. The movement was repulsed with a loss of about one hundred men, the Federals being driven back through the river waist-deep. McClellan had an exaggerated idea of Magruder's force, which at no time then had exceeded 8,000 men, and the reduction of his own force kept him from aggressive movements. His appeals to the President were met by urgent instructions to act promptly. Still McClellan lingered, and even when Franklin's division of 12,000 was sent to reinforce his already large army of nearly 120,000 men, he still remained inactive and in doubt whether to storm the enemy's lines or turn his flank. The Confederates, however, had

GEN. NATHANIEL P. BANKS.

long since decided that the position was untenable, both Lee and Johnston having carefully inspected the works and considered the possibilities. Magruder was therefore instructed to keep up the farce of resistance until a thorough concentration could be made around Richmond. At length McClellan had made his dispositions for an attack, and May 6 was fixed as the time, but this had probably leaked out, as these matters very frequently did, the "spy service" being in full operation on both sides, though the championship in this peculiar class of operations must certainly be awarded to the wily and unscrupulous Confederates. This was partly owing to the devotion exhibited for the Confederate cause by the ladies of the South.

On the 30th of April, Johnston, Lee and Magruder, together with Jeff Davis and some of his Cabinet, held a council in Yorktown and decided on evacuation. On May 3 this was hastily carried out, and the troops from that point retreated to Williamsburg. On the morning of the 4th McClellan found nothing to storm, and after taking possession of the abandoned works, sent General Edwin V. Sumner in pursuit of the fugitives.

GEN. JOSEPH HOOKER.

The pursuing force consisted of the cavalry and horse artillery under Stoneman, the divisions of Generals Joseph Hooker and Kearny along the Yorktown road, and those of Smith, Couch and Casey along the Winn's Mill road. At the junction of these two roads was Fort Magruder, and other works had been thrown up in the vicinity. Here the Confederates had left a strong rear guard, and Stoneman's advance was checked. Hooker, on hearing of this check, pressed on to the Warwick road and Sumner joined Stoneman. At dawn on the 5th of May, Hooker came upon the Confederate lines before Williamsburg. The approach was protected by felled timber and rifle pits. Hooker, knowing he had a heavy supporting force, determined upon immediate attack, and throwing out skirmishers to pick off the sharpshooters, advanced Weber's and Bramhall's batteries. After a hard fight, Fort Magruder was silenced. But now Longstreet's division was sent from Williamsburg to support the Confederate rear guard, and the battle by noon had assumed a serious aspect. Till nearly nightfall Hooker had to repel furious onslaughts, and could get no aid from Sumner, as General Winfield Scott Hancock had the main portion of the remainder of the troops holding the Confederates in check on the right. He held his ground, however, till General Phil. Kearny came up, and dashing to the front, relieved Hooker's exhausted troops, whose loss during the day had been nearly two thousand. Kearny, with his customary pluck, at once began to push the enemy, and under his orders Colonel Hobart Ward charged on and captured the centre rifle pits. In this effort he lost nine officers. This work was completed by the Fortieth New York, under Captain Mindil, and with the aid of reserves under General Jameson a line of battle was established before dark. In another direction General Hancock had seized a couple of redoubts

GEN. PHILIP KEARNY.

near the flank and rear of the Confederate lines, but was compelled to retire before a heavy force under General Jubal Early, till he reached a position near Cub Dam Creek, where he formed his line. Early's troops pressed on, and Hancock calmly awaited the coming shock till just before the moment of impact. Then, by a gallant bayonet charge all along his line, he drove the Confederates back pell-mell, and killed fully five hundred of them. All this time McClellan had been absent, but coming up now, he ordered reinforcements to Hancock's support, who thus held the key of the position.

The total Federal loss was about twenty-two hundred killed and wounded; that of the Confederates was about one thousand

That night General Longstreet hastily evacuated Williamsburg, and followed Johnston toward the Chickahominy, leaving nearly eight hundred of his wounded behind. McClellan occupied the place next day, but failed to follow up his advantage. This delay has been condemned, and it is quite possible that prompt pursuit might have effected very important results, but it is hardly just to criticise such operations from the luxurious repose of a library arm-chair, with facts at command which could not possibly have been within the knowledge of a harassed commander in the field. On the 8th of May McClellan sent Stoneman forward, and by the 22d the headquarters of the General-in-Chief were at Cool Arbor, about nine miles from Richmond and near the Chickahominy, beyond which the Confederates had safely retreated. In the meantime his advance had crossed the river and occupied the heights on the Richmond side.

GEN. JAMES LONGSTREET.

While these operations were in progress an important movement had been made by General Wool, who was in command at Fortress Monroe. He learned on the 8th of May that General Huger, intimidated by the proximity of Burnside and McClellan, was preparing to evacuate Norfolk, and as this had long been an objective point in Wool's plans, he made instant arrangements for an attack. His first attempt to land and seize Sewell's

Point was frustrated by the *Merrimack* (or *Virginia*) coming to the aid of the shore batteries. He then changed his plans, and at midnight on the 10th of May a landing was effected at Ocean View, the troops, some five thousand in number, under Brigadier-General Max Weber, being taken in transports, under convoy of Commodore Goldsborough, from Hampton Roads. President Lincoln and Secretaries Chase and Stanton accompanied General Wool to the point where the troops landed, and then returned to Fortress Monroe. Meanwhile General Wool took command in person, and with Generals Mansfield and Viele advanced upon the works. The bridge over Tanner's Creek had been set on fire, but Huger had fled with his troops to Richmond, leaving his artillery. The Federal troops were met by a flag of truce, and Mayor Lamb made a formal surrender of the city. General Viele was appointed Military Governor, and Wool rode back to Fortress Monroe with the welcome news of this important capture. Next morning the Confederates applied the torch to the Navy Yard, blew up the *Merrimack* (or *Virginia*), abandoned the fortifications at Sewell's Point and Craney Island, and running their gunboats on the James River toward Richmond, left the navigation once more open.

These successes were considered by the President as the most important among the recent events, and he issued an order, through Secretary Stanton, conveying his thanks as Commander-in-Chief of the army to Major-General John E. Wool, and the officers and soldiers of his command, for their gallant conduct in these brilliant operations.

CHAPTER XXII.

CAPTURE OF MEMPHIS—BATTLE OF NEW BERNE—OPERATIONS ALONG THE CAROLINA COASTS—CAPTURE OF FORT PULASKI—DUPONT AND SHERMAN IN FLORIDA—BUTLER AND FARRAGUT ON THE MISSISSIPPI—OPERATIONS AGAINST FORTS JACKSON AND ST. PHILIP—CAPTURE OF NEW ORLEANS—OCCUPATION OF THE CITY BY GENERAL BUTLER.

We must now rapidly run over concurrent events in other sections. We have recorded the capture of Island Number Ten in the early part of April. General Pope's next objective point was Memphis and accordingly Commodore Foote's flotilla prepared to convoy the transports down the Misissippi. To do this, however, the Confederate works along the river, some of which were remarkably strong, had to be subdued. Fort Pillow, eighty miles above Memphis, was the first reached, and on the 14th of April Commodore Foote began shelling the works and soon sent Hollins' flotilla to shelter. The country being inundated, the troops could not co-operate. On the 9th of May Foote was compelled to turn over his command to Captain C. H. Davis, the wound received at Fort Donelson incapacitating him from duty. The next day Hollins with an increased flotilla and some armored "rams" attacked the Federal fleet. After a fierce fight one of the Confederate gunboats was sunk, one of the rams and another gunboat heavily damaged, and Hollins ceased the attack. With occasional interchanges of shots a couple of weeks passed, and then Davis was reinforced by a "ram" squadron under Colonel Charles Ellet, Jr. The rebels had, however, learned of the disaster at Corinth, and on the night of May 4 they evacuated Fort Pillow and went down the river escorted by Hollins' flotilla. Fort Randolph, lower down, was also evacuated and the Union flag was soon floating over both forts. Pushing on in pursuit, Davis' fleet was but a short distance above Memphis on the evening of May 5. The Confederate fleet lay here ready for action. Early on the morning of the 6th of May the *Cairo*, of the Federal fleet, opened the attack. A couple of Confederate rams were promptly thrown forward and as promptly met two similar vessels from Ellet's squadron. The unique naval combat lasted but a short time, during which the rival rams rushed at each other with terrible fury. The *Beauregard* and the *Lovell*, of the Confederate fleet, were sunk, the *Van Dorn* escaped down the river, and the other vessels were abandoned by the Confederates, who made for the shore. All opposition to the Federal fleet being thus swept aside, the fall of Memphis followed as a natural consequence. General M. Jeff Thompson, who had watched the naval fight, fled as soon as the day was lost and Mayor Park surrendered the city to the Union commanders. Shortly afterwards General Wallace, upon the fall of Corinth, was sent to occupy that post and protect the Memphis and Ohio Railroad between there and Humboldt.

In the meantime General Burnside had been busy. After the capture of Roanoke Island he planned an attack on New Berne, North Carolina, and with the fleet, now under command of Commodore Rowan, left Hatteras Inlet on March 12. The next day his troops, about 15,000 in number, were landed at Slocum's Creek and pushed on toward New Berne, eighteen miles distant, the gunboats keeping pace with the army along the shore of the Neuse River. The channel had been obstructed at many points by sunken vessels and powerful torpedoes, but fortunately all these were avoided. On the morning of the 14th, General Foster, with the First Brigade, marched upon Fort Thompson, while Generals Reno and Parke followed with their two divisions further inland. After heavy fighting Foster captured the outlying Confederate works and swept the occupants out of their intrenchments. Meanwhile General Reno had been engaged with another shore battery, but with the aid of the Fifty-first Pennsylvania, under Colonel John F. Hartranft, this position was also stormed. The Confederates fled across the Trent, at the junction of which with the Neuse, New Berne is located. They burned the bridges behind them and made off to Tuscarora, ten miles distant. The fleet in the interim had silenced the works along shore, and at night General Burnside took military possession of New Berne. The capture of this town and harbor was of great importance. A large quantity of guns and ammunition, stores, wagons, etc., together with a couple of steamers and some sailing vessels, were also captured. The Federal loss was about one hundred killed, including Lieutenant-Colonel Henry Merritt, of the Twenty-third Massachusetts. Two hundred Confederates were made prisoners. After appointing General Foster Military Governor of the city, General Burnside prepared to move on Fort Macon, commanding Bogue Sound and the harbor of Beaufort, North Carolina. General Reno was dispatched to make demonstrations in the rear of Norfolk and General Parke was sent to attack Fort Macon. On the 23d of March Parke's troops occupied Morehead City, and then siege operations were begun against Fort Macon. At 6 A. M. on the 25th of April, the siege batteries on Bogue Spit opened fire and were ably assisted by the gunboats. The combat was maintained with vigor on both sides till 4 P. M., when Captain Guion displayed a white flag from the fort and sent an offer of surrender. General Burnside had come over from New Berne and the next morning took possession of Fort Macon and some five hundred prisoners.

Meanwhile, General Reno had been active along Albemarle Sound. Several sharp engagements were fought, including the battle of South Mills, in which Hawkins' Zouaves suffered considerable loss. Finally, Washington, at the head of the Pamlico River; Winton, on the Chowan, and Plymouth, at the mouth of the Roanoke River, were occupied by the Federal forces, and for a time active operations ceased in this direction, the coasts of North Carolina being now practically under the control of the Union troops. On the 17th of July General Burnside was summoned to Fortress Monroe, and he turned over the command of the department to General Foster.

Meanwhile, General Sherman and Commodore Dupont were planning the capture of Fort Pulaski and other important posts between the Savannah River and St. Augustine, Florida. Fort Pulaski, on Cockspur Island, at the mouth of the Savannah River, and Fort Jackson, had been seized by the Confederates early in the war. After some preliminary movements by an expedition under Captain John Rogers, with the gunboats and troops under General Viele, a lodgment was first effected on Jones' Island, where earthworks were thrown up at Venus Point, and then heavy batteries were established on Big Tybee Island. By this means Fort Pulaski was blockaded and the Savannah River in the rear closed. This work was accomplished toward the end of February, and the works were then pushed forward for a bombardment. Under the direction of General David Hunter, who succeeded General Sherman in command of the department, and who arrived at Tybee on the 8th of March, the attack was commenced on the morning of the 10th, a summons to surrender having been disregarded. Throughout that day the heavy batteries of Tybee Island, which General Gillmore had constructed with great skill, kept pounding away at the fort, and before night the return fire of the enemy had become very weak. At intervals of about twenty minutes throughout the night Gillmore kept sending his iron compliments to Colonel Charles H. Olmstead, First Georgia Volunteers, in command of the fort. At daybreak on the 11th the cannonade was resumed with increased vigor, and shortly after noon the masonry was so badly wrecked that Gillmore had determined to storm the works. Before this movement could be set on foot a white flag was shown, and Fort Pulaski, with a number of guns, large quantities of ammunition and stores of all kinds, passed into the possession of the Federal forces. This capture effectually sealed the port of Savannah.

Commodore Dupont and General H. G. Wright, with a mixed force, had in the meantime been moving along the Florida coast. Dupont had proceeded to Cumberland Sound, and was preparing for a vigorous attack on Fort Clinch when the Confederates abandoned the position and Commander Drayton hoisted the Union flag over the recaptured national fort. In like manner Fernandina and Brunswick, the terminus of the Brunswick and Pensacola Railroad, were evacuated. Then Jacksonville was abandoned after the place had been set on fire by order of General Trapier, Confederate commander of the district.

Commander Rogers had meanwhile received the surrender of Fort Marion and the city of St. Augustine. The evacuation of Pensacola followed, after the Confederate General T. N. Jones had destroyed all he could burn in the Navy Yard and in Forts McRee and Barrancas. Brilliant as were these achievements, they had little practical result, it being found inexpedient to attempt to retain possession of Florida at this time, though a loyalist sentiment had been aroused which gave indications of cordial support. General Wright withdrew his troops and Dupont returned to Port Royal. The Vernon and Wilmington rivers, and Wassaw and Ossabaw sounds, had, however, been opened, and General Sherman was in possession of Edisto Island.

DAVID G. FARRAGUT.

The next important event about this time was the capture of New Orleans and its occupation by General B. F. Butler. This had long been a pet project with Butler, and after a conference with Secretary Stanton, on January 13th, 1862, the desired permission had been given. General McClellan opposed the project, fearing to have his own force weakened, but Butler had been recruiting in New England and could find his own men. McClellan's objections were set aside by President Lincoln, and General Butler was placed in command of the newly created "Department of the Gulf." On the 24th of February Butler took leave of the President in Washington, with the declaration that he would not return alive unless he captured New Orleans. The next day Butler embarked at Hampton Roads with some of his troops, but did not effect a landing at Ship Island, on the coast of Mississippi, between Mobile Bay and Lake Borgne, until the 25th of March. This point had long been fixed on as the rendezvous for the land and naval forces of the expedition against New Orleans.

Captain David G. Farragut had been assigned to the command of the naval force, and Commander David D. Porter with a fleet of bomb vessels was instructed to co-operate with him. This latter fleet, consisting of twenty-one schooners, had been constructed specially at the Brooklyn Navy Yard. They were of light draught, but very stoutly built. Each carried a mortar throwing a 15-inch shell and two 32-pound rifled cannon. Farragut, with the armed steamer *Hartford*, had arrived at Ship Island on the 20th of February, bearing orders for Flag-Officer McKean to turn over to him the command of the Western Gulf Squadron. The rendezvous of Porter's mortar fleet was Key West. While the details of the expedition were being mapped out a reconnoissance was made up the river as far as Fort Jackson, and the character of the coast ascertained. Below New Orleans, and about seventy-five miles above the passes of the Mississippi, were Forts Jackson and St. Philip, on opposite sides of the river, besides numerous smaller works, and a powerful water battery attached to the former fort, and a heavy chain cable had been stretched across the river (this, however, a recent flood had swept away). Porter learned, also, that for some miles below Fort Jackson, the shore was heavily wooded, and he took advantage of this circumstance in a most ingenious manner. When he moved up to his position below Fort Jackson, on the left bank, his mortar boats were disguised by tree branches and leaves, so as to be almost indistinguishable from the forest behind them. On the 17th of April all preparations had been completed. General Butler, with 9,000 troops, was at the Southwest Pass, and the fleets were ready to move. The next morning fourteen of Porter's vessels were moored below Fort Jackson, and Farragut with six of his fleet had taken position among the reeds on the opposite side. The bombardment was speedily commenced, and for a couple of days was kept up with vigor, but without result. Farragut then determined on executing the alternative plan of running past the forts and seizing New Orleans, leaving the reduction of the fortifications for after operations. Before this could be done the obstruction in the river had to be removed. This work was begun that night, but the movement was detected, and the enemy sent a fire-raft down the stream from the Confederate fleet, which consisted of thirteen gun-boats, the ram *Manassas*, and an iron-clad floating battery, moored above Fort Jackson. This diversion the Confederates indulged in every night with the double purpose of injuring the Federal fleet, if possible, and at the same time throwing light upon their midnight movements. As a rule the rafts were swung to the shore and left to burn, but some kept on their course weirdly illuminating the river banks.

At two o'clock on the morning of April 24 Farragut began the advance on the flagship *Hartford*, followed by the *Richmond* and *Brooklyn*, keeping along the right bank to attack Fort Jackson, while the gunboats *Harriet Lane*, *Westfield*, *Owasco*, *Clinton*, *Miami* and *Jackson* were to engage the water battery. Porter's mortar boats retained their position to cover the advance. On the eastern side Captain Theodorus Bailey, with the *Pensacola*, *Mississippi*, *Oneida*, *Varuna*, *Katahdin*, *Kineo*, *Wissahickon* and *Portsmouth*, was to engage Fort St. Philip. The attack on the Confederate fleet was left as an independent operation to Captain Bell, on the *Cayuga*, with the *Sciota*, *Winona*, *Iroquois*, *Pinola*, *Itaska* and *Kennebec*. At the moment of the advance the mortar boats opened a tremendous fire on Fort Jackson. The *Cayuga* was the first to pass the boom, and her advance was at once detected, drawing the fire of the hitherto silent forts. Most of the leading division got through the boom, but the *Portsmouth*, in tow of the *Jackson*, got detached in firing a broadside and floated down stream. The *Itasca* was disabled, and also drifted down, while the *Kennebec* and the *Winona* fell back beneath the iron hail. Farragut had got within about a mile of Fort Jackson when the fort opened fire, striking the *Hartford* several times. As the vessels advanced the ram *Manassas* made a dash at the *Brooklyn*, but failed to injure her. Meanwhile the *Manassas* pushed a blazing fire raft against the *Hartford*, and for a moment the condition of Farragut was perilous in the extreme. After less than two hours of this terrible conflict, in which every description of naval vessel and marine monster, together with the heavily armed forts, were making night hideous with noise and blaze, the Federal fleet passed the forts. Eleven of the Confederate vessels had been destroyed or sunk, and the mighty ram *Manassas* went blazing down the river a shattered hulk, till she sunk in the midst of Porter's mortar boats below Fort Jackson.

Farragut, with thirteen of his vessels, moved up to Quarantine, and the fate of New Orleans was practically settled. General Lovell, who had been down the river, hastened back to the city and prepared for immediate evacuation, but he left orders with General Smith, in command of the Chalmette battery, below the city, to resist to the utmost. Farragut and Bailey, however, soon silenced these works, and then Bailey was sent ashore to demand the surrender of the city from Lovell. That worthy declined to surrender, but said he should withdraw his troops and leave the civil authorities to defend the city. In accordance with Lovell's suggestions, Mayor John T. Monroe sent a stupid letter of defiance, which Farragut promptly replied to by a threat to bombard the city without any reference to the danger of innocent citizens. For some days this senseless correspondence was continued, Farragut being well aware that he could afford to smile at the impudence of the Mayor till such time as Butler should arrive. Accordingly, on the 30th, he peremptorily closed negotiations. The first Union flag had been hoisted over the Mint on the 24th by a small force from the *Pensacola*, but this was speedily torn down. It was subsequently replaced by Captain Bell.

While this was going on General Butler had landed his troops in the rear of Fort St. Philip and was ready on the 28th to begin the assault, but the news of Farragut's operations in New Orleans convinced Colonel Higgins that the case was hopeless and he consequently surrendered the forts and the remnant of the Confederate fleet.

On the 29th, Butler joined Farragut, and after looking over the position, went back to expedite the advance of his troops. On the 1st of May the debarkation commenced. The city was in a terrible condition; large quantities of cotton had been burned, and a wholesale destruction of public and private property inaugurated by General Lovell and Mayor Monroe. Excited and seditious mobs roved the streets and Butler found he had as much work before him in adjusting matters of local control as he had got through in approaching the city hostilely. He was equal to the task and again had an opportunity to air some of that large stock of "views" with which, as we have previously shown, this many sided, mysterious man is always amply provided. As our space is limited and these local details hardly come within the scope of our work, we will leave General Butler in full possession of New Orleans, and in another chapter return to the army before Richmond.

We can hardly quit New Orleans, however, without giving a sample of the extremities to which General Butler was driven by the fierce secession spirit of the populace. The document quoted is self-explanatory:

HEADQUARTERS DEPARTMENT OF THE GULF,
NEW ORLEANS, May 15, 1862.

GENERAL ORDER NO. 28:

As the officers and soldiers of the United States have been subject to repeated insults from the women (calling themselves ladies) of New Orleans, in return for the most scrupulous non-interference and courtesy on our part, it is ordered that hereafter, when any female shall by word, gesture, or movement, insult or show contempt for any officer or soldier of the United States, she shall be regarded and held liable to be treated as a woman of the town plying her avocation. By command of

MAJOR-GENERAL BUTLER.

GEORGE C. STRONG, Assistant Adjutant General, Chief of Staff.

Mayor Monroe made this the subject of so insolent a letter that Butler ordered his arrest and General G. F. Shepley was appointed Military Governor of the city.

We shall have occasion to return to New Orleans later on, but may mention here that General Butler remained in command of the Department of the Gulf until superseded by General Banks who was assigned to that duty on November 9th, 1862, and assumed command on December 16th. A week later General Butler left New Orleans by steamer for New York.

CHAPTER XXIII.

STONEWALL JACKSON IN THE SHENANDOAH VALLEY—FIGHT AT WINCHESTER—BATTLE OF CROSS KEYS — M'CLELLAN BEFORE RICHMOND — RETROGRADE MOVEMENT TO THE JAMES RIVER—THE BATTLE OF GLENDALE—THE FITZ JOHN PORTER AFFAIR—BATTLE OF GROVETON—GENERAL POPE RELIEVED OF HIS COMMAND.

We left "Stonewall" Jackson in the month of April, 1862, operating in the Shenandoah Valley. On the 30th of that month he was reinforced by troops under Generals R. S. Ewell and Edward S. Johnson till he had a force of about 15,000 men. Jackson's special work at this time was an attempt to keep General Banks in check at Harrisonburg, while Lee pushed on to cut the Federal communications between Winchester and Alexandria, but he suddenly became aware of the approach of General Milroy, by way of Monterey, with one of Fremont's Brigades, to join Banks. To prevent this, Jackson left Ewell posted near Swift Run Gap, and pushed forward to Staunton, while Johnson went to check Milroy. This was partially successful, and Milroy fell back to McDowell, thirty-six miles west of Staunton. Here Jackson and Johnson gave him battle on the 8th of May. The fight was stubborn, but without practical advantage to either side, except that the Federals, during the next night, abandoned their position and retreated to Franklin. Jackson followed them up until he learned that Banks was preparing to leave Harrisonburg, when he again combined his forces and dashed through the Luray Valley, falling on Colonel Kenly's garrison at Front Royal and driving the Federals out of that position. Kenly crossed the Shenandoah, but was so hotly pursued by Ashby's cavalry that he was compelled to stand and give battle. The result was disastrous, as Kenly and some seven hundred of his troops, with the supply train and several guns, were captured. This was on the 23d of May, and the news reaching Banks next morning, he at once began a retreat from Strasburg, in the direction of Winchester. Though closely pursued, this point was reached, but it was found impossible to maintain a stand even here. The Confederate force of twenty thousand men was nearly three times the strength of Banks' Division; consequently, after a stubborn fight of five hours, on the 25th, Banks was compelled to evacuate Winchester, and fall back first to Martinsburg and then to the banks of the Potomac opposite Williamsburg. Ashby's cavalry were too intent on plunder to join efficiently in the pursuit, and to this may be ascribed the failure of Jackson to annihilate Banks' little force. It was now the turn, however, of the pursuer to become the pursued; for Generals Shields, McDowell and Fremont rapidly concentrated, and Jackson found it expedient to retreat rapidly up the valley and endeavor to cross the Shenandoah by the bridge at Port Republic. The Federals pressed so close on the rear of the Confederates that a sharp engagement ensued between Ashby's cavalry covering the retreat, and a cavalry force under Colonel Percy Wyndham. In this fight Wyndham and some sixty of his men were captured, and next Colonel Kane, of the Bucktail Rifles (Pennsylvanians), was also taken prisoner. The Confederates, though victorious so far, suffered a severe loss in the death of Ashby, whose horse had been killed under him, and then he, while advancing on foot was shot through the body. The Confederates pressed on for Port Republic, but were compelled to give battle again at Cross Keys. The result was indecisive, both sides retaining their chosen positions. Meanwhile, Jackson had crossed the Shenandoah. The Federal troops were still close upon him, and General Tyler made a gallant dash upon Ewell and Jackson. The force, however, was insufficient, and he was repulsed with the loss of four hundred and fifty men taken prisoners. After this, Jackson had little difficulty in keeping Tyler at bay till he had moved his troops across the bridge and destroyed it. Fremont came hurriedly up, but too late to prevent the burning of the bridge, and the river was too swollen to be forded. The Federal forces then fell back; then Jackson recrossed the river, but on the 17th of June left the valley to aid in the defense of Richmond.

We must now return to McClellan, whom we left inactive before Richmond, save for some small skirmishes between outlying divisions on the banks of the Chickahominy. The fact that McDowell was not sent to reinforce him was the cause of constant complaint by McClellan, and was made the pretext for delay, although McDowell's operations on the Shenandoah Valley were really of importance as tending to prevent Jackson's reinforcement of the forces defending Richmond. President Lincoln again urged McClellan to do something, and do it quickly; but the only replies were demands for additional troops and intimations of possible successes in the near future. Instead, however, of moving his main army on the Richmond works, he sent Fitz John Porter to Hanover Court-House to keep open the path for McDowell. Ably supported by General W. H. Emory, Benson's Cavalry and General Morell's Division, composed of Martindale's, Butterfield's and McQuade's Brigades, General Porter, after some sharp fighting en route, captured the Confederate camp at Hanover Court-House on May 28th, with a number of prisoners, two railroad trains and a large quantity of war material. General Sykes' division was sent to Porter's support, and then the Confederate communications in several directions were severed; this work included the cutting of the Richmond and Fredericksburg road, the destruction of the railroad bridge over the South Anna and several other smaller bridges.

The Confederate General Johnston, however, was far from idle. Noting the fact that the Federal army was divided by the Chickahominy, he prepared to attack it in detail, and on May 30th he started to attack Casey's Division, on the Williamsburg road, at Seven Pines, and the divisions of Kearny and Hooker at Savage's Station and the neighborhood of White Oak Swamp, on the Richmond side of the river. About noon on the 31st, Generals Longstreet and D. H. Hill came upon Casey's front, while General Huger was moving on the left flank and General G. W. Smith on the right flank at Four Oaks Station. After a severe fight Casey was forced back, Kearny was driven to White Oak Swamp and Smith had fallen with great fury on the Union right at Fair Oaks Station. The brilliant advance of General Sumner alone saved the army on the Richmond side from total rout. Bringing up Sedgwick's and Richardson's Divisions, he speedily recovered the ground lost by Heintzelman and Crouch; and in the fierce conflict which ensued the Confederate Generals Johnston and Smith were wounded, and carried from the field. To complete the confusion of the Confederates, General Sumner hurled three regiments of Gorman's Brigade and two of Dana's Brigade upon the enemy, in a dashing bayonet charge. This finished the work for that day. By daybreak on June 1st the Confederates renewed the attack on Richardson's Brigade. This had been anticipated, and was met by portions of the Brigades of Generals French and O. O. Howard, forming the first line; a second line was formed by the remainder of Howard's Brigade, and supporting these were General Thomas F. Meagher's Irish Brigade. General Roger A. Pryor and General Mahone fell heavily upon French's Division, but Meagher's men came to the front, and the Confederate attack was repulsed with heavy loss. During that day and evening the Confederates fell back to Richmond, removing their camp equipage and munitions. The next day Hooker made a reconnoissance to within four miles of Richmond, without check, but by McClellan's orders fell back, and began throwing up intrenchments around Fair Oaks Station. The losses in these engagements amounted to nearly half of the entire forces engaged, being about seven thousand on either side. Several prominent Union officers were severely wounded or killed during the battles of Fair Oaks and Seven Pines; among the former being Generals Naglee, Devons, Howard and Wessels and Colonel Cross.

The subsequent proceedings before Richmond were so unsatisfactory that we shall not occupy our limited space by the details, but merely summarize results. We have seen that Stonewall Jackson hastily quitted the Valley of the Shenandoah and started for Richmond. By a series of masterly movements, the wily campaigner, who was as subtle as he was brave and active, had made his way to Ashland, about sixteen miles from Richmond, where he arrived on June 25th with some 35,000 men. General Joseph E. Johnston being seriously wounded, General Robert E. Lee had assumed command of the Army of Northern Virginia, and the Confederate troops were concen-

THE BATTLE OF GLENDALE.

trated in readiness to force McClellan to give battle or to retire from the siege of Richmond.

All this time McClellan was comparatively idle, although General J. E. B. Stuart had made a desperate raid around his position, between the 10th and 15th of June, capturing a number of prisoners and destroying wagons and schooners at Garlock's Landing, above the White House, on the Pamunkey River.

The information of Jackson's arrival at Ashland decided McClellan's course; he had been projecting a retrograde movement to the James River, and this was hastened by the bold advance of Generals Longstreet, A. P. and D. H. Hill on Mechanicsville. This took place on the afternoon of June 26th, but owing to the failure of Jackson to co-operate, the Confederate attack was a failure, and resulted in fearful loss of life. It has been stated that if McClellan had at this time pressed in on Richmond he might have passed between Lee and his base of supplies, but instead of doing this he prepared to withdraw his troops across the Chickahominy. In carrying out this movement several severe battles were brought on. That of Gaines' Farm was especially disastrous, Fitz John Porter's division being terribly cut up. McClellan now abandoned his intrenchments, and leaving his sick and wounded with the medical stores, etc., at Savage's Station, he made a hasty retreat to Malvern Hills, on the banks of the James River, closely followed by the Confederates under Magruder, Huger, Longstreet, Hill and Jackson. Fortunately the Confederates were too late to prevent the passage of the troops over White Oak Swamp Bridge, but a fierce fight was waged here, known as the Battle of Glendale, in which General Meade was severely wounded. General McCall was taken prisoner, and but for a desperate charge by General Meagher, the fortunes of the day must have told heavily against the Federal arms. During the night the Union troops got safely across the Chickahominy, and once more the Army of the Potomac was reunited, on Malvern Hills, with the James River as a means of communication. McClellan meanwhile was alternating between the camp and the deck of the *Galena*, whither he went to confer with Commodore Rodgers.

The approaches to Malvern Hills from Richmond and the Swamp had been covered by Porter's troops, and General Barnard had made other dispositions for defense by the 1st of July. On that day General Lee prepared to carry the position by storm, and had disposed Jackson, Ewell, Whiting and D. H. Hill on the left and Magruder and Huger on the right. The plan was to silence the batteries by a concentrated fire on the centre, and then, with a "rebel yell" and a bold dash with fixed bayonets along the whole line, he expected to sweep the Federal troops into the James River. It did not happen just that way, however. Charge after charge was made with absolute recklessness, but all without avail. Repulsed at every point, the Confederates fell back to the woods, but only to reform and return to the attack. Thus the long afternoon and evening passed, until at length the coming to the front of Meagher's Irish Brigade, and a heavy cannonade from the gun-boats in the river completed the Confederate discomfiture, and they were driven in all directions, utterly demoralized. McClellan had been on board the *Galena* throughout the battle, and when toward evening, in response to urgent entreaties from Heintzelman, he appeared among the troops, it was merely to give orders for a further retrograde movement to Harrison's Landing. This position was occupied on July 3d, and meantime Lee had returned to Richmond, having lost nearly 19,000 men in the previous forty days. The Federal losses from the time of the battle at Mechanicsville amounted in killed and wounded and missing to over fifteen thousand. The failure of McClellan to capture Richmond had been irritating enough, but his rapid retreat still more incensed the President, and he determined on a personal inspection of the state of affairs. Arriving at Harrison's Landing he found at least 75,000 men unaccounted for, and it was with much difficulty that he learned ultimately that the majority had been granted furloughs while McClellan was clamoring for reinforcements. This did much toward undermining the already waning confidence of the Administration. From this time forward, until the 5th of November, when McClellan was relieved of his command and superseded by General Burnside, the communications between the Washington authorities and

McClellan were marked by querulous complaint on his side and kindly remonstrance on the part of the President.

It had been more than suspected by the administration that the abandonment of the siege of Richmond would be followed by aggressive movements northward, by the Confederates, and that the Capital might be again threatened. To meet such a contingency Major-General John Pope had been placed in command of the Army of Virginia, a new organization intended for the special protection of Washington and to co-operate when needful with the Army of the Potomac in the Peninsula. The new organization was divided into three corps under Major-Generals Sigel, Banks and McDowell. On assuming command on June 28th, General Pope placed himself in communication with McClellan, but the latter, who had previously declined to co-operate with McDowell, on the ground that he preferred to have sole direction, was so curt in his replies that, on the suggestion of Pope, General Halleck was made General-in-Chief over the two armies, and assumed command on July 23d. Halleck personally inspected the condition of affairs at Harrison's Landing, and, having further satisfied himself that a Confederate movement northward was imminent, he ordered McClellan to withdraw from the Peninsula and concentrate his troops at Acquia Creek on the Potomac. This order was given on August 3d, but McClellan, with the obstinacy which had now become chronic, occupied some twenty days in carrying out these commands.

We must now turn to the movements of General Pope, who assumed command of the Army of Virginia, in the field, on July 29. Prior to this he had sent General Rufus King to break up the Central Virginia Railroad and General Banks to seize Culpepper Court House. Both these operations were accomplished. General Hatch, however, had not been successful in an attempt to seize Gordonsville, and General John Buford was placed in command of Banks' cavalry, Hatch being relieved from his command. In the meantime the Confederates, finding that they had nothing more to fear from McClellan, began to push forward. Jackson crossed the Rapidan near Barnett's Ford, having been heavily reinforced, and drove the Federal cavalry back on Culpepper. He then pushed on to Cedar Mountain, where he planted his batteries, and threw Early's Brigade, of Ewell's Division, forward on the Culpepper road. On the 9th of August, late in the afternoon, General Banks, with the divisions of Generals Augur and Williams, led by General Geary, advanced upon Jackson's position. The Confederate force, however, was more than double that of the attacking divisions, and after a fierce combat the Union troops were repulsed with heavy loss, the arrival of Ricketts' Division and, later, of Sigel's Corps, putting a stop to the advance of the flushed Confederates. Two days later Jackson retired across the Rapidan. For some days after this there was sharp fighting along the Rappahannock, the Confederates vainly endeavoring to cross. In the meantime General J. E. B. Stuart again executed one of his rapid movements around Pope's army, but did not effect much by it.

RECONNOITERING.

But a more important movement was in progress, for Jackson had rapidly and secretly carried out a flank movement, and crossing the Rappahannock at Hinson's Mill, pushed through Thoroughfare Gap, across Bull's Run Mountains, and being joined by Stuart's cavalry at Gainesville got in Pope's rear at Bristow Station, on the Orange and Alexandria Railroad, on the evening of August 26th, and captured a couple of trains of cars before any intimation of his movements had reached Pope. Not content with this, he sent Stuart to Manassas Junction and that post was captured before midnight, several hundred prisoners and a large quantity of stores, etc., becoming the spoils of the Confederates. Colonel Scammon with the Eleventh and Twelfth Ohio attempted to dislodge the intruders, but was driven back across Bull's Run, and during the fighting Brigadier-General George W. Taylor, who had moved rapidly out of Alexandria to support Scammon, lost a leg. The Confederates scoured the country, sweeping almost round to Centreville.

Pope at once prepared to intercept Longstreet, and also made provision for the capture of Jackson's force at the Junction. The wily "Stonewall," however, was not to be trapped very easily. Therefore, after destroying most of the captured stores, he pushed by a devious route through to Centreville to effect a junction with Lee. By Pope's orders, Sigel should have left Gainesville at dawn, and Fitz John Porter was to have moved on Bristow's Station at one o'clock, but both were several hours behind their appointed time, and Jackson had cleared out of Manassas Junction before Pope arrived there at noon. McDowell was at once sent in pursuit, but his forces encountered Ewell and Taliaferro near the Warrenton pike, and in a furious battle got the worst of the fight. The losses on each side were heavy, and Ewell lost a leg while Taliaferro was badly wounded. Pope had ordered Fitz John Porter up to Manassas, and expecting him there, sent orders for him to move on Centreville while Kearny pushed after Jackson. The attempt failed, for Longstreet had quickened his movements and swept through Thoroughfare Gap, driving Ricketts' division back on Gainesville. On the morning of August 29th, Pope found that his plans were frustrated and there was little hope of hindering the concentration of the Confederates. He determined on an immediate advance. He ordered Sigel and Reynolds to advance from Groveton and attack Jackson at dawn; Heintzelman with Hooker's and Kearny's divisions was to push on from Centreville to Gainesville, while Porter moved from Manassas to turn Jackson's flank and fall on his rear near the Warrenton pike.

But the whole of Lee's army had got through Thoroughfare Gap, and Sigel with the divisions of Carl Schurz, Schenck and Milroy was engaged in a desperate fight from seven o'clock in the morning till noon, when Hooker arrived to aid them. About four o'clock in the afternoon General Pope sent an order to Fitz John Porter directing him to attack and turn the Confederate right, Heintzelman and Reno being instructed to make a simultaneous assault on the left and front. Porter failed to advance, and the whole movement was frustrated.

[We must turn aside to consider this episode, since it has been one of absorbing interest for the past few years; has awakened keen anxiety and severe scrutiny among civilians and military men; has evoked passionate political prejudice and personal pique of most pronounced character, and has placed on record some very prominent persons, whose actions, beneath the calcium light of public opinion, must tend to invest them with the halo of honesty or the stigma of self-earned concentrated contempt. Foremost among these, on the credit side of the account, are Generals U. S. Grant, ex-President of the United States, and General Sewell, U. S. Senator from New Jersey; and on the debit side, General Chester A. Arthur, President of the United States, and General Logan, expectant Vice President of the United States. To these names may probably be added that of Robert Todd Lincoln, Secretary of War.

Let us look to the facts: In the first place, it has been demonstrated that Pope's "FOUR O'CLOCK ORDER" did not reach Porter until dusk, some hours later, when it was too late to make any attempt to execute it. In the next place, Pope was under the impression that Longstreet had not gained his position on Jackson's right when the order was sent; in this Pope was in error, while Porter, better informed, knew that the dreaded junction had been effected by midday, four hours before Pope sent out his instructions. Porter knew further, and the world knows now, that, even had the order been delivered in due time, it could not have been successfully executed, as the force in front of him was overwhelming, instead of being, as Pope surmised, small and scattered. That such are the facts of the case can be proven by the statements of General Longstreet and the careful researches of General Grant, which led that somewhat stubborn, but gallant and honest soldier, to admit the error of his previous hasty judgment. However, setting aside even these facts, and Fitz John Porter's knowledge of them, the whole tenor of his military record forbids even the surmise that he would have hesitated to advance, from any consideration of personal risk, had the order been delivered at a period compatible with a military common-sense view of an obligation to obey it. The plain truth is that he did not receive the order until, by any possible construction of it, all its commands had been vacated or abrogated by the changed condition of affairs, While implicit obedience is a soldier's duty, at any risk, when obedience can be rendered in actual accordance with orders, yet it must be admitted that an attempt to execute a delayed order, merely as a matter of Don Quixotic discipline, to the certain sacrifice of valuable lives and costly property, would have been a piece of criminal folly, justly resulting in the severe punishment which Fitz John Porter has for so many years unjustly endured for being actually well informed, sensible and patriotic. We are forced to this indignant disclaimer by the immediate presence of the yet fouler wrong, which, at this writing (July 3d, 1884), has just been thrust upon this much-abused military man. After many years of struggle and much parliamentary intrigue, the outspoken indignation of a generous public forced a tardy acknowledgment from its Congressional representatives of the wrong which the nation had put on a faithful servant. We all know how slowly the act of Congressional justice, which was intended to restore Fitz John Porter to the army muster-roll, was reached; we all know how Chester A. Arthur dallied with the measure for nearly the statutory ten days; we may suspect how he induced his Pennsylvania Attorney-General to furnish him with a legal quibble on which to base a veto message: but we can be certain that this technical veto, which only a Republican Senate sustained, was a cruel reversal of that honest judgment, on appeal, by the highest authority of the nation, of a conviction and sentence arrived at by an ignorant or malicious military tribunal during a period of doubt and discord. We may be emphatic, but we are sincere.]

With an apology for this digression we will again fall into line, and follow up the battle of Groveton. The non-arrival of Porter, and the aggressive movements of Heintzelman and Reno, drew upon these gallant officers the full tide of battle. Brilliant bayonet charges and stubborn onslaughts were frequent, and the railway embankment on the Confederate left was captured. Kearny's dauntless boys had succeeded in driving A. P. Hill from the left and forcing this part of the Confederate line backward for some distance. Longstreet's troops, however, poured in to Jackson's aid and turned the scale. The fire-eating Texans, under the dashing Hood, pressed forward and forced Kearny back just before dark, capturing several prisoners, a few flags and one gun. When night fell on this scene of carnage, it is estimated that not less than fourteen thousand men, about equally divided between the opposing forces, had bitten the dust or were badly maimed.

In the events of the next day, August 30th, may perhaps be found some explanation of Pope's bitterness in the Fitz John Porter matter, for a renewal of the fighting with his fatigued and dispirited troops in front of an enemy comparatively fresh and receiving constant augmentations can only be considered a brave man's blunder. Pope, however, had relied upon assistance from McClellan until too late to retreat effectively without a battle. In that battle Fitz John Porter proved that he did not shirk fighting. McClellan in his recent role of "the most promising young man of the period" had failed to forward either men, rations or forage, and now promised to furnish the latter needs, on condition that a cavalry escort should be dispatched from Pope's weakened forces. With the desperation almost of despair, Pope prepared to attack Lee's left, and the fact that Lee was contemplating a similar compliment to him led Pope into another error. The withdrawal of Lee from one part of his line seemed an indication of retreat, and Porter was sent with the advance along Warrenton pike, while Reno, Heintzelman and Ricketts were to fall on the left of the supposed fugitives. In attempting this the intruding pursuers came upon an ambushed, heavy force of Confederates who opened a terrible fusilade. Just then a movement on the left indicated the approach of another large body of the enemy, and Reynolds was hastily detached from Porter's support to go to the aid of Milroy and Schenck. Porter, thus imperiled, stubbornly withstood the shock of battle till Colonel G. K. Warren voluntarily went to his aid with his gallant little band of one thousand men and Buchanan's Brigade of regulars. Porter's command rendered very efficient service, and for a time Jackson was forced slowly back. But the odds were against the Union forces. Longstreet's busy batteries and the heavy impact of his masses of troops, together with the dashing charges of Hood's fearless Texans and the resistless advance of five divisions under Evans, Anderson, Wilcox, Kemper and Jones, completed the discomfiture of Pope's army. It was a forced retreat, but not a rout. Still, so heavy had been the blow that during the night, unperceived or at any rate unpursued, Pope's entire force crossed Bull's Run by the stone bridge and took up a position on Centreville Heights. Here he was reinforced by Franklin and Sumner, making up his force to about 60,000 men.

Lee, however, gave him but little rest, for on September 1 Stonewall Jackson with his own and Ewell's divisions had crossed Bull Run and was moving on Fairfax Court House. An attempt to thwart this movement led to another serious engagement, in which General Isaac J. Stevens, leading Reno's Second Division, and the intrepid "Phil" Kearny, were both shot dead. The resultant confusion was somewhat remedied by a furious bayonet charge of Birney's Division, which drove the Confederates back and left Birney in possession of the battlefield of Chantilly. The total losses of Pope's Army from the battle of Cedar Mountain to that just described have been estimated at 30,000 in killed, wounded and missing or captured. In addition to Kearny and Stevens, there were killed in this last fight Colonel Fletcher Webster, son of Colonel Webster; Major Tilden, Thirty-eighth New York; Colonels Broadhead, O'Connor, Cantwell and Brown. Colonel George W. Pratt, Twentieth New York, was mortally wounded, and Major-General Schenck and Colonel Hardin, Pennsylvania Reserves, were also severely wounded.

On September 2d Pope's shattered forces retired within the lines around Washington. General Pope, disheartened and disgusted by the inexplicable conduct of McClellan in withholding prompt aid, and the consequent reverses he had endured, applied to be relieved of his command, and this being granted, the Army of Virginia was merged in that of the Potomac.

On the same day that Pope's army retired, Lee was reinforced by D. H. Hill's Division, and then began the invasion of Maryland by the Confederates, the Potomac being crossed at the Point of Rocks. Lee established his camp near Frederick, and thence issued on September 8th a proclamation inviting the citizens of Maryland to join in the rebellion. Although artfully and boastfully worded, this proclamation proved powerless to procure panderers to the secession schemes.

The boldness of Lee's advance, however, caused considerable apprehension, and McClellan made haste to protect the imperiled Capital. It was not Lee's intention to attack so strong a position just at that time, but he hoped that by drawing McClellan from the lines at Washington, under the feint of a descent on Pennsylvania, the chances of war might afford an opportunity for a successful attack either on Baltimore or Washington.

The draft of Lee's plans fell into McClellan's hands when the Confederate rear guard was driven out of Frederick, and the Union General had therefore an immense advantage. The scheme involved the capture of Harper's Ferry, thus opening up direct communication with Richmond through the valley of the Shenandoah. Acting on the information thus obtained, McClellan was expected to push on and thwart the Confederate schemes, but to the indignation of General Halleck, he actually proposed the abandonment of the Capital even, in order to give him what he deemed a necessary force with which to take the field. Despite his uneasiness, however, he organized an energetic pursuit, and on September 14th the Confederates were astounded to find nearly the whole of McClellan's forces advancing toward their positions at Turner's Gap, Crampton's Gap and South Mountain, the former of which was held by D. H. Hill's Division. As soon as the position of the enemy had been ascertained, Reno ordered an assault, and by noon the battle of South Mountain had became a serious engagement. By this time Longstreet had come to Hill's assistance, and there were about 30,000 Confederates holding the position. The Union forces were also reinforced by the arrival of the divisions of Wilcox, Rodman, Sturgis and Hooker corps. The fighting soon became general along the whole line, the Federal troops pressing steadily up the steep ascent. By nightfall the Confederates had been driven from their position, but the gallant General Reno had been killed and General Hatch badly wounded. Meanwhile General Franklin had dislodged the Confederate force holding Crampton's Gap and driven them down the Western slope.

While these movements were in progress the indefatigable Jackson had crossed the Potomac at Williamsport, occupied Martinsburg and then pushed on to Harper's Ferry. On September 13th he was preparing to invest the Ferry, and during the same day the Confederates under McLaws had captured Maryland Heights, and Walker was in possession of London Heights. A vigorous attack on Harper's Ferry followed next day. Colonel D. H. Miles was in command, assisted by General Julius White, who had brought his troops in from Martinsburg. After sustaining a terrible bombardment Miles decided to surrender, but was killed while exhibiting a flag of truce. All avenues of escape had been closed, and General White, with 12,000 men, became prisoners of war.

After the repulse on South Mountain Lee withdrew and took took up a position in Antietam Valley, near the creek, on September 15th. McClellan hesitated over an immediate attack, and Lee took advantage of this by a show of force which delayed the Federal advance until Jackson, McLaws and Walker had joined him. During the 15th there were one or two sharp outlying engagements, but both armies were actually preparing for the Battle of Antietam—one of the most sanguinary struggles of the War. At dawn on the 16th the Confederates began artillery practice, but McClellan was not ready to respond. It should be noted that Antietam Creek was spanned by four stone bridges: No. 1, at the crossing of the Keedysville and Williamsport road, was the uppermost bridge; No. 2, some two miles below, was on the Keedysville and Sharpsburg pike; No. 3 was on the Rohersville and Sharpsburg road, one mile below No. 2 and Sharpsburg; No. 4 was on the Sharpsburg and Harper's Ferry road near the mouth of the creek. McClellan's lines on the east side of the Antietam extended on the right from Keedysville, where Sumner and Hooker were stationed; General Richardson's Division of Sumner's Corps was nearer the centre and nearer the stream on the right of the Sharpsburg pike; on the left, protecting bridge No. 2, was Sykes' Division of Porter's Corps; Burnside's Corps was near bridge No. 3. On the hill crests above the bridges, east of the creek, were planted batteries, and on Red Ridge, a spur of South Mountain, Major Myers ("Old Probs"), of the Signal Corps, had arranged a signal station, and, being enabled to survey the entire battle-field, was of inestimable service in communicating intelligence of every movement to McClellan's headquarters, which were in a private residence two miles northeast of Sharpsburg.

At 2 P. M. on the 16th McClellan sent Hooker over bridge No. 1 with the divisions of Ricketts, Meade and Doubleday, to turn the Confederate left. Hooker fell heavily on General Hood, and after a sharp engagement the Confederates were driven back half a mile, in the direction of Sharpsburg. During the evening General Mansfield's Corps crossed in Hooker's rear and bivouacked.

At dawn on the 17th both armies were ready for battle, and Hooker, with some 18,000 men, made a vigorous attack on Stonewall Jackson's left. Hooker pressed Jackson heavily, sustained by a galling fire from the batteries east of the creek, and finally the Confederates were driven from the first line of woods. Hooker then pushed forward to seize the Hagerstown road, but Jackson, now reinforced by Hood's troops, fell on Meade, who led the advanced centre. The battle became furious, and a brigade under General Hartsuff went to Meade's assistance, while General Mansfield advanced to the support of Hooker. The ground was stubbornly contested, and at the time that Hartsuff fell, severely wounded, the gallant General Mansfield was also mortally hurt. Hooker was also so severely wounded in the foot that at nine o'clock he was removed to McClellan's headquarters, leaving Sumner in command. The battle had been raging some three hours before McClellan turned out; he had made his dispositions the previous night and retired to bed early. It was but a sample of the Commander-in-Chief's sublime trust in Providence, and furnishes a key to much of his leisurely, methodical movements, by which many an opportunity for dash and enterprise was hopelessly wasted.

General Sumner, on taking command at nine o'clock, sent General Sedgwick to support the attack on Jackson and Hood. These were steadily falling back when McLaws, Walker and Early came to their support, and piercing the Federal lines, compelled a retrograde movement, until Doubleday checked the Confederate advance. During the fierce combat, Generals Dana, Crawford and Sedgwick were wounded, the latter so severely that he turned over his command to General O. O. Howard. About noon, McClellan sent Franklin to the support of Howard on the right, and then a few dashing charges recovered the lost ground. In the meantime, General French had been hotly engaged with Hill's Brigades in the centre, while Richardson's Division moved forward on the left of French. Meagher's gallant brigade fighting an uphill battle in face of a furious fire. The Confederates were driven back to a sunken road, but Hill being reinforced by R. H. Anderson with some four thousand fresh troops, made an attempt to turn the Federal left. This was repulsed, but while Richardson was directing the fire of one of the batteries he fell, fatally wounded. General Winfield Scott Hancock took command, and, in a desperate charge, drove the Confederates from their position. General Meagher was wounded and carried from the field. The Federals then rested on the Sharpsburg road, and at nightfall were holding that position.

We have seen that Burnside was posted near Bridge No. 3. This was held on the west side by the Brigade of General Robert Toombs, of Georgia, and he was supported by batteries on heights behind and by the sharpshooters of Longstreet's Division. Burnside's orders were to cross that bridge early in the morning, storm the heights and then move along them to Sharpsburg. Repulsed at several attempts—for it was a herculean task—Burnside finally accomplished his purpose soon after noon, but was almost immediately driven back by A. P. Hill's division coming up from Harper's Ferry. At the bridge the Confederate advance was checked by the coming up of the Federal reserves under General Sturgis, and when night fell Burnside was holding his position on the west bank of the Antietam. Night closed the carnage and drew a sable veil over a sickening scene, practically of no advantage to either of the combatants. The Federal losses were stated by McClellan at 12,469 men, of whom 2,010 were killed. The Confederate loss was undoubtedly much greater; but, with customary caution, Lee avoided making an official report. There is but little doubt, however, that up to this time he had lost by the invasion of Maryland some thirty thousand men, of whom some six thousand had been taken prisoners. His losses in war material were also heavy, the Federals having captured some 15,000 small arms, thirteen guns, thirty-nine battle-flags and large quantities of stores. He was consequently in no condition to renew the combat on the 18th, and McClellan, despite the arrival of Generals Humphreys and Couch with some 14,000 fresh troops, took a gloomy view of the situation, almost "sulked like Achilles in his tent," and, in opposition to the advice of Franklin and several other generals, he wasted the 18th in masterly inactivity. Lee, however, did not miss his opportunity; he knew that McClellan would wake up some time or other, and he withdrew his shattered legions across the Potomac into Virginia, and left Pendleton on the river bluffs with eight heavy batteries to check pursuit. On the morning of the 19th McClellan found that his foe had escaped him, and in the course of the day he ordered a sortie on the Confederate batteries by the brigades of Generals Griffin and Barnes. A few guns were captured, but the movement was unimportant. Next day part of Porter's brigade, while making a reconnoissance were surprised by an ambushed force of Confederates, under A. P. Hill, and driven back across the river, losing two hundred men, who were taken prisoners. General J. E. B. Stuart's cavalry kept hovering around to cover Lee's retreat, and even recrossed the river at Williamsport, but were checked by General Couch. Lee had meantime reached Martinsburg, leisurely destroying sections of railroad, and then moved up the Shenandoah Valley toward Bunker's Hill and Winchester. McClellan's force had not been quite idle, for General Williams had retaken Maryland Heights, and Sumner, having occupied Harper's Ferry, had thrown pontoon bridges over the Potomac and Shenandoah by the 22d of September.

McClellan now began the manufacture of the last straw which was to break the camel's back of Lincoln's patience. He began clamoring for reinforcements, and announced that he should rest his troops and hold his position, so as to prevent the enemy from returning into Maryland. In vain President Lincoln insisted upon energy and action, for it was not until October 26th that McClellan began to cross the Potomac at Berlin, and then instead of chasing Lee along the west side of the Blue Ridge, he proposed to move southward on the east side. This movement somewhat changed the Confederate plans, and closely followed by Generals Sedgwick and Hancock, they commenced retreating along the Shenandoah Valley, evidently making for Richmond. Lee had meanwhile sent Longstreet rapidly in advance, and by a dexterous movement his troops crossed the

Blue Ridge, and massing at Culpeper Court-House, placed a heavy force between the Army of the Potomac and Richmond. On November 6th McClellan had his headquarters at Rectortown, near Front Royal, and the whole of his army, including the divisions of Generals Sigel and Sickles, who had been sent from Washington to join him, occupied the whole region east of the Blue Ridge. But the grand opportunity had been lost, and McClellan's failure to pierce the gaps of the Blue Ridge, and with his hundred thousand men complete the demoralization of Lee's forces, finally lost him the confidence of the Administration. He had been pampered like a pet child, reasoned with as a willful school-boy, and chided as an obstinate man, but all to no purpose. On November 5th the War Department issued an order relieving him from his command, and superseding him by General A. E. Burnside. This order reached McClellan on the evening of November 7th, while he was still hesitating over his plans. The blow had fallen at last. Here for a while we will leave the Army of the Potomac and resume consideration of its movements under Burnside in a later chapter.

CHAPTER XXIV.

AFFAIRS IN KENTUCKY AND MISSISSIPPI—GUERRILLA MORGAN'S RAIDS—THE CONFEDERATES CAPTURE LEXINGTON AND FRANKFORT—BRAGG RETREATS INTO TENNESSEE—GENERAL BUELL RELIEVED—GENERAL ROSECRANS IN COMMAND OF THE ARMY OF THE CUMBERLAND—THE BATTLES AT MURFREESBORO—SOME VERY HEAVY FIGHTING.

We must now summarize the movements in Kentucky and Mississippi. The Confederates, though driven from Kentucky, were not disposed to consider their repulse as final. On July 4th, 1862, John Morgan, the Confederate guerrilla cavalryman, left Knoxville, East Tennessee, and with 1,200 troopers well nigh as reckless as himself, crossed the Cumberland Mountains and the southeastern border of Kentucky to begin his notorious raids. His operations being those of a bandit, as a matter of course he was an imperious master, prompt ferocity supplying the place of legitimate authority. Upon one occasion he ordered a trooper to perform some deed of especial risk, but the man, after delay, replied to an inquiry as to whether the order was understood, "Yes, Captain; but I cannot obey." Morgan turned and shot him dead, with the remark: "Then good-by!" warning the others that such would be the penalty to all who disobeyed orders. Morgan proceeded to issue his commands as if nothing unusual had happened. His subsequent orders received prompt attention. On July 9th, at Tompkinsville, Monroe County, he captured Major Jordan and several of a detachment of Pennsylvania cavalry, killing and scattering the rest. It was a sharp fight, and Colonel Hunt, who was with Morgan, was killed. Morgan then issued a proclamation calling upon the Secessionists of Kentucky to greet the "liberators" of whom he was the herald. Several recruits flocked to Morgan's standard dazzled by his dash and daring. Thus recruited he attacked and defeated Lieutenant-Colonel Johnson at Lebanon, capturing several prisoners. He next destroyed the railway bridge between Cynthiana and Paris, and then on July 17th, he scattered a force of Home Guards at Cynthiana under

Lieutenant-Colonel Landrum. In the attack, however, he suffered losses of men fully equal to those he inflicted. Cincinnati was his next objective point, but General Green Clay Smith was moving to meet him with a superior force and Morgan fell back southwest by way of Richmond. In the meantime General N. B Forrest, another Confederate cavalryman, was harrying Tennessee and making threatening raids and demonstrations near Murfreesboro and Nashville. These movements were evidently designed to distract attention and divide the Federal forces as much as possible, for while they were in progress two heavy Confederate divisions under General Bragg and General E. Kirby Smith, entered Kentucky from East Tennessee. This expedition included the corps of Generals W. J. Hardee and Leonidas Polk. On August 30th, General Smith reached Richmond, and after preliminary skirmishing dispersed the Federal forces under General Manson, who was taken prisoner with several of his men. Pressing on, Smith captured Lexington and then Frankfort. He was pressing on for Louisville or Cincinnati, but was checked by the vigorous movements of Major-General Lewis Wallace, who, arriving in Cincinnati on September 1st, promptly proclaimed martial law in Cincinnati, Covington and Newport, and assembling the citizens, put some to work on intrenchments while at the same time he mustered an effective fighting force to aid in defensive operations. These measures disconcerted Smith in this direction, and he organized a city government at Frankfort, while waiting to effect a junction with Bragg.

Meanwhile General Bragg had advanced from Chattanooga toward Louisville, and on September 14th his advance under General Duncan appeared before Mumfordsville, where the railroad crosses the Green River, and demanded the surrender of the position from Colonel T. J. Wilder. This was refused, and the next day an assault on the works was made. The Confederates were repulsed, but awaited the arrival of Bragg. When his main body came up on the 16th the battle was renewed. Wilder fought stubbornly all day, expecting aid from Buell; but this did not arrive, and at 2 o'clock on the morning of the 17th he surrendered with 4,500 men to a force of about

65,000 Confederates. From this point Bragg moved northward, and formed a junction with Smith at Frankfort on October 1st. Here he paused long enough to appoint ex-Congressman Richard Hawes Provisional Governor of Kentucky and to plunder the neighborhood of supplies of every kind, though a pretense was made of payment by the tender of Confederate scrip. The loyal citizens, terrorized by these outrages, appealed to the National Government for aid, and Buell hastened to their relief. Bragg was apparently heading for Louisville, and on the 15th of September Buell left Nashville with about 100,000 men, and hastened to intercept him. The Federal forces gained the race for Louisville by one day, and then, on October 1st, General Buell (who had been temporarily suspended because of seeming lack of energy and reinstated on express conditions) divided his army into three divisions, under Generals Gilbert, Crittenden and McCook, and began to move on Bragg. General George H. Thomas, Buell's second in command, led the right wing. Bragg fell back to Springfield, skirmishing all the time to cover the retreat into Tennessee of a train of four thousand wagons laden with Kentucky spoils of which the "liberators" had relieved the "to-be-liberated" from personal control. It was the old story of the wolf acting as shepherd.

In the meantime Kirby Smith had quitted Frankfort and had concentrated with Bragg near Perryville. General Buell becoming aware of this movement, at once went with the centre division under Gilbert in that direction, and on the evening of October 7th had a skirmish with the Confederates, driving them back about three miles. The next day there was hard fighting along all the line, lasting till nightfall, when the Confederates were repulsed at all points. During the night the Confederates retreated to Harrodsburg and thence into East Tennessee, their rear being covered by General Polk and the cavalry of General Wheeler. An ineffectual pursuit was begun, but the Federal troops were too late to strike an effective blow, and returned to Columbia, whence the main army, under General Thomas, was dispatched to Nashville. This unsatisfactory campaign resulted in Buell being relieved of his command. He was superseded by Major-General Rosecrans, and the name of the army was changed

ARMY OF THE CUMBERLAND CREATED. 275

from that of the Ohio to that of "The Army of the Cumberland."

We will trace the movements of General Rosecrans in Mississippi later in this chapter, but now will continue the thread of the Kentucky campaign from the time when he assumed command on October 30th. He found the army utterly demoralized and about one-third of its nominal strength absent, either on furlough or missing. Immediate steps were taken toward reorganization. In the mean time Bragg, finding that he was not pursued, halted at Murfreesboro, thirty miles southeast from Nashville, and began to concentrate for an attack on that city; but Rosecrans, more prompt than Buell, had anticipated such a movement, and on November 4th General McCook's Division moved in the direction of Nashville, and was just in time to repulse a demonstration of the Confederates with cavalry and artillery under General Forrest. The main body of the Army of the Cumberland moved up shortly after, and for some six weeks General Rosecrans remained there making preparations for a powerful attack on Murfreesboro. During the remainder of November and the early part of December there were many engagements with varying success.

At dawn on December 26th, however, the decisive forward movement was begun from Nashville. The Federal force was arranged to move as follows: General McCook with three divisions, 15,933 men, along the Nolensville pike to Triune; General Thomas, with two divisions, 13,395 men, by the Franklin and Wilson's Creek pike; and Crittenden, with three divisions, 13,288 men, on the Murfreesboro pike, toward Lavergne. As the Federal troops advanced the Confederates fell back, but made a stand at Stone's River, a short distance northwest of Murfreesboro, and on the night of December 30th the two armies were facing each other and ready for battle. General Rosecrans had planned to mass his forces on the left and crush the Confederate right wing, under Breckinridge. General Bragg, on the other hand, contemplated the exact counterpart of Rosecrans' design, and had massed his men on the left, under Hardee. These began the battle on the morning of December 31st, and unexpectedly and heavily fell upon McCook's Division almost before dawn. The assault was bravely met, but before noon the Federal right wing had been turned and Bragg's cavalry had reached the rear of Rosecrans' position. McCook's early calls for help had been unheeded, and Generals Sheridan and J. C. Davis, assaulted on front, flank and rear, were compelled to fall back. The brunt of the battle now fell on General Thomas, and despite fierce assaults and a galling artillery fire, the position was held while Rosecrans readjusted his line of battle. Meanwhile a furious onslaught was made on Palmer's Division, holding the right of the National left wing, and which had been exposed by the driving back of Negley's Division. But for sublime heroism the day would have been lost to the Federal arms, and this was supplied by Acting Brigadier-General William B. Hazen, who, with only thirteen hundred men, sustained and repulsed the shock of several thousands of the Confederate troops. This bold stand enabled Rosecrans to carry out his fresh dispositions, and at nightfall the Federal lines were completely reconstructed. The losses, however, had been heavy, nearly 7,000 men being missing from the ranks. Brigadier-General Willich was a prisoner; Brigadier-Generals Sill, Schaeffer and Roberts had been killed; Generals Kirk, Wood and Van Cleve were disabled by wounds, and ten colonels, ten lieutenant-colonels and six majors were missing. The Confederates held possession of a large portion of the battle ground and had captured one-fifth of Rosecrans' artillery.

The Confederates expected that Rosecrans would retreat, but when the morning of January 1st, 1863, dawned, and Bragg found the Federal forces in battle array, his confidence began to wane. During that day there was little beyond skirmishing attempted on either side. During the night Bragg planted some heavy batteries and opened fire on the morning of January 2d heavily on Hascall's division. These batteries were soon silenced, but there was heavy skirmishing along the front. At a council of general officers, held by General Rosecrans after the battle of December 31st, it had been decided that the plan of turning Bragg's right and taking Murfreesboro should be persisted in, notwithstanding the discouragement of the previous engagement. Accordingly, Van Cleve's Division had been reinforced by one of Palmer's brigades, and Rosecrans was personally superintending the disposition of the troops about noon of January 2d, when a heavy Confederate force, consisting of three columns of infantry and three batteries. Breckinridge's entire command, came out of the woods, and by sheer force of numbers threw the Federals into utter confusion. They recrossed the river, followed by the exultant Confederates, whose numbers were constantly added to. The pursuit, however, was checked by the murderous fire of Crittenden's batteries on the opposite bluffs, and then began a terrific artillery duel. At length, a furious charge of the Seventy-eighth Pennsylvania, Eighteenth, Twenty-first and Seventy-fourth Ohio, Nineteenth Illinois, Thirty-seventh Indiana and Eleventh Michigan, drove the Confederates from their position with the loss of over two thousand men. By the time darkness set in the Confederates were utterly routed. During the next day the arrival of a Federal ammunition train enabled Rosecrans to make arrangements for a further attack, but on the night of the 3d Bragg slipped away through Murfreesbro, and on January 5th was at Tullahoma. In his precipitated retreat he left some two thousand sick and wounded in the hospitals. General Thomas advanced to Murfreesboro and drove out the Confederate rear guard, but the Federal cavalry force was insufficient to justify vigorous pursuit. General Rosecrans made his headquarters in the village, and here we will leave him, for the present, having covered the operations in this section up to and beyond the close of 1862.

CHAPTER XXV.

THE BATTLE OF IUKA—MOVEMENTS AROUND CORINTH—GRANT'S COMMUNICATION SEVERED AT HOLLY SPRINGS—GENERAL SHERMAN AT MEMPHIS—THE ATTACK ON VICKSBURG—FAILURE OF THE MOVEMENT—BURNSIDE WITH THE ARMY OF THE POTOMAC—ABORTIVE ATTACK ON FREDERICKSBURG—BURNSIDE RELIEVED OF HIS COMMAND.

During September, 1862, there were some vigorous movements in Mississippi. On the 19th the battle of Iuka was fought. This was a little village on the Memphis and Charleston Railroad, in Tishamingo County, and a large amount of National stores had been collected there. The Confederate General Sterling Price had moved suddenly on this point and, capturing the stores, made his headquarters there. General Grant sent two columns under Generals Rosecrans and Ord to dislodge him. General Ord's instructions were to wait until he heard Rosecrans engaged, and then to go to his support. All through the 19th Ord was within four miles of Iuka, but did not hear the battle sounds, and therefore Rosecrans had an uphill fight. However, he defeated Price, who suffered a loss in killed and wounded of over 800, and about one thousand were taken prisoners. Over sixteen hundred stand of arms and a large amount of ammunition also fell into Rosecrans' possession. During the night following the battle Price fled southward, and succeeded in forming a junction with Van Dorn on September 28th.

In the meantime General Rosecrans had taken post at Corinth with 20,000 men, and General Grant, with the remainder of the Federal forces, had moved toward Jackson, Tennessee. Perceiving, as they thought, an opportunity to profit by the division of the army, the Confederate Generals Price and Van Dorn, the latter in chief command, moved their combined forces to attack Corinth. On October 3d the attack commenced, and a stubborn battle, lasting two days, ensued. By noon on the 4th, however, the Confederate attack had been completely repulsed, and before night they were in full retreat southward.

The fatigued Federal forces were reinforced that evening by

the arrival of General McPherson with five fresh regiments, and these started in pursuit early on the morning of the 5th. At this time another division, under General Hurlbut, had struck Van Dorn's troops near Pocahontas, and drove them across the Hatchee River. McPherson's troops came up next day, and the retreating Confederates were followed to Ripley, when Grant recalled his troops.

On October 16th, a General Order of the War Department extended the department commanded by General Grant, and it was called the Department of the Tennessee, with headquarters at Jackson. Grant promptly made four districts of his command, assigning General W. T. Sherman to the district of Memphis, General S. A. Hurlbut to that of Jackson, General S. C. Hamilton to that of Corinth, and General T. A. Davies to that of Columbus. We have seen that General Rosecrans had been recalled to take the command of the Army of the Cumberland. There were several small battles at various points during October, but the main object of Grant's campaign just then was the capture of Vicksburg. To this end he moved his headquarters on November 4th from Jackson to La Grange, a few miles west of Grand Junction, on the Memphis and Charleston Railroad. McPherson was sent forward and the Confederates were pressed back to Holly Springs. At this point General Grant established a depot for arms and military supplies, the command being intrusted to Colonel R. C. Murphy. The main army was at Oxford, the capital of Lafayette County. On December 20th Van Dorn with his Confederate cavalry dashed upon Holly Springs, then containing about four million dollars' worth of stores, and captured everything. He remained there a few hours, blew up the arsenal, burned the public property, paroled Murphy and his thousand men who had surrendered, and then quitted the place and made several threatening demonstrations along Grant's lines. The most serious effect, however, was the cutting of Grant's communication and forcing him to fall back to Grand Junction. This retrograde movement allowed General Pemberton to concentrate his troops at Vicksburg to meet the attack which Sherman was planning.

On December 20th General Sherman left Memphis with 20,000 troops in transports, and a naval force under Admiral D. D. Porter co-operating. A landing was effected at the mouth of the Yazoo River on the 22d, and on the 29th a desperate battle was fought at Chickasaw Bayou. The heavy Confederate force and the difficult nature of the ground were too much for the Federals, and by nightfall they had been repulsed, with a loss of over two thousand men, the Confederate loss not being one-tenth of that number.

The Federals rested on their arms that night. Sherman and Porter then planned another attack by going up the Yazoo, but the scheme leaked out and was abandoned. On January 4th, 1863, General McClernand arrived and assumed chief command. He approved a plan which Sherman and Porter had concocted for the capture of Fort Hindman, or Arkansas Post, on the left bank of the Arkansas River, at a sharp bend fifty miles from the Mississippi. On January 11th the post was captured, and then after the fort had been dismantled, General McClernand, by Grant's order, withdrew his troops to Napoleon, on the Mississippi, at the mouth of the Arkansas River.

GEN. AMBROSE E. BURNSIDE.

We must now return to General Burnside, whom we left at Warrenton on November 10th, when he assumed command of the Army of the Potomac, *vice* General McClellan, relieved. Burnside promptly reorganized his army, consolidating the six corps into three grand divisions of two corps each. The Right

Grand Division was composed of the Second and Ninth Corps of Generals Couch and Wilcox, General Sumner having chief command of the division. The Centre was composed of the Third and Fifth Corps of Generals Stoneman and Butterfield, with General Hooker commanding the division. The Left Division consisted of the First and Sixth Corps of Generals Reynolds and W. F. Smith, with General Franklin commanding the division. Burnside's plans were directed toward the capture of Richmond, and he, therefore, made Acquia Creek his base, having railroad connection with Fredericksburg. On November 16th he began to move in that direction. An attempt to cross the Rappahannock by Sumner's Division was met by a heavy demonstration of Lee's forces, and hostilities were delayed until the 21st, when the main body of the Federal Army had reached Falmouth, and from that point commanded the city of Fredericksburg, with batteries on the Falmouth hills. On November 21st Sumner demanded the surrender of the city, but the authorities refused to allow its occupation by the National troops. The Confederate forces, now numbering some eighty thousand men, had been pushed forward by Lee, and were disposed in a semicircle behind Fredericksburg, the right wing resting on the river at Port Royal, below the city, and the left six miles above. Burnside having drawn Lee's attention down the river by attempts to cross twelve miles below Falmouth, determined to construct pontoon bridges across the Rappahannock and attempt to divide the Confederate forces. On December 11th the engineers began before dawn and were well advanced with their work, under cover of a fog, before the movement was detected. There had been constructed on Stafford Heights, on the Falmouth side, twenty-nine batteries to cover the operations; therefore, when Lee's sharp-shooters, who had been ambushed in Fredericksburg, opened fire on the engineers and drove them from the pontoons, a heavy cannonading was begun on the city, which was set on fire in several places. Another attempt to work at the bridges was frustrated by sharpshooters, and then volunteers from Howard's Division crossed the river in open pontoon boats and dislodged the enemy. That evening the remainder of

Sumner's Right Division and Franklin's Left crossed, and occupied Fredericksburg, and by the night of December 12th both divisions were across the Rappahannock, leaving Hooker with the centre division on the Falmouth side. On the 13th Burnside ordered an advance of the whole force on the south bank of the Rappahannock, to attempt the assault of the Confederate lines. Franklin began the attack soon after sunrise, and for a time the Confederates were driven back, Meade's Division pressing them closely until they neared the crest of the hill, when Gregg, with his South Carolina troops, compelled Meade to halt. Then Early swept down upon him, and Meade was driven back with considerable loss. Generals Gibbons and Birney came to Meade's support, but in vain, and then Reynolds came up. The Confederates were then again driven back, but kept stubbornly fighting till dark. Meanwhile Sumner's Division had attacked the Confederate front, Couch's Second Corps leading the attack at noon. French's and Hancock's divisions followed. Longstreet, with heavy reserves behind him, was posted behind a stone wall at the foot of Marye's Hill. French, after a fearful struggle at this formidable position, was hurled back, and then Hancock pressed forward to close the gap. The men fought desperately, Meagher's Irish Brigade being especially brave, but the work was beyond their capacity, and in less than half an hour Hancock was driven back, with the loss of over two thousand men. Howard's Division, and those of Sturgis and Getty, advanced to the support of Hancock and French, but even then the odds were against them. Burnside then ordered Hooker across. He took three divisions, and reconnoitered the position, but feeling satisfied that the works could not be carried, he advised Burnside to give up the attempt. The commander, however, insisted that the crest must be carried, and consequently Humphrey's Division, four thousand strong, were ordered to take the position at the point of the bayonet. Gallantly they pressed forward, but a murderous fire mowed down seventeen hundred of them, and the day was evidently lost. By nightfall the Federals had lost nearly fifteen thousand men. During the next two days Burnside was preparing for another attack, but at length yielded to the representations of

Sumner, and on the night of the 15th of December Burnside withdrew to the Stafford Hills, across the Rappahannock, taking up his pontoon bridges, and abandoning all attempts to hold Fredericksburg.

Still bent on the capture of Richmond, Burnside was planning a fresh expedition, when on December 30th he was ordered by the President not to enter upon active operations. Unable to account for this, Burnside went direct to Washington, when the President informed him that private reports from general officers had made it apparent that he did not possess the confidence of the army. Another attempt to cross the river and flank Lee's forces was frustrated by a storm, and then Burnside again proceeded to Washington to ask the dismissal of officers whom he had detected in correspondence with the President for the purpose of fomenting discontent. The President failed to coincide with this demand, and finally, on January 26th, 1863, an order was issued relieving Burnside of the command of the Army of the Potomac and placing him on waiting orders. Generals Franklin and Sumner were also relieved of their commands.

Major-General Hooker was assigned to the command vacated by Burnside. For three months thereafter no active operations were undertaken by either Lee or Hooker in consequence of the terrible condition of the roads, and also because both armies had been severely demoralized by the heavy fighting of the campaign.

Hooker found his men deserting at the rate of about two hundred a day, and a close examination of the muster rolls proved that 2,922 commissioned officers and 81,964 privates and non-commissioned officers were absent. Of course, included in this number were the sick and wounded in the hospitals. It was an appalling state of affairs, but Hooker at once went to work to reorganize, and his effective measures speedily brought order out of chaos. By the middle of April he had a thoroughly disciplined force of about 110,000 infantry and artillery, with 400 guns and 13,000 cavalry. But we must leave him here in winter quarters and turn to the political aspects at the beginning of 1863.

CHAPTER XXVI.

PRESIDENT LINCOLN'S EMANCIPATION PROCLAMATION—FULL TEXT OF THE MOST IMPORTANT STATE PAPER IN THE HISTORY OF THE UNITED STATES—EFFECTS OF ITS PROMULGATION—CONDITION OF THE FEDERAL FINANCES—FURTHER CALLS FOR TROOPS—DEMORALIZED CONDITION OF CONFEDERATE AFFAIRS.

The first day of January, 1863, will ever stand on record as the date of the most momentous event in modern history. On that day the scratch of a pen upon a sheet of foolscap paper burst the bonds which held the African race in subjection on this continent, and swept away an institution which for two hundred and forty-four years had been a shame and an infamy among a people professing to be free and glorying in their freedom. On that day, as an act of sublime necessity, as it was then deemed, but really in full fruition of the destinies of this great nation, President Abraham Lincoln affixed his signature to and promulgated the Emancipation Proclamation, a document second only in importance, if indeed it does not surpass in human interest, the boasted Magna Charta which the British barons wrung from King John at Runnymede.

Before giving the text of this State paper, let us look into the events preceding its issue. As we have shown in our introductory chapter, the slavery question was practically underlying the whole theory of justification for secession, and to such an extent had the idea of property rights, or vested interests become mixed up with the subject, that the days of the early Abolitionists were passed in peril, even among those who had never owned a slave and who could not have been induced to do so. The extreme caution of President Lincoln at the outset of his career had been very discouraging to the Abolition extremists, and when, on September 13, 1862, an influential Christian delegation urged upon him the issuance of an edict in accordance with their views, he still temporized, though admitting his personal sympathy with so grand an idea. But with Lincoln it was "duty first," and then personal inclination, if that could be honorably considered. He promised to weigh the matter, and closed the interview with these significant words: "Whatever shall appear to be God's will, I will do!"

We need not invade the privacy of Lincoln's closet; facts are enough for us. On September 22d, he issued a preliminary proclamation in which, after reciting certain intended recommendations to Congress, he stated that on the first of January next ensuing he would declare the slaves, within every State or part of a State the people whereof should then be in rebellion, to be thenceforward and forever free.

While the Confederates treated this with scorn, on the surface, yet the threat of so heavy a blow goaded them to desperation. Among the loyalists of the North there was mingled hope and doubt. In the wide world outside, among the on-lookers of the fearfully tragic game, the full import of the declaration was keenly appreciated, and the outcome of it was awaited with hungry impatience.

The first of January dawned—and the plebeian became a king—the President of a struggling Republic became an Emperor among men—a towering, colossal embodiment of nature's nobility—an autocrat of Freedom before whom the proudest hereditary despots of the Old World stood mean, pitiful and abashed. We append the text of the

PROCLAMATION.

Whereas, On the 22d day of September, in the year of our Lord one thousand eight hundred and sixty-two, a proclamation was issued by the President of the United States, containing, among other things, the following, to wit:

"That on the first day of January, in the year of our Lord one thousand eight hundred and sixty-three, all persons held as slaves within any State or designated part of a State the people whereof shall then be in rebellion against the United States, shall be then, thenceforward and forever free; and the Executive Government of the United States, including the military and naval authority thereof, will recognize and maintain the freedom of such persons, and will do no act or acts to repress such persons, or any of them, in any efforts they may make for their actual freedom.

"That the Executive will, on the first day of January aforesaid, by proclamation, designate the States and parts of States, if any, in which the people thereof, respectively, shall then be in rebellion against the United States; and the fact that any State, or the people thereof, shall on that day be in good faith represented in the Congress of the United States, by members chosen thereto at elections wherein a majority of the qualified voters of such State shall have participated, shall, in the absence of strong countervailing testimony, be deemed conclusive evidence that such State, and the people thereof, are not then in rebellion against the United States."

Now, therefore, I, Abraham Lincoln, President of the United States, by virtue of the power in me vested as Commander-in-Chief of the Army and Navy of the United States in time of actual armed rebellion against the authority and government of the United States, and as a fit and necessary war measure for suppressing said rebellion, do, on this first day of January, in the year of our Lord one thousand eight hundred and sixty-three, and in accordance with my purpose so to do, publicly proclaimed for the full period of one hundred days from the day first above mentioned, order and designate, as the States and parts of States wherein the people thereof, respectively, are this day in rebellion against the United States, the following, to wit:

Arkansas, Texas, Louisiana (except the parishes of St. Bernard, Plaquemines, Jefferson, St. John, St. Charles, St. James, Ascension, Assumption, Terre Bonne, La Fourche, Ste. Marie, St. Martin, and Orleans, including the city of New Orleans), Mississippi, Alabama, Florida, Georgia, South Carolina, North Carolina and Virginia (except the forty-eight counties designated as West Virginia, and also the counties of Berkley, Accomac, Northampton, Elizabeth City, York, Princess Anne and Norfolk, including the cities of Norfolk and Portsmouth), and which excepted parts are, for the present, left precisely as if this proclamation were not issued.

And by virtue of the power, and for the purpose aforesaid, I do order and declare that all persons held as slaves within said designated States and parts of States are and henceforward shall be free, and that the Executive Government of the United States, including the military and naval authorities thereof, will recognize and maintain the freedom of said persons.

And I hereby enjoin upon the people so declared to be free to abstain from all violence, unless in necessary self-defense; and I recommend to them that, in all cases, when allowed, they labor faithfully for reasonable wages.

And I further declare and make known that such persons, of suitable condition, will be received into the armed service of the United States, to garrison forts, positions, stations and other places, and to man vessels of all sorts in said service.

And upon this act, sincerely believed to be an act of justice, warranted by the Constitution, upon military necessity, I invoke the considerate judgment of mankind and the gracious favor of Almighty God.

In testimony whereof I have hereunto set my name and caused the seal of the United States to be affixed.

[L. S.] Done at the City of Washington, this first day of January, in the year of our Lord one thousand eight hundred and sixty-three, and of the Independence of the United States the eighty-seventh.

ABRAHAM LINCOLN.

By the President:
WILLIAM H. SEWARD, Secretary of State.

It is impossible to over-estimate the effect of this proclamation. In the South, despite bombast and sneers, there was a feeling that the Feast of Belshazzar had been re-enacted and that the handwriting on the wall had been parodied in all its direful portent. It may not be denied that in the North the proclamation was not as heartily received as it should have been. Somehow men seemed to smell, if not to taste, the bitter dose administered to the Confederates. Abroad, however, the effect was to create a bond of sympathy with all the better elements of the various communities. The boldness of the document charmed; its modest Christian spirit impressed; and its sterling philanthropy commanded respect. The Confederate Congress met the proclamation by the passage of retaliatory legislation, and in April an "Address to Christians throughout the World" was issued from Richmond, in which, among other things, the President was accused of attempting to instigate a servile insurrection, the result of which would be that considerations of public safety would render the slaughtering of all slaves a necessity. Subsequently the refusal of the Confederate authorities to recognize negro soldiers as exchangeable prisoners of war obliged the President, in July following, to issue an order declaring that if the Confederates should sell or enslave any Union captive, in consequence of his color, that retaliation upon Confederate prisoners would follow as a punishment. The serious effect of this was to lengthen the imprisonment torments of many a brave Union soldier in the Confederate cattle-pens. Nor was it only in this quarter that trouble arose; the Peace party protested against the act as as unconstitutional, and preparations were made for condemning it by the ballot-boxes. However, Congress and the Executive were as a unit on this point, and laws were passed authorizing the enlistment of one hundred and fifty thousand negroes into the service of the United States. The President declared that the time for compromise had gone by; peace must be obtained and the Union must be preserved. These blessings could only be reached by the suppression of the rebellion, and to that end the administration would bend all its energies. Slowly the tide turned, and that which had been viewed as a fierce faction fight came to be considered as an earnest, noble battle for the permanent advancement of human freedom and the stability of all free institutions.

While we are considering political matters, it will be well to glance at other war measures. As a matter of course, the war debt was assuming gigantic proportions, but this in no degree dispirited the people, and the credit of the Republic was strengthened by a circular issued August 12th, 1863, by the Secretary of State to the foreign diplomatic agents, in which he stated that the country showed no sign of exhaustion of money, material or men, and that the Government loan was being purchased at par by citizens at the average of $1,200,000 daily. He further mentioned that while gold was selling in the North at 23 to 28 per cent. premium, in the Confederate region it commanded twelve hundred per cent. premium. About this time the Confederate debt is understood to have been something like $600,000,000.

There was difficulty in keeping up the quota of the army. The last calls for volunteers had not been fully met. The Conscription Act, therefore, was passed by Congress on March 3d, and two months afterward the President ordered a general "Draft" of three hundred thousand men. All able-bodied citizens, between the ages of twenty and forty-five years, were subject to the requisition. Instigated by the Peace faction, this measure was bitterly denounced, and in many places the draft officers were forcibly resisted. In New York, on July 13th, a vast mob demolished the buildings occupied by the Provost Marshals, burned the Colored Orphan Asylum, attacked the police, and killed about one hundred persons, mostly negroes. For three days the authorities were almost powerless, and then General Wool, commander of the military district of New York, after much difficulty, succeeded in suppressing the revolt. Still, the anti-war spirit was so violent, that on August 19th President Lincoln issued a proclamation suspending the privileges of the writ of habeas corpus throughout the Union. We shall take occasion to notice some of the reasons for and results of this measure later on. The draft was not a grand success, only about fifty thousand men being obtained. Volunteering, however, made up for much of the deficiency. Still, the terrible losses by battle and disease, and the thinning out of regiments by the expiration of enlistment terms, kept the muster roll down to so low an ebb that in October the President issued another call for three hundred thousand men. At the same time it was provided that any delinquency in meeting the demand would be supplied by a draft in the following January. This prompt and energetic course resulted in placing the Union army on a better footing than at any previous time.

Meanwhile the Confederate army was getting into very poor plight. The Confederate Congress had authorized Davis to call into the military service all white residents of the Confederate States between the ages of eighteen and forty-five years. The first call, for those under thirty-five years, was made in 1862, and on July 15th, 1863, Davis called for all who were liable to bear arms, between the ages of eighteen and forty-five years. This had but little practical result in increasing the Confederate forces, and a close inspection of the muster roll revealed the fact that a large proportion of the army existed on paper only. Desertions and fraudulent substitutions were matters of every-day occurrence. On August 1st, Jeff Davis, in another proclamation, called upon the absentees to return to the ranks, and promised pardon and amnesty to those who reported promptly. It will be seen by the tone of this affected clemency, that President Lincoln's keen analysis of the spirit of the Secession leaders was eminently correct. The "people" were nothing—the rulers everything. The term "Confederacy" was merely a cloak for the autocracy of men as despotic as Bismarck, yet without a shadow of his assumed excuses for the exercise of arbitrary power. To emphasize this point we may note that toward the end of 1863 the Confederate Congress passed an act declaring every white man in the Confederate States, between the ages of *eighteen and fifty-five years*, to be in the military service, and subject to the articles of war and military discipline and penalties, and that upon failure to report for duty at a military station within a certain time, he was liable to the penalty of death as a deserter. Beyond this, an agent was appointed in every county, with authority to seize, at the point of the bayonet, any supplies that might be needed. With one more example of the desperate recklessness of the Confederate leaders we can turn from this subject. Late in 1862 an address was issued to the people of Georgia, at the instance, principally, of Robert Toombs (whilom Secretary of State, but subsequently known as "The Humbug of the Confederacy,") in which the following appeal was made : "The foot of the oppressor is on the soil of Georgia. He comes with lust in his eye, poverty in his purse, and hell in his heart. He comes a robber and a murderer. How shall you meet him ? With the sword at the threshold ! With death for him or yourself ! But more than this—let every woman have a torch, every child a firebrand— let the loved homes of youth be made ashes, and the fields of our heritage be made desolate. Let blackness and ruin mark your departing steps, if depart you must, and let a desert more terrible than Sahara welcome the vandals. Let every city be leveled by the flames, and every village be lost in ashes. Let your faithful slaves share your fortune and your crust. Trust wife and children to the sure refuge and protection of God, preferring even for these loved ones the charnel-house as a home than loathsome vassalage to a nation already sunk below the contempt of the civilized world. This may be your terrible choice, and determine at once, without dissent, as honor, patriotism and duty to God require."

We must now turn back to the battle-fields and by a condensed résumé of the events of 1863 secure sufficient of our limited space to give in fuller detail the closing episodes of the great struggle.

CHAPTER XXVII.

RUNNING SUMMARY OF THE EARLIER MILITARY MOVEMENTS IN 1863—SIEGE OF VICKSBURG—SURRENDER OF VICKSBURG BY GENERAL PEMBERTON—GUERRILLA MORGAN'S RAIDS—HIS CAPTURE, IMPRISONMENT AND ESCAPE—THE GLORIOUS FEDERAL ACHIEVEMENTS AT LOOKOUT MOUNTAIN AND MISSIONARY RIDGE.

We have already described the earlier military movements of 1863, the repulse of General Sherman at Chickasaw Bayou, and the subsequent capture of Arkansas Post on the 11th of January, by the land forces under General McClernand with the co-operation of Admiral Porter's flotilla. After the return of this expedition, the Union forces were again collected at Memphis, and embarked on the Mississippi. A landing was effected on the Yazoo River, but all attempts on Vicksburg from this direction were soon abandoned. General Grant occupied the next three months in moving among the bayous, swamps and hills around Vicksburg, seeking an eligible position in its rear. A canal, cut across from a bend in the river, with intent to form a gunboat passage from the Mississippi, gave promise at first, but a sudden flood destroyed the labor of weeks. A second attempt of the same character was likewise a failure. It was then determined to run the fleet past the Vicksburg batteries, and on the night of April 16th the vessels dropped down the river almost unharmed by the furious cannonade they were exposed to when the movement was detected. The fleet took up a safe anchorage below the city, and General Grant, marching his troops down the right bank of the Mississippi, formed a junction with the naval force. General Grant crossed the river at Bruinsburg on the 30th of April, and the following day drove the Confederates from Port Gibson. This repulse was followed by the Confederate evacuation of Grand Gulf, at the mouth of the Big Black River, and then Grant's army swept round to the rear of Vicksburg. On the 12th of May a strong Confederate force was defeated, after a severe battle, at Raymond. Pressing on toward Jackson, the capital of Mississippi, the right wing of Grant's army under Generals Sherman and McPherson encountered General Johnston's division hastening to the support of the Vicksburg garrison. Another heavy engagement ensued on May 14th, and the Confederates being driven out of Jackson, the city was occupied by Sherman and McPherson. The commissary stores had been burned, but seventeen guns and a large number of tents were the spoils of the victors. McPherson then fell back to Clinton, and Sherman after completing the destruction of the bridges, public buildings and property of rebels in Jackson, rejoined the main army, which had been ordered to concentrate at Bolton's Station. The communications of Vicksburg were now severed, and the Confederates under General Pemberton had to choose between standing a siege or coming out to give battle. On the 16th Pemberton with a large portion of his troops met the Union forces at Champion Hills, or Baker's Creek. He was sharply repulsed and in another battle at Black River Bridge on the 17th was so badly shattered by Grant's impetuous attacks that he withdrew his demoralized force within the defenses of Vicksburg.

General Grant pressed on the investment of the city, believing that an immediate assault was necessary and practicable. He had Johnston in his rear, at Canton, being rapidly reinforced from Bragg's army in Tennessee, and it was of the utmost importance to reduce Vicksburg before Pemberton should make a desperate sortie, or Johnston compel the raising of the siege by an attack in the rear of the Federal lines, which extended some twenty miles from the Yazoo to Warrenton on the Mississippi. An assault was ordered on the afternoon of the 19th of May, but though it was boldly and bravely begun and gallantly persisted in for some hours, the Federal troops were repulsed with heavy loss. On the night of the 21st, Grant directed Admiral Porter to engage the water-batteries with his gunboats and shell the city preparatory to another assault on the morning of the 22d. This was done and the city suffered severely.

The second attack began at ten o'clock in the morning, and for a time the troops advanced without serious check, but when the actual assault was ordered the Confederates hurled themselves on the attacking party and again drove them back with serious loss. Several times along the whole line of the intrenchments the Federals gained lodgment only to be again hurled back or mowed down. At nightfall the troops were recalled from the more advanced positions, leaving only a picket line to mark the edge of the battle-ground. It was now evident to Grant that the place could only be taken by the slow process of a siege. Porter, with his gunboats, held the water-front and kept up a constant cannonade. For a month Grant kept the city closely invested. Pemberton in vain appealed to Johnston for aid, and his dispatch fell into Grant's hands. By this it was learned, on the 27th of May, that Pemberton had but 15,000 effective men and one-meal rations for thirty days. Grant's forces after the failure of the two assaults did not exceed 20,000 until the divisions of Generals Lauman, A. J. Smith and Kimball came to reinforce him. On June 11th, General Herron's Division, and on the 14th two divisions of the Ninth Corps, under General Parke, came up, and then the investment lines were completed. Sherman's Corps was on the extreme right, then came McPherson's, and General Ord (now in command of McClernand's troops) held the left, which was still further extended across the bayou to the river bluffs by the divisions of Herron and Lauman. Steadily, day by day, Grant drew his lines nearer and nearer the city, pushing forward his mines in the direction of the strongest of the enemy's works. In the meantime, Johnston had promised to attempt an attack on Grant's rear, simultaneously with a sortie by Pemberton, to cut his way out. But when Johnston moved toward Vernon, Grant sent Sherman on June 22d with five brigades to check his advance. The frequent interception of the communications between Johnston and Pemberton kept Grant well posted as to all their plans. On June 25th the most important of Grant's mines was exploded with terrific force under Fort Hill Bastion. There had been counter-mining, however, and therefore, though the works were badly shattered, the Confederates were ready and able to repulse the storming party. On the 28th another mine was sprung and another fruitless but terrible assault was made. In the meantime the garrison had been reduced almost to starvation, and on July 3d Pemberton ran up a white flag and sent a communication to General Grant proposing the appointment of three commissioners on each side to arrange terms of capitulation. He stated that he made this proposition to save the further effusion of blood, as he felt fully able to maintain his position for an indefinite period. General Grant, however, was thoroughly acquainted with his weakness and the scarcity of food, and therefore, in a firm, but very courteous reply, as due to the gallantry of a brave foe, he declined to agree to the appointment of a commission; he demanded unconditional surrender of the city and garrison, pledging himself to treat the prisoners of war with all the respect due to men who had shown such endurance and courage. General Grant declined to converse with Major General Bowen, who brought the note, but finally consented to meet General Pemberton between the lines. At three o'clock on the afternoon of July 3d General Pemberton, accompanied by Colonel Montgomery, of his staff, and Major-General Bowen, met General Grant on the southern slope of Fort Hill, to the left of the old Jackson road. General Grant was accompanied by Generals McPherson, Ord, Logan and A. J. Smith. After courteous, but brief, introductions, Grant and Pemberton withdrew to the shade of a live-oak tree for a private conference. It was then agreed that a temporary truce should be observed, and Grant arranged to send Pemberton a proposition in writing that evening. General Logan and Lieutenant-Colonel Wilson subsequently submitted Grant's terms. These were that one division of the Federal troops should march in as a guard at eight o'clock next morning; that when paroles had been signed the garrison should march out of the National lines, the officers retaining their regimental clothing—the staff, field and cavalry officers one horse each; the rank and file to take their own clothing only. Any necessary amount of rations and cooking utensils and thirty wagons were also to be allowed the vanquished. Pemberton's reply on the morning of the 4th asked for permission to march out with colors and arms and to stack them in front of the Confederate lines. He also desired to make stipulations as to the treatment of citizens. General Grant was indisposed to make further concessions, but ultimately consented to the brigades marching out and stacking arms, but after that they were to retire inside the lines until paroled. If these modified terms were not accepted at once, Grant intimated that he should open fire at nine o'clock. There was nothing open to Pemberton but compliance, and consequently McPherson's Corps was set as a guard, the Confederates marched out, stacked their arms and fell back. The formal surrender was made by Pemberton to McPherson. The Federal and Confederate commanders afterward rode side by side into the city, and by three o'clock the terrible strain of forty-five days was at an end. On the 11th of July the duly paroled soldiers, furnished with three days' rations, were escorted over the Big Black River and made their way to Jackson.

The prisoners paroled at Vicksburg numbered 27,000, of whom 6,000 were sick and wounded in the hospitals, and only about 15,000 were fit for duty. The entire number of prisoners taken during the Vicksburg campaign was 37,000, including fifteen general officers. Generals Tracy, Tilghman and Green were killed, and fully 10,000 of the rank and file shared the same fate. Grant estimated the Federal losses during the same campaign at 1,223 killed, 7,095 wounded and 537 missing.

This victory was of the utmost importance to the Union arms, and was a terrible blow to the Confederacy.

Meanwhile General Banks, who, as we have shown, had superseded General Butler in command of the Department of the Gulf, had been conducting a vigorous campaign on the Lower Mississippi. Early in January he advanced from his headquarters at Baton Rouge into Louisiana, reached Brashear City and then overthrew a Confederate force at Bayou Teche. Returning to the Mississippi, he invested Port Hudson, which was stubbornly defended by General Gardner until July 8th, when the news of the fall of Vicksburg compelled that commander to surrender with six thousand men. By this victory the control of the whole length of the Mississippi was restored to the National Government.

We will now turn to the movements of General Rosecrans. For some time after the battle of Murfreesboro but little was attempted. Late in the spring Colonel Streight's command, while on a raid into Georgia, was surrounded and captured by a Confederate force under General Forrest. Toward the latter part of June Rosecrans began to be active, and by a series of flank movements drove General Bragg out of Tennessee into

PICKETS ON DUTY.

Georgia. Rosecrans then took up a position at Chattanooga, on the left bank of the Tennessee River. During the next few months Bragg was reinforced by General Johnston, from Mississippi, and General Longstreet, from Virginia. On September 19th Bragg turned upon the Federal army at Chickamauga Creek, in the northwest angle of Georgia, and a severe but indecisive engagement ensued. General Longstreet came up during the following night and was placed on the left of Bragg's army. General Polk held the right and Ewell and

Johnston the centre. Soon after eight o'clock on the morning of the 20th the Confederates advanced to reopen the battle. Bragg's plan was to crush the Union line, force his way through a gap in Missionary Ridge, capture Rossville and Chattanooga, and annihilate Rosecrans' army. His plans were shrewdly laid, but the contract he had undertaken was beyond his ability. In heavy masses the Confederates were hurled against the unyielding Federal ranks, until General Wood, under a misapprehension of orders, opened a gap in the lines. Into this, with wonderful celerity Bragg thrust forward a heavy column and fairly cut the Union army in two. The right wing was driven from the field and retreated in confusion to Chattanooga. The left, however, was held by General Thomas with dogged determination, and until darkness shrouded the scene the gallant Thomas kept his assailants at bay. During the night Thomas withdrew from the field and joined Rosecrans in Chattanooga. The Union losses in killed and wounded and missing amounted to about 19,000, and the Confederates suffered even more heavily.

General Bragg at once pressed forward to lay siege to Chattanooga. He had severed the Federal lines of communication, and now thought he had Rosecrans fairly cornered. General Hooker, however, with two corps of the Army of the Potomac, opened up the Tennessee River and brought relief to the beleaguered Federals. Then General Grant, who had been promoted to the chief command of the Western armies, assumed the direction of affairs at Chattanooga, and when General Sherman, with his division, arrived on the scene, preparations were made for turning the tables on the Confederates, with the now powerful Army of the Cumberland under the boldest of the Federal generals.

The left wing of the Confederate army rested on Lookout Mountain and the right on Missionary Ridge, a position so formidable that Bragg need not be accused of taking his own name in vain when he boasted that it was impregnable and even planned the storming of Chattanooga. With that sublime audacity which was so notable a Confederate attribute, he gave General Grant notice on the 20th of November that he was about to bombard the position, and advised him to remove all non-combatants. A fly alighting on an elephant would attract about as much attention as this notice elicited. General Grant was not in the habit of taking gratuitous advice. In place of preparing to repel an attack, he meditated dealing a stunning blow upon the over-confident Confederates, and he carried out his intentions. On the 23d, General Hooker threw his corps across the river below Chattanooga and gained a footing at the mouth of Lookout Creek, facing the mountain. The divisions of Generals Geary and Osterhaus supported him, and an assault was begun the following morning. The remainder of the Union army was employed

GRANT'S HEADQUARTERS AT CHATTANOOGA.

in preventing reinforcements from Missionary Ridge going to the aid of Lookout Mountain. In the midst of a dense fog which concealed their advance, the Federals moved forward shortly after eight o'clock. Within a couple of hours the Confederate rifle-pits among the foot-hills had been carried. Here Hooker had intended to pause, but the enthusiasm of his troops knew no bounds, and yielding to the wild impulses of his gallant troops Hooker gave orders to charge on the whole Confederate position. Through the dense fog, up the precipitous sides of the mountain the men scrambled and fought with the reckless daring of incarnate devils. The murderous fire of the heavy Confederate batteries merely seemed to increase their valor, and before two o'clock in the afternoon the Union flag was planted on the cloud-capped summit of Lookout Mountain, surrounded by the exultant Federal troops, while the utterly routed Confederates were streaming in hot haste down the eastern slope and across the intervening hills and valleys toward Missionary Ridge.

During the night of the 24th, General Bragg concentrated his forces and prepared to defend this latter position to the uttermost. In the meantime General Sherman had thrown pontoon bridges across the Tennessee and Chickamauga, and gained a lodgment on the northeastern declivity of the Ridge. General Thomas, with his troops in a fever of excitement, held the centre, being on the southern and eastern slopes of Orchard Knob. At two o'clock in the afternoon General Grant gave orders for the advance, and at once a repetition of the desperate scenes of Lookout Mountain was precipitated. The Federal troops gained the summit of Missionary Ridge and the Confederates were again hopelessly routed. During the following night General Bragg withdrew his disheartened and demoralized remant of an army and retreated in the direction of Ringgold, Georgia. The Federal losses in the two battles reached 757 killed, 4,529 wounded and 330 missing. The Confederate losses in killed, wounded and captured exceeded ten thousand. The results of these battles were so decisive as to put an end to the war in Tennessee until it was renewed by Hood, at Franklin and Nashville, in the winter of 1864.

We have mentioned that General Burnside, when relieved of his command of the Army of the Potomac, was placed on waiting orders. The demand for good field officers did not leave him idle for any great length of time, and in March he was assigned to the command of the Army of the Ohio, and with the Ninth Corps proceeded to East Tennessee. For some months his duties were chiefly executive, the Ninth Corps having been taken from him to assist Grant at Vicksburg. After some minor movements, Burnside arrived with his command at Knoxville, on September 1st, and his advent was enthusiastically hailed by the loyalists of that region. After the battle of Chickamauga, General Longstreet was sent to East Tennessee and on his way to attack Burnside at Knoxville, he captured several small detachments of Federal troops. On the 29th of November, after a regular siege of Knoxville, Longstreet attempted to carry the position by storm, but was repulsed with heavy loss. General Sherman advanced to the relief of Burnside, after Bragg had retreated from Chattanooga, but Longstreet raised the siege and retreated into Virginia before Sherman could reach Knoxville.

In Arkansas and Southern Missouri, during the early part of 1863, the Confederate Generals Marmaduke and Price were again active. On January 8th they advanced on Springfield, but were repulsed, and three days later were also foiled in an attack on Hartsville. The post at Cape Girardeau was attacked on April 26th by General Marmaduke, but without result. General Holmes, with eight thousand men, advanced on Helena, Arkansas, on the day of the surrender of Vicksburg, but he lost one-fifth of his troops and retired in disorder.

When the surrender of Vicksburg and Port Hudson and the retreat of Johnston from Jackson had relieved the pressure on Grant's army, General Frederick Steele was sent to Helena to make preparations for the capture of Little Rock, the capital of Arkansas. In this expedition he was joined by General Davidson, and with 12,000 men and 40 guns, Davidson with his cavalry led the advance, and crossing the White River at Clarendon, pushed on to Brownsville. He drove Marmaduke from the town on August 26th, and then pushed on to the Arkansas River. On September 7th Steele, who had taken another route, came up with him. Davidson then pushed on, and crossing the river on a pontoon bridge, reached Bayou Fourche, five miles above Little Rock, on the morning of the 10th. While preparing for an advance on the city from this side, Steele was moving along the north bank of the river, and the combined attack drove Marmaduke back into the city. The Confederates then hastily retreated, after firing the city in several places. They were closely followed by Davidson's cavalry, and by seven o'clock in the evening the civil authorities formally surrendered to Davidson. Steele had by this time occupied the Confederate works on the north side of the river. The Confederate troops were in full retreat toward

Arkadelphia, but the Federal forces were too much wearied to make any effectual pursuit. The occupation of Little Rock by Steele's army practically ended the fighting in this direction.

We have noticed the raids occasionally made by the guerrilla chief John H. Morgan, and must now chronicle the ingominious finale of his adventures for the year 1863. On June 27th Morgan crossed the Cumberland River at Burksville and pushed rapidly northward. After partly sacking Columbia, Morgan, who had a force of 3,500 well-mounted men and six guns, had a sharp fight at Tebb's Bend, on the Green River, with some Michigan troops under Colonel Moore. Morgan lost some two hundred men. He then moved upon Lebanon, and after a severe engagement captured and fired the place, taking prisoners Captain Hanson and his small force and seizing a small battery. After raiding and plundering in all directions Morgan found that the Federal forces were combining to punish him, and he began to look around for a pathway out of his dilemma. Concentrating his scattered pillagers at Harrison, just within the borders of Ohio, he started to attempt the passage of the Ohio into Western Virginia or northeastern Kentucky as the safest route back to Tennessee. General Hobson, however, was close on his trail and the citizens of Ohio and Indiana, aroused by Morgan's daring depredations, were lending vigorous aid to the Federal and State troops. At Berlin, Jackson County, Ohio, he encountered a well-trained militia force, under Colonel Runkle, and was compelled to abandon an intended raid on some State cattle collected there. On the 18th of July Morgan reached Buffington Ford, on the Ohio, but here he dropped into a trap. On the 19th General Judah fell on his flank, the head of Hobson's column, under General Shackelford, attacked his rear, and a couple of gunboats opened fire from the river on his front. About 800 of Morgan's men surrendered, but the daring chief, with a handful of followers, pushed inland, fighting each on his own hook, until fairly cornered near New Lisbon, Columbiana County. Morgan surrendered to General Shackelford, and he and several of his officers had the honor of occupying felons' cells in the Penitentiary at Columbus, Ohio, until November 20th, when the guerrilla chief and six of his comrades dug their way out and escaped to the Confederate lines in northern Georgia. We shall meet with him again, but, for the time being, he drops out of sight.

We will now glance at some movements along the coast and then return to the Army of the Potomac and the eventful campaign in Pennsylvania. We have noticed the operations of Admiral Dupont in the early part of the year. Toward the end of June a land force under General Q. A. Gillmore, and a fleet under Admiral Dahlgren, renewed the siege of Charleston. The Federal army first landed on Folly Island, and then succeded in planting batteries on the south end of Morris Island in such positions as to bear upon Fort Sumter in the channel and Fort Wagner and Battery Gregg at the northern end of the island. On the 18th of July, after a severe bombardment, General Gillmore attempted to carry Fort Wagner by assault, but he was repulsed and lost over fifteen hundred men. The siege was continued, however, with unabated vigor until September 6th, when both the fort and Battery Gregg were evacuated by the Confederates, who retired into Charleston. This gave Gillmore a position within four miles of the city, and enabled him to train his batteries on the wharves and the lower portion of the city. Beyond this it was not possible to operate at this time, but the port of Charleston was effectually closed, though the harbor and city remained under Confederate control.

We have thus rapidly run over the general events of 1863, except the important movements of the Army of the Potomac, to which we will turn in another chapter.

CHAPTER XXVIII.

HOOKER WITH THE ARMY OF THE POTOMAC—DISASTROUS FIGHT AT CHANCELLORSVILLE—DEATH OF "STONEWALL" JACKSON—CAPTURE OF THE HEIGHTS AT FREDERICKSBURG—LEE'S DASH INTO PENNSYLVANIA AND MARYLAND—CAPTURE OF WINCHESTER BY THE CONFEDERATES—HOOKER SUPERSEDED BY GENERAL MEADE.

We left General Hooker, who had succeeded Burnside, in command of the Army of the Potomac, in winter quarters and reorganizing his forces. The Confederates were also preparing for another vigorous campaign, and General Lee had not only increased his army, but had also vastly improved its field equipment. "Stonewall" Jackson's force had been increased to 33,000 men, the artillery had been consolidated and placed under the command of General Pendleton, and the morale of the army had been improved by judicious handling. In addition to this, Lee had constructed formidable works, extending about twenty-five miles, from Bank's Ford to Port Royal. By these arrangements, Lee's position around Fredericksburg had been so strengthened, that an attempt to force it from the front did not seem possible. Hooker therefore decided to attempt the turning of Lee's flank, and by this operation, coupled with demonstrations in the rear, force Lee to quit his intrenchments. While Hooker was perfecting his plans, another of the Confederate guerillas, John S. Moseby, had made a daring dash upon Fairfax Court-House, captured Colonel Stoughton and raided around generally. On March 17th there was a sharp engagement near Kelly's Ford on the Rappahannock, between Federal cavalry under General W. W. Averill, and General Fitz Hugh Lee's cavalry. The Federal forces retired and recrossed the river, but the losses on each side were so nearly equal as to bar any claim for a victory. By this time Hooker was ready to move. On April 12th he ordered General Stoneman to advance with his cavalry up the eastern banks of the Rappahannock, then cross and disperse Fitz Hugh Lee's cavalry at Culpeper Court-House, and by destroying bridges and railroads sever Lee's communications with Richmond. The swollen condition of the river, however, frustrated this movement at that time. On April 27th Hooker began to move his whole force, and the Fifth, Eleventh and Twelfth Corps, under Generals Meade, Howard and Slocum, respectively crossed the Rappahannock at Kelly's Ford, twenty-seven miles above Fredericksburg, during the 28th and 29th of April. They reached Chancellorsville, after wading the Rapidan, in Lee's rear, on the afternoon of the 30th. While this movement was secretly conducted, portions of the Second Corps under General Gibbon kept the Confederates on the watch in front. As soon as the turning column had crossed the decoy troops left their position at Falmouth and hastened to Chancellorsville. General Hooker made his head-quarters in the Chancellor Mansion on the night of April 30th. While these movements were in progress on the right, the three corps, First, Third and Sixth, under Generals Reynolds, Sickles and Sedgwick, the latter in command, had crossed the Rappahannock some two miles below Fredericksburg, and dislodged the Confederate pickets. Sedgwick and Reynolds then held the position while Sickles moved rapidly on to Chancellorsville. Hooker had expected that Lee would retreat to Richmond, but the Confederate chief had called up "Stonewall" Jackson's division and contemplated attacking the Federal army while it was divided. Leaving Early with 9,000 men and 30 guns at Fredericksburg to keep Sedgwick in check, he sent Jackson's column towards Chancellorsville in the small hours of the morning of May 1st, and this was joined by Anderson's Corps. Lee's intent was to secure possession of Banks' Ford and compel Hooker to fight before Sedgwick could form a junction with him. Near the Tabernacle Church, half way between Fredericksburg and Chancellorsville, a plank road diverges from the turnpike, and falls into it again at Chancellorsville. Jackson advanced along the plank road and General McLaws along the turnpike. Hooker's troops had moved out from the other extremity of these roads, and also along a road leading to Banks' Ford. Along the plank road the right column, under

Slocum, had scarcely begun the move when it encountered Jackson's cavalry and was forced back; Sykes' column, which had moved along the turnpike, came to Slocum's assistance, but Jackson's vigorous assaults on the Federal flanks compelled the right wing and the centre to fall back to the works at Chancellorsville. In the mean time Meade's Corps, forming the left wing, had succeeded in getting possession of Banks' Ford, and thus lessening the distance between Sedgwick's division and the main army. During the night of May 1st both armies prepared for a battle. The Federal lines extended from the Rappahannock to the Wilderness Church, two miles west of Chancellorsville. The centre was held by Slocum, with part of Sickles' Corps supporting. Howard held the right of the line, aided by Pleasanton's Cavalry, and Meade's Corps, with a division of Crouch's, held the left of the line. So well had Hooker disposed his troops that Lee hesitated to attack him in front, and yielding to the advice of the daring "Stonewall," he decided to divide his force and attempt a flank and rear movement. Jackson, with 25,000 men, filed off from the plank road and moved through the woods to the Orange plank road, four miles west of Chancellorsville. Although this movement was detected by General Birney and reported to Hooker, and despite a gallant charge, in which Birney cut off and captured five hundred of the Twenty-third Georgia Regiment, yet so boldly and, it must be admitted, bravely, were Jackson's designs carried out, that his men, with the wild "rebel yell," swept down upon the flank and rear of Howard's Corps, the Federal right wing, about supper time. Instantly all was confusion. General Devens was severely wounded, and one-third of his division, upon which the first blow fell, had been disabled or captured in a brief period. The panic-stricken fugitives fell back upon the positions of Generals Carl Schurz and A. Von Steinwehr, any attempts at resistance being swept aside by the exultant Confederates. A brief halt was made, when Steinwehr threw a brigade into some works near Dowdall's Tavern, but the yelling demons swarmed over the works and pushed after the flying Federals until darkness came on. This disaster on the right was speedily communicated to Hooker, who sent forward his own division and

French's Brigade, and ordered Sickles to fall back and attack Jackson's left. A lucky accident enabled Pleasanton's cavalry to check the pursuit until Sickles could extricate himself. In the meantime the Eighth Pennsylvania had been badly shattered in an attack on the Confederate flank, and Major Keenan had been killed. A terrible artillery duel then ensued between Pleasanton's Horse Artillery with part of Sickles' Battery, and the Confederate artillery, under Colonel Crutchfield. In this engagement Crutchfield was badly wounded. But a heavier loss fell on the Confederate army at this juncture. "Stonewall" Jackson, with a small staff and escort, had pushed forward to make a personal reconncissance, with a view of extending his lines to the left and cutting Hooker off from United States Ford. He was on his way back to his own lines, just as Hill had reached the front, when his own troops, mistaking the little party for Federal cavalry, fired into them. Jackson received three bullets, one shattering the left arm below the shoulder, and severing an artery. While he was being borne to the rear on a litter, one of the bearers was shot dead by the canister shot of the Federals. About the same time General Hill was disabled by a fragment of a shell, and the command falling upon General Rodes, the projected Confederate advance was abandoned for the day. "Stonewall" Jackson was first taken to the hospital at Wilderness Tavern, where his left arm was amputated, and three days later, on the arrival of his wife, he was removed to Guiney's Station. He lingered until May 10th, suffering chiefly from pneumonia, and then died peacefully, after an interval of delirium. It may safely be asserted that no individual loss was more keenly felt by the Confederates throughout the struggle, nor was there a death which had a more saddening effect abroad. "Stonewall Jackson's" name was a household phrase in Europe, his daring and dexterity having lifted him into wonderful prominence. Just here it may be pertinent to note the origin of the name. At the beginning of the battle of Bull Run, when the Confederates in one part were routed and in disorderly retreat, General Bee, pointing to an immovable column of men, cried out "Here is Jackson, standing like a *stone wall*." The term fitted the man, and as "Stonewall," more often than as Jackson, he was alluded to among the Confederate troops.

The Confederate troops during Saturday night had been busily preparing for attack or defense as the case might be, but Hooker was too cautious to attempt aggressive operations, and contented himself with dispositions to meet a further attack. He had sent to Sedgwick on Saturday morning for Reynolds' Corps, and its arrival late that evening replaced the shattered Eleventh, which Jackson had so demoralized. In the mean time Sedgwick, in pursuance of further orders, had crossed the Rappahannock and attacked the heights of Fredericksburg. The stone wall at the foot of Marye's Hill, where Burnside's troops had been so fatally repulsed in December, was again the scene of a fearful struggle, but this time with a far different result. The Confederate works were carried in all directions, at a heavy cost of life, however, and Early was driven southward in a demoralized condition. This opened the plank road to Chancellorsville, and Sedgwick pushed along it to threaten Lee's flank and rear.

On Sunday morning, May 3d, the whole of Lee's left wing dashed forward under Stuart, and the Federals were driven back, Sickles holding his position for a time at the point of the bayonet. The Confederate artillery kept up a constant fire, and during the hottest part of the battle General Hooker was stunned by the fall of a pillar of the Chancellor House, his headquarters. This disaster kept Sickles without the reinforcements he had sent for. Lee then threw forward his whole force, and despite a gallant resistance Sickles and Slocum were forced back; then Hancock and Geary, after gallantly holding their position for some time in front of the headquarters, were also broken by overwhelming numbers, and the Confederates took possession of Chancellorsville by ten o'clock, after six hours hard fighting.

We left Sedgwick advancing along the plank road from Fredericksburg. The knowledge of this movement checked Lee's intended advances on Hooker on Sunday afternoon. Appreciating the importance of preventing a junction, Lee sent McLaws with four brigades to intercept Sedgwick. Near Salem Church, on Salem Heights, the opposing forces met and a severe engagement ensued. At one time the Federals had secured the crest of the hill, but finally they were swept back, and by night Sedgwick had lost five thousand men, including those who fell in the assault on the Fredericksburg heights. Although but seven miles from Hooker's main army, Sedgwick found it impossible to effect a junction. Lee at once determined to demolish Hooker in detail, and sent Early, on Monday morning, May 4th, to recapture the heights of Fredericksburg, while Anderson's three brigades were sent to reinforce McLaws. By noon Sedgwick was inclosed on three sides, and when a general attack was made later in the day he was driven back on the river, despite a desperate resistance. Darkness put an end to the Confederate pursuit, and during the night Sedgwick crossed the Rappahannock on pontoon bridges. He had lost more than one-fifth of his command and was cut off from aid to or from Hooker.

Leaving Early and Barksdale to hold Sedgwick, Lee recalled McLaws and Anderson, and determined to crush Hooker that night. This pleasant resolve, however, was frustrated by a furious storm, and in the meantime Hooker, after a conference with his corps commanders decided to retreat across the river. This was accomplished, and on May 6th the Army of the Potomac was again before Fredericksburg, and the Confederates were on the heights in the rear of the city. Each army had resumed its original position, but with vastly depleted strength. The Federal losses footed up to 17,197 men, including 5,000 taken prisoners, and the Confederates had lost 12,277, including 2,000 prisoners. The Federal Generals Berry and Whipple were among the killed. Hooker had also lost thirteen guns, about twenty thousand small arms and seventeen colors.

While these events were in progress General Stoneman's cavalry had been engaged in a dashing raid and had destroyed much Confederate property, but had not effected the main purpose of the expedition, the severing of Lee's communications with Richmond.

About the same time, also, Longstreet had made a vigorous

assault upon General John J. Peck, who had been holding, since September, 1862, a fortified position at Suffolk, on the south side of the James River. After a siege of twenty-four days, during which time both Longstreet's and Peck's forces had fought with desperate gallantry, Longstreet, on May 3d, abandoned the siege of Suffolk and retreated to the Blackwater, closely pursued by Generals Corcoran and Dodge and Colonel Foster. For a time there was a lull in important movements, although several sharp minor engagements between detached divisions of the armies at various points. Early in June, however, Lee, who had been projecting an invasion of Pennsylvania and Maryland, began the advance. His left wing, under Ewell, pushed through Chester Gap, of the Blue Ridge, crossed the Shenandoah River and swept into Strasburg Valley. On the evening of the 13th the Confederate forces were before Winchester, then held by General Milroy. On the evening of the 14th of June, the Confederates with an overwhelming force had substantially invested Winchester, and Milroy, who had but 7,000 effective men, decided to retreat. The Confederate cavalry, under General Imboden, was at Romney, thus preventing reinforcements reaching him by the line of the Baltimore & Ohio Railroad. At one o'clock on the morning of the 15th of June, just as Milroy had spiked his guns, the Confederates fell upon him and the retreat became a rout. The Federal forces made a dash for the Potomac, but were met by Johnson's Division and some 4,000 were made prisoners. Milroy lost also nearly the whole of his artillery and ammunition, the Confederates capturing 29 guns, 277 wagons and 400 horses. Milroy's wagon-train crossed the Potomac at Harper's Ferry, and the garrison at that point retired to the Maryland Heights. The scattered fugitives made their way in various directions into Pennsylvania and spread dismay. Milroy's wagon-train reached Harrisburg by way of Hagerstown and Chambersburg. This rout of the Federal forces left the Shenandoah Valley open to the Confederates. Elated by his success, Lee detached General Jenkins, of Ewell's corps, with fifteen hundred cavalry, in pursuit of Milroy. This force swept up the Cumberland Valley, and after destroying the railroad and other property at Chambersburg, returned and held Hagerstown, Maryland, to await the advance of Lee's main army.

In the meantime, Hooker, distracted by orders from Washington, and wholly unable to penetrate the real nature of Lee's movement, had been kept near the Rappahannock, but when he heard of Milroy's disaster, he at once moved northward with his whole force to Centreville to protect Washington. Lee, however, had the start of him, and Longstreet was sent along the eastern side of the Blue Ridge, where he took possession of Ashby's and Snicker's gaps, thus threatening the Capital and preventing an attack on the Confederates in the Valley. Hooker had taken up his quarters at Fairfax Court-House on June 15th. Several sharp skirmishes occurred from this point between Pleasonton's cavalry and those under the Confederate Stuart. On

GEN. HUGH JUDSON KILPATRICK.

June 17th, General Judson Kilpatrick drove back some Confederate cavalry which made a demonstration from Ashby's Gap, but the general position of affairs was such as to create the most lively apprehension on the part of the authorities of Maryland and Pennsylvania, as well as those at Washington.

While Lee was keeping the Army of the Potomac in suspense around Washington, Ewell's corps crossed the river at Shepardstown and Williamsport, moved on to Hagerstown and then up the Cumberland Valley to Chambersburg, arriving there on June 22d and compelling General Knipe to fall back. Ewell then divided the command into two columns, Rodes pushing on to Kingston, within thirteen miles of Harrisburg, and Early advancing through Gettysburg and York, to Wrightsville, on the Susquehanna. The railroad bridge from this point to Columbia opposite was burned by the retreating Federals. On the 24th and 25th of June the remainder of Lee's army, under Longstreet and Hill, crossed the Potomac, and after concentrating at Hagerstown, pressed in after Ewell, toward the Susquehannna.

Just at this time occurred another of those headquarters complications which so frequently imperilled field successes. Hooker, as soon as he became aware of Lee's movement, crossed the river at Edward's Ferry, with his forces now increased to 100,000 men, but deeming a further force necessary, he urged the abandonment of the post at Harper's Ferry, that the 11,000 men stationed there might be added to his own forces. Expecting that this would be acceded to, Hooker moved on to Frederick, and ordered General Slocum to join General French at Harper's Ferry, and push on with the united force to threaten Lee's rear in the Cumberland valley. General-in-Chief Halleck, however, refused to give him the Harper's Ferry garrison, and Hooker promptly telegraphed to Washington that, being unable to carry out instructions with the force at his disposal, he desired to be relieved from his command.

He probably supposed that this would break down Halleck's opposition, but it seems that this request was precisely what the General-in-Chief had been calculating upon, for on the day the dispatch was received, June 27th, an order was issued, instructing General George G. Meade to assume command of the Army of the Potomac. The acceptance of his resignation was conveyed to Hooker, with instructions to await the commands of the Adjutant-General at Baltimore. Chafing under a sense of unjust treatment, Hooker waited three days, and then failing to receive any instructions, he decided to go to Washington and endeavor to obtain an explanation. In this he again played into Halleck's hands, for there was a standing order prohibiting officers visiting the capital without leave, and Halleck at once ordered him under arrest for violation of rules.

CHAPTER XXIX.

THE CONFEDERATE INVASION OF PENNSYLVANIA AND MARYLAND—MEADE'S MOVEMENTS TO CHECK LEE'S ADVANCE—BATTLE OF GETTYSBURG—DEFEAT OF THE CONFEDERATES—MEADE'S LEISURELY PURSUIT—ENGAGEMENT AT MINE RUN—BOTH ARMIES IN WINTER QUARTERS—CLOSE OF 1863—PERSONAL NARRATIVE OF THE SWAMP ANGEL'S CONSTRUCTION.

"Swapping horses while crossing a stream" was known to be an operation wholly at variance with President Lincoln's methods, and therefore it is probable that some very strong pressure was brought to bear on him before he consented to a change of commanders in the face of an aggressive foe. There was another peculiarity about the new arrangement which seemed to indicate a personal feeling on the part of Halleck against Hooker; and this was that while Hooker's request for the Harper's Ferry troops was bluntly refused, the new commander, Meade,

GEN. GEORGE G. MEADE.

was not only permitted to use them at his own discretion, but he was further assured that the Executive would not interfere with any of his arrangements, and consequently that the authority vested in him was more extensive than that which his predecessors had been intrusted with. The army was at first disposed to resent the change of commanders, but discipline, together with a conviction of the gravity of the situation, speedily overcame discontent, and Meade soon had his troops well in hand and eager to meet the invading foe. General Meade assumed command on June 28th, the very day on which Lee had planned to cross the Susquehanna at Harrisburg, with intent to occupy Philadelphia. The Confederate General Stuart, with his dashing cavalry, had already crossed the Potomac at Seneca, and after destroying a number of canal boats and army wagons, with their stores, passed around the right of the Army of the Potomac at Westminster, and was sweeping on to Carlisle, when on the 29th of June he came in contact with General Judson Kilpatrick at Hanover. The Confederates attacked the flank and rear of Farnsworth's Brigade. The onslaught was sudden and severe, but the arrival of General Custer turned the tide of the battle. Stuart lost some fifty men, but he inflicted a loss of about double that number on Farnsworth before he was driven off. In the meantime Lee found that a further advance would be hazardous, as Pennsylvania was in arms and on the alert, while the Army of the Potomac, largely reinforced, was threatening his rear. He determined, therefore, to concentrate at Gettysburg, by this means keep open a line of retreat, and if successful in shattering Meade's forces, to be ready for an immediate advance on Baltimore and Washington. On June 30th, late in the day, Meade, who was moving forward in force from Frederick, became convinced that Lee intended to risk a grand engagement, and he ordered General French to remove all public property from Harper's Ferry, and guard the line of the Baltimore and Ohio, while occupying Frederick. Meade expected to fight along the line of Big Pipe Creek, between the Potomac and Chesapeake Bay, and after sending Buford's division to occupy Gettysburg, he made the following dispositions for the decisive battle which he was convinced was impending: The centre, composed of the Fifth and Twelfth Corps, under Generals Sykes and Slocum, were sent toward Hanover; the right wing, composed of the Sixth Corps, under General Sedgwick, took position at Manchester, in the rear of Big Pipe Creek, and the left, under General John F. Reynolds, was ordered to push on to Gettysburg. This wing comprised Reynolds' First Corps, the Third, under General

Sickles, and the Eleventh, under General Howard. General Winfield Scott Hancock, with the Second Corps, was stationed in Taneytown, on the road to Winchester from Emmettsburg. This was also the headquarters.

On the morning of July 1st, Buford's cavalry had a sharp encounter with the Confederate advance under General Heth on the Chambersburg road, until the brigades of Generals Cutler and Meredith, of Reynolds' Division, came up to Buford's support. The actual battle of Gettysburg, which was destined to assume gigantic proportions, was soon begun by a severe struggle for the passage of Willoughby's Run, near Seminary Ridge, between the Confederates under Archer, of Hill's right wing, and Meredith's "Iron Brigade," under the personal superintendence of General Reynolds. After a brilliant charge, Archer and some eight hundred of his men were captured, but, unfortunately, Reynolds was killed, having been picked off by a sharpshooter. General Doubleday assumed his command, and soon afterward General Davis' Mississippi Brigade, which had been sadly harassing Cutler's flanks, was surrounded and captured. This not only relieved Cutler and saved Hall's Battery, which had been seriously endangered, but it allowed an extension of the Federal line to the right, to counteract a similar Confederate movement. By noon General Doubleday had secured a commanding position on Seminary Ridge. The Confederate advance under Rodes, of Ewell's division, had, in the meantime, taken possession of another ridge and threatened Cutler's position. Generals Baxter and Paul were sent to Cutler's aid, and, after a sharp contest on the right, near the Mummasburg road, the North Carolina regiments were captured. By this time Howard's corps on the Federal side and the divisions of Pender and Early of the Confederate army, had joined in the contest, which now became serious. General Schimmelpfennig then, under Howard's orders, took chief command in this section, and he sent the divisions of Generals Barlow and Carl Schurz further to the right, thus extending and somewhat weakening the centre. The Confederates under Early fell heavily on Barlow and forced him back, and then Rodes dashed on the centre and throw it back in some confusion. In the midst of this Early, by a rapid advance, pushed into the village and captured about three thousand of the Eleventh Corps. The position on Seminary Ridge was then abandoned, and the Federals, covered in their retreat by Buford's cavalry, fell back to the left and rear of Steinwehr's Division, on Cemetery Hill. Before dark Hill's Corps held Seminary Ridge and Ewell's occupied Gettysburg. The death of Reynolds being reported to General Meade, he at once intrusted General Winfield Scott Hancock with chief command in the field, and sent him forward to act on his own discretion. Satisfied with Howard's disposition of his force, Hancock placed Slocum in command and returned to headquarters, meeting his own corps on the road and placing it in the rear of Cemetery Hill. General

GEN. WINFIELD S. HANCOCK.

Sickles had also moved forward to Howard's support, and before morning the position on Cemetery Hill was well sustained. Meade by this time had become convinced that the invasion was checked, and he determined to force a battle at Gettysburg. When Hancock reported to him, both Generals went to the front and established headquarters in the rear of Cemetery Hill, on the Taneytown road. On the morning of the 2d of July, both armies were only about one mile apart, Lee having made his headquarters at the crossing of the Chambersburg road over Seminary Ridge. General Sykes came up with his division during the night, and was placed in the reserve by Meade. The

Federal right was on Culp's Hill and the extreme left on Round Top, which was held by Hancock and Sickles. Wadsworth and Slocum held Culp's Hill, and were faced by Early and Johnson, of Hill's command, while Hood and McLaws, of Longstreet's command, confronted Hancock and Sickles. Both armies were anxious for battle, but neither Lee nor Meade coveted the distinction of opening the fight. The latter was anxious over the non-arrival of Sedgwick, who with 15,000 men was some miles distant, and the former was not slow to perceive the advantageous position which Howard had secured. As a consequence, the day wore on with merely an occasional skirmish until Lee, probably suspecting the reason of Meade's quiescence, determined to begin the attack by a dash on Sickles, who held the ridge between Hancock and the Round Top. Expecting an attack, Sickles had extended and somewhat weakened his left, but before Meade could change this disposition, of which he saw the peril, the Confederate columns were pressing up with the intent of turning the flank. This work was assigned to Longstreet, and Hill was ordered to make an attack on Meade's centre while Ewell attacked the right. Longstreet sent Hood, supported by McLaws and Anderson, to attack the weakest portion of Sickles' line, the main object of the struggle being the possession of Little Round Top. The pressure of twenty-five thousand men turned Sickles' left, but Sykes came to his support. By desperate efforts cannon were dragged to the summit and hastily mounted behind breastworks of loose stones. A terrible struggle ensued, in the course of which Generals Vincent and Weed and Lieutenant Hazlett were killed, but the eminence was secured by the Federals. In the meantime another hand-to-hand conflict had been waged in the peach orchard and open fields at the foot of the hill, and in this Generals Cross and Zook were mortally wounded. Again the Federals were forced from their position, and for a second time the possession of Little Round Top was endangered. At length General Crawford, Pennsylvania Reserves, with six regiments swept the Confederates down the northwestern side, taking several hundred prisoners and killing General Barksdale.

This ended the conflict at this point, and preparations were at once begun to fortify Little Round Top. During this time severe fighting had been in progress on the left centre. General Willard had been killed, and Sickles had lost a leg. The engagement here was closed by a charge under the direction of General Hancock, who drove the Confederates back to their own lines. In other directions equally serious fighting had been going on. Early had made desperate efforts to storm the batteries on Cemetery Hill, the actual Federal centre, and his men with reckless gallantry had forced their way entirely through one battery and fairly into another. Carroll's Brigade, however, came to the rescue, and the position was saved. On the extreme right Johnson, of Ewell's left division, had penetrated the woods in the rear of Culp's Hill, and just before dark a terrific engagement ensued here, the Confederates penetrating the works near Spangler's Spring despite the gallant efforts of Green's brigade. No attempt, however, was made to follow up this advantage Still, the Confederate line had really been advanced, and Lee claimed this as a victory. The slaughter, however, had been fearful, the lowest estimates placing the killed and wounded on both sides at about forty thousand men.

Though he had certainly suffered a slight repulse, Meade was satisfied to renew the struggle next day. During the night of the 2d Little Round Top was strengthened and the works on the extreme right were also put in readiness to meet the expected advance. As early as four o'clock on the morning of July 3d an artillery fire was opened on the Confederates who had obtained lodgment the previous night, and by eight o'clock General Geary's Division had swept the intruders off the right flank. Lee, perceiving that his original plan had failed, determined to throw his whole strength on Meade's centre, and by noon had one hundred and forty-five guns leveled at Hancock's position on Cemetery Hill. But Meade had been preparing for this, and the heavy cannonade which began about one o'clock from the Confederate lines was promptly answered by an almost equal volume of iron hail. For some hours this furious artillery duel went on, and then a heavy, compact mass of Confederate infantry, led by General Pickett, swept across the plain to the assault of Cemetery Hill. Pickett was supported on the right by Wilcox and on the left by Pettigrew, the entire assaulting column being some fifteen thousand strong. In the face of a galling artillery fire, which made fearful havoc in their ranks, they pressed on till close up to the Federal lines. Then a portion of Doubleday's command opened fire, and this being followed up by heavy fusillades from the divisions of Gibbons and Hayes, threw Pettigrew's troops into confusion, which soon developed into an actual rout. Pettigrew was severely wounded and two thousand of his men, with fifteen battle flags, were captured. The main assaulting column, however, pressed on, scrambled up the hill, broke through Hancock's line, and, driving back part of Webb's brigade, triumphantly raised a Confederate flag on top of Cemetery Hill. The advantage was of brief duration; the Federal troops rallied and stemmed Pickett's advance. Then Stannard's Vermonters riddled the assaulting column, which broke in great disorder. Twenty-five hundred men and twelve battle flags were captured. The Vermonters then fell on Wilcox and shattered his brigade. The death roll in this combat was terrible. Among the killed was General Garnett, and Generals Armistead and Kemper, who led the scaling party, were severely wounded.

While this result was being achieved Meade had sent General Crawford to attack the Confederate right. General William McCandless, with his brigade and a regiment under Fisher, swept along the Emmettsburg road, broke up a brigade of Hood's division, captured two hundred and sixty men, and recovered the ground from which Sickles had been driven the previous day. (General McCandless, one of the heroes of this brilliant sortie, has just died, in Philadelphia, June, 1884, from the effects of a wound probably received in this engagement). The three days' hard fighting ceased about sunset on July 3d, leaving Lee's army shattered and his invasion hopelessly foiled. Although the Federal victory was very complete, yet the morale of the army had been badly shaken, and Meade desisted from pressing his advantage until his men were somewhat recuperated. The Confederates were not only equally fatigued, but they were also in peril, as baffled invaders, and Lee promptly began his retrograde movement. Before night on the 4th of July his whole army was moving along the Hagerstown road, and was making for the Fairfield Pass of South Mountain. By July 12th his force was intrenched on the ridge between Williamsport and Falling Waters, waiting an opportunity to cross the Potomac, swollen by recent storms, into Virginia.

On July 5th Meade sent Sedgwick in pursuit of the fugitives, and Kilpatrick with his cavalry along the Chambersburg road to break up the wagon train. He also sent orders to General French to reoccupy Harper's Ferry, but that vigilant officer had already done so, and had destroyed the pontoon bridges by which Lee had hoped to cross at Falling Waters. The report made by Sedgwick of Lee's strong position convinced Meade that he must advance in force, but he moved cautiously, fearing surprises, and when on the 12th he reached Lee's position, it was found so well fortified that under the advice of a military council an attack was postponed. This delay saved Lee from total destruction, for with the energy of despair the Confederates during the night of the 13th hastily constructed another bridge over which the troops of Hill and Longstreet passed, while Ewell's corps forded the river near Williamsport. The movement was skillfully planned and executed, but did not escape the notice of Kilpatrick, who fell upon Pettigrew's Division of Hill's rear guard, captured 1,500 men, and killed about one hundred and fifty. During the charge Major Webb, of the Sixth Michigan, was killed and the Confederate Pettigrew was mortally wounded.

Lee had escaped with his army, his field equipment, and with some four thousand Federal prisoners, so that the full fruits of the glorious victory of Gettysburg had not been garnered, but, on the other hand, a formidable invasion of the Keystone State had been hurled back and an intended attack upon the National Capital by way of Maryland had been indefinitely postponed.

It was felt that a great peril had been escaped, and therefore, in gratitude rather than in jubilation, the President, on July 15th, issued a proclamation setting apart August 6th as a day of National Thanksgiving. This was devoutly observed throughout the loyal North.

Meanwhile another desperate effort was made by Jeff Davis to obtain some kind of diplomatic recognition from the authorities at Washington, doubtless for the purpose of impressing foreign nations and securing belligerent rights, more than for any other motive, unless it might have been that of passing official spies through the Federal lines. He sent Alexander H. Stephens, Vice-President of the Confederacy, to Fortress Monroe, with a flag of truce, on the *Torpedo* gunboat. Arrived there, Stephens, who carried an official communication from "Jefferson Davis, Commander-in-Chief of the land and naval forces of the Confederate States, to Abraham Lincoln, Commander-in-Chief of the land and naval forces of the United States," required permission of Admiral S. H. Lee to proceed direct to Washington. As a matter of course this demand was referred to the Secretary of the Navy, and, equally as a matter of course, was officially spurned. Stephens did not go to the Capital of the United States, but, returning in wrath to the Confederate capital, Richmond, held a conference with Jeff Davis and Judah P. Benjamin, the result of which was the preparation of an address, ostensibly to the troops under Lee's command, to whom it was read on the day (August 6th) that the North was observing Thanksgiving services, but really designed for effect abroad. This document, unequaled in mendacity, contained among other misrepresentations the following paragraph :

"Your enemy continue a struggle in which our final triumph must be inevitable. Unduly elated with their recent successes, they imagine that temporary reverses can quell your spirits or shake your determination, and they are now gathering heavy masses for a general invasion, in the vain hope that by desperate efforts success may at length be reached. You know too well, my countrymen, what they mean by success. Their malignant rage aims at nothing less than the extermination of yourselves, your wives and your children. They seek to destroy what they cannot plunder. They propose as spoils of victory that your homes shall be partitioned among wretches whose atrocious cruelty has stamped infamy on their Government. They design to incite servile insurrection and light the fires of incendiarism whenever they can reach your homes, and they debauch an inferior race, heretofore docile and contented, by promising them the indulgence of the evilest passions as the price of their treachery. Conscious of their inability to prevail by legitimate warfare, not daring to make peace, lest they should be hurled from their seats of power, the men who now rule in Washington refuse even to confer on the subject of putting an end to the outrages which disgrace our age, or listen to a suggestion for conducting the war according to the usages of civilization."

We have previously summarized the military movements in other sections, and will, therefore, continue to trace the operations of Meade in pursuit of Lee, and thus close the record of 1863.

Meade's army crossed the Potomac in the vicinity of Berlin, on July 17th and 18th, and pushed southward by way of Warrenton, which was reached on the 25th, the various gaps of the Blue Ridge having been seized on the route. There was slight delay at Manassas Gap, where Meade expected to encounter Lee in force, but when the Federal troops pressed on to Front Royal, it was found that the demonstration made by a brigade of Ewell's Corps had been merely a cover, and that Lee's main army had passed by and occupied Culpeper Court House. About this time the needs of Bragg in Tennessee compelled Lee to dispatch part of his force in that direction, and the fact being detected by Meade, he at once moved across the Rappahannock, dislodged Lee and occupied Culpeper Court House. The new position taken up by Lee on the south side of the Rapidan was too well protected to make an assault prudent, particularly as Meade's army had also been depleted by the withdrawal of Howard's and Slocum's corps, which, under General Hooker, were sent to join the the Army of the Cumberland. During August General Buford had a sharp engagement with the Confederate cavalry under Stuart. Early in September General Kilpatrick crossed the Rappahannock, and after driving the Confederates for some distance, burned a couple of gunboats which they had previously captured. On September 16th General Pleasonton, with Generals Buford, Kilpatrick and Gregg, took a large force of cavalry across the Rappahannock fords above Fredericksburg, and supported by the Second Corps, under General Warren, made a reconnoissance in force, which resulted in the discovery of the weakening of Lee by the departure of Longstreet. This decided Meade's plans, and he began preparations for an advance by sending Buford, on October

10th, to take possession of the upper fords of the Rapidan. Before this movement could be carried out Lee had crossed the fords, and sweeping round by Madison Court House, was on Meade's right and attacking Kilpatrick's outlying cavalry with such vigor that they were forced back on Culpeper. This surprise, for such it really was, disarranged Meade's plans, and on the night of the 11th he withdrew across the Rappahannock, blowing up the bridge to cover his retreat. Although Stuart's cavalry pressed closely on the heels of Meade, the main body of the Confederates halted at Culpeper, on the supposition that Lee intended to give battle at this point. Meade recrossed the river next morning, but Lee had begun another movement to gain Meade's rear and the Federals were compelled to fall back. In the meantime General Gregg had been surrounded by the Confederate advance and routed with the loss of five hundred men. Both armies now pushed on for Bristow station, Hill and Ewell with a large Confederate force being sent in advance by Lee, to intercept Meade at this point. When Hill reached there, the main body of the Army of the Potomac had passed and was well on the way to Centreville. Hill was about to charge on the rear guard when Warren's Corps, after a skirmish with Ewell near Auburn, came up behind him. This diverted his attack, and he faced about to meet Warren. A sharp engagement ensued, in which the Confederates were worsted, losing four hundred and fifty men, who were captured. Hill was thus placed in an awkward dilemma, but Warren was not much better off, for before dark Ewell came up. Fortunately it was too late on that October night for a further battle, and under cover of darkness, Warren effected his escape and joined the main army on the morning of the 15th.

Baffled in his attempt to gain Meade's rear, Lee began a retreat, first destroying the Orange and Alexandria Railroad from Bristow to the Rappahannock. Meade was detained by this movement for some three weeks at Warrenton, and then proposed to advance on the Fredericksburg Heights, but Halleck objected, and therefore, on November 7th, an advance was made on Rappahannock Station, General Sedgwick, with the right wing going to this point, while General French pushed on to Kelley's Ford. At Rappahannock Station Sedgwick found a portion of Early's Division in strong entrenchments guarding a pontoon bridge. A furious engagement ensued and at length the First Brigade, under Colonel Ellmaker, 119th Pennsylvania, advanced to storm the works. Soon afterward General David A. Russell ordered a general charge and the position was carried with fearful slaughter. The Federals obtained possession of the pontoon bridge, took some sixteen hundred prisoners and captured a number of guns, small arms, etc. While this was in progress, General Birney, of French's column, the left wing, had waded the river at Kelley's Ford, stormed the rifle-pits, captured five hundred prisoners and drove the Confederates from the position. This unexpected blow again disconcerted Lee, and he rapidly fell back beyond the Rapidan. Here he constructed a line of works along Mine Run, and then, withdrawing Ewell's Corps from Morton's Ford on the Rapidan, and calling up Hill's Division, he prepared to defend his position, which extended over eight miles on an irregular ridge, every conformation of which was seized on and rendered available for offensive or defensive works. On his flank and rear was a forest, on his front the marshy banks of Mine Run, and in addition an abatis of pine trees.

General Meade determined to attempt to turn this position, and getting around to Orange Court House, destroy his foe in detail. Having made all dispositions, he began his advance on November 26th. There were, however, delays and misunderstandings, so that the intended points were not reached with precision. However, on the 28th, after careful reconnoitering, it was decided to attack the works next morning. General Warren was to atack the right at eight o'clock, and Sedgwick to assault the left of Lee's position about an hour later; meanwhile a heavy fire was to be opened on the centre from the batteries. This programme was but imperfectly carried out. The batteries opened fire and a dash of skirmishers across the Rapidan dislodged the Confederate pickets; but Warren found the right too well protected and the Confederates so strongly massed that he hesitated to begin the attack. Sedgwick, of course, refrained from advancing until he heard Warren's guns, and thus nothing was done in that quarter. General Meade, after inspection of the works, concluded that Warren's caution was commendable, and he ordered a suspension of the entire movement. After several days' observation and consultation Meade decided that the risks would be too great, the more especially as Lee had been actively strengthening his position. On December 1st, therefore, Meade began a retreat, and recrossing the Rapidan went into winter quarters between that stream and the Rappahannock. Lee was well content to be severely left alone and did not attempt to impede his movements. The two armies thus confronting each other for nine months, no other events of any importance occurring until May of the following year.

We have previously mentioned, among the movements of 1863, General Gillmore's attack on Charleston and the bombardment of Forts Wagner, Gregg and Sumter, but in skirmishing around for any facts bearing upon the events of the war we have fallen upon the following, in the *Brooklyn Eagle* and it is so pertinent, as well as so quaintly interesting, that we feel impelled to transplant it bodily. "The Swamp Angel," so named by Sergeant. Felter, of the New York Volunteer Engineers, obtained a celebrity that was world-wide, but very few people ever had more than a kind of ghostly notion of the miasmatic monster, therefore the inside history of its construction is decidedly apropos:

"Did you ever hear the story of how the Swamp Angel was put into position before Charleston?" asked a veteran of the engineers of a group of veterans in Brooklyn.

"I've read about it several times," said one of the group.

"Well, I never read an account of it yet that wasn't crooked," returned the engineer. "I was there myself and know the whole inside of the business, and I'll tell you just how it was. General Gillmore was in command of the engineers at the siege of Charleston. One day in the midsummer of '63 he sent Captain Michel, now general at West Point, to see whether there was any point on the coast where guns could be placed to attack Charleston. Michel reported that the coast was all swamp for three or four miles inland—nothing but mud, water and slush forty or fifty feet deep. He had gone half a mile or so in a boat, making very poor progress through the bulrushes, and the stench from the carcasses of animals thrown into the swamp made him sick. Gillmore was in a bush hut eating supper with Colonel (now General) Serrell when he got Michel's report. He turned to Serrell and asked him whether he thought it possible to get guns posted in the swamp. Serrell said he thought nothing was impossible; he called Lieutenant Harrold and sent him to reconnoitre. Harrold was gone half the night, and came back very much bedraggled and tired. He said it was impossible to get the guns through, and impossible to mount them even if they could be got through. Using his utmost efforts he had only been able to get between two and three miles into the swamp. Serrell said it had got to be done. Harrold asked how he was going to do it, and said it would require men with legs forty feet long to get through that swamp. Well, the project of posting guns in the swamp got abroad in the camp, and the soldiers made great fun about it. They said that Drs. Dalrymple and Snow, two of the medical officers on General Gillmore's staff, were appointed to splice the legs of our men to get them to the required length. Next morning Colonel Serrell took Lieutenant Edwards with him and started to look at the swamp for himself. They got as long a plank as there was in the camp and waded into the swamp, each holding one end of the plank. The day was fearfully hot, the work was terrible getting through the rushes and water-plants and thick, slimy slush, and the smell of the swamp was sickening, but they persevered, working slowly out till they came to a creek. Here they were stopped for a time, as it had a considerable current and was deep, but after a while they got the plank fitted so that one held it while the other crawled over and held it still in his turn. Then, with infinite labor, they went on a mile farther toward Charleston. Finally they got to the water's edge, four and a half miles from Charleston. Here the ground was more solid. There were oyster-shells and winkles and spiral aureoles. They took a bearing to the steeple of St. Michael's Church in Charleston, and another bearing to Fort Moultrie, and another to Fort Johnson, and so located their own position in the swamp. Then they worked down the edge of the open water to Block Island, and so returned, terribly played out and dirty, but full of hope. Colonel Serrell told General Gillmore that he thought it possible to get guns into such position in the swamp that they might bombard Charleston, and that night submitted a plan for establishing the wished-for battery. In this plan he estimated that it would require 9,000 days' work to put just one gun into position (we reckoned by the day's work of one man then— 9,000 days' work of one man, or one day's work of 9,000 men). This gun was to be of extraordinary power, and was to rest on a platform composed of three thicknesses of three-inch yellow pine plank; two of the layers of plank crossing, while the other traversed them diagonally; all were to be strongly spiked together and underneath them were loads of brush and sandbags. Piling, consisting of heavy planks with sharp points, was to be driven twenty feet into the mud, so that the tops came flush with the platform which was to surround it: this, again, was to be strongly spiked, and that completed the inner platform. All around this immense quantities of brush were to be thrown into the swamp, and on top of this brush a grillage of logs, strongly fastened together, but totally distinct from the inner platform, was to surround that platform. On the top of this grillage of logs sandbags were to be piled till they sunk it considerably, in spite of the brush. As it sunk it was to force up the platform in the centre.

"Well, the plan was submitted and approved, and men were detailed right away to put it into execution. Meanwhile everybody was laughing at the engineers, and the Charleston papers got wind of the project, and made great sport of it. One of the comic papers had a very funny cartoon about an old negro carrying the 'Swamp Angel's' compliments to General Beauregard in Charleston. Another paper would have it that the Yankees were going to drain the swamp, which, of course, was impossible, as it was fed direct from the Atlantic Ocean; another paper again insisted that we were going to dyke the swamp across; another that we'd sent North for people to bring down bridge structure; another that we had discovered something wonderful in pneumatics, and still another that we were going to use a balloon battery. Well, the engineers went ahead, in spite of all the laughing. They built a bridge to the point of swamp which Colonel Serrell and Lieutenant Harrold had surveyed, and soldiers carried out the planks and logs and 10,000 bags of sand, and the battery was built. The work was mostly done at night, and the hardest job of all was to drive the piling. Many men were killed at the work, for the rebs shelled us, but it was all done at last. We had put up a sham fort a little distance down the coast, just a simple mass of leafy boughs. It bothered the life out of the rebs; they cou'dn't make out what was going on behind it, and shelled it incessantly. Well, when we had got the swamp fort all ready, we built a flat-bottomed scow, put a 7-inch rifled Parrott on her, waited till high water came, floated her through, and got her into position. We couldn't get elevation enough on it at first, thou h, and had to cut away the rear gun carriage; that fixed things to a nicety. Oh, wasn't that gun a daisy—never a cannon before or since had such a range. You can guess how nicely we had it trained when I tell you Lieutenant Nathan Edwards and Colonel Serrell laid the line of fire, calculating to put a shell into the rebel head-quarters, five and a half miles off, and they only missed their mark by a few feet. Smas'ed right through the house next door, that shell did, and Captain Macbeth, who was then on Beauregard's staff, afterward told me that he was sitting at his desk when the thing occured. An old nigger came running into him in a great state of excitement, saying, 'Massa! Massa! dar's a Yankee shell come an' made a hole in de street big nuff to put ter omnibus in.' A lieutenant of Colonel Pleasanton's regiment fired that shot. I tell you it woke the Charleston folks up, and Meerscham and Johnson and other forts fired whole mines of metal at us, but it was all no good. We could fix up in the night all they could knock down in the day, for their shot would go into the sandbags and do no harm, and, besides, we had a reserve platform of sandbags behind the battery. The gun was fired nineteen times that first night and did great execution, but the panic it caused was even greater than the execution it did, for Charleston had imagined that it could not be attacked on this side, and consequently had prepared no defenses. General Gillmore, some days before we had opened fire, had sent a flag of truce to Beauregard telling him that he proposed to open fire on Charleston, and warning all non-combatants to retire, but Beauregard said it was impossible to bombard the city without a fleet. Next morning, after the Swamp Angel's' salute, Beauregard sent a steamship with a flag of truce to us. His communication argued that it was wrong, unfair and altogether against military precedent, to attack him in rear of his works. Gillmore replied that it was both right and fair, and that, as far as precedents went, he was making them, and so the truce ended, and the fight between the 'Swamp Angel' and the forts continued, with the advantage largely on the 'Angel's' side, for, it had so much the longer range and so much the larger mark, it knocked the whole lower part of the city to pieces."

CHAPTER XXX.

EARLY MOVEMENTS IN 1864—GENERAL SHERMAN'S EXPEDITION FROM VICKSBURG—CAPTURE OF FORT PILLOW BY THE CONFEDERATES—BRUTAL MASSACRE UNDER ORDERS OF GENERAL FORREST—THE RED RIVER EXPEDITION—FAILURE OF THE MOVEMENT—COLONEL BAILEY'S REMARKABLE ENGINEERING ON THE RED RIVER—GENERAL BANKS SUPERSEDED BY GENERAL CANBY.

The earliest military movements in 1864 took place in the Mississippi region. General Sherman, after the return of his troops from Knoxville, Tennessee, had been for some time, in January, stationed along the line of the Memphis and Charleston Railroad from Scottsboro to Huntsville, in northern Alabama. At the end of that month he was ordered to Vicksburg, from which point an expedition was planned for the purpose of capturing and destroying the Confederate iron works at Selma, Alabama. In addition to this an advance upon Mobile and the destruction of the Confederate railroad connections of Eastern Mississippi were operations included in the scheme. On February 3d General Sherman left Vicksburg with four divisions, in all about 2,300 men, Generals McPherson and Hurlbut accompanying him at the head of the troops detached from their respective corps. He reached Meridian on the 15th of February, and here, at the

GEN. WILLIAM T. SHERMAN.

intersection of the railroad from Mobile to Corinth with that from Vicksburg to Montgomery, the tracks were torn up for a distance of about one hundred and fifty miles. Bridges were burned, locomotives destroyed, the torch was applied to huge stores of cotton, and, in fact, Confederate property of every description was given to the flames. Here Sherman expected to form a junction with a cavalry force under General W. S. Smith, which was dispatched from Memphis. This, however, was frustrated by the bold advance of the Confederate cavalry under General Forrest, who intercepted Smith about one hundred miles north of Meridian and drove him back to Memphis with the loss of five guns. Smith reached Memphis, after a forced march, on the evening of the 25th of February. In the meantime Sherman had been anxiously awaiting the arrival of the cavalry, but finding that the junction had been prevented, he decided to fall back, and, retracing his route from Meridian to Canton, he reached the latter place on February 26th with some 400 prisoners, about 5,000 negroes and a large number of loyal white refugees. After disposing of Smith, the dashing Confederate Forrest swept northward, entered Tennessee, and on March 24th captured Union City. Pushing on to Paducah, Kentucky, he made a vigorous assault upon Fort Anderson, into which Colonel Hicks, with about 700 men only, had retreated in his advance. Forrest had some 3,000 troops, and threatened to carry the place by storm, but it was gallantly defended, and on the 27th, fearing the approach of reinforcements, the chagrined Forrest was compelled to draw off, with a loss of more than three hundred men. Turning back into Tennessee, he appeared before Fort Pillow, on the Mississippi, about seventy miles above Memphis, on April 13th. Major Bradford defended his post valiantly, but Forrest, under the Confederate trick of a flag of truce, contrived to advance his men secretly along the ravines, and then having demanded a surrender, which was refused, the place was taken by surprise. Then began one of the most atrocious scenes of the war, for Forrest, desiring to avoid the incumbrance of prisoners, inaugurated a wholesale massacre of whites and blacks, men, women and children, at least three hundred persons being butchered in cold blood, under the personal supervision of Generals Forrest and Chalmers, who entered the place at opposite sides at the same time. About the same time Buford demanded the surrender of Columbus, threatening to show no quarter to negro troops should the place be taken by assault. Before he could get ready for attack, however, the approach of General S. D. Sturgis from Memphis convinced Forrest and his myrmidons that their raid had lasted long enough, and he, with Buford, retreated toward Jackson, and subsequently got into Northern Mississippi with considerable plunder. On the retreat, Colonel Bradford, who had been captured at Fort Pillow, was treacherously led out of the ranks and shot dead ; the excuse being that, as a native of a slave-labor State, he was a traitor to the Confederacy by being in the Federal service. Early in June Forrest was preparing for another raid, his main purpose being the prevention of reinforcements reaching Sherman. Sturgis advanced with about 9,000 infantry and artillery, and 3,000 cavalry under General Grierson in the advance, to check Forrest's operations, but on June the 10th Forrest fell upon Grierson's division, and, after a sharp conflict, the Federals were utterly routed, and lost about three thousand five hundred men. Early in July it was learned that Forrest had made his headquarters near Tupelo, on the Mobile and Ohio Railroad, and General A. J. Smith, with 12,000 men, moved forward to attack him there. During some sharp fighting on the 12th, 13th and 14th of July the Confederates sustained severe losses, but the Federals had also received some heavy blows, and therefore Smith led his troops back and rested them for about three weeks near Memphis. When he again moved forward to attack Forrest, that slippery soldier was not to be found. While Smith was endeavoring to solve the mystery of his disappearance, Forrest himself dashed into Memphis at dawn on August the 21st, expecting to capture Generals Hurlbut, Washburn, and Buckland. Failing to find them, he took their staff officers and some three hundred privates prisoners, and retreated with them after about an hour's looting in the city.

We must now turn to the Red River expedition under General Banks. We left Banks in New Orleans at the close of 1863 planning another expedition into Texas. On January 23, 1864, he received a dispatch from General Halleck stating that it was proposed to operate against Texas by the line of the Red River, with the further object of capturing Shreveport, the seat of the Confederate government of Louisiana. General Banks had serious apprehensions of the impracticability of this scheme, but as Halleck insisted that the best military opinions of the generals of the West favored the plan, he did not feel at liberty to press his objections further. That he did object, however, goes a long way toward lifting from his shoulders the responsibility of the disastrous failures which ensued. According to Halleck's plan, a strong land force was to march up Red River, supported by a fleet of gunboats under command of Admiral Porter. The army was composed of three divisions, one from Vicksburg, under General A. J. Smith; another from New Orleans, under General Franklin, to whom General Banks turned over his own column; and the third from Little Rock, under General Steele. On March 7th, Smith's advance began moving forward to Red River, and was joined by the fleet under Porter. On the 14th Fort De Russy was reached, and after some sharp fighting it was taken by assault. The Confederates retreated up the river to Alexandria, but they were driven out on the 16th, and five days later they were surprised at Henderson's Hill by some of Smith's troops under General Mower. The Confederates lost four guns, and about 250 of the men were captured, together with about two hundred horses. Beyond this point the progress of the expedition was slow, the rapids of the Red River being formidable obstacles to the passage of the gunboats. Natchitoches was next occupied, and then the co-operation of the land and naval forces ceased, for the road turned from the river in a circuit to the left. The flotilla, however, proceeded slowly up stream toward Shreveport. On April 8th, as the advance brigades were nearing Mansfield, they encountered the Confederate main force advantageously posted. A severe battle ensued at Sabine Cross Roads, resulting in heavy loss to the

Federals, for the Confederates captured about one thousand prisoners, ten guns and one hundred and fifty-six loaded supply wagons. The retreat of the Federals was stopped at Pleasant Grove, and there the exultant Confederates received a severe check next day. General Banks, who had by this time joined the troops, decided, however, to fall further back to a better vantage ground at Pleasant Hill, and there give final battle. The Confederates came up in great force. The fighting was desperate on all sides. The Texas Cavalry, under General Sweitzer, suffered terribly in a furious charge, not more than ten of the regiment escaping. Toward night the Confederate attack had not only been repulsed, but the right wing of their force had been driven back more than a mile. Although the Federal troops were victorious in this last engagement, yet, under all circumstances, it was deemed advisable to cease further efforts to advance and to fall back on Grand Ecore. On reaching here it was found that the Red River had fallen so rapidly that many of Porter's larger vessels were aground, and the river was still falling. The Confederates, too, were swarming around and at various points had planted batteries on the banks. With some difficulty Porter got his fleet over the bar at Grand Ecore, and then leaving Lieutenant-Commander Selfridge in charge, he went down the river to Alexandria, where the still greater peril of the rapids threatened the returning fleet. Lieutenant-Colonel Joseph Bailey, of Wisconsin, Engineer of the Ninth Corps, had conceived a plan for building a dam at the foot of the rapids, and then, by means of the pent-up water, through a sluice-way, floating the vessels past the rapids. His advice, however, was rejected for some time, and it was not till after Porter had blown up the Eastport, which had grounded sixty miles below Grand Ecore, and several other vessels had been damaged by conflict with shore batteries, that Bailey's scheme received any attention. By April 25th both the land and naval forces were at Alexandria, on the Red River, and it was now all-important to get to the Mississippi. General Grant had meantime ordered the closing of the operations against Shreveport and the return of Sherman's troops for other movements. There were differences between Porter and Banks as to Bailey's scheme, but finally Banks told him to go ahead and gave him authority to employ all the men he wanted. On May 1st the work was begun, and by the 8th, with the aid of nearly all the troops, a dam nearly eight hundred feet in length had been constructed of stone, timber and sunken coal barges. The water on the rapids was raised seven feet, and by evening of the 13th of May, with a few trifling misadventures, the fleet was floated into the deeper water below. The army and fleet then moved cautiously down the river, attacked at various points by the Confederates. Three of the vessels were captured in these engagements and one was burned to prevent the Confederates gaining possession of it. On May 16th the army had a sharp engagement near Marksville, and then on the 19th the troops crossed the Atchafalaya at Simms' Port on an improvised bridge constructed under the direction of Colonel Bailey. On May 20th General Banks was relieved of his command, and General E. R. S. Canby assumed charge of the troops as part of the Military Division of West Mississippi. General Steele had advanced from Little Rock to aid in the capture of Shreveport, but learning of the Federal reverses in other directions and having suffered severely in several engagements, he found himself compelled to fall back on Little Rock. In one of his battles, at Jenkinson's Ferry, the Confederates lost three thousand men, including three general officers, and Steele lost about seven hundred of his troops. After a terrible march through swamps Steele and his scattered forces reached Little Rock on May 2d about the time when Bailey was building his dam at Alexandria. The entire expedition was a lamentable failure and the disgrace of it was keenly felt at headquarters in Washington. We will now turn to more important matters at the Capital.

CHAPTER XXXI.

THE RANK OF LIEUTENANT-GENERAL REVIVED—GENERAL U. S. GRANT MADE GENERAL-IN-CHIEF—RETIREMENT OF GENERAL HALLECK—PREPARING FOR A VIGOROUS CLOSING CAMPAIGN—GENERAL SHERMAN'S MOVEMENTS—THE TWO BATTLES BEFORE ATLANTA—SHERMAN'S OCCUPATION OF ATLANTA—TOTAL DESTRUCTION OF HOOD'S ARMY—"MARCHING THROUGH GEORGIA."

One of the most significant events at the beginning of 1864, and one which should perhaps have taken precedence in this history, was the promotion of General Ulysses S. Grant to the foremost position among the actors in the final scenes of the great national drama.

It had been evident that General Halleck, though animated by loyal zeal, was not ready enough for the continually arising emergencies. Not only did the administration feel this, but Congress and the country perceived it. With the view of solving the problem which seemed to be bothering the President, Representative E. B. Washburne submitted a proposition in the House for a revival of the grade of Lieutenant-General of the army, a rank one degree only below that of Commander-in-Chief constitutionally reserved for the President of the United States. This was amended by Mr. Ross, of Illinois, with the condition appended that General U. S. Grant should be such Lieutenant-General. The motion was introduced on December 14th, 1863, and in its amended form was adopted by the House of Representatives on February 1, 1864.

The House measure was carried to the Senate, and there a further amendment was tacked on, making the office perpetual (whatever that may mean) and prescribing that the Lieutenant-General should be under the President, the General-in-Chief of the armies of the Republic (a profoundly inconsequent provision, seeing that the Constitution almost expressly implied such an arrangement). However, a conference committee agreed upon a bill embodying all these provisions, and this became law by the President's signature on March 1st, who at once appointed Grant to the revived position. The Senate confirmed this appointment on March 2d, and on the 9th General Grant, who had been summoned from the field, was personally presented with his important commission by President Lincoln in the White House. The entire Cabinet, General Halleck and several other important officials were present, the scene and the brief addresses of the chief personages being very impressive. On March 10th the President issued an order formally investing General Grant with the chief command of all the armies of the Republic, and assigning General Halleck to duty as Chief of Staff of the Army after stating that he was relieved from command "at his own request." General Grant at once started for the West to inaugurate the spring campaign, and at Nashville, on March 17th, he issued an order recapitulating his appointment, announcing his assumption of chief command, and that his headquarters would be with the Army of the Potomac in the field.

The first month of Grant's appointment was occupied in planning the campaigns of the year. Two great movements were decided upon, and to these all other operations were to be subordinate. There were now under arms about 800,000 Federal troops, and these controlled by the consummate tact, restless energy and dauntless pluck of such a man as U. S. Grant were destined to achieve results which an Alexander the Great might have envied.

The Army of the Potomac, under command of Meade and the General-in-Chief, was to advance upon Richmond, still defended by the Army of Northern Virginia, under General Robert E. Lee. The army under General William T. Sherman, who succeeded General Grant in command of the Military Division of the Mississippi, was to undertake the destruction of the army of General Joseph E. Johnston, and the capture and destruction of Atlanta, Georgia, with its great machine shops, foundries, car works and depots of supplies, in fact the very backbone of all the Confederate resources. Major-General J. B. McPherson, commanding the Department and Army of the Tennessee, and the armies of the Cumberland and Ohio, were included in Sherman's command. The total number of men in the three armies under Sherman's control was close on one hundred thousand.

Reserving for the close of our history the direct sweep of events by which General Grant, with the Army of the Potomac, put the finishing stroke upon the fortunes of the Confederate hosts, we will by a summary narrative cover the movements of General Sherman up to the time when he received the surrender of Johnston's army at Raleigh, N. C., on April 26th, 1865, just about one year (within four days) of the date on which the advance from Chattanooga was begun.

When Lieutenant-General Grant had developed his plans he sent orders to General Sherman to move on General Johnston, then at Dalton, and afterward press on to Atlanta. These orders were received on April 30, 1864, and the advance was begun on May 6th. The Confederate forces under Johnston, then massed about Dalton, numbered some 55,000 men, infantry and artillery, in three divisions, commanded by Generals W. J. Hardee, J. B. Hood and Leonidas Polk, and about 10,000 cavalry under General Wheeler.

The forces under General Sherman were sub-commanded as follows: Army of the Cumberland, Major-General George H. Thomas; Army of the Ohio, Major-General J. M. Schofield, and Army of the Tennessee, Major-General J. B. McPherson. The entire Federal force numbered about 100,000 men. Opposite the Union Army and between it and the Confederates was the Rocky Face Ridge, through which were a couple of passes known as Buzzard's Roost Gap and Snake Creek Gap, the former, which was nearest the Federal lines, being held in force by the Confederates. Through the latter McPherson pushed his troops and came on the Confederate position, south of Dalton, about the same time that Schofield, with the Army of the Ohio, moved from Red Clay and menaced the position on the north. General Thomas had, meantime, made a demonstration on Buzzard's Roost Gap, in Johnston's front. Finding that this combined movement was likely to turn one or other of his flanks, Johnston fell back to Resaca, and here, on May 14th and 15th, two sharp engagements ensued, the second of which compelled Johnston to abandon his position and cross the Oostenaula leaving four guns and a quantity of stores behind him. Retreating by way of Calhoun and Kingston to Dallas, Johnston had by May 26th very strongly intrenched himself, with his lines extending from Dallas to Marietta. After several days spent in skirmishing and reconnoitering, Sherman was again preparing to turn Johnston's right, when on May 28th the Confederates fell heavily on McPherson, at Dallas. This assault was repulsed, but a similar movement upon Howard was more successful. Sherman pressed on in spite of natural obstacles, and on June 4th Johnston again fell back, and took up a formidable position, embracing Big and Little Kenesaw, and Lost and Pine mountains, with the Chattahoochee River behind him and hastily constructed but powerful works covering his front. By constant manœuvring Sherman compelled Johnston to contract his lines and concentrate on Great Kenesaw Mountain. On June 22d this constant pressure so irritated the Confederates that General J. B. Hood made a dash at Sherman's lines, attempting to sever the communications of Thomas and Schofield. Gallant and sudden as was the attack, it failed utterly, and Hood was driven back in great confusion. Sherman determined to follow up this repulse, and therefore ordered an advance on June 27th upon Johnston's left centre at and south of Kenesaw Mountain. The assault was vigorously made, but was disastrously repulsed, the Federal loss being about three thousand men, including Generals C. G. Harker and D. McCook. Sherman's vigorous policy, however, allowed of no crying over spilt milk; in fact, he never allowed his men to rest long enough to know that they had been beaten. Consequently on July 2d an advance in force was ordered for the next morning. During the night Johnston abandoned his position, and fell back toward Atlanta. The Federal army followed him up, and even pressed upon his new positions on the other side of the Chattahoochee. On July 9th another advance in force virtually forced Johnston within the lines protecting Atlanta. It was, perhaps, fortunate that at this juncture the Confederate President, Jeff Davis, who was constantly meddling in military matters, of which he had about as much knowledge as a goose has of grammar, chose to consider that Johnston's repeated retreats indicated incompetency, and summarily superseded him by turning over the command to General J. B. Hood. For some days Sherman busied himself in collecting his stores and making arrangements for the investment of Atlanta, now only eight miles distant, and from the nature of its converging railroads and its manufacturing and storage capacities, a point of great importance. On the 17th of July the advance began, and on the 20th the various divisions of Sherman's army had closed in upon the city. General Schofield had meantime seized Decatur; McPherson had destroyed much of the railroad track to the eastward, and General Rousseau, with two thousand cavalry, was raiding round west of Opelika, destroying a network of branch railroads. On July 20th Hood made another of his daring dashes, but was again repulsed in an engagement which cost him some five thousand men; the Federal loss was about fifteen hundred men. On the 21st of July General Sherman found that Hood had abandoned his outlying positions and retired into Atlanta. The next day McPherson, with the Army of the Tennessee, prepared to move from Decatur on the Confederate works at Atlanta. In the meantime the Confederate General Hardee, by a night march, had reached the left and rear of the Federal lines, and fell heavily upon them. McPherson came up just as a charge of Hardee's had cut a gap between the troops of Dodge and Blair, and at the same moment a Confederate sharpshooter, a namesake, one Major McPherson, took deliberate aim and shot him dead. The death of General McPherson was a sad loss, but General John A. Logan was at once placed in command of the Army of the Tennessee, and promptly carried out the plans of the dead general. After a heavy day's fighting, the first battle of Atlanta ended by the Confederates falling back within their lines. During the next few days there was skirmishing in various directions, and on July 27th, General O. O. Howard was appointed by the President to succeed McPherson, a proceeding which General Hooker resented by resigning the command of the Twentieth Corps, which was turned over to General H. W. Slocum. There were several other changes of command about this period, General D. S. Stanley succeeding Howard in command of the Fourth Corps, and General Jefferson C. Davis succeeding General Palmer in command of the Fourteenth Corps. On July 27th General Howard, with the Army of the Tennessee, secretly shifted his position from the extreme left, on the Decatur road, to Proctor's Creek, on the extreme right, and early on the 28th, when Hood discovered the movement, he threw Hardee and S. D. Lee with a heavy force upon Logan's Corps, on Howard's right. The Confederates expected that the men in their unfinished works would be taken at a disadvantage, but the assault had been foreseen, and, as a consequence, the second battle of Atlanta, after four hours' heavy fighting, cost the Confederates about five thousand men, and sent the remainder broken and dispirited back to their intrenchments. During the next two weeks Hood remained inactive, and then he sent Wheeler with 8,000 cavalry on a raid. Wheeler reached the railway at Calhoun on July 16th, but, in the meantime, Sherman, who was preparing for a general advance, sent Kilpatrick with a cavalry force to capture and destroy the West Point and Macon Railroad. In this work he was interrupted by part of Wheeler's force, but he cut his way through and returned to Decatur on the 22d. The movement was not sufficiently complete, and Sherman decided to raise the siege of Atlanta for the present. On the night of the 25th this movement was begun and by the 28th Sherman's forces had destroyed a dozen miles of the West Point railroad. Hood, unaware of this, had divided his army and sent one half, under Hardee, to counteract Kilpatrick's raid. On the 31st Howard, when attempting the passage of the Flint River, near Jonesboro, encountered this force, and after a severe conflict Hardee was routed and Jefferson C. Davis, of Howard's army, carried by a gallant charge the Confederate works north of Jonesboro. Hood, with the balance of his army, remained at Atlanta, closely watched by General Slocum, but during the night of September 1st the Confederate general, detecting his error in weakening his force, blew up his magazines, destroyed the foundries and workshops, and precipitately evacuated Atlanta, some of his troops going to Macdonough and others to Covington. On the morning of September 2d Mayor Calhoun formally surrendered the city to General Slocum. On the 4th General Sherman demanded the removal of all citizens and arranged a ten days' truce with General Hood to allow of this being carried out. By September 8th Sherman's entire force was encamped around Atlanta, and the city was occupied in a few days by military only.

We have mentioned that an arrangement for a truce was made with Hood, but that worthy denounced the removal of civilians, and wrote: "In the name of God and humanity I protest, believing that you will find you are expelling from their homes and firesides the wives and children of a brave people." To this General Sherman sent a crushing reply, in which, after reminding Hood that Johnston had removed families all the way down from Dalton, and that he (Hood) had burned or destroyed some fifty dwelling houses that impeded the operations of his forts, Sherman concluded:

"In the name of common sense I ask you not to appeal to a just God in such a sacrilegious manner—you, who in the midst of peace and prosperity have plunged a nation into civil war, 'dark and cruel war'; who dared us to battle; who insulted our flag; seized our arsenals and forts that were left in the honorable custody of a peaceful ordnance sergeant; seized and made prisoners of war the very garrison sent to protect your people against negroes and Indians long before any overt act by the (to you) 'hateful Lincoln Government'; tried to force Kentucky and Missouri into rebellion in spite of themselves; falsified the vote of Louisiana; turned loose your privateers to plunder unarmed ships; expelled Union families by the thousands, burned their houses and declared by act of 'Congress' the confiscation of all debts due Northern men for goods had and received. Do not talk thus to one who has seen these things, and will this day make as much sacrifice for the peace and honor of the South as the best-born Southerner among you. If we must be enemies, let us be men, and fight it out as we propose to-day, and not deal in such hypocritical appeals to God and humanity. God will judge me in good time, and he will pronounce whether it be more humane to fight with a town full of women and the families of 'brave people' at our backs, or remove them in time to places of safety among their own friends and people."

It is evident that General Sherman had learned to write as well as fight in his West Point studies. Nor were his words unsupported by acts, for no distinction was made between the families of friends or foes—all were transported, with their clothes and furniture, averaging 1,651 pounds to each family, whither they wished to go, at the national expense. In fact the abashed Hood was constrained to tender, in writing, his acknowledgments of the courtesy which he (as a Confederate general) and his people had received on all occasions in connection with the removal. In strong contrast to this was the conduct of the Confederate President, Jeff Davis, who hurried to Macon about this period to make a personal investigation, In a speech on September 23d, after commenting on the disgrace of Johnston's retreat from Dalton to Atlanta, he said, "I then put a man in command who I knew would strike a manly blow for the defense of Atlanta, and many a Yankee's blood was made to nourish the soil before the prize was won." Then in attempting to smother the disgrace of the shambles at Andersonville, he pretended that the United States was responsible for the non-exchange of prisoners, and said, "Butler, the beast, with whom no commissioner of exchange would hold intercourse, had published in his newspapers that if we would consent to the exchange of negroes, all difficulties might be removed. This is reported as an effort of his to get himself whitewashed, by holding intercourse with gentlemen." After this display of billingsgate, Davis went off to instruct Hood, at any sacrifice of Confederates soldiers' lives, to lure Sherman out of Georgia, where his presence was dealing a deadly blow to the spirits of the Confederate leaders. In pursuance of this design Hood, who had been joined by Hardee, near Jonesboro, crossed the Chattahoochee and made a sharp raid on Sherman's communications; at the same time Wheeler with his cavalry appeared before Dalton and demanded its surrender, but was driven off before he could do much damage. Then about October 5th a division of Confederate infantry under General French threatened Allatoona, where one million rations were stored. General Corse was sent to the aid of Colonel Tourtellotte, and after some furious fighting French was repulsed, and then fell back in some disorder on the approach of General Cox. By this time General Sherman had rested his army, and falling at first into Hood's trap, began a vigorous pursuit of that wily Confederate, who was striking northward into Tennessee. After following Hood north of the

Chattahoochee, crossing the Oostenaula and pressing into the Chattanooga Valley, Sherman became convinced that Hood's game was that of the shamming lame lapwing in its trick of luring intruders from its nest. In other words, he refused to be drawn away from his main prize, Atlanta, and diverted from his intended "MARCH TO THE SEA." Consequently Sherman determined to return to Atlanta, and he delegated to General Thomas full power over all the troops under his command, excepting four corps with which he proposed to make the now famous march. He also gave Thomas the two divisions of General A. J. Smith, then returning from Missouri, all the garrisons in Tennessee, and all the cavalry of the military division, except a single division under Kilpatrick, which was reserved for operations in Georgia. He believed that Thomas would then have strength enough to more than cope with Hood, and his calculations were correct. The Confederates swept up through Northern Alabama, crossed the Tennessee at Florence, and advanced on Nashville. General Schofield, in command of this section, fell back to Franklin, eighteen miles south of Nashville. Here, on November 30th, he was attacked by Hood; a sharp battle was fought, and at nightfall, after having kept Hood in check all day, Schofield crossed the Harpeth River and retreated within the defenses of Nashville. At this point all of General Thomas' forces were rapidly concentrated. A line of intrenchments was drawn around the city on the south. Hood came on, confident of victory and prepared to begin the siege by blockading the Cumberland; but before the work was fairly under way, General Thomas, on December 15th, moved from his works, fell upon the Confederate army and utterly routed it, with a loss of more than twenty-five thousand men in killed, wounded and prisoners. Despite the intense cold the shattered Confederates were pursued in every direction until they were killed, captured or so completely dispersed that all traces of Hood's army as an organization disappeared, and on the 23d of January, 1865, the dispirited General was "relieved at his own request" of his command (he had already been relieved of his army), at Tupelo, Mississippi. In this campaign General Thomas estimated his losses at about 10,000 men, but he had captured 11,857 officers and men (besides 1,332 who had been exchanged), 72 serviceable guns and 3,079 small arms. He had also administered the oath of amnesty to 2,207 deserters from the Confederate service. On the 30th of December he announced the close of the campaign, but General Grant was not prepared to let anybody rest till the rebellion was suppressed, consequently Thomas was instructed to send Wood, with the Fourth Corps, to Huntsville, and to concentrate the troops of Smith, Schofield and Wilson at Eastport, to await a renewal of the winter campaign in Mississippi and Alabama. Having thus summarized the movements of General Thomas and the destruction of Hood's forces, we will return to General Sherman, whom we left preparing for his tramp across the continent.

CHAPTER XXXII.

SHERMAN'S "MARCH TO THE SEA"—A GLORIOUS WAR RECORD—THE CONFEDERATES' SWEPT BY A FEDERAL BROOM—SAVANNAH CAPTURED—MOVEMENTS IN THE CAROLINAS—CAPTURE OF CHARLESTON—SURRENDER OF THE CONFEDERATE GENERAL JOHNSTON—CAPTURE OF MOBILE—RECORD OF THE CONFEDERATE PRIVATEERS—THE BEGINNING OF THE END.

On November 14th, 1864, General Sherman had completed his arrangements for his "MARCH TO THE SEA." He had cut the telegraph wire between Atlanta and Washington city, probably that he might not be hampered or disquieted by instructions from Headquarters, for although the President and General Grant had been advised of his intentions, their consent to and sympathy with his plans was tacit rather than active. Sherman's entire force was about 60,000 infantry and artillery and 5,500 cavalry. This adventurous army was divided into two grand divisions, composed of four army corps. The right wing, under Major-General O. O. Howard, consisted of the Fifteenth Corps, General P. J. Osterhaus, and the Seventeenth Corps, General F. P. Blair. The left wing, under Major-General H. W. Slocum, was composed of the Fourteenth Corps, General J. C. Davis, and the Twentieth, General A. S. Williams. The cavalry, in one division, was commanded by General Judson Kilpatrick.

The movement began on the morning of November 14th, the left wing under Slocum marching by way of Decatur, for Madison and Milledgeville, and the right wing, under Howard, by way of Macdonough for Gordon, on the railway east of Macon. General Sherman remained in Atlanta to superintend the total destruction of the place, and by the night of the 15th some two hundred acres in the centre of the city exhibited a roaring mass of flames. The following morning Sherman joined Slocum's wing, and the perilous march of two hundred and fifty miles was fairly inaugurated by an army cut loose from its base of supplies, but with twenty days' supply of bread, forty days' of beef, coffee and sugar, and three days' supply of forage in the wagons. Each wing had its separate pontoon train and the instructions to each sub-commander were to "live off the country" as he went along. As Sherman had anticipated, the Confederates could offer no serious resistance, and Wheeler's Confederate cavalry hovering around were kept in check by Kilpatrick. We will not linger on the details of this part of the expedition : the army swept on through Macon and Milledgeville, reached and crossed the Ogeechee; captured Gibson and Waynesborough, and on the 3d of December General Sherman with the Seventeenth Corps reached Millen, where thousands of captured Federals had been imprisoned in loathsome pens. Unfortunately these had been spirited away, and the troops could only wreak their vengeance by destroying the place and its railroad approaches. The army then passed on through swamps and sands, destroying the various obstructions and driving out the Confederates, until on the 10th of December they were driven within the defenses of Savannah, where General Hardee was in command, and General Sherman and his exultant and expectant troops were before the city and preparing to invest it. The destruction of the Charleston railway, at the bridge, by General Slocum, and of the Gulf railroad nearly to the Little Ogeechee, shut off supplies to the city. On the 13th, General Hazen was sent to capture Fort McAllister on the Ogeechee, below the city. This was done by assault in splendid style, and thus Sherman secured communication by that river with Ossabaw Sound, where Admiral Dahlgren and General Foster were expected. General Sherman received by this route several 30-pounder Parrott guns, and then summoned Hardee to surrender. On his refusal, Sherman left for Hilton Head to arrange with Foster for intercepting Hardee's probable retreat to Charleston. As soon as his back was turned, however, Hardee, like a wily old rat, slipped out of his hole on the night of the 20th, covering his movements by a heavy cannonade, during which he destroyed a couple of iron-clads, several smaller vessels, and all the stores he had time to get at. Sherman was notified and hurried back, entering the city in triumph on the 22d, and o-the 26th sending a message to President Lincoln that he made him a Christmas present of the city of Savannah, with 150 heavy guns, 25,000 bales of cotton and plenty of ammunition. During the whole of this adventurous march, the trail of which was nearly forty miles wide, and two hundred and fifty-five miles in length, General Sherman lost in the six weeks occupied, only 560 men. He estimated that he had damaged the enemy some $100,000,000, including 200 miles of railroad, and of this some $20,000,000 was direct Federal profit, while the rest was compulsory waste.

By the 1st of January, 1865, General Sherman had completed his preparations for the continued occupation of Savannah, the removal of obstructions in the river under the supervision of Admiral Dahlgren, and the opening up of communications by the free passage of vessels. He was then ready for a march northward through the Carolinas. On the 15th of January the Seventeenth Corps was sent by water around Hilton Head, to Pocotaligo, on the Charleston and Savannah Railroad, where a position was taken up threatening Charleston, to which city Hardee with his fifteen thousand men had escaped from Savannah. Slocum, with the left wing and Kilpatrick's cavalry, was to have crossed the Savannah River from the city on a pontoon bridge at the same time, but heavy floods prevented this and the delay caused by hunting for a favorable crossing wasted the balance of January. In the meantime General Grant had sent Grover's Division of the Nineteenth Corps to garrison Savannah and had taken the Twenty-third Corps under Schofield from Thomas' command in Tennessee to reinforce Terry and Palmer on the coast of North Carolina, and thus pave the way for Sherman's future movements.

On February 1st Sherman's whole army moved forward against Columbia, the capital of South Carolina. The Confederates were terror-stricken at the audacity of these operations, though they hoped that the swamps and morasses would impede, if not engulf, the Federal army. Governor Magrath summoned every white man in the State between the ages of 16 and 60 to take the field, and desperate attempts were made to establish a line of defense along the Salkhatchie, while

Wheeler's cavalry was ever on the alert, hovering around the advance columns. But impediments merely seemed to whet the appetite of the Federal troops; they pressed on, forced the passages of the river, and by the 11th of February had severed the Confederate lines of communication between Charleston and Augusta. On the 12th the Seventeenth Corps dashed upon Orangeburg, and driving out the Confederates, destroyed rail-

RUINS OF CHARLESTON.

road communication with Columbia. On the 14th the fords and bridges of the Congaree were carried, and on the 16th the right wing was opposite Columbia, while the left wing, under Slocum, had swept by Augusta and was rapidly approaching the same point. Bridges were rapidly thrown across the Broad and Saluda rivers and Columbia's fate was about determined. The failure of Bragg and Beauregard to check Sherman's advance had compelled the Confederate authorities to reinstate General Johnston, one of the bravest and coolest, if most cautious commanders. On the 17th of February Beauregard, Governor Magrath and a number of other officials fled from the city, and Mayor Goodwyn, with a delegation of the city council, came out in carriages and formally surrendered to Colonel Stone, of the Twenty-fifth Iowa Infantry, who, in accordance with general instructions, promised protection to private property. General Wade Hampton, however, who had command of the Confederate rear guard, is alleged to have fired all the cotton, public and private, in the city, before quitting. At any rate, the cotton was fired, and, despite the exertion of Sherman's officers and men, the flames spread rapidly and laid the whole city in ruins. The fall of Columbia convinced General Hardee that Charleston was no longer tenable, and therefore, while Columbia was blazing, the torch was vigorously applied in Charleston. The great depot of the Northwestern Railroad, in which a large quantity of powder was stored, took fire and was blown up, and four squares in the best part of the city were laid in ashes. After further destroying all the shipping he could reach, including two iron-clads, Hardee, with about 14,000 troops, escaped, and made off to join Beauregard, Cheatham and Johnston in North Carolina. The news of the evacuation was received by the Federal forces on James and Morris islands on the morning of the 18th, and within a few hours the Stars and Stripes were again floating over Forts Sumter, Ripley and Pinckney. Lieutenant-Colonel Bennett, commanding at Morris Island, received the formal surrender of the city from Mayor Macbeth, and then hurried up a small force to assist in suppressing the flames. The principal arsenal was saved, as was a large quantity of rice, which was generously distributed among the distracted poor of the place. Colonel Stewart L. Woodford, of the One Hundred and Twenty-seventh New York, was appointed Military Governor of Charleston, and by judicious management speedily effected amicable arrangements with the citizens.

General Sherman meanwhile had remained at Columbia only long enough to complete the destruction of the arsenals, machine shops and foundries, and tear up the railroad tracks. This was done during the 18th and 19th of February, and then he renewed his march northward in the direction of Charlotte, North Carolina, having advised General Grant that he might be expected at Goldsboro any time between the 22d and 28th of March. Kilpatrick's cavalry meantime had raided toward Augusta in the endeavor to mislead the Confederates as to Sherman's line of advance, and was now making for Winnsboro. On the 18th he found that Wheeler had effected a junction with Wade Hampton, and that the combined force was between him and Charlotte.

General Sherman pushed on to Winnsboro, and there effected a junction with the Twentieth Corps, under Slocum, on the 21st of February. The Federal army then crossed the Great Pedee, at Cheraw, driving Hardee from that post, and compelling him to retreat on Fayetteville. He was not allowed to tarry here, for Sherman pushed on, and by March 11th his whole force was concentrated at Fayetteville, Hardee again retreating. Kilpatrick, meanwhile, had met with a misadventure which nearly proved serious. Learning that Hampton was defending Hardee's rear, Kilpatrick, with Spencer's Brigade, made a night march, and cut through Hampton's line; but that night, March 8th, Hampton, by a stealthy movement, surprised Kilpatrick's quarters, captured Spencer and most of the staff, and then began plundering the camp. Kilpatrick, who had escaped on foot into the swamp, rallied his men and again fell on Hampton's troopers, recapturing the guns and holding the Confederates at bay till General Mitchell, with a brigade of infantry, came to his aid. Hampton then gave up the fight, and Kilpatrick joined the main army at Fayetteville. Here the troops were rested for three days, and then the march was resumed towards Raleigh. On the 16th of March Hardee was encountered strongly intrenched, with twenty thousand men, near Averasboro, between the Cape Fear and South rivers. After a hard fight, Slocum drove Hardee into his intrenchments, from whence that night he escaped to Smithfield, where Johnston was concentrating. General Sherman was now confident that he had no further obstacles on his route to Goldsboro, but early on the morning of the 19th, when approaching Bentonville, a skirmish on the left rapidly developed into a formidable attack, and by noon a fierce battle was in progress, for the whole of Johnston's army, reinforced by Hardee, Hoke and Cheatham, were massed in front of Sherman's left wing and were exulting over the prospect of his complete annihilation. But for the almost superhuman efforts of General Jefferson C. Davis, this result would have been accomplished. The impetuous charges of the Federals under such leadership, however, turned the fortunes of the day, and when darkness fell the amazed Confederates were routed. During the night other detachments came up, the right wing moved over to the support of the left, and although there was heavy fighting during the 20th, the Confederates failed to regain their advantage. On the 21st General Terry, with his column from Wilmington, and General Schofield with his troops from Newbern, had reached Goldsboro, and General Johnston finding that the junction of the three armies was now practically accomplished, fled in such haste to Smithfield that he left his pickets and wounded to be captured. On the 23d the entire Federal force, numbering about 60,000, were encamped in and about Goldsboro, and were allowed to rest a while. Placing General Schofield in temporary command, General Sherman went by rail to Morehead City and thence by water to City Point, where he met Generals Grant, Meade and Ord, and President Lincoln. An important conference was held in regard to future movements, and Sherman learned all that had happened "since he had been out of the world." Returning to Goldsboro on the 30th, Sherman superintended the furnishing of needed clothes and supplies to his troops, and then on April 6th he learned of the fall of Petersburg and Richmond. This somewhat changed his plans, and he decided that it was time to finish up his end of the war by demolishing Johnston. On the 10th of April he put his forces in motion toward Smithfield, where Johnston had been concentrating. But the news had reached the Confederate commander, and he hastily fell back on Raleigh. Sherman pushed on to Smithfield only to find the bridges destroyed and Johnston still retreating. The startling news of Lee's surrender reached him here, and he at once dropped his heavy field equipment and in light order pressed after Johnston, receiving the formal surrender of Raleigh on the 13th of April, as he passed on his way to overtake the fugitive Confederates at Hillsboro. On April 14th Johnston sent a note to Sherman asking him to communicate with General Grant and obtain permission to treat for peace. Sherman promptly replied that he was fully authorized to arrange terms and would halt his army to receive proposals. On the 16th a further

PLACE OF JOHNSTON'S SURRENDER TO SHERMAN.

communication was received asking for an interview next day, half-way between Raleigh and Hillsboro. Nothing definite was arranged at this meeting, but on April 18th the two generals met, and Sherman consented to a "Memorandum" as a basis of consideration by the Government. This document was sent to Washington, but its terms were so preposterously lenient that the administration rejected it, and General Grant hastened to Raleigh to announce its rejection and if necessary to relieve General Sherman of his command. Reaching Raleigh on the 24th, Grant instructed Sherman to notify Johnston that his proposals were absolutely rejected and that the truce must close in forty-eight hours. To this message was supplemented a demand for an immediate surrender of Johnston's army on terms similar to those which Grant had made with Lee. It may be here noted that the "Memorandum," said to have been prepared by Breckinridge, was in effect an actual amnesty and a virtual expunging of all records of rebellion. General Sherman as well as General Grant had yearnings for peace, in the interests of common humanity, but, while Sherman was ready to approach the subject as a "man," Grant would only do so as a "soldier"—a subtle distinction requiring no further comment. That Grant fully appreciated the position is shown by the fact that having contented himself with the simple conveyance of the Government's rejection of the "Memorandum," he left Sherman full powers to conduct further negotiations, and waited unobtrusively at Raleigh for the result. It was not long delayed. On April 26th, at the request of Johnston, another meeting was held between the two commanders, and terms of capitulation identical with those granted to Lee at Appomattox Court House were agreed upon. It was stipulated that all arms and public property of the Confederates should be deposited at Greensboro, and that the capitulation should include all the troops in Johnston's military department, comprising the seaboard States south of Virginia. The terms were promptly approved by Grant and the troops formally surrendered, except a body of cavalry under Wade Hampton. This General declined to be included, not being actually part of Johnston's department, and he led his troopers off to Charlotte, to join the now fugitive Confederate President Davis.

Reserving minor episodes for a closing chapter, we can here close our record of important military movements in this section, and, after picking up a few "loose ends," move on with the Army of the Potomac to the actual close of the war and the events incidentally alluded to above.

Coincident with Sherman's operations in the Carolinas was the famous cavalry raid of General George Stoneman. Returning to Knoxville, from his winter campaign in southwestern Virginia, he was ordered on February 7th, 1865, to prepare for a raid into South Carolina in aid of Sherman's movements, but this order was modified by the successes of Sherman's operations, and finally Stoneman was intrusted with a sort of independent command and turned loose as a sort of Nemesis on horseback to wreak destruction on Confederate property. We will briefly sketch his dashing operations. Concentrating the cavalry brigades of Colonels Palmer, Miller and Brown, about six thousand strong, at Mossy Creek, he started out on March 20th, crossed the mountains, captured Wilkesboro and forced the passage of the Yadkin at Jonesville. Turning to the north, he traversed the western end of North Carolina and thence passed into Carroll County, Virginia. At Wytheville the railroad was torn up and the whole line was destroyed from the bridge over New River to within four miles of Lynchburg. Then Christiansburg was captured and ninety miles of railroad track passed out of existence. Turning first to Jacksonville and then southward, Stoneman struck and destroyed the North Carolina railroad between Danville and Greensboro. At Salem the factories were burned, and after tearing up the track in the direction of Salisbury, that town was captured, together with large stores of arms, ammunition, cotton, clothing and provisions. The Confederates were quick enough to get away with the Federal prisoners who had been penned up in the town. Then on April 19th a division under Major Moderwell reached the great bridge of the South Carolina Railroad spanning the Catawba River, eleven hundred and fifty feet in length. This was totally destroyed by fire. After a fight with the Confederate cavalry under Ferguson, the victorious troopers turned back to Dallas, where all the divisions concentrated, and by April 20th the famous raid was ended. During its progress six thousand prisoners, forty-six pieces of artillery and a large quantity of small arms were captured. The amount of destruction effected is beyond computation.

We have now to notice important events on the Atlantic coast and in the Gulf. In the beginning of August, 1864, Admiral Farragut, with a powerful squadron, made a descent upon the defenses of Mobile, which were Fort Gaines on the left and Fort Morgan on the right of the harbor, in Mobile Bay, some thirty miles south of the city. Within the bay, additionally guarding the harbor, was the monster iron-clad ram *Tennessee* and three gunboats, commanded by the Confederate Admiral Buchanan, who floated his pennant on the *Tennessee*. Admiral Farragut's fleet consisted of fourteen wooden vessels and four iron-clads. On August 5th, Farragut was ready for the attack, and about six o'clock A. M. the fleet steamed up to Fort Morgan. The iron-clads were the *Tecumseh*, *Manhattan*, *Winnebago* and *Chickasaw*. Farragut was in the wooden ship *Hartford*, and was lashed to the main top, from which perilous position he gave his orders during the engagement. The *Tecumseh* opened the battle by a shot at Fort Morgan, and soon all the ships were engaged. Before long the *Tecumseh* struck a torpedo, which, exploding directly beneath her turret, made so fearful a rent that she sank, with Commodore Craven and nearly all the officers and crew, only seventeen of one hundred and thirty being saved. The *Hartford* then pressed on, and missing a blow from the *Tennessee*, engaged the other gunboats. After an hour's conflict the Confederate gunboat *Selma* was captured, and the other two forced to seek the shelter of the forts. Then the *Tennessee* came down at full speed to attack the *Hartford*, but the other vessels closed around the monster, and after a terrible battle the powerful ram was so battered that Admiral Buchanan, himself badly injured, was compelled to surrender, The fleet being disposed of, Farragut turned his attention to the forts. During the 6th, Fort Gaines was so severely shelled that on the morning of the 7th Colonel Anderson, the commander, surrendered. Fort Morgan, on Mobile Point, still held out, and its commander General Richard L. Page, of Virginia, severely censured Anderson for cowardice. It should have been mentioned that General Canby had, previous to the commencement of Farragut's operations, sent a land force of 5,000 men from New Orleans under General Gordon Granger, and these had been landed on Dauphin Island, which divides the entrance to Mobile Bay. Having assisted in the silencing and capture of Fort Gaines, these were now transferred to the rear of Fort Morgan, and on the 9th of August began lines of investment. On the 22d, the fleet and batteries commenced a heavy bombardment which lasted all day and seriously damaged the fort. The next morning Page surrendered, after destroying a large portion of the guns and ammunition. The possession of these forts effectually sealed the port of Mobile against blockade runners. One hundred and four guns and fourteen hundred and sixty-four men were captured during these operations. The capture of the city itself by the land forces occurred some months later, but it may be well to incorporate the episode here. At the beginning of 1865 Mobile was defended by three lines of earthworks, completely round the city. The first line, about three miles from the business portion of the city, was constructed in 1862, the second line in 1863, after the fall of Vicksburg, and the third line, about half-way between the other two, in 1864. The entire fortifications comprised forty-eight forts and redoubts with connecting breast-works. On the 7th of March, 1865, a portion of the Army of the Tennessee, having used up Hood, was sent to join Canby's command and was stationed at Fort Gaines, Mobile Bay. Another rendezvous and base of operations was selected on the Fish River, about twenty miles from Spanish Fort, one of the strongest of Mobile's defenses. In the meantime, General Steele, with Hawkins' colored troops and Lucas' cavalry, was approaching from Pensacola to Blakely, ten miles north of Mobile. All general preparations having been completed, Spanish Fort was invested on March 27th, and the siege operations were vigorously kept up till April 8th, when, by a vigorous assault, a commanding outpost was carried, and during the next night General Gibson evacuated the fort. The guns were then turned on Forts Huger and Tracy, which were also abandoned two days later. In the meantime, operations had been pushed against Fort Blakely, on the east bank of the Appalachee. This was carried by assault on the 9th by Hawkins' colored troops, with shouts of "Remember Fort Pillow," but the dreadful massacre alluded to was not avenged in kind. The whole eastern shore of the bay was now in Federal possession, and on the night of April 11th General D. H. Maury, after sinking the rams *Huntsville* and *Tuscaloosa*, abandoned Mobile and fled up the Alabama River with nine thousand men. On the evening of the 12th the authorities formally surrendered the city to General Granger and Rear-Admiral Thatcher. General Canby took possession and thus crushed the rebellion in Alabama. A large number of prisoners and some two million dollars' worth of stores and ammunition, in addition to several guns, were captured with the city.

The only other important operations to be considered in this connection were those against Fort Fisher, commanding the entrance to Cape Fear River, and Wilmington, North Carolina, the last seaport held by the Confederates. In December, 1864, Admiral Porter, with a powerful squadron, attempted the reduction of this formidable fortress. General Butler, with a land force of 6,500 men, accompanied the expedition. On the 24th of December the bombardment began, and the troops were sent ashore with orders to take the works by storm. General Butler remained with the fleet keeping up communication with General Weitzel, who led the storming column, by signals. When Weitzel had carefully reconnoitered the position, he was satisfied that it would be merely murder to throw his men on such works, for if the fleet continued firing they would destroy friend and foe, while if the naval attack ceased, the guns of the fort could annihilate the land forces. General Butler concurred and ordered the troops to re-embark, and they went back in the transports with Butler to Fortress Monroe. The fleet, however, remained off Fort Fisher.

On December 30th General Grant wrote Admiral Porter, requesting him to remain while he organized a more powerful land force. General Alfred H. Terry was intrusted with the command of the new expedition, and leaving Hampton Roads on January 6th, 1865, began debarking, after detention by rough weather, on the 13th. General Terry's dispositions were admirably made, and on the morning of the 15th he was ready for the assault. All through the previous night the fleet had been battering the works, and then at 8 o'clock on the morning of the 15th the land batteries began raining iron hail into the works. By preconcerted arrangement the fleet ceased firing at three in the afternoon, and then began a fearful struggle. One by one the traverses were carried by the dauntless Federals, stubbornly defended as they were by the equally courageous Confederates. By nine o'clock at night the last defensive point was stormed, and the work was done. The whole of the garrison left alive became prisoners, including Colonel Lamb, commander of the fort, and General Whiting, the latter being mortally wounded. Within the next two days Fort Caswell, on the right bank of Cape Fear River, was blown up, the works at Smithville, Reeves' Point and Battery Holmes were abandoned, and the whole position was in the hands of the Federal forces.

We must now hastily glance at the doings of the Confederate privateers during the war, and close this chapter with the memorable naval battle between the *Kearsarge* and the *Alabama*.

We have heretofore incidentally mentioned the privateering commissions issued by the Confederate authorities, and will now summarize the careers of the principal vessels so commissioned. The first of these was the *Savannah*, Captain T. H. Baker, of Charleston, South Carolina, from which port she escaped June 1st, 1861; three days later her captain, mistaking the U. S. brig *Perry* for a merchant vessel, attempted its capture. Finding his mistake he put his ship about, but after a running fight was compelled to surrender, and with his crew suffered imprisonment and trial on charges of piracy. The next was the *Petrel*, Captain William Perry; this privateer evaded the blockading squadron off Charleston Harbor on July 28th, and making a similar mistake with regard to the U. S. frigate *St. Lawrence*, Pirate Perry fell into a terrible trap. His vessel was sunk by an explosive shell and four of her crew were drowned. The remainder were rescued and sent to Moyamensing prison, Philadelphia, also on charges of piracy. The Confederate President threatened reprisals if these men were treated as pirates, and the subject became one of discussion even in the British Parliament. After much argument, the Government, from motives of humanity as well as of expediency, to avoid complications at the outset of the war, consented to treat both sets of captives as prisoners of war, and they were subsequently exchanged. In October, 1861, the

Nashville ran the blockade from Charleston and returned with a cargo worth three millions of dollars. Her career as a blockade runner was closed in March, 1863, when she was sunk by a Federal iron-clad at the mouth of the Savannah River. Among privateers the next in importance was the *Sumter*, which in June, 1861, under command of Captain Raphael Semmes, ran the blockade at New Orleans, and for several months played fearful havoc with merchant vessels. In February, 1862, Semmes was chased into Gibraltar, where he sold his vessel. He subsequently commanded the *Alabama*. As the Southern blockade became more effective the Confederates were driven to British ship yards for their cruisers. The *Florida* was fitted out in the harbor of Liverpool, and, in the summer of 1862 succeeded in running into Mobile Bay. From thence she escaped the following January, and after destroying fifteen merchantmen, was captured in the harbor of Bahia, Brazil. She was brought to Hampton Roads, and there, by an accidental collision, sunk. The *Georgia*, the *Shenandoah*, and the *Chickamauga*, built in the ship yards at Glasgow, Scotland, all escaped to sea and ravaged the American mercantile marine. The *Chickamauga* was blown up by the Confederates at the capture of Fort Fisher, and the *Georgia* was captured in 1863. The *Shenandoah* had the longest record. She left London early in October, 1864, as an East Indiaman, named the *Sea King*, and cleared for Bombay. At Madeira, however, the steamer *Laurel*, from Liverpool, transferred to her an armament and crew of eighty men, nominally Englishmen. She was then rechristened the *Shenandoah*, and Captain James I. Waddell displayed his privateering commission, signed by the Confederate Secretary of the Navy, Mallory. When the character and purposes of the vessel were disclosed only twenty-three of the crew consented to remain. The *Shenandoah* then cruised in the Southern Ocean, preying on American merchantmen. She visited Melbourne, Australia, where her officers were liberally feasted. During June, 1865, she was up among the New England whaling fleet, on the borders of the Arctic Ocean, and on the 28th of that month, taking advantage of a gathering of the whaling fleet by reason of one of the vessels being in distress, Waddell, under the American flag, approached, and then displaying the Confederate ensign, made prizes of ten of the vessels, burning eight of them before midnight. On the 2d of August Waddell learned that the war was over, and, hastening to England, surrendered the *Shenandoah* as a prize to the *Donegal*, a British vessel. The crew claimed to be American citizens, and the British authorities, conniving at the fraud, released them. The most notorious of all the Confederate privateers was the *Alabama*, built at Liverpool, especially for the purposes of Captain Raphael Semmes, formerly of the *Sumter*. There was little disguise about the preparation of this ship, and the American Minister, Mr. Adams, called the attention of the British Government to the matter, but in vain, and the vessel was allowed to depart. In a Portuguese harbor of the Western Isles, she received her armament, and then Semmes and her other officers arrived in a British steamer. During the last three months of 1862 Semmes destroyed by fire twenty-eight vessels, and in the course of the entire career of the *Alabama* it is estimated that not less than sixty-six vessels, involving a loss of ten million dollars, suffered at the hands of this piratical crew. The vessel never entered a Confederate port and confined her operations to European and more distant waters. Early in the summer of 1864, after a cruise in the South Atlantic and Indian seas, the *Alabama* ran into the harbor of Cherbourg, France. Captain John A. Winslow, of the United States steamer *Kearsarge*, was then lying off the port of Flushing, Holland. On being apprised of the *Alabama's* movements, Captain Winslow at once proceeded to look after her. June 14th, 1864, he arrived off Cherbourg, when Semmes, with inimitable impudence, sent a note to Winslow, begging him to remain and try conclusions with the *Alabama*. This fitted in exactly with Winslow's wishes, and he waited the convenience of his would-be antagonist. It seems probable that Semmes had some misgivings, for before coming out of the harbor he sent ashore a quantity of valuables, the product of his recent cruise. On Sunday, June 19th, the *Alabama* steamed out, escorted beyond French waters by the French iron-clad *Couronne*. Captain Winslow, to avoid any possible complications, had moved out to a point about seven miles from the breakwater. When the *Alabama* came within twelve hundred yards of the *Kearsarge* she opened fire, and delivered several broadsides before Winslow retaliated. During the succeding conflict the *Alabama* was kept moving and firing rapidly, each vessel circling so as to keep the starboard side nearest the enemy. Semmes baffled every attempt of the *Kearsarge* to close in on him, but on the other hand, while the firing of his ship was rapid and reckless, that of the *Kearsarge* was slow, methodical and effectual. By about noon, the *Alabama* was disabled as a steam vessel, and was also badly shattered by shells. Then Winslow poured in grapeshot. At length her flag went down, but until a white one was shown the fire was continued. After the *Kearsarge* ceased, in deference to the white flag, the *Alabama* fired two more shots and attempted to reach neutral waters. The *Kearsarge* resumed her fire and ran across the bow of the *Alabama*, intending to rake her, but just then the boats of the *Alabama* were lowered and Winslow was informed that the privateer was sinking. In about twenty minutes the *Alabama* went down and the *Kearsarge* saved sixty-five of her crew. Meanwhile the *Deerhound*, an English yacht, having on board the owner, Mr. Lancaster and his family, which had followed Semmes out of Cherbourg, came rapidly up, rescued Semmes, his officers and some of the men, and ran rapidly with them to English waters.

In England Semmes and his officers were treated as heroes and the claims of Winslow that they were his prisoners were stoutly resisted. It is not necessary to go further into details, as that would involve considerations which became matters of legal decision long afterwards.

We shall now turn to the Army of the Potomac, and with the operations of Grant and Lee approach the end of our war history.

CHAPTER XXXIII.

REORGANIZATION OF THE ARMY OF THE POTOMAC—BATTLE OF THE WILDERNESS—BATTLE OF SPOTTSYLVANIA COURT HOUSE—BATTLE OF COOL ARBOR—OPERATIONS BEFORE PETERSBURG—MOVEMENTS IN THE VALLEY OF THE SHENANDOAH—BATTLE OF CEDAR CREEK—SHERIDAN'S FAMOUS RIDE FROM WINCHESTER—THE ARMY IN WINTER QUARTERS.

On March 23d, 1864, Lieutenant-General Grant returned from his Western visit and joined General Meade at the latter's headquarters, Culpeper Court House, where preparations were at once begun for a vigorous campaign with the Army of the Potomac. The five army corps were consolidated and then reconstructed into three grand divisions, the Second Corps being under the command of General Winfield Scott Hancock, the Fifth under General G. K. Warren, and the Sixth under General John Sedgwick. The cavalry of the entire army was consolidated and placed under the command of General Philip H. Sheridan. In the meantime General Burnside had been at Annapolis, Md., recruiting his old Ninth Corps, and by the end of April his corps, partly composed of colored troops, was merged into the Army of the Potomac, the aggregate of which then amounted to nearly one hundred and forty thousand men.

At this time the Confederate army under Lee occupied a line extending nearly twenty miles on each side of Orange Court House, Va., its right wing protected by the Mine Run works, which had been much strengthened during the early part of the year, and its left wing covered by the Rapidan and the mountain range. The corps of Ewell and Hill were near the Rapidan and that of Longstreet was near Gordonsville.

By May 1st Lieutenant-General Grant had perfected his arrangements for a general advance and had outlined his whole plan of operations. All orders were given through General Meade, who was intrusted with minor details, and was thus virtually in command of the Army of the Potomac. Grant's plans included an overland march of the main army from the

Rapidan to the James, while the Confederate communications with Richmond were to be threatened at various points Thus General Butler, with about thirty thousand men, was to move from Fortress Monroe and take up an intrenched position at City Point, the junction of the Appomattox with the James. At the same time General Franz Sigel was instructed to form his army into two columns, one of which, about seven thousand strong, he was personally to lead up the Shenandoah Valley so as to divert Lee from concentration, while the other column, under General Crook, composed of about ten thousand men, was to march up from the Kanawha region and threaten the Virginia & East Tennessee Railroad.

At midnight on May 3d, the forward movement of the main army was begun, the right column, consisting of the Fifth and Sixth Corps, under Warren and Sedgwick, moving from Culpeper Court House, and the left column, consisting of the Second Corps, under Hancock, from Stevensburg. This latter, preceded by Gregg's Cavalry, crossed the Rapidan and pushed on to Chancellorsville, where it bivouacked on the night of the 4th. The right column, with Warren leading, also crossed the Rapidan and pushed directly for the Wilderness. It had been Grant's intention by a rapid advance to secure a position in rear of the Confederate army, but Lee penetrated the design and sent his army under two columns, led by Ewell and Hill, to meet the Federal advance and force a battle in the Wilderness. The intrenchments at Mine Run were left some six miles in the rear of the Army of Virginia as a safe retreat in case of necessity. There were two roads running through the Wilderness, one a plank road and the other an old turnpike; these ran almost parallel from Lee's centre and intersected the roads from Germania Ferry at which the Federals had crossed.

On the morning of May 5th, Warren's advance encountered the advance skirmishers of Ewell's division and some sharp fighting began at once. At first it was presumed to be merely a rear guard that had been felt, and preparations were made to turn this aside and press on for the Mine Run intrenchments. It was soon apparent, however, that the enemy were in considerable force, and General Wadsworth's Division, supported by General Robinson and by General McCandless, was advanced on the turnpike. The irregular and wooded ground prevented either side from having a thorough knowledge of the opposing movements. There was vigorous fighting throughout the whole day, and at its close the advantage was slightly with the Confederates as to position. Warren had lost nearly three thousand men, and McCandless' Brigade escaped, by the skin of its teeth, from a perilous corner, with the loss of two full regiments. General Alexander Hayes was also shot dead at the head of his troops. By nightfall both armies were within arm's reach of each other, but confused amid almost impenetrable thickets and at no point absolutely conscious of each other's position. Both sides, however, were ready to renew the combat on a field where only luck and brute force could possibly accomplish anything. To cover Longstreet's movement, intended to flank Grant's left, Lee ordered a demonstration on Seymour's Brigade, at the extreme right, but Warren and Hancock had simultaneously made a vigorous attack on Hill's Division, and for a time this was forced back almost to Lee's headquarters. Longstreet's flanking movement had been comprehended, but the countermanding order was, of course, unknown, and therefore when Hancock attempted to press his advance he found himself confronted by an overwhelming force, and before noon was compelled to fall back. About this time General Wadsworth, who had been pressing the Confederate line heavily, was shot through the brain and then captured. He died the next day. This disaster was offset by a Confederate blunder, for Longstreet, coming suddenly upon a detached portion of his own command, was fired upon and so severely wounded as to be disabled. This threw the immediate command of the field upon Lee, whose slower movements enabled Hancock to prepare for the impending attack. By four o'clock, however, Hill and Longstreet fell heavily on Hancock's position, and aided by a forest fire, the Confederates drove the Federal troops back on Chancellorsville. But for the gallant intervention of Colonel J. W. Hoffman with the fragments of several regiments, the result might have been very serious. Lee was still determined to carry his point if possible.

and about sunset threw a heavy column under General Gordon on the Federal right, capturing Generals Seymour and Shaler and about four thousand men. A further advance was checked by General Sedgwick, and thus the day's fighting ended.

That night Lee retired behind intrenchments, and Grant, anxious for a more legitimate battlefield than the tangled Wilderness afforded, determined to push through to Spottsylvania Court House, some thirteen miles to the southeast. This movement was begun by Warren on the evening of May 7th, but Lee was quickly apprised of it, and sending forward General Anderson with the head of Longstreet's Corps, the Confederates were enabled to seize Spottsylvania Ridge and impede the Federal advance. By Sunday night the whole of Lee's army was across the intended southern line of march of the Federal troops. On the 9th the Federal line of battle was formed, Hancock on the right, Sedgwick on the left and Warren in the centre. Hancock had driven the Confederates across the Ny, a little river in front of the Federal line. During the day, to cover the intrenching operations, there were several skirmishes, and in one of these General Sedgwick was shot dead by a Confederate sharpshooter. Brigadier-General W. H. Morris was also severely wounded.

GEN. PHILIP H. SHERIDAN.

In the meantime General Sheridan had been sent with a heavy cavalry force to break up Lee's connections with Richmond. Sweeping over the Ta and the Po, he next crossed the

North Anna, captured and destroyed the Beaver Dam Station of the Virginia Central Railroad, destroyed ten miles of the track and released some four hundred Federals taken prisoners in the Wilderness. After a skirmish with General J. E. B. Stuart's cavalry, he crossed the South Anna, and on May 11th captured Ashland Station on the Fredericksburg road, destroying it, with its stores and seven miles of track. Pushing on for Richmond, he again encountered Stuart's cavalry, but repulsed them and drove them toward the north fork of the Chickahominy, Generals Stuart and Gordon being mortally wounded in the fight. The road was now open to Richmond, and a gallant dash by Custer's Brigade carried the outer works of the city; but this was all that could be accomplished, and after some sharp engagements with forces sent out from Richmond, Sheridan made his way to the James River; rested three days at Haxhall's Landing, and by May 25th rejoined the Army of the Potomac by way of Hanover Court House.

Meanwhile the battle of Spottsylvania Court House had been fought. On the morning of May 10th two desperate assaults were made on the Confederate position on Laurel Hill, across the Ny, by the divisions of Crawford and Cutler, but they were repulsed with heavy loss. Toward night the assaults were repeated, the Second and Fifth Corps being combined for the attack. The slaughter was fearful. The first Confederate line was taken, together with nine hundred prisoners and several guns, but the movement not being supported, the Federal troops fell back. During the day Generals J. C. Rice and T. G. Stevenson were killed. The close of the first day's battle marked no important result, but some nine thousand Federals and eight thousand Confederates were killed, wounded or prisoners. Nothing daunted, however, Lieutenant General Grant in his dispatches of the 11th, took a hopeful view of affairs, and closed with the now historic sentence, "I propose to fight it out on this line, if it takes all summer."

But little was done next day, but at midnight General Hancock, under instructions to strike Lee's line at the right centre, began his preparations for an advance by daylight on the 12th. He formed his attack in two lines, one composed of the divisions of Gibbon and Mott, and the other those of Barlow and Birney. Moving stealthily through a dense fog, the latter column fell upon the earthworks held by General Edward Johnson, of Ewell's Division. The Confederates were at breakfast when the Federal troops, at the point of the bayonet, and with clubbed muskets, dashed in among them. Generals Johnson and George H. Stewart, and about three thousand men, were surprised and taken prisoners. These Hancock sent back to Grant. Hancock had also captured some forty guns. His troops meanwhile were so flushed with success that they pursued the fugitives for more than a mile, when they were checked by another line of breastworks. By this time also some of Hill's and Longstreet's men had been sent to rally the fugitives, and Hancock was forced back to the first line. General Wright was sent to reinforce Hancock, and at the same time Warren and Burnside charged heavily on the whole Confederate front. Lee made desperate efforts to dislodge Hancock, the men fighting hand to hand on either side of the breastworks, but by midnight Lee's troops were compelled to retreat, leaving Hancock master of the position.

On the 13th the Confederates had considerably shortened their lines, but were well intrenched, and for eight days the two armies faced each other watching for an opening. On the morning of the 18th an attempt to force the Confederate position was repulsed, and then Grant resolved upon a flanking movement. Abandoning his position north of the Rapidan, he established another base at Fredericksburg. He still kept his face toward Richmond and on the night of the 21st another flanking movement was begun toward Mattaponax Church. Lee was, however, on the alert, and by a shorter route reached the North Anna River and took up a strong position in close communication with the Virginia Central Railroad. After several desultory engagements and much marching and counter marching, the important engagement of Cool Arbor was fought on June 3d. In this battle, despite desperate bravery, the Federals were utterly unable to force the Confederate position and suffered a loss of some ten thousand men, while the Confederate loss did not exceed one thousand.

Grant now determined to throw his army on the south side of the James River, and for this purpose extended his lines to the Chickahominy, making a feint as if intending to cross it and march directly on Richmond. This ruse succeeded, and Lee rapidly retired into the intrenchments of that city. On the night of the 14th, however, the Federals had thrown a pontoon bridge across the James below Wilcox's, and by noon of the 16th the entire army had crossed and was moving on Petersburg.

While these movements were in progress General Butler had begun a series of operations by which the Army of the James was to co-operate with the Army of the Potomac by a movement against Richmond on the south side of the James River. He moved early in May, and by the 5th he had passed up the James River on transports, accompanied by a powerful flotilla, taking possession of City Point, and had also landed a heavy force at Bermuda Hundred, a triangular strip of land at the mouth of the Appomattox, between it and the James. Strong intrenchments were created, and the gunboats on the two streams protected a position only eight miles from Petersburg and fifteen from Richmond. The movement was a complete surprise. When Grant determined to place Meade's army beyond the James, he sent the command of General Smith back by water to reinforce Butler at Bermuda Hundred, and as soon as Meade's army had effected its passage, Grant went in person to Butler's headquarters to arrange for a plan of co-operation from that base against Petersburg. Butler was heartily in sympathy with these plans, and on the 10th of June he sent General Gillmore with three thousand five hundred infantry, and fifteen hundred cavalry under General Kautz, against Petersburg. Gillmore drove in the Confederate skirmish line, but hesitated to pursue his advantage; Kautz meanwhile had dashed into the city, but the falling back of Gillmore enabled the Confederates to turn their attention to him and drive him from the town. On the 15th another attack was made, this time with the fresh troops of General Smith. The outworks were captured, but Smith, unaware of the smallness of the force within the city, spent some hours in preparing for an assault.

Late in the evening an advance was made in force and the rifle-pits were carried. By this time two of Hancock's divisions had arrived, and then the troops rested. This was fatal to the movement, for in the course of the night the greater part of Lee's army poured into the city, and by next morning the chance of its capture was gone. Then followed a long siege of ten months, upon which we will not waste space here, but merely mention some of the salient points. Convinced now that he had a formidable foe to deal with, Grant instructed Meade to post the main body of the army before the Confederate works at once and open fire on them. During the 17th and 18th of June several assaults were made, but without any material success, for the Confederates, having fallen back on new and stronger works, repulsed the Federals and inflicted considerable loss. Preparations were now made for a regular siege, and Lieutenant-Colonel Henry Pleasants, of the Forty-eigth Pennsylvania, undertook the construction of a mine to blow up one of the principal forts. This was begun on June 25th, and was about ready for use in one month. Most of his men being from the mining regions, their experience made up somewhat for the lack of proper tools.

In the meantime, General Butler, on June 20th, had thrown General Foster's Brigade across the James River, at Deep Bottom, and formed an intrenched camp, connected by a pontoon bridge with Bermuda Hundred, this being intended to aid the assault at the time of the springing of the mine. About five o'clock on the morning of July 30th the mine was sprung, blowing up the fort, guns and garrison of three hundred men, and leaving a crater two hundred feet by fifty feet, and about thirty feet deep. The assault which followed was a terrible failure, the Federals being repulsed with a loss of forty-four hundred men, while the entire Confederate loss did not exceed one thousand. The disappointment was very great, but Grant was not to be disheartened. About the 12th of August he ordered an attempt on the flank of the Confederate works at Baylis' Creek, but little advantage was gained, as Lee was rapidly reinforcing the position. On the 18th of August General Warren succeeded in capturing and holding the

Weldon road. Lee made desperate efforts to recover this important line of communication, but every assault was repulsed, though at a fearful cost of life.

On September 28th Generals Ord and Birney captured Battery Harrison, one of the strongest positions around Richmond. In an attempt to retake this position the Confederates suffered heavily. The Federal loss at the time of the capture had been heavy, for General Burnham was killed, Generals Ord and Stannard severely wounded, the latter losing an arm, and some seven hundred men were killed or severely wounded. The next really important movement, and the last for the season in this direction, was the contest for the possession of the Boynton plank-road, a few miles west of the Weldon road, and nearly the only line of communication open to Lee. To guard this, Lee had extended his intrenchments along to Hatcher's Run, and these works also protected the South Side Railway. At daybreak on October 27th the Ninth Corps, under Parke, Warren's Fifth Corps and Hancock's Second, made a combined attack on these works. In this movement, however, Crawford's division got entangled in a swamp. This left Hancock unsupported, and Hill's leading division under Heth charged down upon him, while Wade Hampton's cavalry were harassing his flank and rear. These, however, were kept off by Gregg, and General Eagan fell so heavily upon Heth's force that it was utterly demoralized. The fight lasted all day without any material advantage, and at midnight Hancock withdrew to the lines before Petersburg and Warren returned to his position on the Weldon road. This practically closed the campaign of the main army, and preparations were made for going into winter quarters. Grant's army built some comfortable cabins, and all active operations ceased until the following February.

We must now trace the other movements which had meanwhile taken place in the Shenandoah Valley, where Lieutenant-General Grant had placed General Sigel. On May 1st Sigel, having turned over his immediate command in the Kanawha Valley to General Crook, moved up the Shenandoah Valley with eight thousand men, intending to cross the Blue Ridge and march to Lynchburg or Gordonsville.

To check this movement Lee sent General Breckinridge, with all the force he could spare. On May 15th Breckinridge encountered Sigel near Newmarket, about fifty miles from Winchester, and, falling furiously upon him, drove the Federal troops down the Valley to Cedar Creek, near Strasburg, a distance of nearly thirty miles. In this disastrous rout Sigel lost some seven hundred men, six guns, a quantity of small arms and much of his field equipment. In great disgust Grant immediately relieved Sigel of his command, and turned it over to General David Hunter, with instructions to push on to Lynchburg after destroying the railroad between Staunton and Charlottesville. Having been reinforced, Hunter, with nine thousand men, advanced on Staunton, but encountered at Piedmont, on June 5th, a large Confederate force under Generals W. E. Jones and McCausland. After a sharp engagement, in which General Jones was killed, the Confederates were utterly routed, some fifteen hundred men being captured, together with several guns, battle-flags and small arms. In the meantime General Averell had moved along the Kanawha Valley, without any other result than losing several men in one or two sharp encounters with the guerrilla Morgan. On the 8th of June the forces of Crook and Averell joined Hunter at Staunton, and thus reinforced, Hunter, with twenty thousand men, attacked Lynchburg, on the southern side, on June 18th. But Lee, penetrating the intent of Hunter's movements, and sensible of the importance of the position, had sent so strong a force to hold it that Hunter quickly abandoned his attack and retreated by way of Salem, up to which point he was closely followed by the Confederates. From thence Hunter made his way across the mountains to Meadow Bridge, in the direction of the Kanawha, where he expected to find some much-needed rations. But a guerrilla force had captured these stores, and for some days the disheartened troops were in great straits.

This retrograde movement, however, left the Shenandoah Valley open, and Lee was prompt to take advantage of it. Hoping by a bold diversion to compel Grant to raise the siege of Petersburg, in order to defend the Capital, Lee despatched General Early, with about twenty thousand troops of all arms, with orders to cross the Blue Ridge, sweep down the valley, invade Maryland and threaten Washington City. On July 5th Early crossed the Potomac at Williamsport; on the 6th he was at Hagerstown, where he made a forced levy of $20,000, and then pushed on, plundering right and left. On July 9th, however, General Lewis Wallace met him at the Monocacy and a fierce battle ensued. The overwhelming Confederate force was such that Wallace at once perceived nothing could be done but keep the enemy at bay, at all hazards. This was gallantly done, for, although the Federals were ultimately driven back with heavy loss, the check to their opponents had enabled reinforcements to reach the capital. Even as it was, there are doubts whether Early, had he risked the adventure, might not have inflicted serious damage on the city. Moving cautiously, however, Early approached Washington in the vicinity of Fort Stevens, but after a sharp fight with a reconnoitering party sent out by General Augur, he retreated across the Potomac at Edwards' Ferry on July 12th, and regained the Shenandoah Valley with a vast amount of plunder. General Horatio G. Wright, of the Sixth Corps, followed them up, and several sharp engagements were had with varying success. The command of the Federal troops was then turned over to General Crook, General Wright returning to attend to his special duties—the defenses of Washington. Crook moved to Harper's Ferry and thence was moving on Winchester, when he unexpectedly encountered the Confederates at Kernstown on July 23d. The next day, after a sharp engagement, the whole of Crook's force was driven back on Martinsburg. In this engagement General Mulligan was killed and the Federals lost fully twelve hundred men. After another fight on the 25th, Crook contrived to get across the Potomac, but he left Early master of the southern side of the river. The Confederates at once spread on raiding expeditions, and a body of cavalry, under McCausland, dashed into Pennsylvania and captured Chambersburg. Failing to extort a forced levy of two hundred thousand dollars, the village was fired and private property of every kind simply stolen. General Averell's cavalry was quickly upon them, but the Confederates had wrought their mischief and were hastening back to Virginia. He came up to them, however, at Moorfield on August 4th, and inflicted a heavy blow.

These continued raids, however, and the necessity for the occupation of the Shenandoah Valley in sufficient force to protect Washington, as well as Pennsylvania and Maryland from these constant distractions and risks, at length determined Lieutenant-General Grant to consolidate the Washington, Middle, Susquehanna and Southwest Virginia departments into one organization. This was called the Middle Military Division and comprised about thirty thousand troops. The command of, this important force was intrusted to the gallant and dashing General Philip H. Sheridan, for General Hunter had expressed a desire to be relieved. Sheridan's cavalry force numbered about ten thousand and was in splendid condition. With his subsequent operations, including his memorable "Ride from Winchester" and his promotion to the rank of major-general, we shall bring up our narrative to the close of 1864.

On August 7th, General Sheridan took up his headquarters at Harper's Ferry and assumed command. His first attention was directed to the thorough preparation of his forces for an actively aggressive campaign, in which he determined to punish the Confederates for their ravages elsewhere. For more than a month he was occupied with his plans and arrangements, and so well had he mastered all details that at an interview on September 16th Lieutenant-General Grant gave him almost unlimited power, with the simple instructions, "Go in." He went in—he went in to win—and he won, acquiring a reputation hardly second to any that was achieved throughout the war.

By various feints and devices, Early attempted to draw Sheridan from his chosen position, which by the middle of September was in front of Berryville, on the turnpike from that town across the Opequan Creek to Winchester, but Sheridan, though a young man (he was but 33 years of age at this time), was "too old a soldier" to be lured into any trap. Early was in front of him, covering Winchester, and on the 18th had sent away a large force toward Martinsburg. This was Sheridan's chance, and he promptly availed himself of it. By three o'clock on the morning of the 19th of September, Sheridan's forces moved forward upon Winchester, Wilson's Cavalry leading, and being followed by General Wright with the Sixth and General Emory with the Nineteenth Corps. Averell and Torbert were sent to menace the Confederate left, while Crook's Eighth Corps, then at Summit Point, was ordered to join the advance at Opequan ford. The cavalry and Wright's troops crossed the Opequan at daybreak; but Emory's troops were somewhat delayed and in the meantime Early had succeeded in recalling his troops from Bunker's Hill, and now was massed to the northwest of the town. The only approach to his position was through a narrow pass between thickly wooded hills. The attack was gallantly made by Ricketts' division of the Sixth Corps, closely followed by Grover's of the Nineteenth, but although the first line of Early's centre was stormed, the Federals were checked and then thrown back in confusion by heavy columns hurled upon them. A rally was made, however, and then the pursuing Confederates were galled by a fire in their rear from Emory's troops and thrown back on their own lines. The fight continued for some hours with varying fortunes until Crook's Eighth Corps fell heavily on Early's left; at the same time Wilson's cavalry pressed in on his right and a general advance on his centre completed the demoralization of his lines. By five o'clock in the afternoon the Confederates were in full retreat, and did not halt till they reached Fisher's Hill, twenty miles south of Winchester. The Confederate loss was very heavy; Generals Rodes and Godwin were killed, together with about one thousand men, while Sheridan captured twenty-five hundred prisoners, five guns and nine flags.

Determined to give his foe no rest, Sheridan attacked him at Fisher's Hill on the 22d and drove him from a strongly fortified position with the loss of a thousand prisoners and sixteen guns. General Torbert, with a heavy cavalry force, had been previously dispatched to seize New Market, in Early's rear, but was checked in the Luray Valley by General Wickham's cavalry, or Early's destruction would have been complete. The fugitives were followed to Port Republic, and thence they escaped into the Blue Ridge with the loss of their wagon train. Then Sheridan began his work of devastation in the Shenandoah Valley, and literally desolated the country. According to his own account he destroyed two thousand barns and seventy mills, filled with grain, flour, etc.; drove off four thousand head of stock and killed for army use about three thousand sheep. Smarting under his defeat, Early rallied his troops and sent his cavalry under Rosser to harass Sheridan's rear, but he was soon disposed of with heavy loss in men and material. On the 12th of October Early attempted a surprise on Sheridan's new position at Fisher's Hill, but was repulsed with severe losses.

Believing that Early had got his quietus for a time, Sheridan posted his forces in a strong position on the east side of Cedar Creek, with pickets extending along the north fork of the Shenandoah to Front Royal, and then temporarily assigning command to General Wright, Sheridan went to Washington.

In the meantime Early, reinforced by Kershaw's Division and six hundred cavalry sent to him from Petersburg by Lee, planned and carried out a surprise. At dawn on the 19th of October, the whole Confederate force broke in on Crook's Division in the immediate front, and hurled it back on the supporting divisions. The Federal guns were turned upon the flying troops, and all efforts to rally the men failing, General Wright, with the entire army, fell back first to Middletown and then a few miles beyond, the confusion being so great that it was almost impossible to form a line. Early pushed on to Middletown, but his hour of triumph was about over. He had captured some twenty-four pieces of artillery, some twelve hundred men and the entire Federal camp and equipage, and probably expecting that the fugitives would fall further back, he allowed his men to rest, plunder and eat. This was fatal. General Sheridan, having transacted the official business which took him to Washington, had returned to Winchester on the night of the 18th, and slept there. The sound of cannonading up the valley in the morning he ascribed to a reconnoissance only, and therefore he breakfasted quietly and then rode leisurely out of the city, southward toward

Kernstown. Here he met the fugitives, and quickly grasped the position. He had twelve miles to ride and an army and a reputation to save. Ordering the parking of the retreating artillery, he put his horse to the gallop and dashed on. As the fugitives thickened he did not draw rein, but waving his hat, shouted: "Face the other way, boys! Come on! We're going to lick them out of their boots!" The change was magical: the disheartened men forgot fatigue, forgot defeat; they were going to follow Sheridan, and they did this with a will. By the time he reached the front General Wright had succeeded in restoring something like order, and had made preparations for an advance. Dashing along the lines Sheridan cheered the men and declared: "We'll have those camps and cannon again!" Approving all arrangements that had been made, Sheridan gave the order for an advance of the entire line at three o'clock. A terrible struggle ensued, but men in such a state of enthusiasm were not to be repulsed to any great extent. There was a slight check when Early opened their own guns on them again, but it was soon over, and then the Confederates, pressed on both flanks by cavalry, were utterly routed. Through Middletown and Strasburg to Fisher's Hill went the fugitives, leaving everything behind them. The Confederate losses were about 300 killed and wounded, 1,000 taken prisoners. and their whole camp equipage, wagons, horses, ammunition, etc. Sheridan lost about 300 men. The Federal troops returned to their old position on Cedar Creek, and Sheridan made his headquarters at Kernstown, near Winchester, being now in full possession of the Shenandoah Valley, from Harper's Ferry to Staunton. With the exception of a few cavalry skirmishes, there was no other fighting until operations were resumed in the spring, for Early's army was virtually annihilated as an organization. On the 4th of November, General McClellan resigned from the Army, and Sheridan was appointed to the major-generalship thus vacated. His gallant achievements took the public by storm and created almost unparalleled enthusiasm, as well in official as in loyal circles outside.

CHAPTER XXXIV.

EVENTS OF 1865—THE CLOSING SCENES OF THE WAR—DESPERATE ATTEMPTS OF THE BELEAGURED CONFEDERATES—EVACUATION AND BURNING OF RICHMOND—OCCUPATION OF PETERSBURG—SURRENDER OF LEE TO GRANT—DISPERSION OF THE ARMY OF NORTHERN VIRGINIA—CLOSING BATTLE AT PALMETTO RANCH, TEXAS—END OF THE WAR.

In the early part of January, 1865, the beleaguered Confederates in Richmond conceived the notable plan of severing the Federal army, lying on each side of the James River, by destroying the obstructions at the lower end of Dutch Gap Canal and the pontoon bridges below. For this purpose the armored vessels *Virginia*, *Fredericksburg* and *Richmond*, and the wooden steamers *Drewry*, *Nansemond*, *Hampton*, *Buford* and *Torpedo*, slipped silently down from under Fort Darling, a formidable battery on Drewry's Bluff, about eight miles from Richmond. There was an interchange of shots as the squadron was detected passing Fort Brady, but the *Fredericksburg* broke through the Dutch Gap boom. The others failed to get through, and the *Drewry*, which had grounded, was blown up by a shell from one of the shore batteries. After sustaining a heavy fire for some time, the rest of the squadron hastened back to cover.

During the first week of February, General Warren, with Gregg's cavalry, succeded after several sharp engagements, in seizing ground for the extension of the Federal lines to Hatcher's Run and the completion of the City Point railroad to that point. On February 27th, General Sheridan started on a raid which Grant had projected, to cut Lee's communications and seize Lynchburg. He had with him about ten thousand men under Generals George A. Custer and W. Merritt, and some of the cavalry of the old Army of West Virginia, under Colonel Capeheart. They moved on toward Staunton, Colonel Capeheart disposing of the Confederate General Rosser at Mount Crawford, where he attempted to hinder the passage of the stream. At Waynesboro' Early was intrenched and determined to prevent the passage of Rockfish Gap. The contract, however, was too large for his ability, and Custer, without waiting for the rest of the force, fell upon him, captured sixteen hundred of his men, and sent the other nine hundred, with their discomfited leader, hunting for shelter across the Blue Ridge. Custer lost but about twelve men, and captured two hundred loaded wagons, eleven guns and seventeen flags. This time Early's boastful bubble was effectually punctured, and he retired into comparative obscurity.

This occurred on March 2d, and the next day the authorities of Charlottesville formally surrendered that place to Sheridan. Deciding that Lynchburg was too strong for him, Sheridan passed round behind Lee's army, and proceeding eastward destroyed the James River Canal, the supply line for Richmond, and pushed on to Columbia. Halting here for a day while his men destroyed the canal as far as Goochland, he next struck the Virginia Central Railroad at Tolersville, and tore up the track for fifteen miles to Beaver Dam Station. There in two columns his men under Custer and Devin completed the destruction of bridges and railroads in all directions, and finally the whole force swept round by the Pamunkey River and White House, and rejoined the Army of the James, on Grant's right, on March 26th. This rapid, daring and successful raid not only seriously imperiled Richmond, but it made confusion worse confounded among the Confederate leaders; in fact, the terror of Davis, his Cabinet and his Congress was such that preparations were made for immediate flight. The usual effects of failure, mutual suspicion and recrimination had been at work for some time, and during January there had been threats to strip Davis of his power and make Lee dictator, to put an end to the egotistical and ignorant interference of the Confederate President with military matters.

To save himself the humiliation of deposition, Davis consented on February 1st, 1865, to the reappointment of General Johnston and the appointment of General Lee, by the Confederate Congress, to the position of General-in-Chief of all the armies of the Confederacy. It was the beginning of the end. About this time also the project of abandoning Richmond and transferring the seat of Government to some point in the Cotton States was under consideration. The rapidly occurring disasters of the next three months, however, left nothing in the shape of a government to be transferred anywhere.

Just before Sheridan's return from his brilliant raid, Grant had perfected his plans for an advance by the Army of the Potomac, under Meade, the Army of the James, under Ord, and the entire cavalry force, under Sheridan, the movement to be begun on March 29th. In the meantime Lee, suspecting that when Grant moved he would do so in force, determined on one desperate effort to burst the bonds which had so long restrained him. He decided on one leap for liberty, and on the morning of March 25th he ordered General Gordon, with a large force, to attack Fort Steadman, on Grant's extreme right, south of the Appomattox, so as to get control of the railroad to Hatcher's Run and open a pass for the army to cross the Roanoke and join Johnston. Twenty thousand men were in readiness to avail themselves of this outlet. At four o'clock in the morning Gordon dashed upon and into Fort Steadman, capturing several of the surprised garrison—Fourteenth New York Artillery and First Division of the Ninth Corps—and driving out those who escaped capture. The surprise had been well planned, for the guns of the fort were promptly turned on the connecting line of intrenchments, and the redoubts were cleared in short order. The advantage was lost, however, by the failure of the reserves to advance. The fort guns were then turned on Fort Haskell, to the left, and an assault was attempted, but the position was gallantly held by Major Woermer, and when General John F. Hartranft's Division of the Ninth Corps came up, the Confederates, caught between heavy artillery fires and faced by a strong force, threw down their arms. Thus nineteen hundred men became prisoners instead of victors, when success had been fairly within their grasp. Those who attempted to escape were mowed down, and the Federal forces, seizing the auspicious moment, pressed forward and captured the intrenched picket line of the Confederates.

Lee's plans had failed and had not even disturbed those of Grant, for on the morning of the 29th, the corps of Warren and Humphreys began the advance, crossing Rowanty Creek and Hatcher's Run, and moving in two parallel columns against the Confederate flank. Sheridan had moved at the same time from Bermuda Hundred and had pushed on to Dinwiddie Court House. At night he was but six miles from Warren and Humphreys, giving the Federals an unbroken line to the Appomattox. Lee quickly perceived the peril of his right wing, and concentrated some fifteen thousand men and Fitzhugh Lee's cavalry across the path of Warren and Humphreys. A heavy rain on the night of the 29th had so damaged the roads that Grant suspended his advance, but Lee was desperate and reckless, and he made a sudden dash on the Federal position. The movement was so heavy and sudden that Ayres' division was forced back on Crawford's, throwing that also into confusion, but Griffin's division, in the rear, remained firm, and Warren was speedily enabled to retaliate. The Confederates were driven back to their intrenchments, but an attempt to dislodge them failed.

In the meantime Sheridan had pushed forward the troops of Devin and Davies and captured the Confederate position at Five Forks. Baffled in his first attempt, Lee now attacked the position with the divisions of Pickett and Bushrod Johnson, and the Federal cavalry were driven back upon Dinwiddie Court House. The Confederate advantage, however, was soon lost, for Sheridan charged on their flank, and sharp fighting ensued until night came on. By dawn, on the morning of April 1st, Ayres had hastened to the support of Sheridan, who then dashed forward and drove the Confederates back into the works at Five Forks, while Warren was moving to the White Oak road on the Confederate left. At 4 o'clock that afternoon Warren advanced in line of battle, with Crawford's division on the right, Ayres' on the left and Griffin's bringing up the rear. After some sharp fighting in the open field, Ayres carried the Confederate works on the right, capturing about one thousand men, while Griffin did the same on the left. Immediately after this the cavalry charged over the works, and the Confederates fled in wild disorder. Five thousand men and several guns and colors were captured.

That night General Grant ordered a cannonade along the whole of the line investing Petersburg, from Appomattox to Hatcher's Run, and at daybreak on the 2d the assault began. The outer works were carried at several points, and the South Side Railroad, Lee's most important line of communication, was cut at three points. Gibbon's Division of Ord's command simultaneously attacked the lines south of Petersburg and captured Forts Gregg and Alexander. The Confederate forces, now strengthened by Longstreet, who had pushed forward from Richmond, were confined within the inner line, and Lee considered himself competent to attempt the recapture of the works on his left. Heth struck the Ninth Corps heavily, but was repulsed, and General A. P. Hill was shot dead. The last hope of holding either Petersburg or Richmond was gone, and Lee, shortly after ten o'clock on Sunday morning, April 2, telegraphed to Jeff. Davis at Richmond that his lines were broken and that Richmond must be evacuated. He proposed himself to maintain a bold front at Petersburg till night, and then try to reach Johnston by the Danville railroad.

It soon became evident in Richmond that Davis and his Cabinet were preparing for flight, and the wildest excitement prevailed. That evening Davis fled by the railroad, the Virginia Legislature, in canal boats, left for Columbia, and the Confederate Congress had dispersed. The Treasury gold had been sent on to Danville early in the day, and by midnight Major Melton, representing the Confederate War Department, had carried out his orders, despite the protests of the civil authorities, and had applied the torch to the warehouses and stores. By noon on April 3d the whole centre of the city was a blazing heap of ruins. The troops had crossed to the south side of the James River by seven o'clock that morning, burning the bridges behind them. Terrific concussions now shook the country around; these were caused by the blowing up of the magazine, the ram *Virginia* and the iron-clads *Fredericksburg* and *Richmond.* General Godfrey Weitzel, who had been watching for some such movement, at once advanced, but with caution, as the approaches were known to be planted with terra-torpedoes. Fortunately, the retreat had been so hasty that the Confederates forgot to remove the little red flags, marking these explosives, which had been placed for their protection. At seven o'clock that evening Mayor Mayo formally surrendered the city, and the Stars and Stripes were soon floating over the Virginia State House, from which the Confederate Congress had just fled in such hot haste and abject terror.

General George F. Shepley, Chief of Staff to General Weitzel, was appointed Military Governor; Lieutenant-Colonel Manning, Provost Marshal, the city being placed under military rule. Vigorous efforts were made by the troops to suppress the flames, but the inhabitants who remained were sullen and refused to respond to the conciliatory advances made. They were therefore allowed to sulk, with a significant warning not to attempt any public meetings to air their disloyalty.

While Richmond was blazing, Lee's troops in Petersburg were quitting so secretly that they were many miles away when the Federal pickets discovered, at dawn, that the intrenchments before them were entirely abandoned. General Grant at once took possession of the city, and sent his columns in rapid pursuit of the fugitives.

When Lee determined on the evacuation of Richmond and Petersburg, he arranged to concentrate his retreating forces at Amelia Court House, and for that purpose ordered up commissary and quartermaster's stores from Danville to that point. The selfish haste, however, of the Confederate authorities at Richmond, frustrated all his plans. With a view of furnishing transportation for the fleeing administration, these supply trains were ordered on to Richmond, and there became involved in the general conflagration. Consequently, when Lee arrived at Amelia Court House, he found himself stripped of all supplies and compelled to forage for food.

Meanwhile Grant had been pressing on his pursuit, and on April 6th nearly the whole of the Army of the Potomac was at Jetersville, ready to advance on Lee at Amelia Court House. By this time it was found that Lee had left that position, had passed the left flank of the Federal army and was moving westward to Deatonsville. Sheridan, with his cavalry in three columns, pushed after the fugitives, and at Sailor's Creek the divisions of Crook and Devin cut off Ewell's Corps from the main Confederate army. After a fierce struggle the Confederates were overwhelmed and General Ewell, four other general officers and six thousand men were taken prisoners. During the night of April 6th the shattered remnant of Lee's army crossed the bridges over the Appomattox at Farmville and attempted to burn the bridges behind them, but succeeded in destroying only one of them. A position was taken up, strongly intrenched, on the stage and plank roads to Lynchburg, a few miles north of Farmville, but the men were absolutely starving and the officers were beginning to show signs of insubordination. Without the presence of Lee, a military council was held and it was decided that the time for surrender had arrived. This was communicated to Lee, but he positively refused to accede to the proposed capitulation.

On April 7th General Humphreys had ordered a combined assault on Lee's fortified position by General Miles on the left and General Barlow on the front. Miles incautiously made his attack before Barlow was in position, and was repulsed with serious loss. This further increased Lee's obstinacy. In the meantime General Grant, convinced that his foe was fairly in his hands, considered that the time had arrived when the promptings of humanity ought to be listened to. With noble magnanimity he sent a note to Lee, from Farmville, to the following effect:

"The result of the last week must convince you of the hopelessness of further resistance on the part of the Army of Northern Virginia in this struggle. I feel that it is so; and regard it as my duty to shift from myself the responsibility of any further effusion of blood by asking of you the surrender of that portion of the Confederate States Army known as the Army of Northern Virginia."

Lee sent an equivocal reply, not admitting the hopelessness of his cause, but asking what terms would be given, and then commenced a hasty retreat. On receiving this note on the morning of the 8th, Grant sent another communication, indicating in general terms his proposition and suggesting a personal conference. Lee was meanwhile struggling to get away beyond Lynchburg into the passes of the Blue Ridge, and, therefore, to gain time he sent another reply, in which, after intimating that he did not think the time had come for the surrender of his army, he proposed to accept the suggestion of a meeting to be held the next morning, between the picket lines, on the Richmond stage road, to treat for peace. To this casuistical communication Grant's reply was terse, but still courteous; many another man would have lost his temper over the thinly disguised equivocation of Lee's letters. He said, in effect, that such a meeting, upon such a basis, would be futile. He had not the authority to treat for peace, but had both desire and authority to grant liberal terms in respect of a surrender.

While this correspondence was going on, General Sheridan, with characteristic promptitude, was making his arrangements to prevent the needless spilling of either ink or blood. With General Custer in the advance, he made a forced march of thirty miles, and reaching Appomattox Station, on the Lynchburg Railroad, captured the four supply trains on which Lee's men depended for their next meal, and on the evening of the 8th he had blocked Lee's last hope of escape, while the rest of his command was hurrying up to be in readiness to annihilate the Confederate Army. Still undaunted, Lee resolved upon another desperate effort. He had but about ten thousand men, and these he hurled upon Sheridan's line on the morning of April 9th with such impetuosity that the Federals fell back, but Sheridan knew that the men in front of him had no staying powers, that they were weakened by want of food and loss of ambition, so he quietly ordered a steady retrograde movement, wearying the foe meanwhile until he had perfected his arrangements. Then when the Confederates were ready for a final charge, they were confronted by a wall of determined men whose fixed bayonets gleamed ominously. It was enough! Sheridan's cavalry were just about to charge when the display of a white flag stopped hostilities.

At this moment, elsewhere, a still more important scene was being enacted. The failure to break Sheridan's line convinced Lee that his hour of humiliation had arrived. He hastily sent a note to Grant acknowledging the receipt of the latter's letter, and asking for an interview to arrange for a surrender. General Grant was just setting out to join Sheridan, but promptly signified his willingness to meet Lee, at once.

About 2 o'clock on Sunday afternoon, April 9th (singularly enough it was Palm Sunday), General Grant, attended by Colonel Parker, his chief aid, and General Lee, attended by his Adjutant-General, Colonel Marshall, met in the residence of Wilmer McLean, at Appomattox Court House. After a courteous interchange of civilities, as became brave men who had faced each other undauntedly for many weary months, each sincere in the conviction of the justice of the cause he espoused, the two commanders rapidly discussed the terms of surrender, and then they were reduced to writing. With great delicacy General Grant made the proposition of surrender and tendered it for Lee's acceptance. Appended is the text of the document:

APPOMATTOX COURT HOUSE, Va., April 9, 1865.

"GENERAL—In accordance with the text of my letter to you of the 8th inst., I propose to receive the surrender of the Army of Northern Virginia on the following terms—to wit: Rolls of all the officers and men to be made in duplicate; one copy to be given to an officer to be designated by me, the other to be retained by such other officer or officers as you may designate. The officers to give their individual paroles not to take up arms against the Government of the United States until properly exchanged; and each company or regimental commander to sign a like parole for the men of their commands. The arms, artillery and public property to be packed and stacked, and turned over to the officers appointed by me to receive them. This will not embrace the side arms of the officers, nor their private horses or baggage. This done, each officer and man will be allowed to return to his home, not to be disturbed by United States authority so long as they observe their paroles and the laws in force where they reside.

"U. S. GRANT, Lieutenant-General.

"To General R. E. LEE."

"HEADQUARTERS ARMY OF NORTHERN VIRGINIA, April 9, 1865.

"GENERAL—I received your letter of this date, containing the terms of the surrender of the Army of Northern Virginia, as proposed by you. As they are substantially the same as those expressed in your letter of the 8th inst., they are accepted. I will proceed to designate the proper officers to carry the stipulations into effect. R. E. LEE, General.

"To Lieut.-General U. S. GRANT."

This important matter having been thus happily adjusted,

General Grant promptly provided for the feeding of the famished Confederate troops from the Federal stores. We have seen that their last hungrily-looked-for rations had been captured by Sheridan. On April 12th, the captives were marched in divisions to a point near Appomattox Court House, where they stacked their arms and accoutrements. The men then received their paroles and, where it was needed, transportation to their homes and food for the journey. General Lee went to join his family in Richmond, and there, for nearly a month, till he could arrange his private affairs, they were furnished with daily rations from the Federal commissariat stores.

General Grant and his staff left for City Point on the 11th, and on the morning of the 14th arrived in Washington, whence he was called to New York that evening, and thus escaped the immediate horror of the assassination episode.

General Meade was intrusted with the details of the surrender, and the army returned first to Burkesville Station and then to Petersburg and Richmond.

In a previous chapter we have detailed the surrender of General Johnston to General Sherman, and we have therefore now to trace only the desultory warfare west of the Mississippi to close our record of the military operations of the civil war.

On April 21st General E. Kirby Smith issued an address relating the disaster which had befallen the Army of Northern Virginia, but counseling continued resistance on the ground of expected aid from foreign nations. General Smith's appeal aroused such manifestations of feeling in Texas that General Sheridan was sent to New Orleans, and began preparations, with a large force, for further operations in Texas and Louisiana. But the end was rapidly approaching. The final battle was fought on May 13th at Palmetto Ranche, near the Rio Grande, between Colonel Theodore H. Barrett, of the Sixty-second United States Colored Infantry, and a Confederate force under General J. E. Slaughter. The battle lasted for nine hours, the odds being largely in favor of the Confederates, both as to numbers and position. Their repeated attacks, however, failed to break Colonel Barrett's line, and they finally retired. It is somewhat remarkable that the carnage of this terrible war ended when Slaughter ceased to fight, and that colored men, the primary cause of the "recent unpleasantness," were the last to fire a volley in the war; and further yet, that a colored man, Sergeant Crockett, of the Sixty-second Colored Infantry, was the last man wounded.

Thirteen days after the battle of Palmetto Ranche, General E. Kirby Smith surrendered his entire command to General Canby, the energetic movements of General Sheridan at New Orleans having convinced him at last that discretion was the better part of valor. Thus ended on May 26, 1865, the entire War of the Rebellion.

In a concluding chapter we shall pick up the thread of political history, narrate the terrible episode of Lincoln's assassination, and trace the fortunes of the fugitive Confederate Government.

CHAPTER XXXV.

POLITICAL MATTERS—LINCOLN'S RE-ELECTION—THE GREAT CONSPIRACY—ASSASSINATION OF PRESIDENT LINCOLN—ATTEMPTS ON THE LIFE OF SECRETARY SEWARD—FLIGHT AND CAPTURE OF J. WILKES BOOTH, THE ASSASSIN—CAPTURE, TRIAL AND EXECUTION OF THE CONSPIRATORS—CAPTURE OF JEFF DAVIS—CONCLUSION.

While the armed forces of the United States and of the Confederacy were wrestling on the final battle-fields of the war, a no less bitter and, perhaps, far more dangerous struggle was in progress in the political arena, and, as has too frequently happened in its history, the Democratic party, with monumental stupidity, allowed a few factious, self-seeking, scheming and utterly unreliable men to place it in the seeming position of being an active factor in the efforts to dissolve the Union. There were anti-war Democrats, it is true, and they aired their opinions freely—but, on the other hand, there were anti-war Republicans also, only in the latter case, as in that of the Spartan boy who stole the fox—there was shrewd, almost demoniac courage in the matter of *hiding it under the cloak.* It may honestly be doubted whether there was at any time during the war either a Republican or a Democrat who could conscientiously have placed himself on record in the language of Rutherford B. Hayes—"my heart bleeds for the poor negro!" The "Knights of the Bleeding Heart" were very scarce in those days, even if the order had been actually instituted. There were Democrats as honestly earnest as the best among the Republicans for the suppression of Secession, and these did not hesitate to call it Rebellion, though just how that stigma could, logically, attach among a "Nation of Sovereigns," is beyond our casuistic powers to comprehend.

The summer of 1864 brought with it the momentous issue of a Presidential election. There were some sharply defined lines. Among the Republicans there were those who condemned President Lincoln for his caution and humanitarian bias; they called it irresolution or cowardice, and desired to elect a more hot-headed, or, at any rate, a more vindictive Executive. There were Republicans who fully appreciated the fidelity, the quiet energy and the sublime Christianity of the man who "never lost his head" and was ever most cool when others were most excited. The former, calling themselves "the Radical men of the nation," held a convention at Cleveland, Ohio, on May 31st. About three hundred and fifty delegates were present, and they adopted a platform, some of the planks of which embraced the following propositions: The duty of the Government to suppress the Rebellion by force of arms; the right of free speech and the enjoyment of the privilege of the writ of Habeas Corpus; the advocacy of the Monroe Doctrine; the policy of restricting the incumbency of the Presidential office to one term; the election of the President and Vice-President directly from the people; the commission of the work of "reconstruction to the people instead of to the President;" the confiscation of the lands of the rebels and their division among soldiers and actual settlers. It will be seen that underlying many of these specious provisions was an actual rebuke to President Lincoln. In accordance with the one-term principle they placed in nomination General John C. Fremont and General John Cochrane, for President and Vice-President, respectively.

The Union National Convention, in reality the legitimate party organization, met in Baltimore, Maryland, on June 7. Delegates were present, regularly elected according to party rules, from all the States not in rebellion. The platform adopted contained a pledge to sustain the Government in its efforts to suppress the Rebellion; an approval of the determination of the Government not to compromise with the rebels; an approval of the acts of the Government in relation to slavery and of an amendment to the Constitution for the prohibition of slavery (a plank which the "Radicals" had rejected or dodged); a proffer of thanks to the soldiers and sailors who had helped to save their country; an expression of perfect confidence in Abraham Lincoln and an indorsement of his acts; a declaration that it was the duty of the Government to give equal protection to all persons in its service without regard to color; an indorsement of the Monroe Doctrine ; favoring encouragement to foreign immigration, and the speedy completion of a railroad to the Pacific Ocean, and declaring that the national faith in regard to the public debt must be kept inviolate. In emphatic sustentation of this platform, the convention renominated Abraham Lincoln for President, and associated with him for Vice-President Andrew Johnson, then Military Governor of Tennessee. They were honest, long-headed men who formulated these resolutions and nominations, for their perfection, directness and essential nationalism took the wind completely out of the sails of the so-called " Liberal " faction. Fremont and Cochrane withdrew from a contest which could only have divided the Republican party and imperiled its existence.

The Conservative party had called its Convention to meet on July 4th, but the serpent crept into their Garden of Eden, and they postponed the meeting until August 29th (for reasons which we shall presently refer to), and then they met at Chicago. Horatio Seymour, of New York, presided, and his speech condemning the war and criticising the administration indicated more than mere political opposition. However, it was part of the programme, and had doubtless been carefully "slated." The construction of a platform was intrusted to a committee consisting of one delegate from each State represented, with James Guthrie, of Kentucky, as nominal " boss carpenter," though the real architect was undoubtedly Clement L. Vallandigham, who, as a Representative from Ohio, had, on July 10th, 1861, made a bitter attack in Congress on President Lincoln, charging him with usurpation in respect of the military preparations ; who had been arrested in Dayton, Ohio, on May 4th, 1863 ; tried and convicted by a court martial of treasonable conduct ; sentenced to confinement in a fortress ; partially pardoned by the President on condition of exile from the United States, and who had now returned from Canada in the hope and expectation that his violation of the conditions would lead to his arrest and precipitate the development of certain acts of conspiracy then under consideration. Under such inspiration it is not surprising that the platform, after the regulation declaration of " fidelity to the Union under the Constitution," proceeded to denounce the Government and embodied the following resolution:

> "*Resolved*, That this Convention does explicitly declare, as the sense of the American people, that, after four years of failure to restore the Union by the experiment of war, during which, under the pretense of a military necessity, of a war power higher than the Constitution, the Constitution itself has been disregarded in every part, and public liberty and private rights alike trodden down, and the material prosperity of the country essentially impaired. Justice, humanity, liberty and the public welfare demand that immediate efforts be made for a cessation of hostilities with a view to an ultimate convention of all the States, or other peaceable means, to the end that, at the earliest practicable moment, peace may be restored on the basis of the Federal Union of the States."

The platform closed with the assurance of Democratic sympathy for the Union soldiers, and a promise of care and protection. The platform was adopted, and then General George B. McClellan, of New Jersey, was nominated for President, and George H. Pendleton, of Ohio, for Vice-President.

As one of those "blunders which are worse than crimes," the action of this convention was unique. Loudly condemned by the public voice, it was silently slain by the ballot boxes in November, and President Lincoln was triumphantly re-elected, only Delaware, Kentucky and New Jersey supporting the McClellan ticket.

We have alluded to reasons for the postponement of the Chicago Convention. There was held in the meantime a kind of Secession Conference by the leaders of the Peace Faction and other sympathizers on the Canada side of Niagara Falls, and Horace Greeley, of the New York *Tribune*, was induced to submit to the President a "plan of adjustment," contemplating the restoration of the Union, the abolition of slavery, a complete amnesty for all public offenses, the payment of $400,000,000 to the owners of the emancipated slaves, a change in the representation of slave-labor States, and a National Convention to ratify and settle in detail such adjustment. After good-naturedly discussing the subject for some days, Mr. Lincoln finally "put his foot down" on anything but unconditional surrender. There was nothing for it then but to try and commit the Democratic party by means of the convention proceedings. As a sequel the convention was committed, but the Democratic party, as such, was not.

The next move made by the Confederate authorities was through the intervention of Francis P. Blair, Sr., of Maryland, who in January, 1865, obtained an interview with President Lincoln, during which he exhibited a letter written by Jeff Davis expressing a willingness to appoint a commission to renew the effort to enter into a conference with a view to secure peace to "*the two countries.*" Mr. Lincoln, with his customary courteous shrewdness, wrote a letter to Mr. Blair, which might be shown to Davis, in which he expressed willingness to treat with any properly accredited person, " with a view of securing peace to the people of *our common country.*" The words italicized by us are the keys of the correspondence : an attempt on the one side to obtain recognition for, and a distinct refusal on the other to grant recognition of, an independent government. Could Davis have had everything his own way, this would have ended the matter, but with the threatened dictatorship of Lee hanging over him, he was compelled to send a commission. He appointed Alexander H. Stephens, John A. Campbell and R. M. T. Hunter, a member of the Confederate Senate, as Commissioners to proceed to Washington and confer with the President of the United States. Davis' instructions "to proceed to Washington" were considerably modified in their result by the refusal of the United States Government to allow said Commissioners to approach nearer than Hampton Roads. They were not allowed to land, but on board the vessel which brought them they had first a conference with Secretary of State Seward, and then, on February 3d, with the President and Secretary jointly. Of course the matter came to nothing, for the President would not yield one iota, and he further told the Commissioners that Congress had, three days before, adopted an amendment to the Constitution prohibiting slavery throughout the United States. Equally as a matter of course, the Confederates were furious when their Commissioners returned. They threatened to make the Yankees sue for peace within twelve months, "and resolved never to lay down their arms until independence was won."

On December 6th, 1864, a month after the re-election of President Lincoln, Congress reassembled, and in his annual message the President alluded to the fact that the question of Union or no Union had been definitely settled. He further said, "In stating a single condition of peace, I mean simply to say that the war will cease on the part of the Government whenever it shall have ceased on the part of those who began it." He further urged the House of Representatives to concur with the Senate in adopting a "thirteenth amendment" to the Constitution of the United States, prohibiting slavery in the Republic forever. This measure, which had been adopted by the Senate April 8th, 1864, by a vote of 38 to 6, was taken into consideration by the House of Representatives on January 6th, 1865. It was adopted on January 31st, by a vote of 119 to 56, amid intense excitement and enthusiasm. When order was restored, Mr. Ingersoll, of Illinois, moved that, "In honor of this immortal and sublime event the House do now adjourn." This motion was adopted by a vote of 121 to 24. This was the measure alluded to by President Lincoln in his interview, at Hampton Roads, with the Confederate Commissioners, and his prediction that it would be ratified was sustained, when, on the 18th of December, 1865, the Secretary of State announced its adoption by the requisite three-fourths of the Legislatures of the States, which made it part of the Constitution.

On March 4th, 1865, President Lincoln was inaugurated for his second term. In view of the calamity then impending, and of the great success of the Federal arms then about to be consummated, we may be excused for quoting a portion of his solemn, pathetic and significant inaugural address. He said:

"Neither party expected for the war the magnitude or the duration which it has already attained. Neither anticipated that the cause of the conflict might cease with, or even before, the conflict itself should cease. Each looked for an easier triumph, and a result less fundamental and astounding. * * * * Both read the same Bible and pray to the same God, and each invokes His aid against the other. It may seem strange that any men should dare to ask a just God's assistance in wringing their bread from the sweat of other men's faces; but let us judge not, that we be not judged. The prayers of both could not be answered. That of neither has been answered fully. The Almighty has His own purposes. 'Woe unto the world because of offenses, for it must needs be that offenses come; but woe unto that man by whom the offense cometh!' If we shall suppose that American slavery is one of these offenses, which, in the providence of God, must needs come, but which, having continued through His appointed time, He now wills to remove, and that He gives to both North and South this terrible war as the woe due to those by whom the offense came, shall we discern therein any departure from those divine attributes which the believers in a living God always ascribe to him ? Fondly do we hope, fervently do we pray that this mighty scourge of war may soon pass away. Yet if God wills that it continue until all the wealth piled by the bondsmen's two hundred and fifty years of unrequited toil shall be sunk, and until every drop of blood drawn with the lash shall be paid with another drawn by the sword, as was said three thousand years ago, so still it must be said, 'The judgments of the Lord are true and righteous altogether.' * * * * With malice toward none, with charity for all, with firmness in the right, as God gives us to see the right, let us strive on to finish the work we are in, to bind up the nation's wounds, to care for him who shall have borne the battle, and for his widow and his orphans—to do all which may achieve and cherish a just and lasting peace among ourselves and with all nations."

These were noble sentiments, welling up from the Christian heart of as pure a patriot as ever drew the breath of life, and yet the shadow of a dreadful death was hovering over and around him. "The Thugs were on his trail," sleeplessly plotting and planning his destruction. Doubtless among those who heard him were those who had already contrived his taking-off; and away in the Confederate capital, so soon to expiate in flames the taint of their presence, were those who were guiltily hugging the horrible secret that with their humiliation should come his doom, dealt by a hireling hand.

For several days prior to the evacuation of Richmond President Lincoln had been at City Point, and on April 4th, the day after Richmond was evacuated, he went there in the *Malvern*, Admiral Porter's flagship. He was enthusiastically received by the colored people, who pressed around him to grasp the hand of their liberator. On the 6th he went again to that city, accompanied by Mrs. Lincoln, Vice-President Andrew Johnson and several Senators. While there a number of leading Confederates called upon him, and propositions were made looking to a permit for the reassembling of the Virginia Legislature, under a pledge that the work of reconstruction should begin at once, and moral and material aid to the Confederacy should be withheld. To this the President assented, but the tenor of the legislation differed so widely from that promised as to compel the President to withdraw the safeguard he had accorded and to instruct General Weitzel to bring about the dissolution of the Legislature.

About this time, April 5th, Jeff Davis, who had made good his escape to Danville (whither his wife had preceded him by some four or five days with all her portable effects), issued a proclamation in which he boastfully declared that the evacuation of Richmond had left the army free to move from point to point and strike the enemy in detail far from his base. He declared his intention to defend the soil of Virginia and repudiated any peace with the infamous invaders of her territory. He further said : "If, by the stress of numbers we should ever be compelled to a temporary withdrawal from her limits, or those of any other border State, again and again will we return, until the baffled and exhausted enemy shall abandon in despair his endless and impossible task of making slaves of a people resolved to be free." This braggadocio flowed vigorously from a pen held by a hand well nigh palsied by apprehension and despair.

It may be here noted that one of the earliest of the Confederate Cabinet to wholly disappear was Secretary Judah P. Benjamin, whose whereabouts could not be traced till he turned up in London. We noted his death in Paris some little time since, and now it appears from a statement in the London *Law Times* of this month (July, 1884), referring to the probate of his will, that he was born a British subject, was never naturalized as an American citizen, though he had been a member of the United States Senate, and one of the Confederate Cabinet, and that he died a French subject. His will disposes of about $300,000 worth of personalty and $200,000 worth of real estate. It is dated April 30, 1883. He undoubtedly had a fine law practice in Lincoln's Inn. Yet it would hardly seem that such an estate, with his habits, could have been accumulated in the time. It is true that a large quantity of treasure was unaccounted for when matters were overhauled, and it may be that some of it went to England when Judah P. Benjamin turned his steps in that direction.

We must now turn to the saddest episode in the whole history of the Civil War. As we have previously mentioned, Lieutenant-General Grant, after Lee's surrender, went to City Point and thence to Washington City, arriving there on the morning of the fatal 14th day of April. He was accompanied by Captain Robert T. Lincoln (now Secretary of War), who was one of his staff officers. The latter breakfasted with his father, the President, and related the occurrences of the surrender, at which he was present. A Cabinet meeting was held that morning at eleven o'clock, Lieutenant-General Grant being present. After the adjournment, he remained in conversation with the President some little time, and it was finally arranged that they should visit Ford's Theatre together in the evening, to witness the performance of " Our American Cousin," which was having a great run. The President sent a messenger to engage a box, and the watchful conspirators were doubtless promptly apprised of the arrangements. Subsequently, General Grant was called to New York, and thus probably escaped assassination, as he was inquired for in the theatre about nine o'clock in the evening, by a man bearing a large package. The party in the box, therefore, consisted only of President and Mrs. Lincoln, Major H. R. Rathbone and Miss Clara W. Harris. The President was in excellent spirits, as indeed he might well be, in view of accomplished facts. For some weeks, at least, a sort of haunting foreboding had depressed him, an indefinable sense of danger had kept him strained and watchful, but now, amused and interested, the black shadow was for the moment forgotten. It has been said that " the darkest hour precedes the dawn," but in this case, as indeed seems fitting, all was reversed.

The identity of the person who at nine o'clock attempted to gain access to General Grant has never been ascertained, but that his movements were part of the Satanic conspiracy cannot be doubted. Be that as it may, shortly after ten o'clock John Wilkes Booth, after sending in a card by the President's messenger, passed rapidly into the President's box, and going behind Mr. Lincoln's chair, shot the President through the head. His rapid entrance had been unnoticed, but the sharp report of the pistol, which fell like the clap of doom on the awe-stricken audience, for a moment stunned the occupants of the box. Major Rathbone sprang to his feet and confronted a fiend who, having thrown down his smoking Derringer pistol, was now pressing to the front of the box, brandishing a dagger. Major Rathbone, hardly yet conscious of what had been done, seized Booth, but he broke from the Major's grasp after inflicting a severe wound on his left arm, and dashing to the front of the box, leaped to the stage, shouting at the same time, "Sic semper Tyrannis." The Presidential box was draped with the National flag, and in this one of Booth's spurs caught. He fell to the boards, breaking one of his legs, but immediately scrambled up and hurried across the stage to the prompter's post and disappeared in the wings, along a passage purposely left clear for him by a stage carpenter who was in the plot; when he gained the exit door, another miscreant was waiting with a horse. Springing to the saddle, despite his injury he rode furiously away. We shall trace his course later on, but will now return to the Presidential box.

The assassin's bullet had entered Mr. Lincoln's head above and back of the temporal bone, and passing through his brain, lodged just behind the right eye. A portion of the brain was oozing from the wound, the President's head having fallen slightly forward. Mr. Lincoln was quite unconscious, and was carried across the street to the house of a Mr. Peterson. The Surgeon-General of the Army and several other medical gentlemen were promptly in attendance, but all human skill was unavailing, and without recovering consciousness, President Lincoln passed away about twenty minutes past seven o'clock on the morning of April 15th. his noble, rugged countenance assuming an expression of perfect serenity.

The screams of Mrs. Lincoln had given the first clear indication to the audience of the nature of the tragedy which had been enacted, and then, amid the wildest excitement, there were shouts of "Hang him! hang him!" as those nearest the stage charged across the footlights. But the miscreant had too well planned his escape, and was on horseback almost before his crime was actually known.

Captain Theodore McGowan, Assistant Adjutant-General to

General Augur, who was in the theatre, gives the following account of what he witnessed:

"Arriving at the theatre just after the entrance of President Lincoln and the party accompanying him, my friend Lieutenant Crawford and I, after viewing the Presidential party from the opposite side of the dress circle, went to the right side and took seats in the passage above the seats of the dress circle and about five feet from the door of the box occupied by President Lincoln. During the performance the attendant of the President came out and took the chair nearest the door. I sat, and had been sitting, about four feet to his left and rear for some time, when a man, whose face I do not distinctly recollect, passed me and inquired of one sitting near who the President's messenger was, and, learning, exhibited to him an envelope, apparently official, having a printed heading and superscribed in a bold hand. I could not read the address—in fact, I did not try. I think now it was meant for Lieutenant-General Grant. That man went away. Some time after I was disturbed in my seat by the approach of a man who desired to pass up on the aisle in which I was sitting. Giving him room by bending my chair forward, he passed me and stepped one step down upon the level below me. Standing there he was almost in my line of sight, and I saw him while watching the play. He stood, as I remember, one step above the messenger, and remained perhaps one minute looking at the stage and orchestra below. Then he drew a number of visiting cards from his pocket, from which, with some attention, he selected one. He stooped and showed the card to the messenger, but as my attention was then more closely fixed on the play, I do not know whether the card was carried in by the messenger or his consent given to the entrance of the man who presented it. I saw, however, a few moments after, the same man entering the door of the lobby leading to the box, and the door closing behind him. This was seen because I could not fail from my position to observe it; the door side of the proscenium box and the stage were all within the direct and oblique lines of my sight. How long I watched the play after seeing him enter I do not know; it was perhaps two or three minutes. The house was perfectly still, the large audience listening to the dialogue between "Florence Trenchard" and "May Meredith" when the sharp report of a pistol rang through the house. It was apparently fired behind the scenes, on the right of the stage. Looking toward it and behind the Presidential box, while it startled all, it was evidently accepted by every one in the theatre as an introduction to some new passage, several of which had been interpolated in the early part of the play. A moment after, a man leaped from the front of the box, directly down, nine feet, and on the stage, and ran rapidly across it, bare-headed, and holding an unsheathed dagger in his right hand, the blade of which flashed brightly in the gas-light as he came within ten feet of the opposite rear exit. I did not see his face as he leaped or ran, but I am convinced he was the man I saw enter the box. As he leaped he cried distinctly the motto of Virginia, "Sic Semper Tyrannis." [Others assert that he also shouted, facing the audience as he ran, "The South is avenged"]. The hearing of this and the sight of the dagger explained fully to me the nature of the deed he had committed. In an instant he had disappeared behind the side scene. Consternation seemed for a moment to rivet every one to his seat; the next moment confusion reigned supreme."

About the time that this terrible tragedy was being enacted, another phase of the diabolical Assassination Conspiracy was occurring at the residence of Secretary Seward. We can best give this in the words of Dr. Verdi, the family physician. He says:

"At nine o'clock on the evening of the 14th of April, 1865, I had left Secretary Seward in a comfortable condition, and his family hopeful of his speedy recovery from an accident which he, several days previously, had met with, his horses having run away and dashed him from the carriage, fracturing his right humerus at the surgical neck, his lower maxillary below the angle, and generally bruising him about the face and neck. At a few moments after ten p. m., I was hastily summoned by the colored boy to attend Mr. Seward, his sons and his attendants, who were, as the messenger expressed it, 'murdered by an assassin.' Two minutes brought me to the spot. I was the first medical man there. As I glanced around the room, I found terror depicted on every countenance, and blood everywhere. Among the bleeding men and terrified ladies I sought for Mr. Seward. He was lying on his bed covered with blood, a fearful gaping gash marking his chin and extending below the maxillary bone. Hastily I examined his wounds, and I had the joy to bring the first consolation to that anxious family in announcing to them that his wounds were not mortal. The carotid artery and jugular vein had not been divided or injured. The gash was semi-circular, commencing just below the high bone of the cheek and extending downward toward the mouth and then backward over the submaxillary gland, laying open the inflamed and swollen part of the face and neck that had been injured by the previous accident. On examining further, I found another stab under the left ear, wounding the parotid gland; but this cut was not very deep. Mr. Seward had lost much blood, and I immediately applied ice to arrest the bleeding temporarily, after which I was informed that Frederick Seward was in an adjacent room, also injured. I hastily went to him, and found him lying on a lounge with blood streaming over his face. He had been wounded in several places, viz.: on the left parietal bone, just about the parietal eminence on the left side of the frontal bone, just about the line of intersection with the parietal; with two other light wounds in that neighborhood. He was not insensible, but could, not articulate. In about an hour, however, after his wounds were dressed. he fell into a slumber from which, for sixty hours, he could not be aroused. I had scarcely finished applying ice to arrest the hemorrhage when I was told to look at Mr. Augustus Seward. I became truly amazed. "What, said I, "is there another one wounded?" His injuries, however, were comparatively slight. One was from a blow with the butt end of a pistol, on the upper and middle part of the forehead; the other a cut over the metacarpal bone of the thumb of his right hand. Here I was again requested to look at another man. My surprise ceased then, I became terrified. This was the man nurse, a soldier in attendance on Mr. Seward. I found his wounds were four in number, all from the blade of a knife—three over the right scapular region and one below it. After giving to this patient the requisite attention, I was called to see another man who was wounded. He had received but one stab in the back over the seventh rib, very near the spinal colum. The knife must have glanced off, as the cut was long but quite superficial; had it been direct his right lung would have received an irreparable injury. The circumstances of the affair, as I gathered them, were as follows:

"At ten o'clock the bell at Mr. Seward's house was rung and answered by the colored boy. As the door opened a very tall man appeared with a small package in his hand, saying that Dr. Verdi had sent him with a prescription for Secretary Seward which he must deliver personally. The boy remonstrated, saying that Mr. Seward was asleep and that he, the servant, would take charge of the prescription. The man said, 'No, I have particular directions and I must deliver them myself.' So saying he walked up stairs, but treading very heavily he was reminded by the boy who was following him to walk more lightly in order not to disturb Mr. Seward. Mr. Frederick Seward was at this time lying, dressed, on a sofa in his room, one adjacent to his father's, and hearing heavy footsteps, came into the hall and met the stranger, who attempted to enter his father's room. Frederick expostulated with him, declaring that his father was asleep and could not be seen. Miss Fanny Seward, who was in her father's room, hearing the conversation outside, opened the door to ascertain what was the matter, but Frederick cried out to her to 'shut the door.' It seems that for two or three minutes the assassin hesitated or endeavored to enter without making a deadly assault upon Frederick, but meeting with determined opposition he dealt several blows on young Seward's head, apparently with a pistol, with the intention probably of disabling without killing him. The door was then opened and the murderer entered, pushing Frederick, already staggering, before him. Then disengaging himself from his adversary he asked Miss Fanny, 'Is the Secretary asleep?' at the same moment making a spring for the bed where the unfortunate man sat, aroused with the frightful conviction of what was to be expected. The next moment the villain dealt him a blow with the deadly knife, which was so violent that, fortunately we may say, it precipitated him from his bed. In falling, however, he must have received the second blow, on the other side of the neck. It must have been at this time that the man nurse Robinson, who had been absent at the hospital, returned and attacked the murderer to prevent him from doing further injury to Mr. Seward. In the endeavor to restrain the ferocity of the assassin, the nurse was struck several times. It was at the moment that the nurse and Frederick, who rallied sufficiently to still use his feeble efforts in behalf of his poor father, were struggling with this man, that Major Augustus Seward, awakened from sleep by the noise and screams of Miss Fanny, came into the room thinking that probably his father was delirious, and had frightened the attendants, or else that the nurse left to watch during the night was in some way misbehaving himself. The major, seeing the struggle, and not at all comprehending the facts, took hold of the man, still believing him to be the nurse, and dragged him to the door. Of course the assassin took advantage of this, and dealing one blow on the head of the major, and cutting his hand, ran down stairs, followed by the major, who did not know the condition of affairs until he came back to his father's room. The assassin then mounted his horse, which he had left before the door, and rode rapidly away. The whole tragedy occupied less time than was consumed in relating the circumstance."

Before proceeding to the narration of Booth's flight and his subsequent killing by Boston Corbett, it will be necessary to trace from scattered incidents some of the features of the entire conspiracy. It would appear that some time in the year 1861 Booth conceived the idea, or had it suggested to him, of kidnapping the President and confining him in a house within the city limits; this house, belonging to one Mrs. Greene, was discovered in the course of the investigations after the assassination. The underground apartments were fitted with manacles, and the whole place was mined, ready for explosion, if it should be found impracticable to run the President, after he had been caught and gagged, within the Confederate lines. He failed, however, to get the right associates, and this scheme was abandoned. He then began to contemplate murder. He visited Canada several times, and it is pretty well understood that he had conferences with the Confederate agents who were implicated in the schemes known to have been devised for operation on July 4th, 1864, and in consequence of which the Democratic Convention was postponed. On one of these occasions Booth deposited at the Ontario Bank in Montreal some four hundred and fifty dollars. It was through these Canadian visits that Booth became connected with Lewis Payne Powell, alias Wood, alias Payne, the miscreant who attempted the life of Secretary Seward. Booth had previously made the acquaintance of Mrs. Surratt, whose career it is now necessary to trace in order to make our story intelligible.

Outside the District of Columbia, to the south, in Prince George County, is a village called Surrattville. At the time in question it consisted of a few cabins at a cross-road, surrounding a hotel, the master whereof, giving the settlement its name, left to his widow, Mrs. Mary E. Surratt, the property. Not making much of the business she moved into Washington with her son and several daughters, renting the hotel to John Lloyd, who also engaged to look after the rebel mail route from Matthias Creek, Virginia, to Port Tobacco, which struck Surrattville, as one collection and distribution point. Mrs. Surratt was frequently at this hotel and Booth was a visitor there and at her house in Washington. During the latter part of 1864, Booth went from this point as far as Leonardstown, in St. Mary's County, ostensibly to buy lands, but really to locate the rebel postal stations and make acquaintances. One of these was George A. Atzeroth and another David E. Herrold or Harold, who was a gunner, and had friends at every farm-house between Washington and Leonardsville. Atzeroth was a house-painter, of German descent, who had led a wild life at Port Tobacco, and had been a blockade runner across the Potomac and a mail carrier. When the conspiracy was broached to him by Booth and Mrs. Surratt with the promise of a large sum of money, he at once went into the scheme and bought a dirk and a pistol. Two others, Sam Arnold and Michael O'Laughlin, were detailed each to kill a Cabinet officer, but they backed out of actual violence. Atzeroth took his knife and pistol to Kirkwood's, where Vice-President Johnson was stopping, and secured a room directly over his. But some accident disarranged his plans, and without making an attempt on Johnson's life, according to programme, he fled, leaving everything behind him. There were found in his room a big bowie knife, a Colt's cavalry revolver, secreted under the mattresses of his bed, Booth's coat, in the pockets of which were three boxes of cartridges, a map of Maryland, gauntlets for riding, a spur, and a handkerchief marked with the name of Booth's mother. Atzeroth was captured at the house of his uncle in Montgomery County, Maryland.

That the murder had been some time in contemplation and the route of escape laid out by Booth and Mrs. Surratt, is shown by the facts that six weeks before the assassination young John Surratt took two repeating carbines to Surrattville and told John Lloyd to secrete them. He did so by making a hole in the wainscotting and suspending the weapons from strings so that they hung within the plastered wall of the room below. On the afternoon of the "Assassination Day." Mrs. Surratt drove over to Surrattville and told John Lloyd to have the weapons ready as they would be called for that night. Herrold was made quartermaster and hired the horses. He and Atzeroth were mounted between eight o'clock and the time of the murder, and riding about the streets of Washington together. Three weeks before they had been in Port Tobacco and Herrold told "the boys" that when they heard of him again he would be in Spain, where there was no extradition treaty, while Atzeroth boasted that when he came again, he would be rich enough to buy the whole place. Mrs. Surratt sent her son northward on Thursday, April 13th.

We come now to events immediately preceding the tragedy. At seven o'clock on Good Friday evening, April 14th, Booth came down stairs from his room in the National Hotel, looking abnormally pale; this was commented upon by some of his acquaintances and he ascribed it to indisposition. Turning to the hotel clerk, Booth asked him if he was going to Ford's theatre, adding significantly, "*There will be some very fine acting there to-night!*" He was next noticed by Mr. Sessford, ticket agent of the theatre, as he passed in soon after the doors were opened. He visited the stage under his privilege as a professional, and took note of the surroundings; it was probably for the purpose of making sure that his confederate, the stage carpenter, had not forgotten his instructions in regard to so shifting the scenes that instead of the usual tortuous path, a clear exit should be left. It was also worthy of note that, at a later period, the discovery was made of a gimlet hole in the entry door of the Presidential box, which had been carefully cleared by the aid of a penknife. Through this peep-hole Booth, doubtless, scanned the position of his victim before entering the box. Between the time at which Booth was first seen to enter the theatre and the period of the assassination, he visited the restaurant next door, and rapping impatiently on the bar, called for "Brandy! brandy! brandy!" this was supplied and hurriedly swallowed by the miscreant. We now come to Booth's flight.

Immediately after the assassination Booth met Herrold in the next street, and together they rode at a gallop past the Patent Office and over Capitol Hill, one of the horses being that on which Atzeroth had previously been mounted. Within fifteen minutes after the murder the telegraph wires were severed entirely round the city, with the single exception of a secret wire, for Government uses, leading to Old Point. By means of this the Government reached the fortifications around Washington, first telegraphing all the way to Old Point and then back to the outlying forts. As Booth and Herrold crossed the Eastern Branch at Uniontown, Booth gave his proper name to the officer at the bridge, a shrewd trick, as it afterwards threw the detectives off his track, for they naturally supposed that this was a device on the part of an accomplice, and they therefore hunted in other directions. At midnight the fugitives reached Surrattville, ten miles distant; Herrold dismounted and thundered at the door. When it was opened by Lloyd, Herrold pushed in and got a bottle of whisky, which he took out to Booth, and then hurried upstairs, returning with one of the carbines. Lloyd started to fetch the other, but Herrold said: "We don't want it; Booth has broken his leg and can't carry it." As they rode off Booth called out to Lloyd, "Don't you want to hear some news?" to which Lloyd replied: "I don't care much about it!" Booth then said: "We have killed the President and Secretary of State!" They then dashed off across Prince George's County, and before sunrise stopped at the house of Dr. Mudd, three miles from Bryantown. They contracted with him for twenty-five dollars, in greenbacks, to set the broken leg of Booth, who was introduced, under another name by Herrold to Dr. Mudd, a previous acquaintance of Herrold's. Dr. Mudd remarked that Booth draped the lower part of his face during the operation, and while evidently in great pain was silent. Having no splints, an old fashioned wooden band-box was split up for the purpose. An assistant of Dr. Mudd's also hewed out a pair of crutches. Booth's riding-boot had to be cut from his foot; within were the words "J. Wilkes," but this Dr. Mudd professed not to have seen. The inferior bone of the left leg was broken vertically across, and therefore it did not yield when Booth walked on it.

All that day the men hung around the house, but towards evening the murderers slipped their horses from the stables and rode off along the belt of the swamps below Bryantown. They came across a negro named Swan, and they gave him seven dollars to show them the way to Allen's Fresh; their reat intent, however, was to reach the house of Sam Coxe, a notorious Maryland rebel. They reached there at midnight, and after calling for some time, Coxe came to the door with a candle. As soon as he recognized his visitors he blew out the light, pulled them into the house and left the negro outside with the horses. Here they stopped till four o'clock on Sunday morning, the negro observing that they ate and drank heartily, but when they came out they abused Coxe for his want of hospitality. This was done to mislead the darkey, and when he had led them another three miles they handed out another five dollars, saying they now knew their road. The cute contraband, however, watched them and saw that they returned to Coxe's house.

The next trace of them is on the following Friday, when some men at work on Methxy Creek, in Virginia, saw them cross in a boat which some white man had tied to a stone in the morning. They struck across a ploughed field for King George Court House. It is not necessary to trace their further movements till we find them at Garrett's farm, where their capture was effected by a force under Lieutenant-Colonel E. J. Conger and Lieutenant L. B. Baker. This force had been dispatched from Washington and steamed down to Belle Plain, seventy miles from Washington, upon Potomac Creek. Here they disembarked and began to scour the country. At Port Royal Ferry they found a negro who had driven the fugitives towards Bowling Green in a wagon. Next they came across a cavalry captain, one of Moseby's disbanded command, and when he learned why the men were wanted, he promptly gave information which took the searching party back to a house which they had passed, occupied by one Garrett. About midnight they surrounded the house, and when Garrett appeared Baker seized him by the throat and demanded the whereabouts of his guests. The old man hesitated, and finally attempted to assure the officers that the men had left. His son, however, came upon the scene, and taking in the situation said: "Father, we had better tell the truth about the matter. Those men whom you seek, gentlemen, are in the barn, I know. They went there to sleep." The barn was promptly surrounded, and then Colonel Baker shouted: "To the persons in this barn I have a proposal to make. We are about to send in to you the son of the man in whose custody you are found. Either surrender to him your arms and then give yourselves up, or we will set fire to the place. We mean to take you both or to have a bonfire and a shooting match." Baker had obtained the key of the padlock and now suddenly opened the door and pushed the boy Garrett in. He was heard appealing to Booth, and the latter, in reply, cursed him for betraying them. Finally the boy came out, reporting the failure of his errand. After several other summonses to surrender, Booth asked that the force be withdrawn to give him a chance, as he would not be taken alive. To this Baker replied, "We did not come here to fight, but to capture you. I say again appear, or the barn shall be fired." At this Herrold weakened, and, after being cursed by Booth, came to the door and was dragged out. Colonel Conger then slipped around to the rear of the barn, drew some loose straws through a crack and lit them. In a moment a big blaze went up, and Conger saw Booth, who at first attempted to beat out the fire, but finally made a dash for the door with the carbine in his hand. Contrary to orders, Sergeant Boston Corbett drew a bead on him, and the assassin fell headlong to the floor. Conger and the two sergeants picked up the body and bore it from the fierce flames. After water had been dashed in Booth's face, and a rag soaked in brandy and water passed between his teeth, the miscreant revived sufficiently to articulate, "Tell mother I died for my country. I thought I did for the best." He died about sunrise, and the body was sewn up in a blanket and the cortege moved back to Washington, taking Herrold and two of the Garretts along with the corpse. After identification in Washington the Secretary of War committed the body to the disposal of Colonel Lafayette C. Baker, of the Secret Service. Of its ultimate disposal there is no trace beyond the fact that on the night of April 27th two men in a small rowboat carried it off. The Secret Service has since resolutely refused to give any further details.

In the meantime the authorities in Washington had been on the alert, and at length a descent was made on the house on H street, North, near Sixth, in Washington, occupied by Mrs. Surratt, it having been ascertained that a number of suspicious people had gone in and out of there in various disguises. Major H. W. Smith, of General Augur's staff, and Captain Wurmerskirch, assistant to Colonel Olcott, found in the house and arrested Mrs. M. E. Surratt, Miss Anna Surratt, Miss Honora Fitzpatrick and Miss Holahan. They were separately examined and made contradictory statements. In the meantime the house was searched and evidences of communication with the rebel lines, and quite recently with J. Wilkes Booth, justified their prompt removal to the Old Capitol prison. Before their removal, however, a light knock was heard at the front door, and Major Morgan, on opening it, found a young-looking man, about five feet eleven inches in stature, light complexion, peculiarly large gray eyes and hair that had evidently been dyed. He wore a gray cassimere coat and vest, fine black cloth pantaloons and fine boots; the latter were well covered with mud and he had the appearance of having been lying out in the rain. He had a pickaxe on his shoulder. As soon as he saw the officers standing with pistols in their hands, he remarked: "I believe I am mistaken," and turned to go away. Major Morgan, however, asked who he wished to see; he replied, "Mrs. Surratt." Major Morgan then said: "Mrs. Surratt lives here; she is at home; walk in!" Fairly trapped, the assailant of Secretary Seward walked into custody.

Lewis Payne Powell, or Payne, as he called himself, when quitting Seward's house galloped for the open country, but when near Post Lincoln, on the Baltimore pike, his horse threw him headlong. Afoot and bewildered, he resolved to return to the city, guided by its lights, and taking an abandoned pick from the deserted intrenchments, struck out for Mrs Surratt's house, where he had boarded under the name of Wood. When questioned by his captors as to his business at that time of night, he said he had been sent for to dig a trench. Mrs. Surratt denied all knowledge of him, and his own statements were quite irreconcilable with the facts of his appearance. His hands being washed they were found to be soft, and in his pockets were tooth and nail brushes and a delicate pocket knife. This destroyed all his "poor laboring man" pretensions. Gradually a suspicion arose that he was the assailant of Secretary Seward, and the domestics of that house were sent for. The colored boy threw up his hands in horror, and pointing to Powell, said: "That's the man! I don't want to see him! He did it; I know him by that lip."

One by one the various parties implicated in these atrocious crimes were hunted down, and after trial by a Military Commission, found guilty of murder and conspiracy. On the 9th of July, David E. Herrold, George A. Atzeroth, Lewis Payne Powell and Mary E. Surratt were hanged. Of the other persons arrested for complicity, Michael O'Laughlin, Dr. Samuel A. Mudd and Samuel Arnold were sentenced to imprisonment, at hard labor, for life, and Edward Spangler was sentenced to six years' hard labor imprisonment.

We can now turn from this revolting subject. As we have seen, Atzeroth abandoned his part of the conspiracy, which included the killing of Andrew Johnson, the Vice-President, and thus the absolute anarchy, which had doubtless been part of the scheme, was averted. Six hours after Mr. Lincoln's death, Chief-Justice Chase administered the presidential oath of office to the Vice-President, and thus Andrew Johnson became President of the United States. The Lincoln Cabinet, consisting of William H. Seward, Secretary of State; Hugh McCulloch, Secretary of the Treasury; Edwin M. Stanton, Secretary of War; Gideon Welles, Secretary of the Navy; John P. Usher, Secretary of the Interior; James Speed, Attorney-General; and William Dennison, Postmaster-General, were invited by the new President to retain their portfolios.

On the 19th of April the funeral services were held in the East Room of the White House, where the body of President Lincoln had been taken after being embalmed, and then the solemn funeral procession started on its route through sorrowing cities. In Baltimore, Philadelphia, New York and Albany the remains were viewed by hundreds of thousands, and then from his private home, in Springfield, Illinois, the honored remains of the great Martyr were laid in their final resting place.

On May 2d President Johnson issued a proclamation in which a reward of one hundred thousand dollars was offered for the arrest of Jefferson Davis and twenty-five thousand dollars for the arrest of each of the following : Jacob Thompson, C. C. Clay, George N. Saunders and Beverly Tucker ; and ten thousand dollars for the arrest of William C. Cleary, late clerk of C. C. Clay, the proclamation setting forth that there was evidence in the Bureau of Military Justice that there had been a conspiracy formed by them and other rebels and traitors against the Government of the United States, harbored in Canada, to assassinate the President, the Secretary of State and others.

On June 2d Lieutenant-General Grant issued an address to the army, the work of disbanding having already commenced. The address was in the following words :

Soldiers of the Armies of the United States: By your patriotic devotion to your country in the hour of danger and alarm, your magnificent fighting, bravery and endurance, you have maintained the supremacy of the Union and the Constitution, overthrown all armed opposition to the enforcement of the laws, and of the proclamation forever abolishing slavery—the cause and pretext of the rebellion—and opened the way to the rightful authorities to restore order and inaugurate peace on a permanent and enduring basis on every foot of American soil. Your marches, sieges and battles, in distance, duration, resolution and brilliancy of results, dim the lustre of the world's past military achievements, and will be the patriot's precedent in defense of liberty and right in all time to come. In obedience to your country's call, you left your homes and families and volunteered in her defense. Victory has crowned your valor and secured the purpose of your patriotic hearts ; and, with the gratitude of your countrymen, and the highest honors a great and free nation can accord, you will soon be permitted to return to your homes and families conscious of having discharged the highest duty of American citizens. To achieve these glorious triumphs, and to secure to yourselves, your fellow countrymen, and posterity, the blessings of free institutions, tens of thousands of your gallant comrades have fallen and sealed the priceless legacy with their blood. The graves of these a grateful nation bedews with tears, honors their memories, and will ever cherish and support their stricken families.

We might properly close here, but feel impelled to relate the capture of Jeff Davis and a little personal reminiscence which has some significance in connection with the assassination conspiracy. We will deal with the latter subject first.

Early in January, 1867, the writer was dining with a friend, Mr. Hill, son of an English M. P., at the Café Trois Frères, in the Palais Royale, Paris, when a massive looking man took a seat at a neighboring table. He had some difficulty in making an unusually stupid garçon understand his wants and Mr. Hill volunteered assistance, being a fluent French scholar. The offer was accepted, but in a very ungracious manner. However, when the dinner had been eaten, and it was a capital meal, seasoned with some very fine wine, the ungraciousness of the stranger disappeared, and with some reference to the rumors of an intended yacht race between the Prince of Wales and James Gordon Bennett round the Isle of Wight, he opened a conversation and invited us to join him over a bottle of wine. The offer was accepted on condition that we were allowed to reciprocate. In the course of conversation some remark was made by the stranger which indicated a very intimate acquaintance with the affairs of the South. The writer remarked, "You seem to be very well informed, sir, as to some inside history." Quickly, but with much dignity, came the response, ' I should think, sir, that the ex-Secretary of State of the Southern Confederacy should know whereof he speaks!" and he laid down a visiting card on which, in plain, unpretentious script, was printed "*Robert Toombs*, of Georgia." Of course an exchange of cards ensued and then my friend Hill, whose sympathies were intensely Union, being the son of an English liberal politician, drew out of the conversation. Incautiously, perhaps, the writer said: "Mr. Toombs, I should like to ask you one question?" "Do so, my young friend," was the reply; "if it is anything about the South, I can tell you something!" Then came the embarrassing query, "Mr. Toombs, did you—that is, the Government of which you were a member—know anything of Booth's intentions with regard to Lincoln's assassination?" The face of Mr. Toombs was a study. There was an awkward pause, and then slowly, but distinctly, he remarked, "*I am very sorry that you have asked me that question!*" Quick as a flash went the retort, "And I, sir, am still more sorry that you cannot answer it!" For a moment Mr. Toombs looked annoyed, and then, with a motion of his hand, he said, "Let us drop that subject." It was never broached again, though we spent some time together the next day, during which he stated that he had almost daily interviews with Louis Napoleon, and ventured the prediction that another war, in which the West would be hand in hand with the South, would certainly occur within ten years. Seventeen years have rolled by since then, however, and the prediction of Mr. Toombs has not been verified.

Now let us take up the Jeff Davis matter. General Debrell was engaged in the battle near Raleigh, N. C., when he received intelligence of Lee's surrender, and at the same time General Wheeler got a dispatch from Jeff Davis, dated at Greensboro, N. C., calling for one thousand picked men to escort him and what remained of his government to Washoe, Ga. Accordingly Debrell was dispatched with the required force, and after a march of three days reached Greensboro, at which point he found Jeff Davis with his family, Judah P. Benjamin, John C. Breckinridge, Senator Burnett, of Kentucky; J. H. Reagan, Postmaster-General; Gustavus A. Harris, of Tennessee, and other Confederate officials. As soon as Debrell arrived the party prepared to march and they set out on the following day. Jeff Davis and the other officials rode in front, followed by ambulances containing the women and children and the specie, currently reported among the officers to amount to eleven millions of dollars. It was put up in heavy iron bound kegs and boxes and had a guard of one thousand men led by General Debrell. At a point five miles from Greensboro they encamped, Davis and his family taking up their quarters in a house in the vicinity. The following day Davis visited the camp and made a stirring speech adverting to the disasters that had overtaken their beloved Confederacy, but giving them every assurance that they were not irrevocably lost.

On again taking up the line of march, Jeff Davis had by his side young Colonel Johnston, son of General Albert Sidney Johnston. They camped next at Charlotte, N. C., and here Davis harangued the men again, extolling their patriotism. Here they were joined by Basil Duke, Ferguson and Vaughn, with some troops, increasing the escort to five thousand men. The new-comers began to talk, and then the whole party were suddenly reminded that the Government was slightly indebted to them, and as the treasure was at hand, the idea of presenting their bills very naturally arose. Davis still tried to conciliate, but it was evident that a crisis was approaching. They reached Abbeville, S. C., and on the 6th of May, Davis found that something more potent than promises was necessary. The treasure was opened and the division of Debrell, with the brigades of Duke, Ferguson and Vaughn, were formed in line. Some of the men were paid $30, some $28, and some $20 in gold and silver, the coin being chiefly Mexican dollars.

In the evening Duke sent his Adjutant-General, Captain Davis, to notify all his men who wished to go west of the Mississippi River to report at 11 o'clock the following day. At the appointed time all the men reported, but Duke would take only those who were armed, leaving the rest to shift for themselves. Heaping curses on Duke they went with heavy hearts to Washoe, Georgia, and surrendered to General Wilson, together with the brigades of Ferguson and Vaughn. The command of Debrell escorted Jeff Davis to Vienna Valley, on the west bank of the Savannah River, about twenty miles from Washington, Georgia, where the grand dissolution took place on the 9th of May.

At this point Benjamin, Breckinridge, Burnett and several others took their departure. Jeff Davis and suite crossed the river and the other portion of the government galloped off to Washington. The division of spoils was very unequal. Some of the officers got one hundred dollars and others a bare pittance. Stoneman's cavalry were close on the party, and Davis supposed he could deceive them into following the Confederate troops. So in the mêlée over the division Davis and his followers escaped across country. Davis and Postmaster Reagan, with Colonels Lubbock and Johnston, were in Washington to "settle some business," as they said, and did not join the party, in the camp which was surprised, until the 10th of May. This camp was in a pine forest on one side of the Abbeyville road, about one mile from Irwinsville, Irwin County, Georgia. It consisted of a large wall tent, containing only Davis and his family, and an ordinary "fly" containing the male portion of the caravan. Surrounding and contiguous to these were two common army wagons, two ambulances, and the usual camp paraphernalia. Here, on the morning of the 11th, Lieutenant-Colonel Pritchard, Fourth Michigan Cavalry, and Lieutenant-Colonel Hardin, First Wisconsin Cavalry, coming from opposite directions, surprised them; but the surprise was partly destroyed by the fact that the two commands, mistaking each other in the early dawn, fired upon one another. This stirred the camp, and Davis attempting to escape in his sleeping dress, with a shawl thrown over his head, was captured. There appears to be some discrepancy in the accounts of his costume, and probably there is exaggeration in the "woman's dress" disguise about which so much sensationalism has been written. At any rate the whole party were captured, and, under escort of Colonel Pritchard, were taken to Macon, where they arrived on the afternoon of May 12th.

Arriving at the Lanier House, General Wilson's headquarters, the prisoners were treated to an excellent dinner. After dinner Reagan obtained an interview with General Wilson and begged permission to accompany Davis, as he had shared his prosperity and did not wish to desert him in adversity. On his expressing gratitude for the permission, General Wilson replied, "You are under no obligation, sir; for I should have sent you, whether you wanted to go or not. You are a civilian prisoner, and he is a prisoner, both military and civil." The party were joined here by Clement C. Clay and wife, they having come from their home, Lagrange, and surrendered to General Wilson. From here they were sent to Savannah, and then Davis was sent by sea to Fortress Monroe, where he was confined in a casemate until released on bail, when he went to Europe and remained there for some time. Judge Reagan and Alexander H. Stephens, who were arrested about the same time, were sent to Fort Warren, Boston Harbor. They were released on parole a few months afterward.

We approach the close of our task. For many omissions we ask pardon, but feel that in contemplating the vastness of the field of operations we shall not be harshly dealt with for some unavoidable errors.

The army was rapidly disbanded after the 1st of June, 1865, and by the autumn some 786,000 officers and men had been mustered out of service. The Records of the War Department show that the whole number of men called into service during the war was 2,656,553. Of these, 1,490,000 were in actual service. Nearly 50,000 were killed on the field, about 35,000 were mortally wounded, and about 184,000 died of disease in the hospitals and camps. The total loss on both sides has been estimated to reach fully one million able-bodied men, but of the money cost not even an approximate estimate can be formed.

Long live the Republic! May the Stars and Stripes never again meet the Stars and Bars to disturb the peace of the greatest Republic that ever flourished in the history of the world!

APPENDIX.

As an illustration of the world-wide sympathy evoked by the cruel assassination of Mr. Lincoln, the following poem, from the London *Punch* of May 6th, 1865, may be quoted. It should be noted that this professedly comic periodical had almost exhausted its stock of satire in efforts to belittle the United States, President Lincoln and the Union party, but in the face of so abominable a crime as that of Booth, the motley of the jester was exchanged for sable, and even the bells on his doffed cap were muffled:

ABRAHAM LINCOLN.

BORN FEBRUARY 12th, 1809, DIED APRIL 15, 1865.

He had been born a destined work to do,
    And lived to do it; four long-suffering years—
Ill-fate, ill-feeling, ill-report lived through—
    And then he heard the hisses change to cheers,

The taunts to tribute, the abuse to praise,
    And took them both with his unwavering mood;
But as he came on light, from darkest days,
    And seemed to touch the goal from where he stood,

A felon hand, between that goal and him,
    Reached from behind his head, a trigger prest,
And those perplexed and patient eyes were dim,
    Those gaunt long laboring limbs were laid to rest!

The words of mercy were upon his lips,
    Forgiveness in his heart and on his pen,
When this vile murderer brought swift eclipse
    To thoughts of peace on earth, good will to men.

The Old World and the New, from sea to sea,
    Utter one voice of sympathy and shame!
Sore heart, so stopped when it at last beat free,
    Sad life, cut short just as its triumph came!

A deed accurst ! Strokes have been struck before
   By the assassin's hand, whereof men doubt
If more of horror or disgrace they bore;
   But thy foul crime, like Cain's stands darkly out !

Vile hand ! that branded murder on a strife,
   What e'er its grounds, stoutly and nobly striven,
And with the martyr's crown crownest a life
   With much to praise, little to be forgiven.

www.ingramcontent.com/pod-product-compliance
Lightning Source LLC
Chambersburg PA
CBHW051743300426
44115CB00007B/674